MW00606855

TALES FROM THE BORDERLANDS

TALES
FROM THE
BORDERLANDS

Making and Unmaking the Galician Past

OMER BARTOV

Yale

UNIVERSITY PRESS

New Haven and London

Published with assistance from the foundation established in memory of Philip Hamilton McMillan of the Class of 1894, Yale College.

Copyright © 2022 by Omer Bartov.
All rights reserved.
This book may not be reproduced, in whole or in part, including illustrations, in any form (beyond that copying permitted by Sections 107 and 108 of the U.S. Copyright Law and except by reviewers for the public press), without written permission from the publishers.

Yale University Press books may be purchased in quantity for educational, business, or promotional use. For information, please email sales.press@yale.edu (U.S. office) or sales@yaleup.co.uk (U.K. office).

Set in Janson type by Integrated Publishing Solutions.
Printed in the United States of America.

Library of Congress Control Number: 2021951341
ISBN 978-0-300-25996-4 (hardcover : alk. paper)

A catalogue record for this book is available from the British Library.

This paper meets the requirements of ANSI/NISO Z39.48-1992 (Permanence of Paper).

10 9 8 7 6 5 4 3 2 1

In memoriam
Alan Mintz, 1947–2017
and
Esti Amit (Eichenwald), 1954–2019

Contents

PART IV THE FINAL JOURNEY (MY MOTHER)

Preface

THIS BOOK TELLS A largely forgotten story through the lens of first-person history. The story it tells is of a place and a civilization that vanished in the wake of World War II. The place was Europe's vast eastern borderlands, stretching from the Baltic to the Balkans, where the emerging great empires of the early modern period expanded, overlapped, clashed, and disintegrated. The civilization was by its very nature a mix of multiple cultures, languages, ethnic groups, religions, and eventually nations. They too often overlapped, clashed, and were ultimately brutally sorted out in a manner that sucked out the spirit of the borderlands that had previously animated them.

Telling this story in its entirety is impossible, and attempting to do so would also deprive it of what makes it both fascinating and unique. It is an important story because in many ways it traces the emergence of our own contemporary world from a distinctly different reality. We tend to regard the past as nothing more than a gateway to our more progressive and evolved present. But erasing or marginalizing the past means that we not only fail to understand the present but also do not know what we have lost. The point is not that we can go back in time, but rather that we can learn how life was led and understood in the past and why what we have created for ourselves may not at all be the best version of human civilization. But that borderlands world, which was one of the breeding grounds of the modern age of nations, is too vast and complex to be taken as a whole. Nor is there any need to do that. Instead, we can sample some parts of it, look at them more closely, examine them in the light and in the shade, listen to their sounds more carefully, and interrogate what they have to tell us that we have forgotten, if we ever knew.

Still, even by examining only a small segment of that world, we may find ourselves mired in the kind of endless demographic, ethnographic, and bureaucratic data that obscure even as they quantify the spirit of a civilization. And, in any case, they do not tell a story, which is what this book hopes to do. For this book wants to tell history as a story, and to tell that story as a first-person history. By "first-person history" I mean history with a lowercase *h*. It is the history of the men and women who populated the universe of the borderlands, their fates and hopes, dreams and disillusionment. It is also a history of the stories they told themselves and others about who they were, where they came from, and where they were heading. In this sense it is both a history from below and a history from within. It tells us about the protagonists of this world, those who lived and experienced it, rather than those who ruled and subjugated it, and it tells us what they thought, believed, and felt, in their own words. These people may or may not be typical or representative, but they represent the world in which they resided in fascinating and at times profound ways.

Because I envision this book as a new exercise in writing history through a first-person prism, it is also a personal book. It is personal in that it is concerned with the mentality and emotions of real and fictional people. It is also personal in the sense that I have a personal, indeed an intimate relationship to that world, even though it vanished before I was born. In that sense it was only natural for me to end this book with my own mother's first-person account and her transition from that world on the eve of its destruction to the new world of Palestine on the eve of its re-creation as the Jewish state. This personal link between me and the world I write about through my mother's story makes it into my own first-person history, which is, I think, the only way to delve into this territory in the first place, that is, from within one's own biography, or, perhaps, one's heart.

The Polish-Lithuanian Commonwealth, 1569. Chris Erichsen, cartographer.

Galicia through the ages. Chris Erichsen, cartographer.

TALES FROM THE BORDERLANDS

Mark Epstein, *Woman with a Yoke*, 1920s.
Used by permission of the National
Art Museum of Ukraine.

Introduction

Out into the World (Before the Apocalypse)

THE THREE GENERATIONS BORN between the Spring of
Nations—the revolutions of 1848 that swept across Europe—and
the outbreak of World War I in 1914 lived through a time of rapid
economic, social, political, and cultural changes. These were decades of growing hopes for a better future, in which political liberaliza-
tion, greater freedom of movement, and new-fangled ideas about people's
ability to break the chains of traditional family, community, and religious
authority and to redefine themselves in previously unheard-of ways filled
the hearts of youngsters with a sense of adventure and unlimited possibilities. Yet by the end of this period, a newly emergent nationalism that was
intolerant, aggressive, and militant succeeded in mobilizing large numbers
of the increasingly impatient younger cohorts, whose hopes for change had
been repeatedly dashed by a traditional elite loath to relinquish its power.
The war that broke out unleashed death and devastation on a scale that
no one could have foreseen. None of the survivors of the slaughter was
unscathed by its horrors, and the generations that followed them were of
a very different breed, less hopeful and naïve, more cynical and uncompromising than the men and women of the pre-1914 "world of yesterday,"
as the Jewish-Austrian author Stefan Zweig called it in a book written
shortly before he committed suicide in exile in 1942.[1] The world we live
in today still bears the scars of the "age of total war" and in some ways has
internalized the mentality of the great social, ideological, and military con-
frontations of the twentieth century. For that reason, it is hard for us to

imagine the world that existed before that time, and the men and women who lived in it. Yet it was their hopes and dreams, twisted and perverted into the stark realities of industrial warfare and genocide, that were at the root of it all.

Nowhere is this more evident than in the case of eastern Europe's former borderlands, that "shatterzone of empires," where the German, Austro-Hungarian, Russian, and Ottoman Empires touched each other along a vast swath of territory populated by people of multiple ethnicities and religions, languages and traditions.[2] From the point of view of the empires they belonged to, these regions were on the periphery, made up of a bewildering mix of humanity of dubious loyalties. From the perspective of the inhabitants of the numerous villages, towns, and cities of the borderlands, the empires were distant, somewhat amorphous entities, whose representatives, when they appeared, were perceived as disrupting their traditional way of life for no particular reason. The empires sought to understand the nature and characteristics of the people residing in these borderland territories—which were usually annexed in the course of a larger political or military event of which the local population knew very little. As they were categorized and counted, divided into groups, and assigned particular characteristics by imperial agents and a host of curious ethnographers, the people of the borderlands, who had lived side by side since the Middle Ages, began seeing themselves through the lens of their observers. Internalizing the qualities attributed to them by outsiders, the "borderlanders" also began identifying more clearly and antagonistically what distinguished them from their neighbors beyond the traditional religious, linguistic, and socioeconomic differences.

The rise of nationalism in these regions in the second half of the nineteenth century further hardened these distinctions and added to them a new urgency and militancy. The idea that nations should dwell in their own ancestral lands and separate themselves from those of other ethnicities—ethnicities that were often grafted onto religious affiliations—implied that the mixed populations of the borderlands should be sorted out and unmixed, each into its own space. It also meant, of course, that the vast multi-ethnic empires to which these newly emerging nations belonged were no longer relevant or legitimate and could at best play the role of managing relations between these groups. Hence the traditional friction between religious and ethnic groups in the borderlands was elevated to a matter of self-determination, pride, and dignity, and relations with the distant empires became increasingly fraught as each nation sought independence and the ability to conduct its own business without what came to be seen as foreign interference.

As new nations came into being, they invariably claimed to have ancient historical roots and a unique connection to the land of their ancestors. The creation of this ethnic and territorial nationalism was the project of intellectual and religious leaders, and it was only under conditions of a modernizing society that they could reach the masses and begin the process of nationalizing them. Once the desperately poor and almost universally illiterate peasants, who constituted the majority of the population, were liberated from serfdom in the wake of 1848, the nationalizers saw it as their task to teach them how to read and write so as to be able to implant in them the idea that they were, indeed, a nation with a glorious past and an even better future. The promise of that future, however, was usually tied to liberating themselves from the other groups in their midst as well as from their distant imperial masters. Nationalism, in this context, was thus a recipe for conflict and bloodshed.

The province of Galicia is a good example of this historical moment. Made up of territory annexed from the Polish-Lithuanian Commonwealth by the Austrian Empire in 1772, this newly named province was the easternmost, poorest, and most populous part of what later came to be known as Austro-Hungary; it also had the largest concentration of Jews in the empire.[3] While western Galicia, which nowadays makes up southeastern Poland, had a majority Polish population, in eastern Galicia, which is now part of West Ukraine, the largest ethnic group was Ruthenians (later known as Ukrainians), alongside a large Polish minority. More than 10 percent of the population were Jews, who predominated in many of the region's mid-sized towns and formed substantial minorities in its larger cities.

Galicia has come to be known as the birthplace of Ukrainian nationalism in the latter part of the nineteenth century and the early twentieth century; local Ruthenians increasingly came to view themselves as the indigenous population of a region that had been colonized by the Poles and exploited by their Jewish helpers and lackeys.[4] Yet Galicia was also a major stronghold of Polish nationalism, which believed Galicia to be part of its national patrimony, brutally torn off from its body by the Austrian Empire. Poles referred to Galicia then—and many still nostalgically think of it today—as part of the "kresy," Poland's historical borderlands, where fortified towns and castles protected Western civilization against Cossack and Tatar invasions from the east and encroachments by the Ottoman Empire from the south.[5]

Thus Ruthenian and Polish nationalists vied with each other over the same piece of land. The nationalist Ruthenian goal was to expel the Poles and create an independent West Ukraine, potentially linked to the larger territories of Ukraine across the border under Russian imperial rule. Polish nationalists tended to describe Ruthenians as their somewhat less developed siblings, who, under benevolent Polish rule, could be integrated into the Polish nation as fellow Slavs and Christians. Where both national movements agreed was on the issue of the Jews, who had no place in their respective visions of future nation-states.

The Jews had begun arriving in these regions in the sixteenth century, invited by Polish magnates—owners of vast agricultural estates—to develop their towns, manage their properties, and expand commerce. With the growth of exclusionary Polish and Ukrainian ethnonationalism, Jews increasingly came to be described as a foreign, parasitic element sucking the blood of the indigenous population. The reluctance of Jews to support either national movement for fear of being labeled as the other group's enemies, and their support for the empire as the only power that could maintain the balance between competing national movements, only exacerbated their situation on the eve of World War I.[6]

One Jewish response to the new politics of the era was to develop a national movement of their own, which in Galicia came to be increasingly influenced by Zionism. Galician Zionism had much in common with Polish and Ukrainian nationalism; it was both ethnic and territorial. But the territory in which the Zionists hoped to create a Jewish national home was not where they dwelled at that point, but rather in Eretz Israel, at the time a distant region under Ottoman rule.[7] Many other Jews hoped to continue their traditional lives; vast numbers immigrated to North America, where they believed they would have better economic prospects and be less exposed to ethnonationalism. Still others tried to integrate into the larger European society and adopt one of the available national identities. And not a few embraced revolutionary thinking, believing that the only way for Jews to find a place in the world was to change the order of things from top to bottom.[8]

I have written extensively on eastern Galicia. Over the last two decades I have traveled there often, both for reasons of archival research and in order to get to know the land and its people. The population of West Ukraine is almost exclusively Ukrainian today, although people there often refer to themselves as Galicians. And while my research focused on events in the region leading to World War II and its aftermath—by which time the population had been "unmixed" through policies of genocide, ethnic cleansing, deportations, and population exchange—I was struck by the collective amnesia I encountered there. Indeed, I had a profound sense that all the rich and complex history I had come to research, largely the product of the interactions between the different groups of Galicia's multiethnic population and the impact of its multiple rulers, had been completely rubbed out and forgotten, including any memories of the violent manner in which this demographic "simplification" had been accomplished. In 2007 I published a sort of geographical and historical travelogue, which takes the reader on a journey through a series of towns and cities in eastern Galicia. The book depicts life in each of these sites before the great destruction of World War II, reconstructs how that world was shattered during the Soviet and German occupations, and then outlines the current politics of memory in West Ukraine, geared toward an erasure of that past along with a glorification of Ukrainian freedom fighters, often the same men who collaborated with the Germans in the genocide of the Jews and then carried out the ethnic cleansing of their Polish neighbors. Not surprisingly, the book is titled *Erased*.[9]

Precisely because *Erased* was concerned with depopulation and forgetting, my next book sought to repopulate the region by reconstructing its long multiethnic past. For that purpose, I focused on the Galician town of Buczacz, to which I also had a sentimental and personal connection. As a teenager growing up in Israel, I read and loved the stories by Shmuel Yosef (Shai) Agnon, the only Hebrew-language author to have received the Nobel Prize in literature, who was born in Buczacz and dedicated much of his subsequent vast oeuvre to that town as a microcosm of small-town East European Jewish life, utterly destroyed in the Holocaust. In 1966, on his way back from receiving the prize in Stockholm, Agnon stopped for a few days in London, where my father was then serving as Israel's cultural attaché to the Court of St. James. When Agnon came to our home in Golders Green, my mother welcomed him by saying, "Mr. Agnon, you should know that I too am from Buczacz." Being the Galitzianer that he was, Agnon shot back: "Now that I have been awarded the Nobel Prize, everyone claims to come from Buczacz." He was right in the sense that it was only through his writing that this remote eastern Galician town received the public attention that it did; he also, I think, hurt my mother's feelings, since she had never boasted about her origins and only wanted to make him feel welcome. But the fact of the matter was that she did indeed come from that town, and that the story of her childhood, which she recounted to me just once, shortly before her death, and only upon request, created an intimate and powerful link between me and a site that at the time I had still never visited. To be sure, that link was largely not to the town that I did travel to for the first time a few years after my mother's death, but to the town as it had been before the war. Yet stepping on its soil did, so to speak, stir up the ghosts of the past, and set me on a quest for those who had inhabited Buczacz for several centuries and whose memory had been largely wiped out.

After World War II, Agnon spent much of the next quarter of a century writing a vast tome on his city of Buczacz. He described the task he had taken upon himself as being akin to building a city, the Jewish Buczacz that was no longer.[10] Inspired partly by Agnon's stories and partly by my mother's memories, my book *Anatomy of a Genocide*, published in 2018, attempted to explain how communities of multiethnic coexistence, which had lived side by side since the sixteenth century, were eventually transformed into communities of genocide during World War II. While the book reaches back to the early beginnings of the town, the bulk of it is dedicated to the unfolding of ethnonationalist hatred and violence first unleashed in 1914 and continuing throughout the interwar period, when the town came under Polish rule, all the way to the aftermath of World War II and the Holocaust. In this sense, *Anatomy of a Genocide* is an analysis of both the long-term roots and the daily manifestations of local mass murder.[11] And while it brings back to the town the people who are missing from it in *Erased*, its own inner trajectory is toward the catastrophe at the end of the story. Additionally, even as the book tries to provide what I have called a "biography" of Buczacz (that is, it strives to "build a city"), and does so not only from the Jewish perspective, as in Agnon's case, but from that of its Polish and Ukrainian residents, compressing so many voices between two covers meant that I could not greatly elaborate on the protagonists' lives or let them speak for themselves for more than a few paragraphs.

In my next book I tried to address this last issue. *Voices on War and Genocide*, published in 2020, put together three lengthy accounts of the world wars in Buczacz by a Polish headmaster, a Ukrainian high school teacher, and a Jewish radio technician.[12] Each of these accounts is unique, yet together they provide us with a much deeper understanding of how daily life at times of crisis was experienced by members of different generations and national groups, creating a sort of "*Rashomon* effect" of seeing similar events from three distinct perspectives. Added to the three-dimensional view of events, which simultaneously involved pitting one ethnic group against another, is the personal prism. By reading these lengthy diaries, we become intimately acquainted with their writers—their worries, fears, and hopes—as well as the writers' family members and neighbors; in brief, we empathize with them as human beings, even as we may find some of their opinions despicable and reject their prejudices. And because what they recount are often events of terrible inhumanity and violence, we can picture ourselves more clearly in such situations than we could if we were reading about them in detached, scholarly narratives. Thus, what happened in the distant town of Buczacz many decades ago feels eerily and at times threateningly similar to what may happen in our own towns and neighborhoods.

But because *Voices on War and Genocide* is precisely that, a compilation of first-person accounts of a time of unprecedented and often fraternal violence, it remains part of the trajectory and focus sketched out in *Anatomy of a Genocide*, namely, the long-term path to, and the intimate observation of, local interethnic violence. And yet, the "biography" of such distant provincial towns as Buczacz, as of any other town and neighborhood, cannot be told only as inexorably leading to a foretold end of horror and devastation, just as the biography of an individual should not be told only from the perspective of their foretold death. Before the catastrophe occurred, many other paths were open, many other opportunities were sought, many hopes and dreams and aspirations were articulated and embraced. The end is always inevitable after the fact; but things could have been different, and no one could have imagined how they actually turned out.

As I was researching and writing *Anatomy of a Genocide*, I became increasingly fascinated with the stories people told about how they came to these borderland regions, how they were changed during their centuries-long residence there, and where they ended up once they began leaving the borderlands in the second half of the nineteenth century. In other words, I grew interested in three prisms that, to my mind, could be combined in telling a different kind of history of Europe's eastern borderlands and, to some extent, of borderlands more generally, using Galicia as a representative and at the same time quite distinct example of those long-vanished multiethnic lands. The first of these prisms is the *longue durée*, that is, viewing the history of a region over an extended period of time. The second involves perceiving this era as one made up of three distinct, albeit somewhat overlapping elements, namely, of origins (where did we come from?), transformation (what did we become?), and transition (where did we go?). The third prism entails seeing this complex and ever-changing history as an amalgam of legends and myths, stories and tales, personal biographies and fictionalized accounts, which, when put together and recounted, breathe life into a world that is no more, bring us closer to its protagonists, and, perhaps, aid us in better understanding our own predicament.

I begin at the beginning, with competing myths of origins and bloody struggles over time and space. "Where did we come from?" is a perennial question in mythology, history, and identity: Were we always here, or did we come from elsewhere? Were we forcefully brought, or were we invited to come? Did we conquer by fire and sword, or were we subjugated and colonized? When did we begin to tell these stories to ourselves and to others? When were such stories transformed from tales we tell ourselves about our origins to narratives of exclusion and oppression? The tales of the borderland's origins date back several centuries but were also retold in the new national literatures of the nineteenth century and helped to establish a sense of historical continuity and a meaningful trajectory that fueled much of the violence of the following century and is still at work today. Yet these tales have their own internal richness, beauty, and meaning that can extract them from the limits of events and the logic of history to tell us more about the human spirit and the inevitable loss of what had once been.

By the end of the seventeenth century the borderland region of eastern Poland that would become Galicia settled into an era of relative peace and tranquility. The bloody and turbulent events of the previous decades set up a new struggle between two powerful movements over the minds and souls of the region's population. One was the Enlightenment and the mindset of reason, which called for a rational organization of society rooted in a belief in the orderly functioning of nature and the ability of science to decipher the universe; the other was the pursuit of faith and spirituality as a means to heal the soul and bring about divine intervention in the seemingly irrational and destructive universe created by humanity, or at least to shelter from the world in the embrace of mysticism. The borderlands of Galicia experienced a flowering of architecture and art, and, with the Austrian annexation, an increasingly rational form of government; at the same time they saw waves of mysticism, expressed, not least, in the struggle of Hasidism against the Haskalah, or Jewish Enlightenment. This was the rich soil from which many of the tales and myths of the borderlands sprouted, tales that have filtered through to the contemporary world and have made our image of the borderlands as a region floating between the harsh realities of strife and conflict, on the one hand, and myth and fantasy, on the other.

Those born in the borderlands about halfway through the nineteenth century were often the first to be exposed to the modern world. Some of them left their distant and isolated towns altogether and began living lives unimaginable to their ancestors. Others traveled out "into the world" but then returned, bringing with them new ideas but also slipping back into provincial realities. Still others never left but were indirectly influenced by the vast changes happening at "the center," echoes of which reached out all the way to the periphery. The following generation had already been exposed at times to new ideas about society, politics, culture, and technology in their own provincial homes, thanks to their parents' prior interests. But they were also keenly aware of the older generation's disillusionment at being shunned by the "outside world" they sought to join and having to resign themselves to a provincial existence they had hoped to leave behind. This younger generation was both edgier and more idealistic, hoping to change things more radically from within, in their own provincial settings, or to go out and change the order of things in the world altogether. Because they had greater hopes and more idealistic aspirations, their disillusionment was also deeper and more shattering. Some of them lived long enough to see what the ideologies they had embraced actually wrought on the world, and in old age they could look back in horror at the vast gap between idealism and destruction.

The last generation, some of whom served as soldiers in World War I and others who were exposed to it as teenagers or children, often ended up being mauled by the annihilatory dynamics of modern warfare, endless fraternal conflicts, and vicious, bloodthirsty regimes fueled by hopeful ideologies turned cynical and homicidal. Yet they were not merely subjected to the whims of others, but also became actors in a world of their own making. They accommodated themselves to the new logic of absolute power that transformed youthful idealists into useful cogs in that vast undertaking of remaking humanity through radical surgery and faceless bureaucracy. Some surviving members of this generation spent the rest of their lives serving these new systems; others left in time, living their remaining lives haunted by what they had seen, or done. Others still retained a measure of optimism and faith in humanity, either because they had never abandoned their old values and faith or because they adopted what appeared to be more humane and pragmatic ideologies; the most fortunate among them died before the inevitable disillusionment that comes with time and old age.

This book tells the story of making and unmaking the past of a place that no longer exists, a borderland of cultures and fantasies, tales and myths that made it into what it was; a place that was part of the making of those who discarded it as they stepped out into our own brave new world. Most people, of course, stayed where they were, and waited for the world to come to them, which it eventually did, in the form of the telegraph and the telephone, the railroad and motorcar, tanks and airplanes. The few who ventured out into the world before it stretched out its hand into their provincial towns hoped to change their own lives and, in some cases, believed they could change the world in turn. Coming from a backward, traditional, seemingly unchanging periphery, they burst out onto the larger scene with the energy and hopes and creativity of outsiders striving to fit in. In coming out into that world they did, in their different ways, transform it as much as it transformed them. The sites from which they came no longer exist as they once knew them; the world they helped remold and transform is the world in which we still live today. But it is not the one they had aspired to join or erect. In retrospect, and not only because of the dreaded nostalgia of old age, the world of yesterday may have ultimately appeared to them more appealing than the one they had helped create. But it is difficult not to admire them for their momentous leap into the future and to wonder whether any of us would similarly dare transform our own dreary realities into a better place.

In the last part of this book, I go back to my beginning, the story of my own family's journey from Galicia to Palestine, as told by my mother. Although she was born after World War I, her parents belonged to the pre-1914 generation, and the world she lived in as a child was still suffused with memories, customs, and traditions of old Galicia, the borderland of empires. Her family also made the great leap of leaving everything behind and transforming themselves into something entirely different; yet they always remained tied, like many of the other people I describe, with a thousand strands, to the world they had come from. And because my mother both was from there and at the same time had completely embraced her new existence, I too, however belatedly, internalized some of the ambiguity that I recognized in her toward the end of her life, especially once I reached an age that allowed me to think more critically about my own seemingly self-evident identity, roots, and place in the world. My mother's tale leads this book from the world of those I studied and researched to the internal world of family and self. I suspect that not a few readers can undertake a similar journey in their own time and place, from the confines of the family and the opaque regions of the borderlands "out into the world," and back again.

PART I

Where Did We Come From?

(*With Fire and Sword*)

The linden tree in Buczacz, 2008. Photo by the author.

CHAPTER ONE

Origins

The Linden Tree

ON 18 OCTOBER 1672 the town of Buczacz stepped momentarily into international history. That day, Polish king Michael I and Ottoman sultan Mehmed IV signed the Peace Treaty of Buczacz. The treaty is remembered as a humiliating moment in Polish history, one of many that dotted the topsy-turvy fortunes and ultimate precipitous decline of Polish power in the seventeenth and eighteenth centuries. In signing this document, King Michael agreed to surrender the seemingly impregnable fortress of Kamieniec Podolski, along with all of Ukraine and Podolia, and pledged to pay a heavy yearly tribute to the sultan.[1]

Preceded by decades of unprecedented bloodshed and destruction in the far-flung lands of the vast Polish-Lithuanian Commonwealth, the peace was but a prelude to war, which followed the signing ceremony almost before the ink of the Ottoman Turkish document had dried. Buczacz was born into an era of violence and was designed to stem the surge of invading armies and to facilitate the expansion of Polish rule. Buczacz was baptized with fire and sword, and the manner and purpose of its birth heralded its bloody demise. But in the intervening centuries, Buczacz led a full and vibrant life; as in all towns around the world, it was a life of beauty and dread, sorrow and joy, inspiration and ruin in varying measures. For without the pain of birth and the grief of death, the sheer pleasure of existence would be but a rumor.

The earliest chronicler of Buczacz, Friar Sadok Barącz, was a Polish Dominican of Armenian origins. Ordained in 1838 and variously employed as a librarian, religious instructor, and professor of Bible, Barącz wrote extensive histories of the Armenians in Poland, the Dominican Order, and several cities in Galicia. His colorful account of Buczacz, largely based on sources no longer available following the devastation of two world wars, is tainted with the biases of a strong defender of the Roman Catholic faith and the Polish nation, but it is also a rich source of local myths and anecdotes.[2] His account of the treaty's signing ceremony has been recycled in most subsequent chronicles of the town: "Some say that Mehmed negotiated with the plenipotentiaries of the Polish king under the linden tree. But others say that the negotiations could not have taken place under the linden tree since it was planted on the site where the agreement was signed. The tree survives to this day, but it is in a lamentable condition, because some of it was destroyed in the storm of 1852. This linden tree, just like an old lady, should be cared for, since only one branch of it still survives."[3]

So wrote Barącz in 1882. The tree has survived, although whether it is the original linden tree under which the treaty was signed, or one that was planted to commemorate the signing, or, finally, one that was misidentified and has nothing to do with an event that took place well over three centuries ago, cannot be determined with certainty. Be that as it may, it is indeed a splendid tree; its roots reach deep into the ground and its branches soar high into the sky, partly obscuring the derelict Soviet-era tenements behind it. The sixteenth-century Polish poet Jan Kochanowski had a particular fondness for the linden tree, which symbolized, he believed, repose and peace of mind; for although it produces no fruit, it provides shade and tranquility, shelter and comfort.

> My guest, seat yourself beneath my leaves and take a rest!
> The sun will not reach you here, I promise,
> Even if it is high, and straight rays
> Make the short shadows run back under the trees.
> Here cool breezes always blow from the fields,
> Here the nightingales and starlings comfortably complain.
> From my fragrant flowers hard-working bees
> Draw honey which ennobles the tables of lords.
> While I know how to murmur so softly
> That one falls easily and sweetly asleep.
> I do not bear apples it is true but my master praises me
> As if I were the best tree in the garden of Hesperides.[4]

If the roots of this linden tree are firmly entrenched in its hometown's soil, its long branches reach out in every direction, each shaped differently and striving toward another point in the sky. It is, in that sense, a symbol of Buczacz, an icon of shared habitation and diverging aspirations and fates. I first saw and photographed the tree on a gloomy, overcast day in October 2008, just after visiting the nearby, newly erected monument to Stepan Bandera. Leader of the Organization of Ukrainian Nationalists (OUN), Bandera was intimately linked to the explosion of violence that sealed the fate of Buczacz as a community of several ethnicities and faiths; he represents a generation in which brother turned against brother and torrents of blood were shed in the name of purity, liberty, and justice. The tree had seen it all; but the people in the banged-up cars driving on the road next to it, or those in their crumbling apartments across the untended lawn, the pedestrians with their meager shopping in small plastic bags, their shoes and pants spattered with mud from the unpaved path, remembered none of it; they gazed down at the ground, never seeing those branches silently curling their way toward a steel-gray heaven.

Officially designated a city in the late seventeenth century, the estate of Buczacz appears in the records of the noble Polish Buczacki family as early as 1260. This clan's "Abdank" coat of arms dates back to the earliest myths of Polish history. Curiously, this designation makes a fleeting appearance in Polish author Henryk Sienkiewicz's great 1884 historical novel, *With Fire and Sword*. There, the leader of the 1648 Cossack uprising, Bohdan Khmelnytsky, initially presents himself as "Zenobius Abdank, a landholder in the Kiev Territory, and a colonel in the Cossack regiment of Prince Zasławski." But while this reference suggests that the Buczackis were at least partly Ruthenian, they are remembered in Polish history as proud defenders of Poland's eastern borderlands and disseminators of the Roman Catholic faith in these regions. It was the Buczackis who first constructed a wooden castle on a hill overlooking the village and the Strypa River that winds its way in the valley below.[5]

Nineteenth-century Polish accounts of these early times of territorial expansion and Catholic proselytizing are filled with heroic figures, sweeping landscapes, dramatic battles, intrigue and passion, sacrifice and love. The borderlands (kresy) and "green Ukraine" have lodged themselves deep in the Polish romantic imagination, with the "Wild Lands" of the eastern steppe playing a role somewhat akin to that of the Wild West. Indeed, when Sienkiewicz sought a model for seventeenth-century Ukraine, he traveled to the American West for inspiration.[6] Writing at about the same time, Friar Barącz, who spent his entire life in Galicia, insisted that already in these early times the Buczacki clan's warriors had "defended Rus [Ruthenia] and Galicia with their own bodies against the invasion of the wild oppressors, for this was the route of the Tatars. They were like Shepherds protecting their flocks from hungry wolves." And even as "the brave youth of Poland clashed with the enemy throughout the homeland, the elderly worked at home, extracting profits from the land and the forests, and watching over their abundant springs." Barącz had no doubt that God was on the side of Poland, just as long as Poland was Catholic. "In that laborious work," he exclaimed about the Buczacki knights, "their lives were fortified by the Catholic faith, the faith into which they entrusted their lives, and in which their progeny—nestling securely at home—continued to be raised."[7]

Warriors of the Borderlands

In 1340 the Polish king Casimir the Great annexed territories of Red Rus (Ruthenia) in which Buczacz was located, parts of which later came to be known as Galicia. Poland expanded much farther, to Volhynia, Podolia, and Ukraine, following the creation of the Polish-Lithuanian Commonwealth at the Union of Lublin in 1569. These new territories provided the kingdom with vast grain-growing areas that greatly contributed to its wealth, but also brought it into constant conflict with the Ottoman Empire. In waging war against the Ottomans and their Tatar proxies, Poland made use of large numbers of Cossacks who came directly under its rule. But farther to the east, the fiercely independent Zaporozhian Cossacks, who congregated in fortresses below the great Dnieper rapids, resisted Polish expansion. Finding support among the peasants, who were oppressed by their Polish landlords and Jewish estate managers, the Zaporozhians rose against the Poles several times in the first half of the seventeenth century. These uprisings were brutally suppressed, but their fundamental causes were not addressed, and disgruntled peasants, townspeople, and gentry fled to Zaporozhia. Adding fuel to the fire was the Orthodox Cossacks' vehement opposition to the Uniate (Greek Catholic) Church, established in 1596 by formerly Orthodox Ruthenian bishops who pledged loyalty to the pope in Rome while keeping the Eastern rite. The resulting great uprising of 1648 permanently changed the human and political landscape of Poland's far-flung eastern territories and did not spare Buczacz and its vicinity.[8]

As freedom-seeking, ruthlessly brave, and brutally fierce warriors, the Cossacks have a mixed reputation in Ukraine, Poland, and Russia, as well as among Jews. Isaac Babel's "Red Cavalry" stories are only one illustration of the love-hate relationship many authors have had with these proud outlaws.[9] That a Jew from Odessa opted to serve in the Russian Civil War with a Cossack Bolshevik formation that also played a prominent role in the anti-Jewish violence accompanying the fighting in Ukraine is ironic but not untypical.[10] As early as 1881, the Narodnaya Volya, a revolutionary organization of Russian intellectuals to which several Jews belonged, issued a broadsheet urging Ukrainians to take part in the pogroms of that time—which in turn triggered the first wave of Zionist immigration to Palestine—and depicting the same mythical past of a Cossack-ruled, Pole- and Jew-free Ukraine that anti-Bolshevik Ukrainian nationalists strove to restore six decades later:

> That is not how things were in Ukraine back then, in the days of our forefathers. The peasants owned all the land; back then there were no Polish lords or Jews. The people were free Cossacks, they answered only to the elected community elders and to the Atamans [Cossack leaders]. That's how things were until the Russian tsars came to Ukraine. As soon as they arrived, this cheerful country was shrouded in sorrow. They deprived the people of all the land, handing part of it to the Polish lords, their close associates, and selling part of it to the kikes, while handing the freemen to them as slaves.[11]

Indeed, even the Polish nationalist Sienkiewicz, keen as he is to present the Polish hero of *With Fire and Sword*, Jan Skrzetuski, as a faultless knight in shining armor, ends up sketching his rival, the savage Cossack warrior Jurko Bohun—loosely based on Khmelnytsky's Colonel Ivan Bohun—as the most romantic and tragic figure in the novel.

Magnificent horsemen that they are, the Cossacks have ridden all the way into the present century. A lavish Russian film production of Nikolai Gogol's novel *Taras Bulba*, some of it filmed on the site of the finely restored fortress of Kamieniec Podolski in present-day Ukraine, arrived in theaters as recently as 2009. This tale of a heroic fictional Cossack's exploits unleashed a debate over whether the Cossacks are an essential part of the Ukrainian national heritage or represent the "great Russian soul" of which Ukraine (or "Little Russia") is merely a part.[12] The fact that a twenty-first-century cinematic production of a nineteenth-century novel written in Russian by a Ukrainian of Cossack origins about a seventeenth-century conflict with the Poles could still spark an international dispute indicates how central these events still are to these nations' collective memories. Indeed, the Russian film was preceded by a no less extravagant Polish production of *With Fire and Sword* in 1999, presenting Poland's nostalgic view of its lost eastern territories. As nationalism rises in all three countries, these "memories" of the past come to feature ever more prominently, all engaged in that perennial question of humanity: where did we come from?

Firstcomers

The earliest records of Buczacz and its Galician surroundings are murky, mixing legend and myth with ideological bias and fragmentary archeological and documentary evidence. Excavations carried out in the interwar period uncovered signs of human habitation in the vicinity of Buczacz as far back as 25,000–40,000 years ago, while traces of Bronze and Iron Age humans, including some indications of Scandinavian culture, have also been found. Between the fifth and second millennia BCE the region was likely populated by the Trypillya culture, which made use of animal husbandry and agriculture as well as domesticated horses. Subsequently the inhabitants apparently came under raids by nomadic Scythians, and graves dating back to 800 BCE contain numerous harnesses. In the early centuries of the Common Era this area was inhabited by the Goths, a Germanic people that probably came from Scandinavia and that gradually merged with the local population. There is also evidence of Iranian-speaking Alans in the region between the ninth and the fourteenth centuries.

Basing himself on this complex record of human habitation, the Ukrainian chronicler of the Greek Catholic Basilian monastery in Buczacz, Yaroslav Stotskyi, has suggested that it demonstrates the deep roots of indigenous identity: "All these and other races that inhabited Buczacz and its region in different centuries created together a pre-Ukrainian identity: in the shape of their language, character, religion, culture, and customs."[13]

Conversely, for the Polish priest Barącz the history of Buczacz unfolds as a mission of bringing Roman Catholic Polish civilization to the lands of the barbarous heathen in the east. Hence the efforts by the Buczacki lords of the city "to solidify the faith among the urban population," not least by providing funds in 1379 for the restoration and upkeep of the Roman Catholic Church. The suggestion that a church had already existed there even earlier is consistent with the assertion that Roman Catholicism pre-dated the establishment of Polish rule there and was therefore native to the region.[14]

Ukrainian writers dispute this view. Father Iosyf Kladochnyi, for instance, presents the construction of a Roman Catholic church in Buczacz as an act of colonization. Noting that according to the 1379 document recording the church's reconstruction, the local population was ordered to pay a tenth of their wages toward the cost of this undertaking, he concludes: "the Poles wanted to Polonize the native population with the assistance of Catholicism in its Roman form and to pressure the Ukrainian nobility into supporting the Latin rite. Since the latter resisted these efforts, Ukrainian nobles were not allowed even into the lowliest state offices and their properties were confiscated. Thus they accepted the Latin rite, and their clans became Polish."[15]

There is little doubt that the rebuilt church symbolized Polish domination of Buczacz and its surroundings. Following the transfer of the city into the hands of the Potocki clan in 1612, for instance, several of its renowned lords are said to have been buried there. And when the church was replaced by a grander structure in the mid-eighteenth century, all those entering the new edifice were greeted with the Potocki Pilawa coat of arms and an inscription over the main gate declaring that the church had indeed been built by the current owner of the city. And while Buczacz was in fact taken over by the Austrians only nine years later, the church continued to serve the town's Roman Catholic population for almost two more centuries, until the ethnic cleansing of World War II and the imposition of Soviet rule put an end to Polish and Roman Catholic presence in the region.[16]

Forty-five years later, writing from his Canadian exile just before the collapse of the Soviet Union and the long-sought declaration of Ukrainian independence, the Greek Catholic Father Kladochnyi—who had served in World War II as chaplain of the Ukrainian Waffen-SS Division "Galicia"— wryly commented that "the parish church of The Assumption of Mary in Buczacz, which remains there to this day, was rebuilt in stone in the eighteenth century," and contains "a marble panel with inscriptions honoring important Polish statesmen of that period."[17] In fact, under communist rule, and lacking a congregation, the church fell into a state of increasing disrepair. But shortly after Kladochnyi penned these comments and following the change of regime, the Roman Catholic Father Ludwik Rutyna returned to Buczacz after decades of exile and spent the last years of his life restoring the church to its former glory.

Father Rutyna also ended up serving a small congregation mostly made up of Ukrainians who turned to Roman Catholicism. Some cynics have suggested that these men and women were primarily motivated by the hope that the Roman Catholic Church would provide them with better opportunities for travel and work in Poland and the rest of the European Union. Father Kladochnyi would likely not have been surprised, since that was the way he viewed the region's Polonization from the very beginning. Indeed, he argued, even the original "owners of Buczacz—the Buczackis—were Ukrainian," but "following the occupation of Galicia by the Poles [in 1340], they accepted the Latin rite and were Polonized in the fifteenth century."[18] This competition of origins itself dated back to the town's early records. The very same document of 1379 ordering the construction of the church described Buczacz, which was already protected by a wooden fortress, as "the seat of the Abdank clan, the meritorious protector of the borderland and the disseminator of western culture and Catholicism."[19]

Pious Rulers

Stefan Potocki, the first member of his clan to rule Buczacz, was forty-four years old when he took over the town.[20] Engaged in several wars in the very first year of his rule, Potocki ended up falling into the hands of the Ottomans, who incarcerated him in Istanbul. The common practice at the time, especially with wealthy or important prisoners, was for their families or communities to pay handsome rewards in order to gain their release.[21] And indeed, according to Barącz, in this case too, after having "sustained many humiliations, injustices and troubles," Potocki was finally released when "a ransom of 300,000 ducats [about $13.5 million in today's currency] was assembled and rushed" to Istanbul.

But Barącz has another, more edifying tale to tell about this event. The real reason for Potocki's rescue, we are told, was the utter devotion of his wife, Marya Mohylanka. Having found himself in "this sad situation," relates Barącz, Potocki "wrote to his wife, telling her to sell everything to anyone in order to pay out the sum demanded." But Marya "sought another source of finance," and, "donning a hair shirt, she gathered poor virgins, widows and orphans, and tearfully begged for alms, unceasingly beseeching God to show mercy toward her captive husband." It was this dedication to her husband and persistent appeal to heaven that brought about the miracle of Potocki's release. For as the city's new lord recounted upon returning home, his liberation was accomplished through no crude bartering of souls but by way of divine intervention:

I sat in prison weighed down by shackles and prayed according to my custom . . . [when at] midnight I heard a voice: "Believe in me, son! Think of your possessions! God is with you!" Carefully listening to the voice, I perceived that the shackles had fallen off from me and the door of the prison had opened. Gripped by fear I fell down in rapture, from which I arose, sadly convinced that no human being would be able to liberate me; hence I passionately said my prayers and lifted my shackles in my hands. With that a most venerable old man approached me and cried out: "Do not be afraid! Come with me!" I myself do not know when it was that I left the prison and was put on a boat, which the old man piloted; but that same night he delivered me to Venice.

Upon hearing this tale of wonders, Marya Mohylanka, we are told, "rose up, tears of joy streaming down her face," and pointed out her own role in the affair: "My most pleasing husband, champion of the wives of Polish magnates! Listen to me. Look at these members of my household, impoverished and abandoned, with whom I spent thirty days and nights in prayer, and behold these hands of mine, into which alms abundantly poured, obtaining through persuasion the liberation of my most beloved husband."

This, too, however, is not the end of the story, which has yet another moral of special importance to Barącz. For as it turns out, prior to his capture, Potocki had taken up Calvinism, which became popular in Poland at that time. In Barącz's telling, then, Potocki was rescued not only from an Ottoman prison but also from the Calvinist heresy, for his rescuer was none other than Saint Dominic. As he "appeared before him," the saint "urged him to abandon his erroneous apostasy and to pass on to his son the following prophetic utterance: 'Quo usque religio Dominicana, eousque Domus Potociana.' The Potockis will continue to exist as long as they remain Dominicans." It was for this reason that upon his safe return, Potocki "furnished a Dominican cloister, where he lived piously, in hope for good salvation as a righteous and pious Catholic, and there he ended his life in 1631."[22]

But Marya Mohylanka was Eastern Orthodox, and never abandoned her faith. This union, between the newly fervent Roman Catholic Polish magnate and the no less devout daughter of a Moldavian prince, whose Orthodox faith was commonly identified with the region's Ruthenian population—which in turn was in the process of being converted to Greek Catholicism—encapsulates the intimacy, complexity, and increasingly fraught relations between religion, ethnicity, and myths of origins in Buczacz and Galicia as a whole. And while this first Potocki ruling family, according to Barącz, "possessed many noble qualities," and "contributed greatly to the city," it was in fact Marya Mohylanka who left the greatest impression on the population. "Even today," exclaims Barącz, referring to the late nineteenth century, more than 250 years after these events took place, "the grateful people keep in their living memory the name of Mohylanka, or 'the proud one,' as she was commonly called."[23]

Two major contributions are ascribed to Mohylanka, both of which have remained distinct features of the town's appearance and reflect its borderland nature on the frontiers between Poland and Ukraine. First was the erection of the Orthodox church of Saint Nicholas, consecrated in 1610, and thus apparently two years before Potocki officially assumed power in Buczacz. Taken over by the Greek Catholics probably toward the end of the century, this was the first stone church in the city, and remains its oldest surviving structure.[24] A recent account by the Polish chronicler of Buczacz, Stanisław Kowalski, describes "this old church, surrounded by a high wall," as "undoubtedly one of the greatest monuments in the city." But because the church also came to symbolize the divide between Roman and Greek Catholicism, later identified as the respective religions of Poles and Ruthenians, Kowalski finds that "this heavy and gloomy religious building evokes certain reflections." These thoughts concern not only "its founder, Marya Mohylanka," but also "later generations of the Potocki family," not least its eighteenth-century ruler and "zealous propagator of the Greek Catholic Church," Mikołaj Potocki, whose mixed reputation hinges, among other things, on his abandonment of his ancestors' Roman Catholicism.[25] Little wonder that contemporary Ukrainian writers recall Mikołaj, whose story will be told below, as "an outstanding figure,"[26] while Polish patriots have viewed him as a traitor to his nation, since, as one author put it, the Roman Catholic Church had "sought to propagate Catholicism, and thus Polishness, to the eastern territories of the Polish crown." From that author's perspective, one could only lament that the rulers of "Buczacz, whose Ruthenian population constituted the smallest ethnic group" in the city, had built and supported "more Orthodox churches than was required by the local Orthodox faith and then the Greek rite."[27]

Besides supporting her faith, Marya Mohylanka appears to have also engaged in improving the fortifications of her new abode. Upon their arrival in Buczacz, the Potockis found the remains of the old wooden fortress. The same site was now used to build a massive new stone castle, while incorporating the basement vaults dating back to the fourteenth and fifteenth centuries. The total area of the castle was somewhat smaller than that of the original structure, but this time the entire city was also surrounded with a complex of ramparts and trenches, which are still visible from the current layout of the city.[28] The road leading to the castle passed by a tower built on the eastern perimeter of the town, whose ruins can still be seen today, and then proceeded to a drawbridge over a water-filled ditch, which would block the main gate to the castle at night. Long after it was abandoned, the castle's thick and high walls, complete with embrasures for cannons, could still be seen, although they have been gradually falling apart. The view of the town from the castle hill remains striking even today, and must have been all the more pleasing before the progressive destruction of the city in the two world wars.[29]

There were clearly good reasons to vastly improve the city's fortifications. By the time of Stefan Potocki's death, trouble was brewing in the borderlands.[30] The violence that was about to sweep across the vast eastern territories of Poland spared no one, but it had an especially tragic impact on the Jews of the region. This was also the case in Buczacz, for when the Potockis arrived in the city, they also found there a significant Jewish community.

Where the Crooked Became Straight

Shmuel Yosef Agnon was born in Buczacz in 1887, just five years before Barącz passed away in his monk's cell in the beautifully situated monastery of Podkamień, seventy-five miles north of Buczacz. Fifty years later, in mid-March 1944, Podkamień was the site of a massacre of hundreds of Poles seeking shelter in the monastery and its surroundings, committed by troops of the Ukrainian Insurgent Army (UPA), a nationalist formation engaged in the ethnic cleansing of Galicia. Agnon died in Jerusalem in 1970, just four years after receiving the Nobel Prize in Literature, in a place and a time vastly different from the Galicia he had left behind before World War I. Agnon's original name was Czaczkes, and the tombstone over his father's grave bearing that name can still be found in the Jewish cemetery on the outskirts of Buczacz, where he was put to rest in 1913.

Agnon's mother died, aged forty-three, in 1909, less than a year after he immigrated to Palestine; her gravestone has only recently been discovered in the same cemetery, oddly situated at some distance from her husband's.[31]

Although he left Buczacz at the age of twenty-one and only visited it twice, much of Agnon's writing was dedicated to the life and culture of Galician Jewry. Three years after his death, Agnon's daughter, Emuna Yaron, published his book *Ir u-Melo'ah* (*A City in Its Fullness*), a complex and immensely rich chronicle of Jewish Buczacz and the small-town East European Jewish universe to which it belonged. The epigraph that opens this vast amalgam of myth, fiction, and history, which Agnon never completed, succinctly summarizes the author's state of mind as he constructed this literary edifice in the decades following the destruction of his town in World War II: "This is the history of the city of Buczacz, which I have written in my grief and sorrow, so that our sons, who come after us, will know that our city was full of Torah, wisdom, love, piety, life, grace, kindness and charity from the day of its founding until the arrival of the blighted abomination and their befouled and deranged accomplices who wrought destruction upon it. May God avenge the blood of His servants and visit vengeance upon His foes and deliver Israel from all its sorrows."[32]

Agnon's great tome is not a story of his hometown's devastation, but a monument to its life, a multifaceted biography of Buczacz as a Jewish town. A master of delving into the deepest recesses of the human soul and the tortured relations between his characters, Agnon rarely takes time to observe his natural surroundings. Yet he introduces his book with a much-cited passage on the town's physical setting. Opening with an implicit analogy to the biblical poetic metaphor of Jerusalem as the geographic and spiritual fortress of the Jews, he then proceeds to depict Buczacz as akin to paradise: even those who come from afar would never wish to leave and soon become indistinguishable from the locals, for it is a place of harmony where the crooked has become straight:

> My city is situated upon mountains and hills, coming in and out of forests filled with trees and bushes, and the Strypa River flows through the city and alongside the city, and streams bring forth water and feed the reeds and the bushes and the trees, and good springs abound with fresh water, and birds dwell in the trees and twitter from them. Some of the birds were conceived and born in our city, and some have flown to our city and have remained in it, having seen and recognized how superior our city is to all the other

places. They have found themselves a home in our city and have taught themselves to chirp like the birds of our city. And he who can distinguish between one song and another, he can distinguish between a bird born in our city and a bird that has come from elsewhere.

Below the hills you will find straight places. Some of them were made by heaven and some were made by man. Some are intertwined and some complement each other. For this is one of those instances where the work of heaven and the work of man live side by side in peace and allow each to complement the other. Most likely these places were created in the early days, when man's heart was whole, without crookedness and without deceit.[33]

This, then, was Buczacz before it all began, as re-created by Agnon in his mind's eye half a century after leaving it: a small town in a lovely valley, surrounded by forests and fields, intersected by a stream, its people living in harmony with God, nature, and each other, waiting patiently for the waves of history to crash onto its walls. And yet, for those familiar with Agnon's voluminous writings on his hometown, this idyllic perception was always mixed with another, far more critical view. In much of his fiction, Agnon does not call the town by its real name but rather refers to it as Szybusz, a name derived from the Hebrew word for "disruption, going wrong, going astray, or deviating." And, indeed, his biography of Buczacz is filled with tales of things "going wrong" and of its Jewish inhabitants' deviation from the path of righteousness, beginning with their decision to stop there "for the night" on their way to Eretz Israel and ending with the community's destruction in the Holocaust.[34] From this perspective, Agnon's Buczacz, and by extension the imaginary shtetl writ large, was both an idyllic setting resembling mythical Jerusalem as the sacred heart of Zion, and a fundamental error that could only be corrected by resuming the journey to the Holy Land.[35]

Guests for the Night

Polish Jews have a long and complex history. For centuries Jews lived as a distinct yet officially recognized and formally ordered entity within the Polish kingdom. This has meant that just as Jews were not fully integrated into Polish society, much of Polish and Jewish history were written separately from each other, demonstrating that even historians are often unable to liberate themselves from the legacy of the past and the biases of their own time. And yet, as some recent studies have documented, any comprehensive history of Poland and European Jewry must recognize how closely the two were bound together.[36]

Jewish communities are known to have existed in Poland since the early eleventh century, when the first Polish coins with Jewish inscriptions were minted. More permanent Jewish settlements in western Poland date back to the twelfth and thirteenth centuries. The first major charter to the Jews in Poland was issued by Prince Bolesław the Pious in 1264, establishing Jewish juridical and communal autonomy and abstaining from any residential or economic restrictions in his principality of Great Poland. These privileges were confirmed and expanded by King Casimir the Great in the mid-fourteenth century and were subsequently applied to other areas incorporated into Poland in the east. This was the legal basis for Jewish life in Poland, assuring Jews of the king's protection and defining their duties to the royal treasury, an arrangement that largely remained in force until the end of independent Poland in the late eighteenth century. But in 1539 King Zygmunt I relinquished full jurisdiction over the Jews residing on the lands of the nobility. This meant that Jews living in private towns such as Buczacz came directly under the rule of their magnates, who defined their rights and duties by granting them particular privileges. By 1765, more than half of the Polish-Lithuanian Commonwealth's 750,000 Jews were living in privately owned estates and towns under the direct jurisdiction of Polish magnates.[37]

It is assumed that some Jews may have come to Poland from the Crimean Jewish kingdom of Khazaria, as well as from Byzantium and Kievan Rus. Additionally, small numbers of Sephardic Jews seem to have arrived in Poland as a result of the expulsion from Spain in 1492, mostly by way of the Ottoman Empire and Italy. But the vast majority of what became Polish Jewry arrived from Ashkenaz—the Jewish name for German and Bohemian lands west of Poland. This migration was prompted by increasing persecution, especially during and after the Black Death of 1347–51 that killed at least one-third of Europe's population. By the early sixteenth century, as a result of repeated pogroms and expulsions from Central and Western Europe, most Jews in the world were living either in the Ottoman Empire or in Poland. The Jews of Poland were multiplying at a particularly rapid rate, with an estimated population of 50,000. This demographic trend stimulated the migration of Jews farther east to Ukrainian lands, especially after the 1569 Union of Lublin transferred these territories to Polish rule. As the king handed out vast tracts of land to the nobility, these magnates came to rely on the Jews for the development of their lands and towns by leasing their estates to them and granting them monopolies for the manufacture and sale of such products as flour and alcohol.[38]

The Jews, for their part, were motivated to move farther east also because the emerging Polish bourgeoisie in the more established towns of central Poland strove to limit their economic activities. Consequently, on the eve of the great Cossack uprising of 1648, a significant share of Poland's 450,000 Jews—by then the single largest Jewish community in the world—were living in the kingdom's Ukrainian possessions. And as the colonization of Ukraine by the Polish nobility inflamed resentment among the Ukrainian population, the Polish magnates' Jewish leaseholders and townsmen were regularly depicted as bloodsuckers living off the wretched peasants as well as representing the age-old "enemies of Christ."[39]

Official documents mention Jews in Buczacz as early as 1500. The oldest tombstone in the town's Jewish cemetery has been dated to 1587, with four more dating to the 1590s. This confirms census data listing a Jewish community in Buczacz in the sixteenth century.[40] Legends about the origins of the community provide a flavor of how Jews living there explained to themselves the circumstances of their arrival. Agnon, who collected such tales for most of his lifetime, assured his readers that his version of the story was a reliable account of how the Jews came to Buczacz: "When was our city founded, and who was its founder? Long have all the historians grown weary from researching this. But a little has been revealed to us, and I am setting down a faithful record of what I know."[41]

The tale Agnon relates conforms in its general outlines to the history of the Jews' arrival in the eastern borderlands of Poland. It also confirms the good relations and shared interests between the Jews and the town's owners, and depicts the prosperity and sense of security of the Jewish community of Buczacz despite occasional bouts of violence and destruction. Just as important, the story sets out from the premise that the Jews had always been on the way to their true destination in Eretz Israel, even though they ended up staying in Buczacz for an extended period of time. In other words, Agnon describes the Jews of Buczacz, and in a larger sense Polish Jewry as a whole, as a transitional population, albeit one that found a comfortable, long-term, much beloved, yet essentially temporary abode in Poland.[42]

The Jews of Buczacz, in Agnon's telling, originally set out from the Rhineland in western Germany, "motivated by their pure hearts' desire to go to Eretz Israel, along with their wives and their sons and their daughters. They sold their fields, their vineyards, their male and female servants, their houses, and all their property that could not be transported. They obtained permission from the governor to leave their city. They took along travel gear and set forth on the road."

To be sure, the Jews "did not know the road to Eretz Israel," but they "knew that it was in the East. And so they turned their faces to the East, and that was the way they went." They had set out in the spring, "when the highways are merry and the fields and vineyards are filled with people, but as they kept going, people became scarce, vineyards and fields were not to be seen, and all the roads led into boundless forests, with birds and animals and beasts." Finally, they "stopped and camped to celebrate Rosh Hashanah, Yom Kippur, and the holiday of Sukkot." But "in those regions, as in most of the lands of the Gentiles, winter comes early," and by the end of the holidays, "when they should have set forth, snow began to fall." Soon "the roads were blotted out and one could not distinguish land from water or tell where there was solid ground and where there were rivers or lakes. Despite themselves, the pilgrims were compelled to tarry in their camp."

And so they remained, "sheltered in their booths in the snow, tranquil and secure from the raging stormy winds and from the terrifying bears and other beasts that would come one by one or in groups to their doors and growl." And then, helpless and stranded in this foreign land, the Jews were rescued. One day, they "found themselves surrounded by some kind of people who looked like animals, with huge and fearsome dogs at their heels and great trumpets at their lips. But they had no evil intent and had only come there to hunt animals, for they were great and distinguished noblemen, and it is the way of noblemen to hunt game in the forest."

Asked by one of the noblemen where they had come from and where they were heading, the Jews "told him their whole story, how they had intended to go to the Holy Land and because winter had overtaken them had made camp there until the end of the winter and cold." The Jews then described everything they had seen on the way, and "the noblemen were amazed by their wisdom and eloquence and so taken by them that they forgot the game and gave up the hunt and began to urge the Jews to come and stay with them, for winter was very hard in that land," especially because "they came from the Rhineland, and would certainly never survive winter in the forest."

It was from that point on, Agnon suggests, that a new relationship developed between the Jews and the local nobility, ultimately leading to the long sojourn of the Jews in Buczacz. "The noblemen who had taken the Jews into their homes enjoyed prosperity in everything they did. They realized and knew that their success was due to the Jews . . . They began to urge them to stay with them, saying, the whole land is at your disposal; make your home wherever you wish, and if you want to engage in commerce in the land, better still, for no one here knows anything about trade."

And so the Jews stayed, initially still hoping to resume their journey at an opportune moment, until one day they realized that for now their travels were over. "To leave this place and to go to Eretz Israel was not possible, for by now they already had a stake in the land and had built themselves homes and were in favor with the nobility. As for the women, some were pregnant, some were nursing, some were worn out and weak. And the elders were even older than before, so that traveling would have been hard on them."

And thus the Jews "agreed unanimously to establish a permanent house of prayer." Once they informed the local lord of their decision, "it so pleased him that he gave them the house and all its furnishings as an outright and perpetual gift, and before his death he ordered his sons to treat the Jews with benevolence, for it was thanks to the Jews that God had granted him prosperity and all that they would come to inherit."

From these humble origins, "little by little, the entire place was settled by Jews." Soon Buczacz "acquired a reputation and people began coming from far and near on the days of the holidays, to see and to be seen. Noblemen and noblewomen also came on horseback. Then the local lord built himself a stone house and later built a castle up on the mountain facing the River Strypa, a great castle befitting one of the great princes of the land. This castle stood for many years as a fortress and shelter for the lord of the city and his many servants . . . Its ruins are still there." That, concludes Agnon, "is how Buczacz began," and the Jews "dwelled there for several generations in peace and tranquility, except in years of war and revolution . . . until the Enemy came and eradicated them all."[43]

Agnon's tale of the Jewish origins of Buczacz was first written as a parable of the beginning of Jewish life throughout Eastern Europe. That early version was penned by Agnon during World War I, when he was living in Germany, and published in a German translation in Berlin in 1916 as part of a volume Agnon co-edited under the title *Das Buch von den polnischen Juden* (The Book of Polish Jews). Ironically, that very year the German army declared a *Judenzählung*, or "Jew count," of Jewish German citizens serving in uniform, in an attempt to show that Jews were not doing

Napoleon Orda (1807–83), *Buczacz on the Strypa*, drawing.
Author's private collection.

their part for the Fatherland. The story was later published in Hebrew
under the title "Origins" (Kedumot) as the first of sixteen tales in the collection *Poland: Fairy Tales* (*Polin: Sipurei agadot*, which can also be translated as "legends"):

> This story is the traditional legend we received from our fore-
> fathers who went to Poland. When Israel saw that the persecu-
> tions were continuing and the suffering constantly renewed and
> the oppression becoming ever greater and the wicked rulers issu-
> ing one evil decree after another, to the point that they could no
> longer resist the enemies of Israel, they went out to the road and
> asked, which path should they take to find rest for their souls?
> Then a note fell from heaven saying, Go to Poland. They set out
> and reached the land of Poland and gave the king a mountain of

gold. The king received them with great honor, and God took
mercy on them, and they found favor with the king and the nobles. The king allowed them to dwell in all the lands of his kingdom and to trade in the entire length and breadth of the land and
to worship God according to the precepts of their religion. The
king protected them from every foe and enemy. And Israel dwelled
securely in Poland for many years . . . And why is it called Polin
[the Hebrew name for Poland, which can be read as *po-lin*, "here
we shall spend the night"]? For Israel said to God, master of the
universe, if it is not yet my time to be redeemed from this exile,
which is akin to night, our people will spend the night here until
You bring us to Eretz Israel.[44]

In Agnon's telling, then, this is a story of exodus and exile, of the much
delayed but finally to be completed return to the Promised Land, in the
wake of many more catastrophes, a return justified and earned all the more
precisely because of the seemingly interminable wait for the completion
of the journey. And while Agnon somewhat skews the chronology of settlement in the site, which was already inhabited when the Jews arrived,
there is no doubt that the Jews soon came to constitute the core of urban
life and commerce in Buczacz, transforming it into a significant economic
hub. In this sense, the Jews fulfilled the purpose for which they were en-
ticed to migrate to Poland with various economic and religious privileges
and protection from enemies internal and external. And yet, in Agnon's
telling, the Jews ended up in Buczacz accidentally rather than by design, for
this was not their destination but merely a rest station on the way to the
Holy Land. In that sense, from Agnon's perspective, the Jews of Buczacz,
Galicia, and the borderlands of Europe as a whole were, to paraphrase the
title of the author's last–World War II novel—based on a visit to his
hometown two decades after leaving it—merely guests for the night.[45]

Stumbling Stones

Others have also speculated that the Jews were among the very early settlers in Buczacz even before it came under Polish rule in the mid-fourteenth
century. One interesting example is Stanisław Kowalski's history of Buczacz.
Born in Jazłowiec (Yazlovets, ten miles south of Buczacz), Kowalski attended school in Buczacz for eight years before his conscription into the
Polish army in 1938; the following year he was taken prisoner by the Red

Army and spent two years in the murderous Soviet gulag of Kolyma. Subsequently he joined the newly established Polish Anders Army, fought with the British in Normandy, and was wounded in combat in Germany shortly before the fall of the Third Reich. After the war Kowalski immigrated to the United States and wrote several books on his hometown, the gulag, and Buczacz.[46] Kowalski insists that his account of Buczacz aims to "reconstruct what has now disappeared in the abyss of oblivion." For him, although "the beginnings" of Buczacz "are completely unknown," the town "became important once it returned to the homeland during the reign of Casimir the Great." In other words, Kowalski believes that Buczacz, along with the rest of Galicia, had always been Polish, even prior to the existence of any historical records of the presence of a Polish state in the region. Precisely because "circumstances do not allow a reconstruction of what was destroyed by time and war," writes Kowalski, "the only way to keep it in human memory is the written word," which is the goal of his book. "For the sake of our nation," he proclaims, "we should wish that what guided the generations that lived during the partitions"—namely, those Poles who kept the memory of independent Poland alive after it disappeared as a political entity in the late eighteenth century—"will become a model to be followed by contemporary Polish scholars, and that the destroyed and transformed past will again find its eulogists in historical essays and literature."

Kowalski, then, is a Polish romantic nationalist who accepts current political circumstances but believes deeply in the Polish nation's duty to remember its glorious past, historical and mythical alike. This history, documented or mythological, should be reintroduced to "Polish schools, libraries, and homes, in order to become educational material for Polish youth and to enlighten every Pole." In this endeavor, Buczacz serves as Kowalski's template. "Unknown and forgotten Buczacz is not only a historical subject to be fixed in memory, and not only a tale about people living in distant times. It is a rich history of our Borderlands which we must not forget or allow to be eroded by time, destruction and people of ill will." Kowalski's models for writing such national histories include, of course, Sadok Barącz's own history of Buczacz.[47] His fervent hope is that "a new cadre" of such nationally minded scholars "will arise and take up the task of passing on to new generations what was created by our ancestors and what has been maintained in the memory of the inhabitants of the eastern borderlands, of Podolia and of Buczacz, [a cadre] that will understand the value and historical importance of the large and small towns of this former Polish land."[48]

And yet, unlike many Polish accounts that either ignore the Jewish population of Poland and its contribution to the nation's history or see the Jews as a foreign and generally malign implant, Kowalski devotes a great deal of space to the Jews of Buczacz. And while his narrative has mythical elements not unlike Agnon's tale of origins, it does provide a window into a different perception by a dedicated Roman Catholic and Pole of his former Jewish neighbors and their long history in the region.

Basing himself on patterns of habitation described in accounts of the town written at the end of the seventeenth century, Kowalski argues that by the time Buczacz came under Polish rule, it already had a Polish-Ruthenian population living next to the castle's walls, and a Jewish community that resided in a separate part of the town, protected by walls and defensive towers. Kowalski also relates that members of the town's interwar Jewish community claimed to possess two ancient Torah scrolls, one dating back at least a millennium, and another said to be six hundred years old. This would indicate, he believes, that the origins of the community go back to a Khazar settlement that began at the turn of the previous millennium, while a second community established itself there under Casimir the Great some four centuries later. But since Kowalski does not provide any information on his sources, there is no way to determine their reliability.[49]

What is remarkable about Kowalski's account, therefore, is not just that it is based on pure speculation, but also that it suggests Jewish presence in Buczacz at least as ancient as that of Poles, whose own claim of indigeneity is rooted in myth rather than any scientific findings. In other words, Kowalski's tale of origins ties the fate of Polish Roman Catholicism and Judaism (albeit professed by Khazars, who were not ethnically Jews but adopted the Jewish faith) tightly together, going back to the town's very beginnings, however mythological. More cautious scholars, such as the historian Nathan Michael Gelber, have eschewed such speculations. Born in Lwów in 1891, Gelber grew up in the Galician town of Brody, acquired a PhD in history from the University of Vienna in 1916, and served as an officer in the Austro-Hungarian army in World War I. He was general secretary of the Austrian Zionist Organization in the 1920s and immigrated to Palestine in 1934. Over the years, Gelber published many works on Jewish and Zionist history, and after the Holocaust devoted much of his remaining years to writing on the destroyed Jewish communities of Galicia, including a well-documented chapter on the history of Buczacz in the town's memorial book. According to Gelber, although Jews were apparently living in Buczacz when it was still a feudal estate, only by the sixteenth century did they become a major commercial presence, actively

participating in the local fairs that linked Poland and the east, and forging
contacts with merchants in Lwów, Kraków, and Constantinople. As Gelber shows, this reflected a general trend within the larger context of Polish
settlement in Volhynia, Podolia, and Ukraine, where the Jews soon mo-
nopolized much of the trade, handicrafts, and branches of manufacture
related to agriculture.[50]

Documented histories such as Gelber's notwithstanding, legends and
fictions about the beginnings of Buczacz, as of the rest of Galicia, came to
play an important role in how people imagined who they were and where
they had come from. With the rise of nationalism in the second half of the
nineteenth century, new popular forms of historical poetry and fiction retold the past through a national prism and suggested exhilarating visions
of the future; in imagining the past and fantasizing the future, the assertion of descent from the first inhabitant of the land or the builders of the
city came to be associated with rights of ownership and belonging. This
comes to show once again that, rumors to the contrary notwithstanding,
history plays a crucial role in the lives of people and nations; yet its impact
does not necessarily depend on the accuracy of its reconstruction. All too
often, fanciful tales of the past have nourished ideologies and motivated
politics far more effectively than carefully researched and documented historical accounts. At times, we stumble onto history as one would stumble
over a mass grave: we know that something terrible, perhaps also decisive,
but in any case gruesome, happened in the past. But we don't know who
the perpetrators and the victims were, or why it happened; hence, we cannot tell what lessons can be drawn from this discovery. And so, we set about
imagining and narrating the tale, and soon enough we can draw those lessons that serve our purpose best.

This trajectory can be reversed; we can stumble on empirical remind-
ers of a past that we know all too well but wish to repress and forget. For
close to three decades, the so-called *Stolpersteine*, or Stumbling Stones project, has installed more than 70,000 brass plates into the pavements of numerous German cities and towns, recalling the names of mostly Jewish, as
well as some Sinti (Romani), handicapped, homosexual, and other victims
of the Nazi regime; the plates are located at the victims' last place of residence or work before they were taken to their deaths by the authorities.[51]
A very different kind of stumbling upon a known, yet also murky, and
clearly deadly past is related in Agnon's "biography" of Buczacz. Once upon
a time, he writes, the beloved beadle of the great synagogue in Buczacz,
curly-haired Shalom, decided to hire laborers to clear away the debris and

trash that had piled up over the years on the path to the synagogue, and to pave it anew:

> As they were removing the rocks and the garbage, they dug into the ground in order to fill the ditches. They had not been digging very deeply when they struck human skulls buried in three rows, ten skulls to a row, all with undamaged teeth. Thus they knew that these were remains of soldiers, which had been lying there for many years. Perhaps they had been there for a century, perhaps for a millennium, for Buczacz, as you know, is an ancient town and over the years had seen many wars, because before the Slavs came to our region other unknown tribes and peoples whom we do not know had dwelled there, and before them there were still other tribes and peoples. They killed each other over and over and inherited each other one after the other until the Slavs came and wiped them out and dwelled in their place. And even they did not have peace, because then came the Turks and the Tatars and they did to Poland what she had done to those who had been there before. And for that reason, they used to say that in Buczacz there is not a single spot without a grave, if not of a Turk then of a Tatar, and if of neither then of a Pole, and if not of a Pole then of the nations that had dwelled here before.[52]

Buczacz, in Agnon's telling, like so many other towns in Europe's borderlands, marched into history over piles of corpses; three centuries later, it made its exit in a similar fashion, leaving behind far bigger mass graves of freshly killed residents.

CHAPTER TWO

Massacres

Grandfather Simcha

Toward the end of World War II, Nathan Nata Hanover's Hebrew-language book *Yeven Metsulah* (*The Deep Mire*), originally published in Venice in 1653, was reissued by the publishing house Hakibbutz Hameuchad in Palestine.[1] The book is the most detailed eyewitness account available of the destruction of Jewish communities during the Khmelnytsky uprising. Traditionally referred to by Jews as "the evil decrees of 1648" (גזירות ת״ח-ת״ט), these events are described in Ukrainian, Russian, and Marxist historiography as Ukraine's war of liberation and national rebirth or as the revolution of 1648.[2] The timing of this reissue was hardly coincidental, coming as it did when news of the mass murder of Ukrainian Jewry by the Germans and their Ukrainian collaborators was filtering into what was still Mandatory Palestine. One important player in the violence was the Organization of Ukrainian Nationalists, whose leader, Stepan Bandera, has been celebrated as a national hero, especially in the towns and cities of West Ukraine, the former eastern Galicia, since the fall of communism and Ukrainian independence in 1991. Conversely, the gruesome slaughters by Banderite units that proudly carried his name are remembered with rage and horror by Jewish Galician survivors.

An earlier modern edition of Hanover's account was published in 1923 by Klal-Verlag in Berlin, this time in response to the widespread pogroms that accompanied the Russian Revolution and civil war in Ukraine in 1918–21.[3] Many Ukrainians view Symon Petliura, the anti-Bolshevik chief of the military forces and leader of the short-lived Directorate of the Ukrainian National Republic in 1919–20, as the symbol of yet another glorious chapter in Ukraine's ongoing struggle for independence. For many Jews, the massacres were seen as the moment in which Ukrainian nationalism became closely linked to antisemitic violence. Because Petliura was assassinated in exile in 1926 by the Bessarabia-born Jew and anarchist Sholom Schwartzbard, whose family was murdered in the pogroms, Petliura's name has also become associated for many Ukrainians with Jewish perfidy, whereas popular Jewish opinion perceives Petliura as Khmelnytsky's successor and Bandera's forerunner, while glorifying Schwartzbard as the avenger of Jewish blood.

The chief Hebrew editor of Klal-Verlag at the time was the Hebrew-language poet Hayim Nahman Bialik.[4] Celebrated in Israel as the "national poet," Bialik was born in 1873 and spent his childhood and early youth in the village of Radi (Radivka) and the nearby town of Zhytomyr. After a stint at the Lithuanian Volozhin yeshiva in the early 1890s, in 1900 Bialik settled in Odessa, where he lived for the next two decades, spanning the 1905 and 1917 Russian Revolutions and the civil war in Ukraine. Leaving Russia in 1921, Bialik spent the next three years in Berlin, finally immigrating to Palestine in 1924.[5] His funeral in Tel Aviv ten years later was attended by thousands of people; it is also part of my own family lore, remembered as the only time my paternal grandfather missed a day of work.

Simcha Helfgott (later Bartov), a diminutive, proud man, was born in Pyzdry (Pizdri) in 1898. Located about midway between Kalisz and Poznań (Posen), on the eastern bank of the Warta (Warthe) River, Pyzdry was part of Russian-ruled Poland from the early nineteenth century until it reverted to Polish rule in the wake of World War I. A town of little consequence, Pyzdry briefly entered the annals of that war thanks to its geographical position. As the military commentator Hilaire Belloc noted at the time: "When the critic measures the minimum distance between some point of the Russian frontier and the Prussian capital of Berlin he is struck by the shortness of the line between the one and the other. That point upon the Russian frontier nearest to Berlin," wrote Belloc, "is to be found at Pyzdry, where the river Warta leaves the territory of Russian Poland to enter the territory of Prussian Poland, and from this point to Berlin itself is almost exactly 282 kilometers, or between 175 and 180 miles."[6]

From Grandfather Simcha's perspective, this geographical location on the border between Russia and Germany also implied that the distance between "civilized" modern Jewish life and his own traditional upbringing as an *Ostjude* could be easily traversed. Indeed, growing up as one of eleven children in a wretchedly poor family, Simcha was regularly sent to spend the summer months with his wealthier relatives across the river, so as to lighten the burden on his parents. Years later he recalled that each time he arrived at his relatives' home, they would see his long sidelocks and dirty, patched-up coat, and exclaim in horror: "Vos iz dos, a vilde khaye!" (Yiddish: What is that, a wild beast!). They would shave his hair and dress him in proper "German" clothes. But at the end of the summer, when he returned home, his dismayed parents would exclaim, "Vos is dos, a Goy!" (Yiddish: What is that, a Gentile!), and swiftly remove his foreign clothes and let his sidelocks grow.

Literally raised on the line separating "West and East," Grandfather Simcha did not develop much respect for the alleged sanctity of national borders and showed little enthusiasm when he was called upon to risk his life to defend them. Conscripted into the Polish army during the Russo-Polish War of 1919–21, he saw no reason to fight and die for a country that treated him as a second-class citizen. According to one apocryphal family tale, he is said to have deserted and hidden in his aunt's attic when his military unit arrived at her town of Baranowicze (now Baranovichy in Belarus). Coming from a culture that preferred to tell stories rather than to express opinions outright, he illustrated his feelings on this issue with a tale about a visit paid by the tsar to the trenches of World War I. Seeing a Jewish soldier wrapped in a prayer shawl and praying fervently in his foxhole, the tsar calls down from his stallion: "Jew, what are you praying for?" The Jew looks up and answers, "I am praying for the victory of Your Majesty over the Kaiser may his name be erased." The tsar frowns and barks back, "Jew, don't you dare intervene in family matters!"

Grandfather Simcha arrived in Palestine in 1925, just a year after Bialik. My grandmother Miriam was not at all happy about leaving, and even after her entire family in Poland was murdered, she never reconciled herself to having been dragged against her will to a hot and strange land, far from all her loved ones. But Simcha was determined to raise his children in Eretz Israel. One family rumor maintained that Grandmother Miriam made sure to get pregnant as soon as they married, hoping that her condition would prevent Grandfather from setting out to Palestine. Instead, the pregnancy made him all the more eager to leave right away, considering that in those days travel to the distant Middle East could take several

Grandfather Simcha *(front row, first on the right)* marching with the
civil guard in Palestine. Author's private collection.

months. Thus my father was born in Palestine in 1926, which in turn
facilitated my own identity as a second-generation sabra, quite a rarity
among members of my generation in Israel.

Almost as soon as he disembarked in Palestine, Grandfather Simcha
proceeded to the Polish consulate to relinquish his passport. He had no
more need for Polish citizenship, and in order to prove it, he made a characteristically Polish gesture of pride and dignity. To his dying day in 1979
he never left the country. Whenever any member of the family went abroad,
Grandfather evaded the issue, but when we returned, he would greet us at
the airport as if we had just arrived for the first time in the Promised Land.
Nor was he ever a pacifist. Well into middle age he volunteered for civil
defense units in Palestine. As a proud Zionist, he no longer faced any di-
lemma as to whom he was serving and for what cause. And so, on that hot
July day of 1934, saving the cost of public transportation, my grandfather
walked all the way from his town of Petah Tikva to Tel Aviv in order to
attend the national poet's funeral, along with a hundred thousand others—
almost one-third of the entire Jewish population of Palestine at the time.[7]

This was likely the most moving public event of Simcha's life, with the possible exception of the United Nations resolution on the establishment of a Jewish State on 29 November 1947. He was a man of conviction. But childhood experiences also played a role. The following event, reported in the *Jewish Chronicle* on 16 April 1920, must have been one of many that marked his childhood and youth: "The disappearance of three Christian boys at Pizdri, near Kalish (Poland), led to a blood accusation panic in the townlet. Despite the protests of the Rabbi, who declared that the Jews did not require Christian blood for Passover, the Synagogues and the residences of the Rabbi, Reader, and Beadle, and a few Jewish notables were searched. In the meantime a large crowd gathered in the streets and threatened to massacre Jews. When the excitement was at its height the missing boys returned from the neighbouring village, Toporova, and the mob dispersed."[8]

The City of Slaughter

Bialik made his reputation with the poem "In the City of Slaughter," written in the wake of the Kishinev pogrom. Located at the time in the Russian Empire's province of Bessarabia, Kishinev (Chişinău) is now the capital of Moldova. Citing a cable sent from St. Petersburg to the *Jewish Daily News*, on 28 April 1903 the *New York Times* described the "anti-Jewish riots" that had occurred in Kishinev a few days earlier as "worse than the censor will permit to publish," and commented that the Jews "were slaughtered like sheep." Incited by false accusations of Jewish ritual murder and other anti-Jewish propaganda, the two-day pogrom saw widespread murder, gang rape, torture, and mutilations. Altogether 47 Jews were killed and 424 wounded, scores of women raped, as many as 700 houses burned and 600 shops looted.[9]

The 1903 pogrom was preceded by an earlier series of anti-Jewish riots in Russia in 1881–82, whose victims have been estimated at anywhere from fifty to several hundreds, as well as tens of thousands of families displaced as a result of property damage. In turn, the Kishinev pogrom heralded a much greater wave of violence. Between 1905 and 1906 alone a total of 657 pogroms took place in the Pale of Settlement, claiming the lives of 3,103 Jews. The next wave of pogroms was on an entirely different scale. During the Russian Civil War in the years 1919–20 mass murders of Jews took the lives of anywhere between fifty thousand and two hundred thousand; the most recent estimate puts the toll at one hundred thousand, while another scholar has suggested that some 10 percent of Ukrainian Jewry, which numbered 1.6 million at the time, perished, with many more raped, maimed, orphaned, and deprived of their homes and livelihood.[10]

In 1903 Bialik was sent by the Jewish Historical Commission in Odessa—headed by Simon Dubnow, the great historian of Polish and Russian Jewry—to interview survivors of the Kishinev pogrom and prepare a report. His findings inspired a powerful poem that not only meticulously documented the horrors of the pogrom but also provided insight into the phenomenon of mass murder of civilian populations by incited mobs, facilitated by indifferent, prejudiced, or ideologically driven authorities and leaders.[11] The poem looks back to the horrors of the seventeenth century, and portends the devastation of World War I and the Russian Revolution. It is only because of the unprecedented extermination policies carried out by the Germans in World War II that we tend to relegate these earlier events of brutality and cruelty to the status of marginal events or mere harbingers of state-organized genocide.

Growing up in Israel in the mid-twentieth century, I studied "In the City of Slaughter" in school. For those of my generation, born in the immediate aftermath of the Holocaust and the establishment of the Jewish state, the poem carried a powerful message, for it was filled with rage, not only against the murderers, or the authorities, but rather against the Jews who submitted to such violence without fighting back. This cowardice, as Bialik saw it, was the product of centuries of living in the Diaspora as a people unwanted, hated, and despised, lacking dignity and pride, oppressed and eternally the target of violence, whether in retaliation for real or imagined Jewish misdeeds or simply because Jews could be attacked with impunity. The underlying motif here was vigorous Zionism: the Jews should become "like the Gentiles" and learn to fend for themselves in their own land. And so Bialik's poem became a text that in its own way could be used to justify violence for the sake of self-preservation as individuals and as a nation, in the name of both sheer existence and national pride.

And yet, unlike my generation, which was largely ignorant and contemptuous of the way of life in the Jewish Pale of Settlement on Europe's borderlands, Bialik himself was also imbued with love and empathy for all the poor, downtrodden, and helpless Jewish inhabitants of the old shtetl in which he was raised and from which he escaped. Additionally, as Steven Zipperstein has shown, Bialik was also well aware of Jewish resistance during the pogrom, and profusely documented it, yet he set it aside because he apparently thought that such instances of fighting Jews would distract from the poem's main thrust of existential Jewish impotence and despair in the Diaspora.[12] Rereading the poem all those years later, I find in it the same sense of horror and astonishment at man's endless capacity to perpetrate violence, and God's shrieking silence in view of man-made atrocity—that terrifying combination of slaughter and indifference—which overwhelms one even after a lifetime studying war and genocide.

The poem begins with an admonition of God for allowing such horrors, and the poet's inability to reconcile the natural beauty of spring with man's inhumanity:

> Arise and go to the city of slaughter and come to the courtyards,
> see with your eyes and touch with your hand, on fences
> and trees, on stones and on plaster,
> the congealed blood and dried brains of the slain . . .
> You'll wade through feathers and stumble on heaps upon heaps
> of broken fragments, shattered shards, vanquished books and
>   scrolls,
> the extinction of prodigious effort and the fruit of hard labor;
> you will not stop on the wreckage but move on to the road—
> the acacias will blossom ahead, and you'll smell their scent,
> their branches half-covered in feathers and smelling of blood;
> against your will, your heart will fill
> with this strange incense and the sweetness of spring—you will not
>   be repelled . . .
> For God has called forth both spring and slaughter together:
> The sun shone, the acacia blossomed, and the slaughterer
>   slaughtered.

The poet then recounts the sights of slaughter and brutality, already shrouded in silence, determined to document them before their traces are washed away and forgotten as just one more instance of human cruelty and divine indifference:

> You run off and come to a courtyard, and in it a pile—
> on this pile two were decapitated: a Jew and his hound.
> One ax cut off their heads and they were thrown onto the trash,
> and in this bloody mix of both the swine will rummage and thrash;
> tomorrow's rain will sweep it all to the drainage ditch—
> And the blood will no more cry from the sewage and the filth . . .

It will all be gone, and things will be as they had always been . . .
And who but God can bear this silence in the land?
Look up to the roof—its tiles too are still,
darkening wordlessly over you, then ask the spiders;
living witnesses, onlookers, they will tell you all:
the tale of a belly slashed open and stuffed with feathers,
the tale of noses and nails, skulls and hammers,
the tale of slaughtered human beings hung from beams,
the tale of a babe found by its stabbed mother's side,
sleeping with her cold nipple still in its mouth;
the tale of a child ripped apart, its life extinguished just as it cried
    "Mama!"

It is here that Bialik descends to the depths of what he perceives as the greatest evil and horror of all, the rape of Jewish women and their betrayal by Jewish men.

Descend from there into the dark cellars,
where your people's innocent daughters were defiled amongst the
    dishes,
one woman under seven Gentiles,
the daughter seen by the mother and the mother seen by the
    daughter,
before the slaughter and during the slaughter and after the
    slaughter;
touch with your hand the soiled featherbed and bloodied pillow . . .
Look and look again: in that dark corner,
under that bench and behind that barrel,
crouched husbands, bridegrooms, brothers, peering through
    cracks
as the holy bodies twitched under the flesh of beasts,
suffocating in their defilement and gagging on their own throats'
    blood,
and just as they shared their food the loathsome Gentiles shared
    their flesh—
they crouched in shame and watched—and made no move,
they did not poke out their eyes nor go out of their minds—
each one perhaps uttering a silent prayer:
God in heaven, make a miracle—and spare my soul.

As he considers the men's shameful groveling and fear, Bialik's contempt knows no bounds:

> Now come and I'll bring you to all their hideouts:
> the outhouses, the pigsties and all other sites of excrement.
> And you will see where they hid,
> your brethren, sons of your people and descendants of the
>   Maccabees . . .
> They escaped like mice and hid like lice,
> they died like dogs wherever they were found . . .
> Look and see, they still wallow in their grief,
> they weep and groan out their laments,
> they beat their hearts and confess their sins,
> they say: "we are guilty, we have betrayed you"—and their heart will
>   not believe their lips . . .
> Why do they beseech me?—Speak to them and they should rage!
> Let them shake their fists at me and demand revenge,
> For all the generations of insults from beginning to end,
> And may their fists shatter heaven and my throne.[13]

Bialik's friend and disciple, the poet, editor, and translator Yaakov Fichman, introduced the 1944–45 edition of *Yeven Metsulah* in the same spirit. Although he was born in Bessarabia in 1881, Fichman spent most of his life in Palestine/Israel and viewed the republication of Hanover's book entirely within the context of what he saw as the unbroken chain of Jewish persecution and massacres. For him, this history served both as a warning and as a lesson for the future—a tale of endless repetition that cannot be prevented or avoided. "At times of war," he wrote, "when great calamities suddenly occur, we read history books differently, we understand them differently. We realize, tragically, that in each generation and each epoch the same events happen over and over again, the same terror, the same opportunity to prepare for the evil, to prevent it—an opportunity that was not exploited, and that, it seems, could not be exploited. The same predicament, which allegedly could have been resolved in time—and yet was resolved (or appeared to have been resolved) only after immeasurable bloodshed and atrocity."

Fichman is not making a mere theoretical statement about the predilection of history to repeat itself. He is speaking here very specifically about the events of his time. "Since my childhood," he recalled, "I did not return to reading Yeven Metsulah. Only after the slaughters in Ukraine, which occurred after the last war, did I read it in Berlin in the new edition issued at the time by the Klal publishing house. This little essay made a great impression. Not only the horrors of Ukraine in 1648 emerged from it but also—that eternal martyrdom, which had just occurred again and shattered us in the years 1919–1921—that repetition that was also similar in many details to the catastrophe of 1648."[14]

What Fichman admires most in Hanover's essay is "the lucidity of the narrative, which makes waves for a few moments, and then returns to its measured pace, while its depths rumble with ceaseless sorrow and tears." To his mind, "this lucidity, which is kept even as the heart fills with horror, demonstrates a strength of spirit, and in no way indicates dispassion."[15] Fichman praises Hanover for his objectivity, despite having been a victim of the events he describes. As Hanover strongly asserts, the Ukrainians (or Greeks, as he calls them, because of their Orthodox religion) were enslaved by the Polish "dukes and noblemen," who compelled them to do hard labor, taxed them heavily, and tortured and abused them. Indeed, he re-marks, the Ukrainians "were so wretched that almost all the nations, even that lowliest of all nations, ruled over them," implying that the Jews were also to blame for mistreating Ukrainians.[16] But ultimately for Fichman, Hanover's greatness is rooted both in his ability to provide the specific details of several events in a way that brings to life the horror and atrocity of the time, and, conversely, in the universal applicability of this narrative for Jewish history and fate as a whole. He therefore concludes:

> When reading this book, one necessarily makes analogies between those events and the events of our own time . . . The great tragedy was then that although some courageous Jews stood out for their ability and willingness to avenge their persecutors, they could not carry this out. Typical of this is the episode of Tulczyn, where the Jews [were prevented from fighting back by their rabbi's words] . . . "If this is God's will, we shall gladly accept our fate" . . . This was the Diaspora mentality, which we have been laboring to up-root for three hundred years, and to our great misfortune, we have failed in this task; to this day we are ruled by this malign fatalism, this tradition of "stretching out our neck," which is precisely what incites the beasts.

For Fichman, Hanover's book and the events he describes, just like all the massacres that have occurred since, must lead to only one conclusion:

> Even today, when we have the ability to stand on the battlefield, when there is no more need to hesitate and question, who should we join and what should we die for, the nation has not yet developed its sense of dignity and has brought forth from itself only a handful of people, men of honor, while the many tens of thousands, to our shame, have not stirred and moved; they still wait for others to rise and rescue them, and they have not yet understood that the future of Israel, their lives, and more than their lives, depend on the extent of our own willingness to sacrifice both body and soul.[17]

This was the Zionist understanding of the Holocaust at the time, and perhaps even more so today, founded on the claim of having identified the historical logic of Jewish catastrophe, and proposing a national remedy to this condition. It was neither fair nor just as far as the Jewish multitudes in Europe were concerned, based as it was on ignorance of the realities of existence there. But it did not lack a certain understanding of the tragedy of Jewish life on Europe's borderlands in an era of nationalism. It weaponized Hanover's essay in the service of Zionism; but it did not entirely distort his meaning or the meaning of the events he described.

Uprising

Nathan Nata Hanover was born in Ostróg (Ostroh), Volhynia, in the early 1620s. Located 125 miles northeast of Buczacz, Ostróg is also just 100 miles west of Zhytomyr, where Bialik spent the formative years of his youth 250 years later. But while Bialik grew up in the Russian Empire, Hanover lived under Polish rule, although his family may have come there from the German town of Hanover, whose Jews were expelled a few decades before his birth. At that time, Ostróg had a considerable Jewish population and was a renowned center of learning. Hanover's father may have been a rabbi, and Nathan himself studied at the Ostróg yeshiva, but after his marriage he moved to his wife's paternal home in nearby Zasław (Izyaslav), where he was occupied with preaching. We know that he had two daughters, but there may have been more children.

In 1648 Zasław was conquered by Khmelnytsky's Cossacks and most of its Jews were slaughtered, including Hanover's father. Hanover and his family managed to escape, and eventually made their way to Italy. In 1652 Hanover was living in Venice, where he published *Yeven Metsulah*. Two years later he moved to Wallachia, in present-day Romania, where he served as a rabbi, and in the 1670s he was employed as a judge (dayan) in the Moravian city of Ungarisch-Brod (Uherský Brod, in the present-day Czech Republic). But in 1683 the town was occupied by Hungarian troops fighting alongside the Turkish army marching on Vienna. The Jews, who were gathered in the synagogue for morning prayers, were attacked by the Hungarians; Hanover was one of the victims. Thus his death at the age of about sixty occurred under circumstances similar to those he described three decades earlier in *Yeven Metsulah*.[18]

Hanover's account is an exceptional document because it relates in detail the events of 1648–49 from the victims' perspective, while at the same time attempting to remain objective and to keep the narrative within its appropriate historical context. For the Hebrew-language reader it is also an astonishing encounter because, save for some passages in Aramaic and a few obscure terms, the text is easily accessible and beautifully written. This does not mean, of course, that Hanover's historical understanding of the period, or the figures he cites for the size of armies or the numbers of victims, are accurate. But this should not detract from the importance of his book. Just as in the case of eyewitness testimonies by survivors of the Holocaust and other genocides, the point is not the precision of dates or figures, but the insights they provide into aspects of such events on which other documents remain silent: the horrors as experienced by the victims, for whom official reports or chronicles have little time and space.

Bohdan Khmelnytsky, the instigator of the events described by Hanover, served as hetman—initially commander of the Cossack host of Zaporozhia and then head of the Cossack state he established—in the years 1648–57. The final outcome of this political and social upheaval was that about half of Ukraine was torn off from Poland and eventually ended up under Muscovite/Russian rule. It also contributed to a gradual change in direction of Jewish migration back toward the west, as well as to the rise of Messianism and Hasidism in response to the traumatic destruction of Jewish life and culture in Ukraine. Another consequence of these events was that the ephemeral Cossack state subsequently inspired generations of nineteenth- and twentieth-century Ukrainian nationalists to struggle for national independence.[19]

Khmelnytsky was probably born in 1595 near Chyhyryn, south of

Kiev, as the son of a registered Cossack of gentry origin and was educated by the Jesuits in Galicia. In 1620 he was taken prisoner by the Ottomans while fighting in Moldavia, and by the time he was ransomed two years later, he had learned Turkish and become acquainted with Crimean and Ottoman politics. His chances of achieving the status of a nobleman on par with the Polish aristocracy were diminished when Poland reduced the number of registered Cossacks under its rule following the failed rebellions of 1637 and 1638. Subsequently, following a conflict with a local Polish nobleman, Khmelnytsky fled to the Zaporozhian Sich, and was elected hetman of the Cossack host soon thereafter. Having concluded an alliance with the Crimean Tatars, Khmelnytsky then set out to do battle with the Poles. Several early victories over Polish armies led many registered Cossacks to desert the Polish forces and join the Zaporozhians, which in turn unleashed a general revolt by the peasants in the Kiev palatinate, targeting their Polish landlords and Jewish estate managers.[20]

Although Khmelnytsky attempted to negotiate with the Poles, the revolts in Ukraine, led by other Cossack leaders and peasants, continued unabated, accompanied by widespread massacres of Roman Catholic Poles, Uniate Ukrainians, and especially Jews. Estimates of Jewish victims run as high as forty thousand to fifty thousand people, representing a loss of up to one-tenth of the entire Jewish population of Poland-Lithuania.[21] Khmelnytsky's responsibility for these massacres is disputed. Ukrainian sources tend to argue that, not unlike Symon Petliura and Stepan Bandera in the twentieth century, he had little control over events. This view obviously also makes it possible to remember these men as national heroes rather than as butchers. Be that as it may, the fact remains that those who swore allegiance to them perpetrated extensive bloodshed and brutality.

Some scholars, among them several North American Ukrainian historians, have pointed out that the Jews were victims not only of their religious identity but also of their economic role and position in society. According to Frank Sysyn, the "symbiotic relations of great lords and Jews aroused hatreds in other strata of the population that were a combination of the anti-Semitism endemic throughout Europe and socio-economic grievances against the noble order in Ukraine." For that reason, in 1648 "the Jews, including the urban poor who had little to do with the nobility, were to be the major victims of the wrath against the nobles' social order."[22] Orest Subtelny blames the victims more directly, commenting that the Jews "exploited the properties and peasants mercilessly, without regard for future consequences." Hence, in 1648 "Jewish losses were especially heavy because they were the most numerous and accessible representatives of the szlachta [Polish gentry] regime."[23] And Paul Robert Magocsi argues that because "the Jews, alongside the Poles, had come to represent the oppressor," in 1648 they "found themselves caught between the proverbial hammer and anvil, and the result was the destruction of many of their communities."[24]

Although Khmelnytsky's forces reached as far as Zamość, just 170 miles from the major Polish city of Kraków, in summer 1649 a peace was declared, which created a Cossack state, free of Poles, Jews, and Jesuits, in what are now the central provinces of Ukraine. Yet Khmelnytsky's ongoing battles with the Poles finally led him to sign an agreement with Muscovy in 1654, in which the Cossack-held territories were united with Muscovy, making Ukraine into part of what later became the Russian Empire for the next three centuries.[25]

The Deep Mire

Nathan Hanover's account of Jewish fate in this period is a relentless chronicle of horror and despair. Upon hearing of Khmelnytsky's victories east of the Dnieper River, he writes, the Jews living west of the river "ran to save their souls" and tried to find shelter in the fortified cities of the region. "Whoever did not or could not flee paid with his life." This was a century, as we learn from Hanover, in which a quick death was considered a blessing. Instead, people "had many wounds inflicted upon them without killing them and were then thrown on the street to die a slow death, writhing in their blood to their last breath." The Cossacks, he writes, "did not spare them any strange death in the world, and perpetrated all four ways of execution: stoning, burning, beheading, and strangling." Not even babies were spared: "They hanged children from their mothers' breasts," and "took the children of the Hebrews and made from them bridges over which they crossed." The Tatars, for their part, "tortured women and virgins and raped women in front of their husbands." In this manner, according to Hanover, "several thousand Jews were killed west of the Dnieper River." And while "several hundred were forced to convert," Jewish religious symbols were desecrated. "They tore the Torah scrolls into strips and made from them bags and footwear; they used the straps of the phylacteries to wrap around their feet and they tossed the boxes of the phylacteries onto the streets, and they paved their streets with the rest of the holy scrolls and some of them they used to stuff into the barrels of their guns."[26]

These and many other graphic descriptions of violence, brutality, and sacrilege that fill this account may appear as mere figments of an author's sick imagination. But if statistics are difficult to substantiate for this era, there is ample evidence that its capacity for the most grotesque forms of violence was only surpassed in the twentieth century. The extraordinary lengths to which the perpetrators went to inflict pain and humiliation on fellow human beings instilled such terror in the victims that they all too often betrayed each other in order to save themselves. One of the first towns to be attacked in June 1648 was Niemirów (Nemyriv), located 180 miles east of Buczacz, and home to one of the largest and most influential Jewish communities in the Vinnitsa (Vinnytsia) region.[27] Initially, when the Jews saw the rebel army nearing the town, "they were filled with terror," and "went into the fortress with their wives and children and silver and gold and sealed the fortress with the double gate and bars so as to fight them." But then the approaching Cossacks "made themselves flags just like those of the Poles," and because "the townspeople knew about this trick," they "called to the Jews in the fortress: 'Open the gate because this is a Polish army that has come to help you against your enemies, should they come.'" But once the Jews

> opened the gate, the Cossacks entered with drawn swords as did the townspeople with swords and spears and scythes and some used clubs and they killed a great many Jews. They tortured women and virgins as they pleased, and some of the women and virgins were leaping into the pool of water next to the fortress, so as not to be defiled by the gentiles, and they drowned. And many of the people, who could swim, jumped into the water . . . but the Ukrainians swam after them with swords and scythes and killed them in the water. And some were shooting with their guns into the water and were killing them until the water turned red from the blood of the murdered.[28]

Side by side with his emphasis on betrayal by neighbors, Hanover also highlights the heroism of Jewish women, who refused to submit to the enemy. In one case, he recounts, a young woman

> from a well-respected and wealthy family . . . was taken captive by a Cossack who married her. But before he came upon her, she told him cunningly that she could perform such magic that no weapon

would do her harm. And she said to him: "If you don't believe me try this, shoot me with your gun and it will do me no harm." And her husband the Cossack assumed that she was saying the truth and shot her unwittingly with his gun and she collapsed and died a martyr's death, so that the Gentile would not defile her, may God avenge her blood.[29]

In yet another story of suicide, Hanover relates how "a beautiful maiden, whom a Cossack wished to marry, asked him to have the marriage performed at their church, which stood behind a bridge. And he fulfilled her wish and took her to the ceremony attired in ceremonial garb, accompanied by drums and dances. Once they reached the bridge, she jumped off it and drowned as a martyr, may God avenge her blood. And there were many more such cases, which cannot be described in writing."[30]

The theme of women's martyrdom runs through the annals of Jewish history. The modern version of female sexual abuse, however, has been clouded by less edifying allegations. Bialik, we recall, denounced the cowardice of Jewish men observing the rape of their wives. The successors of those fainthearted Diaspora Jews, the "new," fighting Jews of Palestine, the men Bialik hoped for and inspired, then turned against the female Holocaust survivors who landed on their shores, alleging that they had only survived by "sleeping with the enemy." Perhaps out of ignorance and narcissism, perhaps driven by a sense of impotence and guilt for having failed to protect them, the young male products of the Zionist experiment thus victimized the victims, in line with David Ben Gurion's depiction of the surviving remnant of European Jewry as the "dust of humanity."[31]

The theme of Gentile betrayal is similarly inherent to the Jewish collective memory and has carved a prominent place for itself also in the Zionist worldview. Unlike Bialik, Hanover does not eschew depictions of Jews arming themselves and fighting for their lives. But in many cases, they are betrayed by their neighbors. Even more painful, and remaining an open sore in Jewish memory to this day, is the rift within the Jewish community such betrayal can cause and the resort to reliance either on God's will or on accommodation with the enemy, which invariably ends in humiliation and massacre. One prominent example is the siege of Tulczyn (Tulchyn), which followed soon after nearby Niemirów was sacked. In the well-defended fortress of Tulczyn, writes Hanover, "there were six hundred soldiers of the Polish nobles, along with two thousand Jews who had gathered there, among them soldiers and seasoned warriors." Perceiving the looming danger, "the Jews and the nobles signed a treaty that they would help each other fight their enemies, and they swore not to betray each other. They greatly strengthened the fortress and the Jews armed themselves with various weapons and stood on the walls alongside the nobles. And each time the Ukrainians tried to approach the walls those who stood on them shot at them with arrows and guns and killed many of them, until they fled from the Jews, and the Jews were filled with courage and chased after them and killed several hundred of them."[32]

Hoping to end the stalemate, the rebels then "sent a message . . . to the nobles in the fortress in order to make peace with them on condition that they hand over to them the Jewish spoil as ransom for their lives." In response, the nobles "called the Jews to them one by one and removed all their weapons from them." Soon enough,

> the Jews understood this trickery and wanted at first to attack the nobles and oppose them, because they were the first to betray the alliance. But the head of the yeshiva of . . . Tulczyn . . . Rabbi Aaron, called out to the Jews: "Hear, my brethren and people, we are in the Diaspora amongst nations, if you attack the nobles, all the kings of Edom [i.e., the Christian rulers] will hear of this and will, God forbid, exact their revenge from all our brethren in the Diaspora. Therefore, if this is the will of Heaven, we must gladly accept our fate, for we are no better than our brethren in the holy community of Niemirów and the Almighty will treat us mercifully in the face of our enemies, and perhaps they will accept our treasures as ransom for our lives." And the Jews obeyed him and brought all their possessions into the fortress courtyard.[33]

Rabbi Aaron's arguments were not unreasonable. But by making them he sapped the morale of his community and unwittingly condemned it to complete destruction. Ironically, he was one of the few members of the community to survive the ensuing massacre, not least thanks to his father's vast wealth. As Hanover tells it, once the Jews laid down their arms and handed over their possessions,

> the Ukrainians entered [the fortress] and the head of the [Polish] nobles, Duke Czetwertyński, said to them: "Here is what you asked for." And the Ukrainian oppressors took all the loot from the Jews and said to the duke that he should put all the Jews under guard . . . And on the third day . . . the Ukrainians came to the nobles

and told them to hand over all the Jews to them. Immediately the nobles pushed the Jews out of the fortress so as not to suffer the same fate . . . And the Ukrainians put them under guard . . . And after that an intermediary came to them and planted a banner in the ground and called out to them: Whoever wishes to convert and live should sit under this banner. But no one responded . . . He then opened the gates . . . and all of them surged in and massacred them, some one thousand five hundred souls killed in the cruelest ways imaginable . . . And they took from them ten rabbis and put chains on their legs and put them under guard for ransom . . . among them was . . . Rabbi Aaron son of . . . Rabbi Meir . . . For the Ukrainians knew that he was very wealthy and would ransom his son for any amount demanded of him.[34]

Almost precisely three centuries later, a besieged community of Jews was faced with a similar conundrum. On 4 September 1942, the chairman of the Łódź Ghetto Jewish Council, Chaim Rumkowski, addressed his community:

The ghetto has been struck a hard blow. They demand what is most dear to it—children and old people . . . I never imagined that my own hands would be forced to make this sacrifice on the altar. In my old age I am forced to stretch out my hands and to beg: Brothers and sisters, give them to me!—Fathers and mothers, give me your children . . . I must carry out this difficult and bloody operation; I must cut off limbs in order to save the body! I must take away children, and if I do not, others too will be taken, God forbid.[35]

By the end of 1942, most of the Łódź Ghetto's population had been gassed in Chełmno. The final remaining workers, along with Rumkowski, were taken to Auschwitz and murdered there in August 1944. Rumors had it that Rumkowski never made it to Auschwitz; he was killed by other Jews in the railcar. Within three years, some 200,000 Łódź Jews, many of whom had worked as hard as they could for the German war machine, had been murdered.[36]

Rumkowski, it appears, consulted his own conscience in making this diabolical demand. In other cases, the morality of sacrificing some so as to save others was deliberated by the religious authorities. On 15 September 1941, Rabbi Ephraim Oshry of the Kowno (Kovno, Kaunas) Ghetto was asked whether it was just for the Jewish Council to distribute work permits to only 5,000 out of a total of 10,000 craftsmen, who in turned made up only one-third of the ghetto's total population. Considering that the permits protected the workers and their families from imminent deportation, they were swiftly snatched by the strongest craftsmen, dooming the others to certain death.

After hedging for a while, Rabbi Oshry finally ruled in favor of the council and the stronger craftsmen: "For it is not a matter of a specific person; it had been the intention of the evil ones . . . to destroy all, but now there is a way to save a few by means of the permits that have been issued, and thus acceptance of the cards and their distribution becomes a matter of saving [persons]." The following month, the council consulted the ghetto's Rabbinical Court again: should they comply with the order to assemble all the Jews, "for it was known that a great part of those who assembled would be doomed to die." Once more the court ruled: "If the order was made that a community in Israel be destroyed, and if by some means it was possible to save a small part of the people, then the heads of the community must gather the courage in their souls, and it is their responsibility to act and to save those who may be saved."[37]

This was the same logic as that of Rabbi Aaron in 1648. But as in the case of Tulczyn, the question was not only whether the community should comply with the orders of its oppressor but also whether it should allow armed resistance even at the risk of retaliation. This question came up more than once during the Holocaust. On 15 May 1943 Jacob Gens, head of the Wilno (Vilna, Vilnius) Ghetto, addressed the leaders of labor brigades, supervisors, and policemen in the ghetto on that very topic:

> Why did I call you together? Because today another Jew has been arrested for buying a revolver. I don't yet know how this case will end . . . But I can tell you that if it happens again we shall be very severely punished. Perhaps they will take away those people over 60, or children . . . As long as the ghetto remains a ghetto those of us with responsibility will do everything we can so that nothing shall happen to the ghetto . . . You will have to watch each other, and if there are any hotheads then it is your duty to report them to the Police . . . Because it is we alone who pay![38]

This was the slippery slope. For soon the question was no longer only whether to prevent resistance, or denounce resisters, but also whether to participate directly in the rounding up and handing over of victims to the perpetrators. In this matter, Gens had his own moral code. He believed in facing up to reality, being tough and strong-willed, and preserving the most valuable members of the community at the price of those who were expendable. On 27 October 1942, Gens reported to the Jewish leadership in Wilno on a mass killing in the nearby town of Oszmiana:

> Gentlemen, I asked you to come here today in order to relate to you one of the most terrible tragedies in the life of Jews—when Jews led Jews to their death . . . A week ago Weiss of the SD [*Sicherheitsdienst*, Security Service of the SS] came to us . . . with an order . . . There were about 4,000 Jews in the Oszmiana ghetto, and it was not possible to keep so many persons there . . . The first to go should be children and women whose husbands were taken away last year . . . The next to be taken would be women and families with a large number of children. When we received the order we replied: "At your command." . . . The Jewish police saved those who must live. Those who had little time left to live were taken away . . . They were a sacrifice for our Jews and for our future . . . Today I will say that it is my duty to soil my hands, because terrible times have come over the Jewish people. If five million people have already gone it is our duty to save the strong and the young . . . and not to indulge in sentimentality . . . Today we must just be strong . . . To survive it all and to remain, after the ghetto, a human being fit for the great Jewish future.[39]

As Gens saw it, his men were not engaged in demeaning and immoral collaboration, but in waging a proud and glorious, indeed patriotic fight. His words were eerily similar to those used by the architect of the "final solution," SS and Police Chief Heinrich Himmler, in a notorious speech he made to SS leaders on 4 October 1943 in Posen:

> I also want to talk to you quite frankly about a very grave matter . . . I am referring to the Jewish evacuation program, the extermination of the Jewish people . . . To have stuck it out and—apart from a few exceptions due to human weakness—to have remained decent, that is what has made us tough. This is a glorious page in our history and one that has never been written and can never be written . . . We had the moral right, we had the duty to our people,

to destroy this people which wanted to destroy us . . . All in all, we can say that we have fulfilled this most difficult duty for the love of our people. And our spirit, our soul, our character has not suffered any injury from it.[40]

The final act of betrayal by Gens was to hand over Itzik Wittenberg, head of a partisan organization in the ghetto, to the Wilno Gestapo in July 1943, using the motto, "one or 20,000." Fearing that he might reveal the names of other fighters under torture, Wittenberg committed suicide. With this, the last deportations of the Jews from the ghetto began; on 14 September Gens was summoned to the Gestapo headquarters and shot. Many of the deported were sent to work on fortifications against the advancing Red Army, but almost all of those who were still alive were murdered in September 1944, just before the Soviets marched in.[41]

In 1648 Tulczyn, as in many other sites in seventeenth-century Ukraine, conversion remained one path to rescue. Indeed, so many Jews converted in order to save their lives during the uprising that in May 1649 the king of Poland allowed them to convert back to their own religion without penalty, recognizing that conversion had occurred under duress and threat of death.[42] Once people came to be defined by race rather than religion, conversion ceased to function as a rescue mechanism. But there were still instances in which Jewish children were saved by being baptized and handed over to monasteries or Christian families, who hid their Jewish background, at times even from the children themselves.[43] This time, too, Jewish religious leaders often opted in favor of life rather than collective identity. In March 1944, for instance, Rabbi Oshry wrote that at a time of "killing and loss and terrible fate . . . of our offspring . . . our children and infants, the children of Israel," he had been asked whether it was permissible for parents to provide their children with Christian birth certificates and hand them over to orphanages as abandoned Christian children, or to hand them to priests, saying that the children had been converted from their faith, even though the parents might subsequently be killed and the children would thus remain for the rest of their lives in Christian hands. The rabbi chose survival over martyrdom:

> If the child is not given to the unbelievers it is certain that it will die, and if they are among the unbelievers they will live, and it is possible that the parents may remain alive and take the child back and return it to Judaism, and it is possible that the unbelievers

themselves may return the child to a Jewish institution, and there are many possibilities in favor. And the Almighty in His goodness will have mercy on the remnants of His oppressed people and not add further to their suffering, and we shall witness the consolation of Zion and of Jerusalem.[44]

The historical veracity of Hanover's exemplary tale of resistance, betrayal, and martyrdom in Tulczyn has been recently investigated. It is clear that Hanover was inspired both by other tales and tropes of martyrdom, and by his desire to provide greater meaning and significance to what was essentially a narrative of mayhem and massacre. Yet apart from the story of the Jews' refusal to accept conversion, which may have been lifted by Hanover from another story—itself possibly apocryphal—on the massacre of the Jews of Gomel during that same period, most of the historical details about the local Jewish alliance with the Polish nobles, their subsequent betrayal and massacre, as well as the ensuing killing of the Poles, appear to be historically sound.[45]

In Tulczyn, as Hanover recounts, the Polish nobles paid a steep price for their duplicity:

After the killing of the Jews [the rebels] turned to the fortress in order to make battle, and the nobles said to them: "Have you not made an alliance with us and why are you breaking it?" And the Ukrainians responded: "As you have done with the Jews and broken your alliance with them, so too we will do with you, measure for measure." And . . . [they] burned the fortress to its foundations, and killed many of them, all the nobles, a mass killing and much looting . . . And as they had done so God paid them back for having broken their covenant with the Jews.

As Hanover concludes, "all the nobles who heard about this accepted this punishment as just, and from that day on the nobles supported the Jews and would not deliver them into the hands of the criminals." Indeed, he believes, "had it not been so, no remnant of the Jews would have remained, God forbid."[46] But over time, such lessons are not easily remembered. Three centuries later, far too many Poles (as well as Ukrainians and other East Europeans) collaborated in the German murder of their Jewish neighbors, and even larger numbers perceived the "removal" of the Jews from Poland as the one good act performed by their otherwise loathed

German occupiers, whose rule cost them a horrendous price in blood and material destruction. Grandfather Simcha knew something about the Khmelnytsky massacres and much more about recent events in Ukraine and his Polish neighbors' antisemitic sentiments. In 1925 he drew his own conclusions and stepped into another history, of which I became an unwitting part three decades later. The vast majority of his and my grandmother's families stayed in Poland; none of them is known to have survived the Holocaust.

CHAPTER THREE

Divine Justice

Assigning Blame

IN JULY 1648, WHEN Hanover heard that the Tatars and Ukrainians were besieging nearby Połonne—whose Jewish community was eventually butchered—he and his family fled from their town of Zasław, becoming outcasts and fugitives in the land, in constant fear for their lives: "Every time we slept in a Ukrainian inn we thought that the Ukrainians would murder us at night, since they were all rebels, and when we awoke in the morning, we would recite the prayer: 'Blessed are You who brings life to the dead,' for having remained alive." As the relentless advance of the Cossack and Tatar forces continued, the local "Ukrainians rebelled against their lords and would kill all the nobles and Jews who lived there in all kinds of terrible ways." This was, writes Hanover, "an unprecedented time of trouble for the Jews," and many of them "fled to the fortified towns," among them the city of Buczacz. In October Buczacz also came under siege. But in Buczacz, as in other strongly fortified towns in the region, the soldiers and citizens of the town defended its walls and drove back the attackers: "All the nobles and the Jews . . . stood against them and shot at them with big guns and killed large numbers of the rabble and they could not conquer them," so that eventually the rebels "abandoned them in great humiliation." But "the plague and famine were great in these places and several thousands and tens of thousands of Jews fell victim to them."[1]

In his own account of these events, clearly relying on various Jewish sources, Agnon notes that before the Cossack siege, "Buczacz had become a town of refuge for the survivors of the slaughter from several other sites, who fled for their lives from the sword of the oppressor and found there a fortress and a shelter among their brethren of Buczacz, who received them with love and treated them fraternally not only with bread and clothes but also in all other communal matters." In accordance with Hanover, Agnon adds that "historians count Buczacz among six sites where they stood up against the rebels" and "fought bravely," so that his hometown became "renowned in war, for having driven out and humiliated the rebels." The historian Gelber similarly stresses that in Buczacz, which had taken in many Jewish refugees from Ukraine, "the Jews fought shoulder to shoulder with the [Christian] city dwellers . . . equipped with guns and powder," and "at times the Jews also served the cannons."[2]

The town's owner at the time was Jan, son of Stefan Potocki and Marya Mohylanka. In Sadok Barącz's recounting, it was Jan who "courageously resisted the siege," so that the Cossacks, "unable to capture the fortified city, retreated and burned down the surrounding villages." But the devoutly Roman Catholic Jan, true son of his father, had meanwhile also observed that "the Greek schism had already begun to spread" in his town; and since this naturally "displeased him greatly," the lord of the city "contemplated using repressive measures." Hence, in 1652 Potocki seized the opportunity when "the terrified non-Uniate population" had abandoned their churches, and established a Dominican monastery of Polish monks on the site of an abandoned Orthodox cloister, hoping that the monks would help "root out the heresies." In Barącz's view, it was the failure of the Dominicans to accomplish this goal that eventually brought catastrophe upon Buczacz and its population, for "in His pure justice, God strengthened the Turkish hordes, so that by fire and sword they would carry out a just sentence against the dissidents. Buczacz was completely ruined!"[3]

This divine punishment, however, came almost a quarter of a century after Buczacz repelled the Cossack attack. In the intervening years, although the town and its surroundings repeatedly came under Tatar raids, Buczacz gradually rebuilt from the devastation of the uprising.[4] Ulrich von Werdum, a German tourist who visited the town in February 1672, glimpsed it at the height of its restoration. Buczacz, he found, was quite large and agreeable, located on several hills and "surrounded by a stone wall." Apart from its well-built houses, the town boasted three Roman Catholic churches, a Dominican monastery, an Armenian church, and a synagogue, as well as a formidable stone castle on a hill overlooking the city and the Strypa River that flowed through it.

While von Werdum concedes that Buczacz was rebuilt mostly by the Jews, who made up the majority of the population there and in many other towns in the region, he has a rather dim view of these particular inhabitants of the borderlands. Indeed, as the German tourist sees it, the Jews were and remain the main source of trouble in Ukraine. As he explains to his readers, because the Jews

lease inns and most other concessions from the Polish lords for money, they are granted a great deal of power over their subjects, and especially over the peasants, whom they roguishly abuse in such a manner, that they berate, whip, and trample over these poor Christians whenever they wish, as I saw with my own eyes, and it made me wonder, that Christian lords could also see this, yet that they do not pay attention as long as they get their money, because quite apart from this [Jewish abuse of power] the Polish lords maltreat their peasants worse than slaves or dogs.

From von Werdum's perspective, then, the uprising of 1648 was none other than an act of divine retribution, whereby "God in His righteousness did not allow them to go unpunished for this for long."

For when they let the Cossacks in Ukraine be tyrannized likewise in this manner by their servants and especially by the Jews—to whom the Polish lords had leased estates—when the Christians were tortured, indeed even hanged and killed daily by the Jews, then the Cossacks, led by General Bogdan Chmielnicki [Bohdan Khmelnytsky], finally rose up, and not only eradicated and strangled right away all Poles and Jews in Ukraine, but broke away, along with all their estates and those of the Polish lords, from the Polish crown, established their own free regime, and with the assistance of the Turks, Muscovites, and Tatars once more went to war against Poland and devastated the kingdom, so that through the Cossack rebellion the majority of Polish lords were impoverished.

Von Werdum has little difficulty in drawing harsh conclusions from his account: "And to my mind," he states, "one of the main causes for the gradual desolation and depopulation of the Ukrainian, Podolian and Ruthenian provinces is that the Jews have often lived there, that they had almost more say than the Christians there, that their synagogues were also built in many sites more magnificently than the Christian churches, and that in these synagogues as in all their words and works, they abuse and slander the name of our Holy Land and bring with them the curse of devastation wherever they come."

This alleged Jewish rule in the region, as von Werdum suggests, also led to a general deterioration of values among the peasant population, which eventually had to account for its sins:

> Besides this also the Christians, who live in these sites, on account of their blasphemy, oaths, murders, incest, adultery, whoring, and other bestial vices, compelled God Almighty . . . to make the lands disgorge their inhabitants, and to make fruitful lands turn into utterly fruitless soil, because of the sin and disgrace which have occurred there. Thus over time the provinces of Podolia, Rus, and Volhynia have become in many places so desolate and depopulated through annual abductions of people by the Tatars, that the fields have turned into deserts . . . [and] one can travel for three or four days without seeing a single house or hostel, a dog or a chicken, even though the soil is everywhere fruitful and luxuriant.[5]

And so, whereas Hanover depicts the Jews as the main victims of Ukrainian peasants and marauding Cossacks, from von Werdum's vantage point, the Jews are in fact the main culprits of the land's devastation, the brutalization of its inhabitants, and its ultimate depopulation. These polar perspectives have seeped through the generations well into the modern age, so that while the stereotype of Ukrainians as barbaric murderers became part of the Jewish collective memory and representation, anti-Jewish stereotypes merging religious prejudice and popular superstitions with economic resentment and new ideologies became part and parcel of the emerging Ukrainian national literature.[6]

Heroes and Villains

One of the earliest authors in this genre is Panteleimon Kulish, whose influence on the Ukrainian Romantic movement and literature can only be matched by that of his friend, the poet Taras Shevchenko. But while Shevchenko is celebrated today as Ukraine's national bard, Kulish is much less well known. Nonetheless, Kulish's novel, *The Black Council* (*Chorna Rada*), is considered the first sustained work of prose and the most successful for its time in what became the modern Ukrainian language. Born in 1819 to a father who traced himself to the Cossack gentry but had been denied his rights of nobility, Kulish published *The Black Council* in 1857. The book depicts the "Period of Ruin," the years following Khmelnytsky's death in 1657, which saw a struggle between competing Cossack factions supported by Muscovy, on the one hand, and Poland, on the other, and the eventual loss of the Cossack state's independence. It is thus both a lament on the failure of early modern Ukrainian statehood and a celebration of a renewed language and national consciousness derived from those earlier heroic and tragic times.[7]

Unlike other works about this period, such as Nikolai Gogol's far better known *Taras Bulba*, the main confrontation in *The Black Council* is not between Ukrainians and Poles, adherents of Orthodoxy and Roman Catholics, but rather a class conflict between estate owners and serfs, magnates and petty gentry, and free, anarchic Cossacks and those who wish to establish some social and political order. Indeed, Kulish is said to have thought of his book as a response to *Taras Bulba*, not only because Gogol wrote in Russian, but also because *The Black Council* was supposed to present the greater complexity of the conflict over Cossack and Ukrainian statehood and the reasons for its ultimate failure.[8] But in one respect both authors shared the same sentiment—strikingly absent from Polish author Sienkiewicz's own literary saga on the same period—namely, an unquestioning and deeply seated antisemitism. This anti-Jewish animus can be almost casual and nonchalant, as in the case of Kulish, or entirely inherent to the plot and positing a ubiquity of malign Jewish influence, as in *Taras Bulba*. It is, in this sense, a sentiment not far removed from that expressed by von Werdum two centuries earlier.

Kulish's main protagonist is Shram, described as "the son of a priest who attended the church brotherhood school in Kiev and became a priest himself." Shram, whose name means "scar" to indicate his many battle wounds, had already fought in the 1638 Cossack uprising. He "was a fiery man and could not sit quietly in his parish while blood was flowing in the war between the Polish overlords and the Ukrainians, between the Catholics and the Greek Orthodox Christians." The uprising was against Polish oppression, but the main and most resented beneficiaries of the oppression were the Jews: "Polish soldiers used to requisition food and drink in cities and villages, rape and kill defenseless women, make people pull

plows across the ice in the middle of winter and let the Jews whip them and
sneer at them as they plowed the ice." Even the enmity between the two
churches served the interests of the Jews, writes Kulish, for "the Catholic
gentry, with some Ukrainian renegades, tried to force a church union with
Rome and called the Orthodox faith a peasant religion. Their churches
they rented to the Jews." And so, eventually, the Zaporozhian Cossacks
"rose with fire and sword against the enemies of their native land."[9]

As the novel opens, Shram is forced out of retirement by the threat of
fratricidal conflict among the Cossacks. The year is 1663, and in the meantime Shram had become "a devout supporter of the church," convinced
that "Ukraine . . . has taught the Poles something: she has expelled their
minions, repulsed the union with Rome and has punished the Jews." He
had believed that Ukraine would be able to "live by her own wits." But
things did not turn out that way, and he has been compelled to return to
command his old unit, for "the Lord is about to try us again with fire and
sword. We need," he says to the men, "a colonel who will know a fox from
a wolf." Shram is clearly such a man and is reelected colonel. And indeed,
along with his loyal friends, and his son Petro, Shram can distinguish the
true from the false and the brave from the fainthearted. When they celebrate their reunion, Shram and his old comrades raise their goblets from
an amusing "silver-plated tray. It bore an engraved design which made
everybody laugh. It represented a Jew and a Cossack. The Jew was offering
the Zaporozhian a drink yet at the same time his hands were trembling
with fear of the Cossack. On top it bore an appropriate inscription."[10]

Subsequent events do not unfold as well as the Cossacks had hoped.
But however history turns out, even as they ride away at the end of the
novel into an uncertain future, Shram's son Petro has a brief exchange with
his indomitable Zaporozhian Cossack friend and enemy: "'Kyrylo Tur,'
said Petro, 'you have a true Cossack's heart?' 'Certainly a Cossack and not
a Jewish one,' replied the Zaporozhian."[11]

Despite his importance as the pioneer of Ukrainian-language fiction,
Kulish has not left us with any memorable literary characters. Conversely,
Gogol is rightly considered one of the giants of modern world literature
and the father of Russian prose. Referring to one of Gogol's most celebrated stories as well as to his vast influence as a whole, Fyodor Dostoevsky famously remarked, "We all came out of Gogol's 'Overcoat.'" This
is why the antisemitism that pervades *Taras Bulba*—which I admittedly
entirely missed when I first read it as a teenager in Israel, mesmerized as I
was by Cossack heroics and just as contemptuous of slimy Diaspora Jews—
is so unsettling. It is also, of course, not particularly surprising, consider-

ing the propensity for stereotyping and prejudice of so many other great writers of the modern era, such as, to cite just two, Ferdinand Céline and Dostoevsky himself. While it may cast doubt on the author's moral character, prejudice in the hands of a gifted writer can infect readers much more readily than the rantings of a pamphleteer. Additionally, unlike *The Black Council*, where Jews are largely incidental and metaphorical (there were no Jews in the Cossack state), in Gogol's novel the relationship between Taras and his Jewish counterpart is at the core of the plot and propels it forward. Indeed, it is striking that *Taras Bulba*'s tale, a work central to the formation of Ukrainian—or Russian—identity, hinges to such a degree on the Cossack's relationship with a Jew.

Nikolai Gogol was born in Sorochyntsi, eastern Ukraine, in 1809, to a family of noble Cossack lineage. His best known works, all written in Russian, include the play *The Inspector General* and the novel *Dead Souls*, as well as such hugely influential short stories as "The Overcoat." Toward the end of his life, he veered toward religious fanaticism and insanity. He died in 1852 at the age of forty-three. The novel *Taras Bulba*, completed in its final version ten years earlier, tells the story of a rebellion by the Zaporozhian Cossacks against Polish rule. The main protagonist, Taras Bulba, is clearly modeled on Bohdan Khmelnytsky, but in Gogol's last version of the story, the Cossacks become the personification of the Russian spirit and Orthodox faith rather than of Ukrainian nationalism. Yet Gogol's stark prose does resurrect—or, perhaps, creates in fantasy and immortalizes in literature—the wild, brutal, passionate, and freedom-loving Cossacks of the Zaporozhian Sich, who have haunted the Russian, Ukrainian, Polish, and Jewish imagination ever since the great uprising.[12]

The relationship between Taras Bulba, the embodiment of the Cossack, and Yankel, the personification of the Jew, is established early on in the novel and is carried through to its conclusion, as the central sustaining element of the narrative. It begins, appropriately enough, with a pogrom. Among the Cossacks, writes Gogol, "were those who, like aristocrats, could not keep a single brass coin in their pockets, and those who would have thought such a coin a fortune, but who, thanks to the Jewish moneylenders, had pockets you could turn inside out without the slightest fear of anything dropping out."[13] The intrinsic Jewish skill of draining the Cossacks' pockets is linked directly to the Cossacks' own celebrated capacity to spend all they have on drinking and feasting, up to the point at which they are called to war. As the Ataman, the elected leader of the Cossacks, tells his men: "Word has it—and you may well know more about this than I do—that many Zaporozhians have run up such debts in the stores of the

Jews and their cohorts that no devil will give them any more credit. Word also has it that there are many young fellows whose eyes have never seen battle, and, as we all know, a young man cannot do without war. What kind of Zaporozhian can he be if he had never killed a heathen?"[14]

Soon enough, the need to go to war and the rage against the Jews converge, producing a dynamic of massacre vividly depicted by Gogol. The pogrom is incited by the report of a fellow Zaporozhian about events in Ukraine: "As things stand," he calls out to the assembled Cossacks, "our own holy churches no longer belong to us!" How has that come about? "The Jews are holding them in pledge. If you don't place money in the Jew's hand, there is no midday mass!" Worse still, "if a dog of a Jew does not scratch a sign with his unclean hand on our holy Easter cake, then we won't be able to bless the Easter cake either." It is, reports the messenger, bad enough that Roman Catholic "priests are swarming over the whole of Ukraine in carts," having "harnessed Orthodox Christian men instead of horses" to these carts. But now, even "the Jews' women have begun sewing themselves skirts from the [Orthodox] priests' cassocks!"[15]

No more is needed to unleash the Cossacks' fury: "Hang the Jews!" someone shouts from the crowd: "Drown the rascals in the Dnieper!" And so the pogrom is unleashed: "These words darted like lightning through the crowd, and the Cossacks surged toward the [Jewish] settlement to slaughter the Jews. The poor sons of Israel, losing the little courage they had, hid in empty vodka barrels and inside stoves; they even crawled beneath the skirts of their women. But the Cossacks found them all."

One Jew, "tall and thin as a stick, his pitiful face twisted with fear," tries to stop the massacre, calling out: "We have never hobnobbed with your enemies . . . And as for the Catholics, we want nothing to do with them, may the devil visit them in their dreams! To us all Zaporozhians are like our very own brothers." But this assertion of virtual kinship is even more offensive to the Cossacks than any sins against the Orthodox Church the Jews have allegedly committed. Someone yells out: "What! Zaporozhians your brothers! . . . You won't live to see the day, you damn Jews! Into the Dnieper with them! Drown the whole lot!" And with this, the pogrom takes its natural course: "These words were like a signal. The Cossacks grabbed the Jews by the arms and hurled them into the river. Pitiful cries from all around, but the grim Zaporozhians only laughed at the sight of the Jews' shod and stockinged legs flailing in the air."[16]

Only the lanky Jew, Yankel, survives, having persuaded Taras Bulba to spare his life because he had once loaned a large sum of money to the

Cossack's deceased brother. This is the beginning of a long association, though by no means friendship, between the two. For Yankel is set up in the novel as the precise opposite of Bulba: the Jew is of course cowardly, but also crafty, skillful in making a profit from even the worst situations, and an eternal survivor; the Cossack, for his part, though not lacking intelligence and a degree of cunning, is ultimately straightforward, fearless, cares nothing for material goods and benefits, and has an intimate, passionate relationship with war and death. Gogol therefore posits this polar relationship between the Cossack and the Jew as the point of origin of this tale on the emergence of the Ukrainian (or Russian) nation. As the novel proceeds, we also find that, perhaps by dint of the extremity of their differences, the Cossack and the Jew, however much they detest each other, also develop what appears at times to be a degree of mutual, albeit grudging admiration.

This peculiar relationship between the Cossack and the Jew, between the blinding light of fire and the uncanny darkness of deceit, follows the Zaporozhian host as it goes to battle. Even as the Cossacks were preparing to set out on the warpath, writes Gogol, "Taras Bulba saw how his Jew, Yankel, had set up a makeshift booth with an awning and was selling flint, gunpowder, and all kinds of military supplies necessary for the campaign. He was even selling bread and buns. 'That devil of a Jew,' Taras muttered to himself, and rode over to him." Bulba warns "his Jew" that he is "begging to be picked off like a sparrow from its twig," since, as he implies, Jewish blood is about to flow and there can be no expectation of protection. But Yankel has his own plan, proposing to join the Cossacks on the campaign with his wagon full of goods: "Along the way I will sell provisions at prices lower than any Jew has ever managed. By God I will, yes, by God I will." To which the old warrior responds by shrugging his shoulders, "amazed at the feistiness of the Jewish spirit."[17]

But Yankel not only serves as a one-man supply train for the host, he also becomes a spy and source of intelligence about the enemy, another characteristic attributed to Jews well into the world wars. It is thus from Yankel that Bulba learns about his own son Andri's betrayal of the Cossacks. For only a Jew like Yankel can penetrate the besieged city of Dubno—whose Jewish inhabitants were eventually massacred by the Cossacks when the Polish nobles refused to let them into the fortress—where he spots Andri dressed as a Polish knight.[18] Andri, as it turns out, has fallen in love with a noble Polish woman and gone over to the enemy. In his rage and disbelief, Bulba almost kills the messenger: "'You are lying, you devilish Judas!' Taras yelled in a frenzy. 'You are lying, you dog! It was you who nailed Jesus to the Cross, you fiend cursed by God! I shall kill you, Satan!' Taras shouted, unsheathing his saber."

Yankel flees on "his thin, spindly legs" as fast as he can from the raging Cossack.[19] But he does not run far enough to relinquish his central position in the novel. Later on, after Taras kills Andri in a fit of rage for this act of betrayal, his other son, Ostap, is taken prisoner by the Poles and transported to Warsaw for a public execution. Desperate to see his remaining son, Taras turns again to Yankel, requesting the Jew to help him sneak into the enemy's capital. By now "his" Jew is residing in the town of Uman, in precisely the kind of setting that exemplifies his nation's character, as Gogol imagines it. At first sight, he writes, Yankel's abode was but "a grimy little hovel with tiny soot-covered windows. The chimney was stopped up with rags, and the roof, leaking and full of holes, was covered with sparrows. A pile of litter lay in front of the door." In fact, however, this is a mere façade for wealth and power. For, having returned from the war, Yankel "had already managed to set himself up in Uman as a leaseholder and tavern keeper, and had gradually managed to get all the surrounding Polish landowners and noblemen under his thumb, sucking them dry of all their money and firmly establishing his Jewish presence throughout the region."

Worse still, this "Jewish presence" is not just about Jews getting rich; it is also about decent Christians becoming penniless: "Every house within three miles was derelict, destitute, sold for drink. Poverty and rags were everywhere. The whole region was devastated as if ravaged by fire or plague, and were Yankel to live there another ten years the whole province would doubtless have been laid waste."[20]

And thus, in Gogol's account, what has devastated this region is not the uprising, the fighting, the sacking of towns and the massacres of civilians, but rather the continuing presence of the Jews, intent on sucking what little has remained of the Ukrainian nation's lifeblood. Yet once again, as Bulba walks into the hovel, a sense of personal gratitude motivates Yankel to suppress his natural urge to denounce the Cossack and gain a handsome reward: "Yankel was praying, covered in a somewhat soiled prayer shawl. He turned to spit one last time, as is the custom in his faith, when he saw Bulba out of the corner of his eye. The first thing that flashed through the Jew's mind were the two thousand gold ducats on Bulba's head, but he felt shame at his greed and struggled to stifle his eternal craving for gold, which like a serpent encircles the soul of every Jew."[21]

Yankel's moment of decency turns out to be a blessing, for before he even has time to reconsider, the proud Cossack promises him five thousand gold ducats, of which he pours out on the table a handsome advance: "The Jew grabbed a rag and quickly covered the ducats with it. 'Oy, what magnificent money! Oy, what good money!' he crooned, twirling a ducat between his fingers and biting it to see if it was real."[22]

Now Bulba can make his request. And in doing so, he once more highlights the distinction between the Cossack and the Jew: the former may not be complicated or sophisticated but is constant and consistent, so that one always knows whom one is dealing with, whereas the latter is a trickster, a man who can be all things to all people, so that one never knows whom one is dealing with. The Cossack, in other words, can be trusted, whether as friend or as enemy; the Jew can never be trusted, and thus can never be a true friend and is always potentially an enemy. Yet it is precisely for this reason that Bulba, who longs to see his son one last time, turns to Yankel: "I wouldn't have asked you—I'm sure I could have made my way to Warsaw myself. But it wouldn't surprise me if those cursed Poles somehow recognized me, as I am not good at tricks and ruses. But you Jews are made for that sort of thing! You could hoodwink the devil himself! You know all the tricks, and this is why I came to you."[23]

But Yankel has good reason to be anxious about secretly transporting a Cossack leader with a price on his head straight to the lion's den. He imagines what the Poles would say if they became suspicious about his cargo: "'Something fishy must be going on! Catch the Jew! Tie up the Jew! Take away all the Jew's money! Throw the Jew in Jail!' And all this because everything bad is always rained down on the Jew's head, because everyone takes a Jew for a dog! Because everyone thinks a Jew is not a human being!"[24] Nevertheless, this unlikely couple makes the long journey to Warsaw and heads straight into the Jewish quarter. As depicted by Gogol, this site too has all the attributes of the European imagination's perception of the ghetto as an infected, disgusting, poisonous sore, either because Jews naturally have this effect wherever they live, or because so many Jews have been crammed into it. The ghetto protects the world from the Jews, but threatens to infect the surrounding Christian population because of its overflowing disease; it should evoke empathy and compassion, but instead it provokes a desire to eradicate it entirely.

And thus Yankel's cart rolls in, pulling "into a dark, narrow back alley, called Dirt Street or Jew Street."

The alley looked like a backyard that had been turned inside out. It was as if the sun never shone there. The grimy wooden houses

and the masses of poles sticking out of their windows made the
alley even darker . . . All the waste and refuse was thrown into the
street, assailing the senses of the passerby. A man on horseback
could practically touch the clothes poles stretching across the alley
from one house to another, on which hung Jewish stockings, short
pantaloons, and smoked geese. Sometimes the pretty face of a
Jewess, decorated with faded beads, peered out of a tiny, decrepit
window. A swarm of mud-smeared, tattered urchins with curly hair
was yelling and wallowing about in the dirt. A red-haired Jew, his
face packed with freckles like a sparrow's egg, was looking out a
window and began talking to Yankel in their gibberish.[25]

Bulba cannot save Ostap, or even meet him to bid farewell. Instead,
he watches in the town square as his son is tortured and executed. Then,
for the rest of his life, he wreaks revenge on all those he believes have
oppressed his people and destroyed his family. The boundless vengeance
Bulba seeks stretches far beyond his death, resurrected as a major literary
trope in Gogol's novel and reincarnated in the form of avenging, merciless
champions of liberation in the following century. Gogol created a literary
model, keenly and methodically followed, for giving birth to a nation by
pulling it out from an ocean of blood. If "The Overcoat" signified the
birth of Russian literature, Taras Bulba's orgy of revenge sketched out the
future of popular uprisings led by charismatic, ruthless men whose hearts
had turned black with rage and hatred:

> Taras tore through Poland with his regiment, burning down eigh-
> teen towns, and close to forty Catholic churches . . . He slaugh-
> tered many Polish noblemen and plundered the most magnificent
> and wealthy castles, smashing barrels and spilling rare wines and
> meads . . . "Spare nothing!" Taras told his men again and again.
> The Cossacks did not even spare the dark-browed Polish beau-
> ties, white-breasted virgins with radiant countenance, who found
> no refuge, not even in churches as they clung to altars. Taras or-
> dered them burnt along with the altars . . . In the street they
> speared infants with their lances and hurled them to their mothers
> in the flames.[26]

This, then, was one legacy of the years of fire and sword, recycled and
sold to the increasingly literate masses in the later decades of the nine-

teenth century. Indeed, it was only with the stirring of modern nationalism that the memory of the Cossack uprising gradually became part of the
popular repertoire. And once it stepped into the national collective memory, it replicated and mutated in accordance with the changing political
realities and forms of media, yet always preserving intact its core of resentful mayhem and vengeful violence. The mighty, joyful, and cruel warriors
of Zaporozhia cast a vast shadow over the borderlands, the tales of their
heroism and conquests, as of the brutalities and massacres they perpetrated,
dominating the collective imagination of nation-making and -unmaking.[27]

Total Destruction

Just over two decades after the destruction of Buczacz by the Cossack
armies, a vast Ottoman host approached the city's newly constructed walls.
The Frenchman François-Paulin Dalairac, who served as a courtier to the
Polish ruler, King Sobieski, and visited Buczacz several years later, wrote
in his memoirs: "Buczacz was once a very considerable and well defended
city, and was clearly of vital strategic importance," for which reason, during
the Ottoman assault on Poland, "in 1672, the Sultan Mehmed IV came
himself to its siege." But this first Turkish siege of Buczacz was a relatively
harmless affair. At the time, Jan Potocki was away fighting elsewhere, leaving his wife, Teresa, and their children behind in the castle. Without the
presence of the lord of the city, Buczacz was in no position to fend off
the enemy effectively and submitted to the invaders after a mere symbolic
show of resistance. Because Teresa had surrendered to the sultan, writes
Dalairac, the victor treated her graciously: "Mehmed was not such a savage
as to be unaware of civilized manners. He asked to see the children, whom
he tenderly caressed, and refused to accept a costly jewel offered him by
the mother, who was tormented by fear. But concerned that his rejection
of the gift would offend her, he thankfully took the jewel from the mother
and handed it with his own hands to one of the children."[28]

This tale made the rounds in subsequent histories of the city. Other
versions of the siege insist that Teresa was determined to defend Buczacz
on her own, and locked herself up in the castle with her children, noblemen, and townsmen. The Turkish Janissaries, we are told, then surrounded
the castle and fired with cannons on the town, burning down part of it.
Only then, having realized that she would be unable to defend her city any
longer, did Teresa send a message to the sultan, observing that he would
gain no fame by winning a battle against a single woman. But the tale of

Mehmed's gracious behavior toward the lady of the city was subsequently confirmed by the Polish emissaries who arrived in Buczacz for the signing of the peace treaty between Poland and the Ottomans. Indeed, in this more elaborate version, we read that, after searching the castle's treasury, the sultan took as trophy two sabers and a cap, as well as choosing for himself two horses from the lord's stable, but otherwise did not harm a soul. Mehmed's chivalry made a great impression in Poland, we are told, not least, it appears, because it contrasted so sharply with the horrors inflicted on the country and its people in previous decades.[29]

Unfortunately, the city's luck did not hold out for long. Expecting another Ottoman assault, the nobles, royal and municipal officials, and representatives of the Jewish community met in 1674 to discuss the defense of the town. The assembled group decided to appoint a special superintendent for each of the city's neighborhoods; the head of the Jewish community, Yerachmiel, was charged with the defense of the Jewish quarter.[30] But the following year, while besieging the nearby castle of Trembowla (Terebovlya), the Ottoman general Ibrahim Shyshman (Şişman: "Abraham the Fat") sent several detachments to occupy Buczacz. In the ensuing fighting, the town was taken over and torched, and while many of the nobles and some city dwellers managed to escape into the castle, numerous Jews were locked out of its gates. As Agnon describes this episode, "those who managed to escape to the castle lived, and those who did not have time to escape to the castle were slaughtered by the Turks like rams and sheep and their corpses found their graves in the stomachs of wild animals and birds of prey." Nonetheless, writes Agnon, "God took pity on our town and it was saved from the Turk's calamity." Alongside divine intervention, he adds, "King Sobieski of Poland should also be well remembered, for he and all his armies came and drove out the Turks from the city and its surroundings. They did not leave even one Turkish horse in Buczacz and its environs."[31]

But the final calamity was still ahead. In 1676, writes Agnon, "before Buczacz had had time to dress its wounds, the Turk returned and conquered the city and destroyed it. He spared not a single house from destruction."[32] As Dalairac succinctly summarizes the fall of the city and its castle, this time "the Turks accomplished a lasting destruction" of the town, "so severe that only debris remained from the walls and the towers, and from the buildings almost nothing could pass for more than a ruin."[33]

How was the powerful castle of Buczacz overcome by the Ottomans? Wishing to deny military victory to the enemy, Barącz suggests a mere stroke of luck or possible betrayal from within. Initially, he writes, "the

Turkish armies spread out in Buczacz in the shape of a crescent," and "began to fire at the walls of the castle" from the center of their positions. But "the fearless garrison replied vigorously, whereby many Turks were killed. Seeing that their side would not be able to overcome this obstacle," the Turks "began to fire from the Fedor," a hill overlooking the castle. "But here too they could not achieve anything, because what the Turks damaged" in the castle's fortifications, "the garrison promptly repaired." What finally brought about the fall of Buczacz, then, was not the overwhelming force and tenacity of the attackers. "In the end," writes Barącz, "it was either the treachery of a woman, or breaching a hole in the wall at the right spot, which enabled [the Turks] to enter the castle."[34]

The tale of female treachery has been further elaborated over the years. Stanisław Kowalski cites an interwar account published in Buczacz, which transformed the old myth into a ghost story with a nationalist twist: "A legend had it that the castle was conquered by the Turks because of betrayal by a local woman, who pointed the Turks to a secret passage into the castle. According to the legend, this woman's ghost still appears in the castle's gateway on Resurrection Day, weeping and repenting her sin of betrayal. This comes to show that the population of Buczacz had a deep sense of national ethics and considered a severe afterlife penance as fair punishment for one's crimes against the nation."[35]

Whether it was captured thanks to an act of treason by a perfidious woman, or was overwhelmed by superior forces and good fortune, Buczacz suffered a bitter fate. Relief units sent to the besieged castle arrived too late to stop the assault and ended up surrendering to the Turks. Once the castle was breached, the garrison was mostly slaughtered; only those who managed to hide underground escaped with their lives. Thanks to the geography of the town, many houses were built on slopes of hills, and people could more easily construct underground hideouts—a practice that became common three centuries later during the German occupation.[36]

Buczacz did not remain in Ottoman hands for long. That same year, King Sobieski defeated the Ottoman army in Żurawno, sixty miles northwest of Buczacz, and the treaty signed there brought the Poles back to Buczacz; yet for the next few years the Strypa River intersecting the city marked the boundary between the two powers. Visiting Buczacz in 1684, the Frenchman Dalairac described it as a devastated borderland town whose days of glory were well behind it:

The city of Buczacz lies deep in the land, by the Strypa River, which divides it into two parts. According to this division, one half of Buczacz belongs to Red Rus [Polish Ruthenia], while the second belongs to Podolia [under Ottoman rule until 1699]. The Strypa is regarded as the boundary between the two provinces. Encircling the city are little hills, and even inside the city itself there are somewhat smaller hills. Buczacz was once built of stone and surrounded from all sides by quadrilateral towers, from which now only the walls remain, no taller than a man.

Inside the city Dalairac saw "many ruined and partly burned buildings, and only a few wooden taverns with thatched roofs. In the middle of the town flows a brook, which propels two or three watermills." As for the remaining population, Dalairac noted that "around the city, from both sides of the heights, that is to say, behind the hill of the castle, a large number of gardens are situated next to a great many springs." The peasants cultivating these orchards, he observed, "build their huts according to the old Polish pattern and locate their homes next to the gate of the city and under the guns of the castle." Conversely, "inside the city, which is completely open to attacks by the infidels, live only Jews and some Poles."[37]

For Agnon, writing from the hindsight of the Jewish community's utter destruction in World War II, it was important to point out that following the liberation of Buczacz from the Ottomans, the Jewish population experienced two centuries of growth, prosperity, and security. For that reason, he wrote, "we gratefully recall King Sobieski of Poland and all his warriors who came to rescue Buczacz and saved the city and drove the Turks out. Not one of them remained. Ever since, until Buczacz was destroyed by the evil decrees of the blighted abomination [the Nazis], people would pump water for Passover matzos from the well known as the King's Well, from whose water Sobieski had drunk when he came to save Buczacz."[38]

Indeed, Dalairac already noted the "remarkably cold and clear water" that "regularly springs out" from a "very beautiful fountain" he found located in the center of the ruined castle. It was likely from this fountain, which no longer exists, that Sobieski quenched his thirst. Today, many of the town's residents obtain water from a metal pipe linked to that well, over which an old plaque assures visitors that this is, after all, the spot where the king of Poland had once stopped. But Sobieski, it appears, was not actually present in Buczacz at the time of its liberation, since his only known visit occurred in 1687, on the way to a failed assault on the great fortress of Kamieniec Podolski. And while the king pitched his camp in

The Buczacz marketplace with city hall and well in World War I. Österreichisches Staatsarchiv, Vienna, AT-OeStA/KA BS I WK Fronten Galizien, 5490.
Used by permission of the Österreichisches Staatsarchiv, Vienna.

the plain facing the castle, "the royal court," in Barącz's disparaging words,
"did nothing for the city."[39] Instead, the arduous work of restoration fell to
the city's young lord, Stefan Potocki, a man of energy and enthusiasm who
did much to ensure his town's progress and security in the early decades
of the following century. An important element of rebuilding the city was
the construction of a new well in the marketplace, which became the main
source of water for the residents of Buczacz until the introduction of running water after World War I. But that well, too, has since disappeared.

The years of fire and sword were finally over.[40] Not until the outbreak
of World War I would Buczacz again see the kind of destruction it had
experienced in the seventeenth century. From now on, as it increasingly
receded into a provincial existence, first on the borderlands of one declining power, and then on the rim of another, Buczacz, like much of the region in which it was situated, ceased being a city to which outsiders would
come; instead, it gradually became a site that people sought to leave. But
before that became possible, or even thinkable, it first had to raise itself from

the ashes and become a place worth living in, a town that would serve as the source of nostalgia for those who would eventually recount their memories of life on its hilly slopes along the banks of the Strypa before the catastrophes of the twentieth century wiped everything out.

PART II

What Did We Become?

(*Faith and Reason*)

The Buczacz city hall in World War II.
Generallandesarchiv Karlsruhe 309 Zugang
2001-42 Nr. 878 (136). Used by permission
of the Landesarchiv Baden-Württemberg.
All rights reserved.

CHAPTER FOUR

Stones and Souls

The Beating Heart

I N THE 150 YEARS between the end of the seventeenth century's devastating wars and the 1848 "spring of nations" revolutions, large parts of Eastern Europe were torn between two opposing forces. One was the Enlightenment, which reached across the continent from France and transformed in myriad ways the views and lives of millions, from mighty monarchs to their lowliest subjects. The other was religion, which sought to provide a renewed sense of meaning to the faithful, traumatized by the inhumanity they had experienced and fearful of the change and upheaval brought about by new ideas and institutions. The struggle over faith and reason was not simply a confrontation between light and darkness, or divine truth and godlessness. The enlightened state soon imposed its will in the name of reason, and religion attracted new adherents by opting for mysticism and superstition. By the end of the period, creed and faith were about to become identified with ethnicity and nation, while modern bureaucracy and technology increasingly enhanced state power and control. But none of this could have been predicted in advance, and very few foretold the catastrophic consequences of combining technocratic prowess and fanatic ideologies.

Today's Buczacz, like many other towns in Europe's eastern borderlands, bears some of the marks and scars of this process. The city's most attractive edifices were erected in the Age of Enlightenment. They stand out in a largely dilapidated urban landscape that has witnessed the effects

of two world wars and the rule of corrupt, ineffective, and at times outright murderous regimes. Old photographs of Buczacz depict a vibrant
and picturesque provincial site; it is now a desolate and tasteless backwater
still clinging to a charming natural setting.

The Polish and Austrian rulers of Buczacz labored to beautify and
improve their town, eager to demonstrate their power, taste, and faith.
They also sought to maintain a manageable balance between their Polish,
Jewish, and Ukrainian subjects. Occasionally they could be cruel, callous,
and prejudiced. But for much of the time, this was a period of reconstruction, economic growth, and demographic expansion, at the end of which
Buczacz began to hesitantly step into the modern era.

Stefan Potocki, who had inherited Buczacz after the death of his father in 1675, set about rebuilding it with much energy and determination.
Like other members of his clan, Potocki catered to the material and spiritual needs of all religious communities. In 1712 he brought from Lithuania six Greek Catholic Basilian monks and an abbot, and awarded them
land and an endowment for their maintenance. The monks were housed
in a small fourteenth-century formerly Roman Catholic church situated
on Fedor Hill across the Strypa River. In return the monks undertook to
teach theology and to pray for the souls of the Potocki family's departed
members; they were also destined to play an important educational role in
Buczacz.[1]

The city's commercial revival had much to do with rebuilding its dec-
imated Jewish population. In 1699 Potocki renewed and expanded the privileges accorded to the Jews by his predecessors, whose records had been
destroyed in the many wars and sieges of the previous decades. The Jews
were allowed to reside in the city, to work in all trades and commerce, and,
in consideration of the human and material losses they had sustained, were
temporarily exempted from paying taxes and rents; the rabbi, the cantor,
and the Jewish hospital were relieved of taxation altogether. Potocki's positive disposition toward the Jews of his town was exemplified in the following passage of his decree: "I allow the Jews—as was stated in the previous bill of rights—to use the road leading from the walls of the church
and the house of the priest to their synagogue, which is on the banks of the
Strypa River. With this I also affirm the use in perpetuity of this synagogue,
which their fathers had built with their own funds, as well as of the cemetery outside the city, and I allow them to expand this cemetery in case of
need . . . and to build there a wall."[2]

The wooden synagogue, built on the banks of the Strypa following the loss of an earlier structure in the Turkish wars, was replaced in 1728 by a massive stone edifice. Legends about the Great Synagogue proliferated well into the twentieth century. A common myth held that it was designed by the same Italian architect who later built the town's famous city hall. But the latter was in fact erected almost a quarter of a century later by Bernard Meretyn, a Galician architect of Bohemian-Austrian origins. While Italians greatly influenced art and architecture in early modern Poland, none is known to have reached Buczacz. Associating the synagogue with Italian artistry was largely meant to add to its glory. One lucid commentator wryly observed in a letter to a newspaper in Palestine in 1938 that such "rumors and tales" as those told "about Count Potocki and the architects he brought from Italy" were "rife in every little town in Poland and Lithuania, and each of us heard them in his childhood." The same writer noted that the date of the synagogue's construction was inscribed in Hebrew and Roman numerals over its side door.[3]

The Great Synagogue recalled by Jews in the 1930s likely looked quite different from the original structure, which was severely damaged in the great fire that swept through Buczacz in 1865. The only house of worship saved from the fire was the church of Saint Nicholas, the oldest and one of the largest stone structures in Buczacz. This probably had to do with its location on a hill overlooking the town. But a popular tale making the rounds among the Jews of Buczacz offered a different explanation. The Pole Stanisław Kowalski, who lived there in the 1930s, recalled this story:

> During the fire all the houses near the church were burned except for a small wretched cottage with a roof of shingles. A poor Jew lived in that cottage with his family. He used to sit on a stone in front of his house to warm his bones. When the Jew saw the burning houses in the town and the flames threatened his property, he fell to his knees and began yelling toward the church, which had still not caught fire: "Oh, Saint Nicholas, if you rescue yourself, rescue me too!" His prayer must have been heard, because his small cottage was the only house that was saved in the center of town.[4]

A few days after the fire, a horrified eyewitness reported the event to the Hebrew-language newspaper *Hamagid*: "From midnight on Saturday until Sunday morning all we could see was fire and plumes of smoke," during which time "the city of Buczacz was transformed into rubble." In the course of the fire "more than three hundred Jewish homes" and their contents "were entirely destroyed," and "a thousand Jewish families" were "made homeless." Not least, "the great and glorious synagogue and two other small synagogues and ten study houses with all their precious books and some holy scrolls were consumed in the flames."[5] Fourteen years later, the author of this report, Berish (Bernard) Stern, became the first Jewish mayor of Buczacz, a position he held for the next four decades, spanning World War I and the fall of the Austro-Hungarian Empire: an extraordinarily successful career bracketed by two catastrophes. After both events, the damage to the city was repaired. But while the famous city hall still attracts tourists to Buczacz, the Great Synagogue has vanished without a trace. In the immediate aftermath of World War II its broken hull was demolished under Soviet orders. It has been suggested that in 1960 some of its stones were used to build a new cinema, located not far from where the Great Synagogue had once stood.[6]

Dismantling the synagogue, even after it was pounded by modern artillery, tank shells, and aerial bombs, took several years. Like many other early modern "fortress synagogues" in this region, it was designed to withstand enemy attacks and to serve as a refuge for the community in times of war and violence. With walls up to 15 feet thick at its base, its floor was dug well below street level. This also allowed for a high ceiling while preserving the building from towering over any nearby churches. Yet very few images have remained of this imposing structure in the heart of the city, and it is rarely mentioned in Polish and Ukrainian travel accounts, or in French, German, and Russian tourist guides.[7]

For Agnon, who often attended it as a child and a teenager, the Great Synagogue was the beating heart of the community. Since its construction, he writes, "for as long as Buczacz existed, prayer in it never ceased, neither by the living nor by the dead. By the living, because they would pray there every day, evening and morning. By the dead, since those who guarded the synagogue at night would hear the sound of prayer rising from it, and the sound was different from that of living people, and thus they knew that these were the dead who had come to pray in public."[8]

Agnon recalled the Great Synagogue shaped as "an erect ark, its walls smooth, their texture resembling old parchment, like that of the Torah books brought back by those who returned to Buczacz" after the Cossack and Turkish wars. In his version, the synagogue was not built partially underground in order to conceal its actual height, nor had it simply sunk into the city's soggy ground because of its great weight, as others have speculated. Instead, the building's design was meant to serve as a metaphor of Jewish fate, so that "Israel's house of prayer prays with Israel." For, "just as Israel calls God from the depths, from the depths of trouble, as it is written: 'From the depths I have called you, Lord,' so too Israel's house of prayer calls God from the depths of the earth." Nonetheless, Agnon agrees that the structure's massive construction "helped our fathers, for when the Tatars came to make war on the city, the Jews would hide in the synagogue, and since it was sunken into the ground and the women's section was built on top of it, no harm came to them from the tools of war."[9]

Stepping into the synagogue's cavernous interior, visitors were filled with awe. The opulently decorated space, complete with murals of flowers and angels, was lit by twelve opaque windows, of which the one over the Torah ark by the eastern wall was made of tinted glass. The bronze chandeliers in all four corners of the building, as well as the wooden doors of the ark, were made by local craftsmen. On either side of the stairs leading to the ark stood iron rams topped by metal palms; in World War I a Russian general apparently removed one of the palms, which ended up in a museum in Moscow. The *bimah*, or raised reader's platform, at the center of the hall was made of marble. Other objects included a ceremonial Chair of Elijah, traditionally used for circumcision; a copper sink and washbasin; a menorah; and an old, illustrated prayer book. In 1931 some of these items were exhibited at the regional capital of Tarnopol. But none is known to have survived the war that followed.[10]

What mattered most to the community was not the monetary value or artistic quality of the objects in the synagogue, but rather their symbolic meaning, as expressed through tales about their genesis. Agnon, who collected the legends that breathed life back into loss and oblivion, writes: "What is left of the splendid artifacts that were in the Great Synagogue? Only the stories remain."[11] One such tale recalls the origins of the great chandelier that was suspended over the reader's platform. As Agnon tells it, the chandelier was brought to Buczacz by the successful merchant and beadle of the Great Synagogue, curly-haired Shalom. On one of his many business trips, Shalom came to Trieste in Italy, where he was hosted by a Christian colleague. The man's dining hall was adorned with a beautiful chandelier, but its candles were unlit. In response to Shalom's query, his host explained that his great-grandfather used to light the chandelier during the Jewish Sabbath and Holidays; but when his business failed, he was compelled to convert to Christianity, and all his offspring were subse-

Interior of the Great Synagogue in Buczacz, 1920s.

quently raised in the Christian faith. Since then, the chandelier had never been lit. But now, Shalom's host feared that later generations would forget this family heritage and use the chandelier for other purposes. The following morning the chandelier was delivered to Shalom to take back with him to Buczacz, where it lit the synagogue for many generations, until the community was destroyed "and the light went out."[12]

Besides the beautiful chandelier, the Great Synagogue also boasted a six-branched bronze candelabra; the tale of its various transformations evoked the entire span of Jewish life in Buczacz. As Agnon relates it, the candelabra dated back to Nachman, who had served as keeper of the seal to the king of Poland. As a reward for Nachman's sage advice, the king presented the synagogue of Buczacz with a copy of the seven-branched candelabra that had once stood in the Temple in Jerusalem, unaware of the prohibition to reproduce any of the Temple's destroyed objects. Fearful of offending the king by rejecting his gift, the community decided to simply remove one of the candelabra's branches. During the Cossack Wars, the candelabra was hidden in the Strypa River and forgotten. When the wars ended, the candelabra was accidentally discovered, fished out, and placed in the newly built Great Synagogue. Within a few generations, no one could recall any longer why the candelabra was damaged; in order to repair it, a white brass eagle, the symbol of Poland, was welded to the spot where the seventh branch had been sawed off. But when Poland was partitioned and Buczacz came under Austrian rule, the community prudently replaced the white Polish eagle with the double-headed eagle of the Habsburg Empire. Many years later, during World War I, the candelabra was hidden again, and when the fighting ended, it was once more miraculously found. But this time, although the double-headed eagle of the now defunct empire was promptly removed, it was no longer replaced by the old symbol of the newly established Polish state, since "the Ruthenians were rebelling against Poland, and were they to see the Polish eagle in the synagogue they would say that we are fighting against the Ruthenian people." As Agnon concludes, "rulers come and go, and Israel remains forever."[13] But under German rule the candelabra was lost again; this time no miracles occurred, and it was never found.

If the Great Synagogue was the community's heart, the study house (*beit ha-midrash*) was its soul. The modest stone house built next to the synagogue also replaced an older wooden structure; for many decades, it accommodated members of the community who had time and inclination to study.[14] Admired for its library, the study house also burned down in the fire of 1865. While the house was rebuilt, the library was destroyed. Stern lamented this loss in his contemporaneous report: "It is this that pains our hearts, the precious books that burned in our town . . . filled with wisdom and knowledge . . . to whose loss we cannot attach any price tag. We are

now," he grieved, "as sheep without a shepherd, without synagogues and
study houses and without a book to consult, and all are filled with mourning."[15] Such lamentations became commonplace in the following century.

In his celebrated 1939 novel, *A Guest for the Night*, Agnon depicts his
protagonist's visit to his hometown a decade after the destruction of World
War I. In Szybusz, as he calls the city, signs of devastation, depopulation,
and impoverishment are everywhere. On Yom Kippur, the Jewish Day of
Atonement, the visitor heads to the old study house, only to discover that
it "had become misshapen. Cabinets once filled with books had been emptied," and "the long heavy benches where the old Torah scholars once sat—
were now part empty and part occupied by simpletons." He recalls that
"the ceiling had once been black from smoke and soot," but "now it was
whitewashed," while "the walls that had been scratched were now plastered." The point, he thinks, is not that "black is better than white and that
scratched is better than plastered," but rather that "the soot came from the
smoke of our forefathers' candles, with which they illuminated the Torah,
and the scratched walls indicated that someone had been sitting there."
But now "these plastered walls make it appear as if no one had ever sat
there."[16]

Despite its new coat of paint and desultory occupants, the study house
remains a site of fond childhood recollections for the visitor; but it also
evokes echoes of past violence and premonitions of future catastrophe.
Although it is the holiest day of the Jewish calendar, most of the men arrive with no prayer shawls: "They have either gone up in flames to heaven
or served as bed sheets for prostitutes." As the visitor looks out of the
window, "one of the two in our old study house that faced the mountain,"
he recalls how, "when I was a lad, I would study there while standing, and
write poetry." Just then, he relates, "a wonderous light shone from the
study house to the mountain, and from the mountain to the study house.
A light, the likes of which you have never seen. It was one light and within
it many radiances. Such a place you would not find anywhere in the world.
I stood there and thought to myself, I will not move from here until He
decides to take my soul from me. And although my own death had occurred to me, I was not sad."

This is his hometown. But with the recognition of its beauty come
thoughts of death: "Again I looked out to the mountain facing our study
house and thought to myself: from this side you can be sure that they will
not come to kill you. Our forefathers used to build their study houses close
to a mountain, so that if the murderers came to kill them, they could hide

in the study house, which is protected by the mountain from one side and by the government from the other. As long as one's time has not come, there is no better place."[17] Yet shortly after the novel was published, neither the mountain nor the government came to the rescue, and that very protective mountain became a site of mass murder. Fifty years later, the local authorities sent in a bulldozer and tore down the abandoned study house.[18]

The Crazy Pasha

All that lay far in the future. As memories of the Cossack and Turkish wars gradually receded, their outlandish violence appeared increasingly inconceivable. Like other town dwellers in the borderlands, the inhabitants of eighteenth-century Buczacz lived in largely segregated religious and ethnic communities, and interethnic violence was far less ubiquitous than popular accounts influenced by more recent events would have us believe. Most people peered beyond their immediate religious, social, and economic preoccupation only when a major event impinged directly on their lives. In Buczacz one such event was the death in 1727 of Stefan Potocki, who had ruled the city for more than half a century, and, following a brief interim period under his widow Joanna, the city's takeover by the couple's maverick twenty-one-year-old son Mikołaj in 1733.[19]

Also known as governor of Kaniów (Kaniv), Mikołaj Potocki was by all accounts a larger-than-life figure: passionate, ambitious, and generous, he was also callous, prejudiced, and cruel; a man of great appetites and uncontrollable urges, he was given as much to deep religious faith as to dissoluteness, licentiousness, moral corruption, and bouts of violence. Mikołaj's decades-long rule over Buczacz extended through the entire period leading to the Austrian annexation of 1772 and the end of the city's private ownership by his clan; it left a strong stamp on Buczacz, not least thanks to the splendid edifices he commissioned there. In the romantic Polish literature of the nineteenth century, he was portrayed as the epitome of the *szlachcic*, the archetypal Polish nobleman, whose ample merits and flaws were accentuated all the more against the backdrop of Poland's unraveling eastern borderlands. For their part, Ukrainian accounts of his life stress his apparent discovery of his Ruthenian roots and conversion to Greek Catholicism.[20]

Educated by the Jesuits in Lwów, Potocki took an early liking to literature, history, and theology, publishing eight slim volumes entitled *The*

Succession of Polish Dukes and Kings in 1731. Once he became lord of Buczacz, this "wealthy and immensely obliging lord," as Barącz describes him, was drawn into an array of administrative and political positions and, having "distinguished himself in every post," eventually became "as famous as his ancestors."[21] Yet this was no unblemished fame, containing as it did more than its share of scandal and outrage, which in part explains its longevity. In 1860 the Polish magazine *Tygodnik Ilustrowany* (*Illustrated Weekly*) asked: "Why was the Governor of Kaniów such a popular figure that he still lives on in the tales and songs of Ruthenian commoners, possibly fragmented by now, yet still quite fresh? Why does he live on also among the more educated class in tales and anecdotes that seemingly proliferate every day?"

Perhaps, the writer speculated, this renown could be ascribed to a certain "devilish, even mythical" quality about the man, considering that while "history knows very little about him, legends tell a great deal, indeed much more than there really was." It appears, concluded this article, that an individual's "greatest popularity cannot burst beyond the country cottage threshold if he does not hold a sword in one hand and a torch in the other; if he does not leave behind streams of blood and heaps of ashes, or, if operating within a more limited scope—if he does not harm people by his madness and eccentricities."[22]

A couple of decades later, Barącz expressed a similar sentiment, noting that Mikołaj Potocki was "rightly or wrongly renowned in all of Poland . . . Feeling very powerful, and having a great deal of money, he selected evil councilors, who advised him to lead a rakish life. He increased the corruption in the city to such an extent, that in order to restrain his arbitrariness, a chief justice had to be kept in the city." And yet, Barącz finds Potocki "admirable" precisely because, despite his "confused corruption," which Barącz attributed to the "crowd of flatterers, people of ill will, who always swarmed around him and falsely applauded him," this great magnate "maintained his noble intellect." Indeed, exclaims Barącz, "his golden heart beat magnanimously to his last breath. Obedient to the calling of his good heart, in buoyant passion he came to realize the wrongs he inflicted, generously compensated for them, and, with old Polish devotion, beseeched the mercy of God for himself and forgiveness for his sins at the foot of the altar. He did not fritter away his property, nor did he exploit his lands, but rather wanted to leave behind good memories throughout the country."[23]

Unlike Barącz, who concedes that this particular Potocki had many sins to atone for by the time he fell at the foot of the altar, some Ukrainian commentators have a more resolutely positive view of the man. The chronicler of the Greek Catholic Basilian monastery in Buczacz, Yaroslav Stotskyi, depicts him as "an outstanding personality in Polish-Ukrainian history." The reason for this full-throated endorsement, as Stotskyi explains, is Potocki's "positive attitude toward Ukrainianness and toward the Basilian monks, for he converted from the Roman Catholic to the Greek Catholic faith, spoke the national Ruthenian language, liked the Basilians in Buczacz, and did not abandon this love until the day he died."[24] In other words, this proud member of the Polish *szlachta* (gentry)—said by some to have led a "Cossack lifestyle"—was recruited posthumously by later generations as a representative of their particular ethnic and national identity.

In fact, Potocki's far more ecumenical inclinations led him to donate vast sums of money to all religious institutions and faiths. In the nearby town of Horodenka alone, he provided funds for a Paulinian cloister; an Armenian parish priest; Roman Catholic, Orthodox, and Greek Catholic churches; and even the Jewish community. Elsewhere he also supported the construction of Bernardine, Reform, Capuchin, and Dominican churches and cloisters. As an investment in the afterlife, Potocki spread the risk as widely as possible.[25]

And yet it is true that Potocki made a crucial contribution to Ruthenian—later seen as Ukrainian—religion, identity, and education, especially in Buczacz. Most important, he funded the construction of the Basilian Monastery on the slope of Fedor Hill, completed in 1753, along with an adjacent two-story school in 1757–58, and the building of the monastery church, completed in 1771, all designed by the Silesian architect Gottfried Hoffmann.[26] These vast investments clearly combined Potocki's interests in religion and education, influenced, no doubt, by his years of schooling by the Jesuits, as well as his fondness for imposing edifices.

The new school building housed the theological seminar, known as the Buczacz Collegium, established by royal charter in 1754 and funded by a foundation set up for that purpose by Potocki. The school served both regular students and candidates for the priesthood, and its dormitory also supplied food and clothing. The goal of this first formal educational institution in Buczacz was to "provide youngsters with education and piety." By 1769 its enrollment reached 343 male students from both major Christian denominations in Buczacz and its environs; they took courses in theology, history, geography, physics, Latin, and Greek, to which philosophy was added following the Austrian annexation three years later. But while the Collegium did not discriminate on the basis of heritage or property, it

The Basilian Monastery in Buczacz, 2007. Photo by the author.

was not open to Jews, who made up a growing share of the population by the early decades of the nineteenth century.[27]

The significant presence of Jews in Buczacz attracted occasional anti-Jewish pranks by the older students. In wintertime they made a habit of riding their sleds down the hill from the school, ending up in the Jewish residential area and causing havoc. But there were also other distractions. A Czech traveler reported that in spring and summer the students sought more amorous engagements by spraying salt on the monastery's lawns, so as to attract the cows being taken out to the meadows on Fedor Hill by young maidens from the town.[28]

Even the patriotic and strict Roman Catholic Barącz, whose displeasure about Potocki's conversion is palpable, concedes that "for all this, it is impossible to deny him the merit he can claim for Buczacz" as "a builder of the city." Not least, notes Barącz, by establishing the college, Potocki "revived the dormant desire for education among the youth." But the governor's darker side could not be ignored, for even as he invested in educating the young, he also became involved in multiple incidents of hooliganism and violence. Since he was responsible for the city's defense, he maintained his own military unit, and stored "gunpowder for cannon in the tower of the castle on the mountain, along with heavy weapons." But instead of protecting the population, Potocki's private army quickly acquired "a bad reputation," and as early as 1738 he and his troops were reported to have repeatedly "perpetrated a great deal of violence and excesses" in Lwów. Eventually, following appeals to the king by the city's inhabitants, Potocki was ordered to leave the provincial capital. Yet for years thereafter "people still remembered his bloody brawls."[29]

Potocki's army was, in fact, a political tool in the service of far greater ambitions than the protection of Buczacz. Indeed, Potocki was increasingly drawn into the power struggles that proliferated in the last decades of the Polish-Lithuanian Commonwealth.[30] In 1733 his troops unsuccessfully supported one of the candidates for a new king of Poland; six years later, while purportedly defending Podolia against invading Russian forces, his hired Cossacks reportedly "terrorized the local gentry, peasants, and Jews." By the early 1740s this private army had expanded to as many as three thousand troops, and Potocki increased his political influence by obtaining a mandate to the Warsaw Sejm (Parliament). But the unruly force under his command became progressively more difficult to control, and following yet another drunken, bloody brawl in Lwów in 1755, Potocki was tried by the city's garrison commander, proclaimed guilty, and forced to pay a hefty fine.

The "crazy pasha," as Mikołaj Potocki came to be nicknamed, still played a part in Polish negotiations with Prussian and Ottoman representatives, aimed at stemming the growing Russian influence in the region, during the late 1750s and early 1760s.[31] But with Europe embroiled in the Seven Years' War (1756–63), Poland's political and military irrelevance became ever clearer. In 1772 Poland was partitioned for the first time, and the newly named Kingdom of Galicia and Lodomeria—more commonly known as the crownland or province of Galicia—was created from the southeastern parts of the commonwealth annexed by the Habsburg Empire. Buczacz was one of the many towns and villages that slipped out of Polish rule. Following the third partition in 1795, Poland ceased to exist as an independent political entity altogether; it was not until the aftermath of World War I that the Polish state was resurrected.[32]

Mikołaj Potocki began to disengage from politics and society almost a decade before the annexation. In 1764 this magnate, who had previously been the third richest member of his powerful clan, began dividing his vast

landed property among his relatives. Perhaps this had to do with witness-
ing the progressive disintegration of the kingdom, or with his advancing
age. Barącz suggests that Potocki had become "discontent with himself: In
his matrimonial life he did not find happiness, and in governmental politics he constantly appeared terribly distressed, and visibly bored." Others
believe that he sought "expiation for his immoral life." Yet, as one modern
account points out, however one judges Potocki's moral character, "art historians have no doubt in calling him a generous patron."[33] There is good
reason to conclude that the governor's greatest legacy was the works of art
and architecture he so unstintingly funded.

Living Water and Sculpted Jews

Potocki's most significant contribution to the architectural prominence
of Buczacz was the city hall. Completed in 1751, it is the joint creation of
the architect Bernard Meretyn and the sculptor Johann Georg Pinsel, who
carved for it sixteen sculptures, including allegorical representations of the
Twelve Labors of Hercules. The two men collaborated on various other
projects, including Saint George's Cathedral in Lwów. A well-balanced
and elegant ensemble topped by a 115-foot tower, the city hall is praised
by one Ukrainian art critic as "an original synthesis of arts . . . unparalleled
in eighteenth century architecture," whereby "architecture and sculpture
are combined so harmoniously that one cannot imagine the city hall without the statues." Unfortunately, many of these sculptures were either partially or completely destroyed in the fire of 1865. Of the six that survived,
some found their way to local museums.

The remaining sculptures were ruined or stolen during the world wars.
In the postwar period the building underwent several modifications, including the replacement of the tower's original roof with a more Slavic-
looking Byzantine dome. Recent attempts to preserve the city hall have
been repeatedly hampered by lack of funds.[34] Not much is known about
Pinsel, who seems to have come from Germany or Austria to Buczacz
around 1750, where he served as court artist to Potocki; he remained there
until his death in 1761 or 1762, a couple of years after Meretyn's passing.
Although many of the figures he created for the city hall had already been
lost by then, his renowned "Samson and the Lion" can still be seen perched
on the building's parapet in a photograph taken during World War II. Pinsel's interest in biblical themes is evident from his other, strikingly realistic
works. A series of painted and gilded wooden figures he created in 1758

Johann Georg Pinsel, *Samson*, Lviv National
Art Gallery, 2016. Photo by the author.

for the high altar of the Church of All Saints in Hodowica (Hodovytsya),
near Lwów, includes the "Sacrifice of Isaac" and a rendering of "Samson
and the Lion," both currently displayed at the Lviv National Art Gallery,
alongside a better preserved stone version of Samson.[35]

Many tales have been told about the construction of Potocki's city hall
and the heroic figures that adorned it. For Agnon, the story begins with
the origins of the well that once stood in the marketplace where the city
hall was later built: "At the center of the marketplace there is a well whose
water never runs dry, day and night, summer and winter. This well at the

marketplace existed before the town, for even before the town was built the well flowed with water and cattle and animals and birds would come and drink and occasionally passersby also quenched their thirst from it. But the water pump and the fence and the two spouts date back four or five generations, as explained in the story I will now tell."[36]

Since the Torah is conventionally compared to a well of fresh, or "living," water, in Agnon's telling the existence of the well in Buczacz is necessarily linked to Jewish life, just as its disappearance symbolizes the end of that life—and of God's presence—in Buczacz:

The sage and Hasid Rabbi Chaim, author of The Well of Living Water, was born in the village of Privolok [Przewłoka, Perevoloka, five miles north of Buczacz], and like all seekers of knowledge in the environs of Buczacz he studied the Torah in Buczacz in our old study house . . . From the end of the Sabbath to the following Sabbath Eve, Rabbi Chaim would not budge from the study house. He would drink from the sink and eat his father's bread . . . for a different lodging and dining table is a waste of one's time . . .

One day at noon Rabbi Chaim paused his study and went to wash his hands before the meal. He encountered an old man, not from his town, sitting there. He invited him to eat with him, but the man refused. He begged him and he would not listen. He said, "Don't beg me to eat, but I would gladly drink some living water."

Because he heard the words living water, Rabbi Chaim understood that the old man meant spring or well water, and not transported water, for had he wanted just any water the sink was there.

Rabbi Chaim dashed off to the well and brought him water. He drank and said, "You have revived my spirits." The old man had been fasting from one Sabbath to the next and his spirits had waned, and now he broke his fast with a little water. Rabbi Chaim said, "I'll go and fetch you more." He said to him, "I will go and drink from the source."

They walked together to the well.

The old man looked at the water flowing from the well. He stuck his cane in the wet earth and rested his beard on the cane and watched the water bubbling from the earth and returning to it.

Rabbi Chaim saw how the old man's face progressively lit up, like those tzaddiks [righteous men] who, whatever they observe, they see in it the deeds of God and His wonders.

The old man raised his head and said, "A well of living water."

He bent down and filled his palms with water, and added, "Pure water, pure water." He blessed again and drank.

And after he prayed by the well he left, for he was one of those who fulfil the verse "I am a stranger in the land," and where they spend the day they do not sleep at night, and where they sleep at night they do not spend the day, for their sole desire wherever they dwell is to seek a place for their soul where God does not turn his gaze away as much.[37]

It is this encounter, relates Agnon, that instigated the construction of the well facing the newly built city hall. Not only did the well symbolize the living water of the Torah and the holiness of the Jewish community of Buczacz, but it was also named after the meeting between the wandering tzaddik and the future author of *The Well of Living Water*, a foundational Hasidic text. Rabbi Chaim, who was born in 1760, later became the rabbi of Czernowitz, and eventually left Europe in protest against the new Austrian authorities' prohibition of public prayers and their insistence on public education, ending his life in 1817 in Jerusalem; he is buried in Tsefat (Safed), and to this day is celebrated as a tzaddik. Thus Agnon's story makes the well in the heart of Buczacz into the fountain of life and wisdom—the Jewish counterpart of the Enlightenment-era city hall and its neoclassical sculptures, with which it once shared the town's main marketplace.

Having established a relationship between the well and the city hall, Agnon turns to locating this magnificent eighteenth-century rococo edifice itself within the larger narrative of Jewish history:

> Next to the marketplace well stands a glorious building, most elegant and very beautiful. This is the great city hall of our town, on account of which all of Poland's cities have envied us. Thanks to its great beauty people used it as a metaphor, so that whenever they saw anyone dressed elegantly, they would say, look at him, he is trying to put on the Buczacz city hall. And just as the building served as a metaphor, so too the fine sculptures made by the craftsman to adorn the city hall served as a metaphor, so that when anyone was at a loss of words from astonishment, they would say, he is so astonished that he has become as speechless as the sculptures of the Buczacz city hall.

In Agnon's tale, the building's architectural and artistic accomplishments are traced back to its Jewish origins. It is not unlikely that the fable he relates was told by members of the Jewish community in pre-1914 Buczacz, and that he merely embellished it in his own inimitable style. Ultimately, the tale he spins is an allegory of Jewish fate. And since he retells it in the aftermath of the Holocaust, it is also an attempt to justify the memory of his hometown as having been populated by a pious Jewish community, despite its members' admiration for the array of barely clothed heroic stone figures overlooking the very marketplace where most Jews lived and traded: "Now that Buczacz has been destroyed, and our brethren, the residents of Buczacz, who used to elevate the city with their beauty and enrich their conversation with fine phrases, have all been killed, I must interpret their sayings, lest you wonder why pious Jews who adhered to the living God in life and in death spoke about those sculptures."[38]

Agnon resolves this conundrum by reimagining the biography of the city hall's maker. This was, we read, the craftsman Theodore, who had worked on the building for six years, during which time he also sculpted the figures that adorned it: "Theodore made many stone sculptures for the house, at the corners of the lower part and at the southern front. And he called them all by name, names taken from the Holy Scripture. Their faces were the faces of the Jews whom Theodore saw in the town of Buczacz and of those Jews that he saw in his nightly dreams and visions."[39] Why did Theodore dream of Jews? As we discover, what animated the sculptures that had once adorned the city hall were not only the living faces of the town's Jews, all now dead and gone just like the sculptures that represented them, but also regained memories of a lost Jewish identity:

> One evening Theodore went for a walk in the town. He came upon the Jewish street. He saw that the street was empty, not a single person was out. Theodore went on walking. He saw a house lit up with many candles and filled with people. They were wearing white and were barefoot and were holding books in their hands and one man was standing among them, entirely wrapped in a white garment, and his voice was like the voice of a man praying for his soul. Theodore did not know whether he actually saw this, or it was a dream.
>
> Yet what he saw was not a dream but reality, which he had already seen as a child. For when he was a boy of about four or five, his mother took him to a house full of candles, and there were many people in the house, all wearing white clothes just like the people that Theodore saw that second time, and an old man stood

among them and was sweetly singing, and they answered him in their own voices. The boy sat at his mother's feet and slept. His sister took him home with her. And as they walked a group of people dressed in black came toward them and took him out of his sister's arms . . . and brought him to the man who built houses and made sculptures, and the man called him Theodore after himself. Theodore lived in Theodore's home and made together with Theodore all that Theodore made. And he grew and became a man and the older he grew the more his name spread as one of the great craftsmen who builds halls and makes sculptures. Mikołaj Potocki heard of Theodore's fame. Potocki came to him and brought him to his land and to his town to build for him his city hall, which he desired. Theodore built for him the city hall. And he adorned it with beautiful images in the likeness of the men and women that Theodore had seen in the town and had seen in his dreams. Because since he had seen the House of God on Yom Kippur Eve he could not forget the faces of the people he had seen in his dreams and the faces of the people he had seen with his eyes on the Jewish street in the town of Buczacz, and Theodore made with his hand what his eyes had seen and what his heart had seen.[40]

In Agnon's fable, the entire city hall complex, otherwise known as the masterpiece of a unique collaboration between an architect and an artist famed for their contributions to Christian edifices, morphs into the creation of a crypto-Jew—a man whose distant childhood memories, dream world, and reencounter with Jewish life in Buczacz culminate in that magnificent edifice and its gallery of Jew-like figures. It is precisely because his repressed childhood memories resurface in Buczacz that Theodore—whose name would be pronounced Fedor or Fedir by the locals—is inspired to transform the spiritual beauty of the Jews into the glorious plastic representations on the city hall. And because Agnon relates this fable in the wake of the Holocaust, he also gives Theodore a death that presages the fate of the community. For, as he tells us, Fedor Hill, upon which Agnon gazed as a youth from the windows of the study house, and where much of the Jewish community was subsequently murdered and buried, was named after the man who created the city's most prized possession.

Theodore, in Agnon's fable, became a victim of his own genius. For once his work was completed, he found himself imprisoned by Potocki within the very edifice he had built, so that he would never be able to re-

produce such a masterpiece for any other city. In desperation, Theodore
made himself "wings to fly with" from "the leftover planks of wood and
ropes and rags." These, explains Agnon somewhat mysteriously, "were not
like the wings of airplanes that are flying now, and not even like the wings
of the first airplane, which were made by a Jewish man many years later,
the very first airplane ever made." Tragically, Theodore's wings did not
carry him very far. Jumping from the tower, he "flew and glided across the
Strypa," but then "his strength was exhausted, and he fell down and died."
In death, he gave his name to Fedor Hill, upon which he crashed. "This is
the hill," writes Agnon, "where five-hundred Jews were buried alive," while
others were led "with truncheons and pistols to the city hall," where they
"surrounded them with barbed wire and poured gasoline on them and set
fire to them and they were all burned alive. And from the bowels of the
earth, from the depths of the pit, all the way to the highest heaven rose the
cries of the Jews . . . And the Gentiles were laughing and saying, there they
go again, wailing just as they do in their synagogue."[41]

Theodore's fable has made the rounds through different generations
and national-ideological configurations. The Polish historian Stanisław
Grodziski, for instance, relates the following version in a book about travels in Galicia: "Long ago, a Polish nobleman from an ancient clan, or a
magnate, invited the learned Italian named Fedorini. Fedorini constructed
a machine in which, like Icarus, he wanted to rise upward or perhaps gently glide down into the Strypa ravine. Unfortunately, he paid with his life
for that brave goal. But he has survived in memory. The people called the
hill from which he set off on his last journey by his name." For Grodziski,
then, the first flyer in history, appropriately named Fedorini, while apparently not an architect, was also not a Jew but an Italian, predating the
Wright brothers by a good century and a half, not to mention the Italian
Giulio Gavotti, whose claim to fame is to have been the first man to have
dropped bombs from an airplane on an enemy target in 1911.[42]

A rather different version of this tale, this time adapted to the circumstances of Soviet Ukraine, is offered by Ihor Duda, who authored a tourist
guide to Buczacz published in Lviv in 1985. In Duda's telling, the city hall
was built by three "skillful craftsmen," whose work "everybody admired."
But Potocki, "consumed with envy," removed the ladder from the tower
they were building—presumably, as in Agnon's tale, for fear of their ac-
complishing a similar feat in other towns. Left with no other choice, the
"builders" began "making something out of wooden planks." The three men
"worked day and night," and at long last the spectators below saw them

"sprouting wings." We already know their fate: "The oldest master flew first," but as "he lacked sufficient strength," he "fell on the market square." The second master "made for the hill but was unable to reach it and fell into the river." But "the third—the young apprentice Fedir—landed on the hill that was then named after him."

In this socialist Ukrainian rendering, local workingmen try to escape the tyrannical rule of a degenerate Polish aristocrat. But if Agnon connects the crypto-Jew Theodore's crash on the hill to the mass murder of the city's Jewish community on the site two centuries later, Duda conforms to the conventions of Soviet history and leaves the Jews entirely out of his narrative. Instead, he recalls that "on top of Fedir Hill, in the shadow of old trees, there is a common grave for the Soviet soldiers who fell fighting for the liberation of Buczacz and its district from the German-Fascist occupiers." Guiding his readers to the Red Army memorial erected on the hill not long before his writing, Duda can only comment that the "Hitlerites" had "exterminated about 7,500 civilians," avoiding any reference to these victims' identity or to their neighbors' complicity in the killing, and falsely stating that "the population did not submit to the fascists."

In a final twist to this local Soviet myth, Duda adds that in 1953, workers "discovered fragments of wings, an airplane engine and a cockpit caked with clay" near the hill. The pilot's remains contained "his documents and personal belongings. The pilot's name was Fedir Ivanovych Vlasikov." This Fedir was an authentic Soviet man: raised in the Orel region of Russia, he later worked in Donetsk in eastern Ukraine, joined the Komsomol (communist youth organization), and became a candidate for Communist Party membership. As a fighter pilot in the Great Patriotic War, the official name of World War II in the Soviet Union, Fedir was shot down on 11 April 1944, while heroically fending off five German fighter planes. His remains "were carried to the common grave in Buczacz. The ancient name of the hill," Duda assures us, "had acquired new meaning."[43]

What Duda does not tell us is that in October 1944, half a year after Fedir was shot down, representatives of the Soviet Extraordinary Commission for the Investigation of Nazi Crimes exhumed some of the thousands of Jewish victims buried on Fedor Hill, only to quickly rebury them and file away the report on their findings. Thus the Jewish victims were erased from the official Soviet record of the Great Patriotic War, as they were from local recollection and commemoration. It took until 2005 for the webpage of the city to acknowledge that "most" of the "nearly 7,500 inhabitants of the town and the district" murdered by the Germans "were of Jewish nationality." But subsequent versions of the webpage once again consigned the identity of the victims to oblivion. Instead, the mythical three heroic builders of the city hall were resurrected and celebrated, this time as local boys, proving that "Buchachians were good craftsmen."[44]

This mix of splendid esoteric legends, parables, and myths, on the one hand, and stark, sordid reality, on the other, tells us a great deal about how the identity of the people who came to the borderlands was shaped over time. In Agnon's tale, the Jews attempt to create for themselves a sense of ownership, however internal and impractical, over objects and works that are entirely divorced from their traditions and daily existence. Setting out to explain why the Jews' love for the Buczacz city hall and its figurines was no blasphemy, Agnon ends up depicting these statues as the stone representations of ghostly images stamped on the unconscious mind of a stolen Jewish child. Since World War II, when the frozen floor of the forest begins to thaw, fragments of bones will occasionally resurface from the mass graves on Fedor Hill, as the only indication of the horror whose traces were erased and forgotten. Other fragments of the prewar past will also emerge every so often from oblivion. In 2008, the head of a statue that had once adorned the city hall was discovered; it may have belonged to the original stone version of "Samson and the Lion," modeled, allegedly, on the long-lost Jews of Buczacz. But a well-preserved statue of the Virgin Mary, also found at that time, has since been restored and returned to its pedestal, a column designed by Pinsel and Meretyn, in the city. Nowadays the Holy Mother is once more watching over Buczacz.[45]

Pinsel's numerous contributions to the city, all funded by Mikołaj Potocki, include two altars made for the Roman Catholic parish church, whose interior, damaged in World War II and badly dilapidated during the communist period, has recently been beautifully restored. The Greek Catholic St. Pokrova Church, built in 1764 to replace an old wooden church on the eastern outskirts of the town, also included a series of remarkable bas-reliefs carved by Pinsel on its northern door, which count among his most precious works, and are now exhibited in the art museum of Ternopil. But the church is now known in Buczacz for another recent discovery of a gruesome past. In 1990 a mass grave of 136 adults, children, and a priest was uncovered next to the church. This massacre is now commemorated as a Soviet crime, although it may well have been the work of the Germans. Just a few minutes' walk up the hill from the church is the Jewish cemetery, where several thousand Jews lie in unmarked mass graves, their slaughter unremembered.[46]

Undivine Comedy

Despite his generous support not only to art and architecture, but also to all denominations in the region, Mikołaj Potocki's growing investment in the Basilian Monastery appears to be related to his conversion to the Greek Catholic rite. Why did he convert? According to Barącz, although Potocki made countless donations of gold and silver to the Roman Catholic church in Buczacz, the clergy "boldly reproached him for his misdemeanors." Tired of being constantly harangued, the magnate finally "abandoned the Roman rite, and was left to cling to the Ruthenian rite with the Basilian order, where he conversed in broken Ruthenian." Having "poured more than two million złoty into their monastery" in Buczacz, Potocki went on to lavish even greater sums on the splendid Greek Catholic monastery of Poczajów (Pochayiv, eighty miles north of Buczacz), which later came under the Orthodox Church. The magnate's devotion to Poczajów provides the occasion for a miraculous tale about his conversion. One day, as Barącz relates, Potocki was traveling past the monastery, when one of the wheels of his carriage broke. Enraged by this mishap, Potocki drew his gun and repeatedly shot at his terrified cart driver; but the poor man turned his face to the monastery and prayed so fervently for his life that none of the shots harmed him. This miracle, which spared him from taking an innocent man's life, led Potocki not only to convert but also to tie his fate to the monastery, funding and closely following the erection of a grand complex designed by the same Gottfried Hoffmann who had built the Basilian monastery.

For the powerful and irascible Mikołaj Potocki, the Austrian annexation was a blow that he simply could not withstand. Heir of a proud line of generals and magnates, this last independent ruler of the vast Potocki domains was compelled to observe the occupation of his properties without even a semblance of resistance. As Barącz writes, Potocki "watched sadly when on 3 October [1772] the [Austrian] armed forces marched in; both infantry and hussars, they spent the night in his Buczacz, and the following day set out to Czortków. But on 15 April 1773, at noon, a fire began by the gate of Jazłowiec, that is, in the suburb of Pokrowski. The flames were whipped up by strong winds and consumed 130 houses. This transformed him and made him completely lose heart."

It was in the wake of these events that in 1774 Mikołaj drew up his will, handing over the governorship of Kaniów and the ownership of Buczacz to his relative Jan Potocki, to whom he referred as his son-in-law, although he is not known to have fathered any children. Mikołaj then left the territory that had come under Austrian rule and moved to a small wooden manor house built for him in the courtyard of the Poczajów monastery. Located in the nearby province of Volhynia, the monastery remained under Polish rule until the third and final partition of 1795, when it was annexed by Russia. But by then Mikołaj Potocki, who had refused to live under foreign rule, was long dead, buried in 1782 in a crypt beneath the Assumption Cathedral, whose construction he had heavily subsidized.[47]

Although his hagiographers assert that he spent his last years in Poczajów "virtuously," other accounts suggest that to the very end Potocki's alleged virtues conflicted with his other, less savory predilections. Ensconced on the grounds of the magnificent monastery he had built, away from the Habsburgs who had occupied and imposed Austrian order on much of the land he had owned and the towns he had built, the former governor apparently sought other ways to entertain himself. As one account tells it, Potocki did indeed go to church "in the morning and in the evening to say monastic prayers," where he "admonished neglectful monks." But, at the same time, "he kept several prostitutes at his house, whom he used to wake up in the morning for the rosary, which he recited together with them; if any of the girls laughed out, he would lash her back with the stem of his pipe to make her stop offending God, as he put it."[48]

Late in life, Potocki married Marianna Dąbrowska, his steward's beautiful daughter, but they separated soon thereafter. There were rumors that he had been adopted by his parents, since they were relatively old by the standards of the time when he was born. Described as "extremely tall with a ruddy, withered face and a gray, thick moustache," the governor of Kaniów became a legend in his time, not least thanks to his notorious "lifestyle" and "the cruelties committed by him and his retinue when drunk." A Ukrainian folk song recounts how he killed the beloved cooper's daughter in Łuck, and a recent Polish author describes him as a "queer man, a psychopath and a brute," who featured as "the negative hero of many brawls and commotions." Yet the same author also praises Potocki as a "pious, though dissolute despot," noting that he "had a considerable share in the development of Buczacz and other towns."[49] Tales about the magnate relate that his "castle in Buczacz was considered at the time a hotbed of unbridled revelries and debauchery." The nineteenth-century Polish poet Zygmunt Krasiński referred to him in his 1835 drama, *Nie-Boska komedia* (The Un-Divine Comedy), as a governor who "shot women on trees and baked Jews alive" (*Ów, starosta, baby strzelał po drzewach i Żydów piekł żywcem*).[50]

This peculiar concoction of religiosity and dedication to education and art, on the one hand, and drunkenness, brutality, and exploitation and murder of women and Jews, on the other, was part of the making of the borderlands. Generosity and violence, enlightenment and savagery, fear of God and contempt for morality, a will to build and an urge to destroy, resided side by side, at times in ample, overflowing quantities, even in the very same individual. Perhaps it is true that, quite apart from the edifices he left behind, what immortalized Mikołaj Potocki the man was his abundance of excesses. Yet in retrospect one must concede that if living under his capricious and arbitrary rule may not always have been pleasant, he did leave behind a considerable cultural legacy that later generations—which at times far outdid him in cruelty and destruction—would learn to admire but could never match.

CHAPTER FIVE

Communities of Spirit

False Messiahs, Forbidden Loves

WHILE THE JEWS WERE by no means insulated from their Christian neighbors, they did reside in their own unique organizational, religious, and cultural universe, distinguished from the rest of society by their physical appearance, religion, dress, and language. For two centuries, the Council of Four Lands, the supreme body of Jewish governance in the kingdom, and its regional offshoots both regulated internal Jewish existence and negotiated the Jewish minority's relationship with the Polish authorities. The abolition of the council in 1764, followed shortly thereafter by the obliteration of Poland itself, heralded the emergence of a world that precluded the old Jewish way of life. Looking back, Agnon expressed a sense of wonder at how the largest Jewish community in the world had managed its internal affairs without any state-like enforcement mechanism:

> There had been nothing like it in any nation or tongue. A people that had been scattered and frayed, which has no authority of state and ministers but only the power of the Torah, comes together and issues edicts and formulates regulations, and these are accepted by the entire people as are the king's decrees; yet they would not have obeyed the king's decrees had he not appointed policemen to enforce them with batons and whips, and even then there are numerous rebels and criminals who break the king's law. But Israel is

a holy people and willingly accepted all that the heads and leaders of the Council of Lands had decreed . . . Then came King Stanisław August of Poland who abolished the councils that had existed for two hundred years. But God avenged the Kingdom of Poland. She abolished the Council of Lands—and He, may He be praised, sent against them three powerful states and they abolished the Kingdom of Poland.[1]

And yet, in each community, the authority of the local *kahal*—the ruling Jewish elite—largely remained in place in the early years of Austrian rule, although its ability to act as tax collector and the first judicial instance was gradually attenuated. Internally, members of the community who contested the authority of the *kahal* could still be deprived of a burial spot in the Jewish cemetery or be excommunicated.

The rabbis acted as scholars, teachers, and judges within their communities. The Jews of Poland had brought with them from Germany the tradition of Talmudic learning and further developed it to the highest level. Alongside lively scholarly activity the rabbis engaged in intensive correspondence with each other throughout Europe over matters legal and religious. While Polish Jews with a Western education were not common, they were also not entirely absent, not least among Jewish doctors. Most learned Jews in Galicia referred to ancient Greek philosophers and scientists as points of contact with foreign cultures, but more recent influences of the Enlightenment, as expressed in the writings of the eighteenth-century German philosopher and dramatist Gotthold Ephraim Lessing, or of the German-Jewish herald of the Haskalah—the Jewish Enlightenment—Moses Mendelssohn, were also seeping in.[2]

Yet unlike Western Jewry, which underwent gradual reformation, emancipation, and modernization, in Eastern Europe the gap between the learned religious elite and the mass of uneducated Jews produced a new movement of spiritualism and mysticism known as Hasidism. Founded in Galicia in the early eighteenth century by Rabbi Israel ben Eliezer (born in the village of Okopy, seventy-five miles southeast of Buczacz, and known widely as the Baal Shem Tov, or Besht), Hasidism sought to reform Orthodox Judaism and revive religion and faith by bringing it closer to the people. As evidence of the fact that Jews were not only separate from, but also influenced by their Gentile environment, the Hasidic movement borrowed a great deal from the Polish gentry, such as its rejection of all forms of sadness, its fervent call to serve God with joy, the use of alcohol, and the focus on exuberant, almost cathartic gatherings, as well as the practice of establishing "courts" of particularly charismatic rabbis.[3]

Jewish mysticism was first brought into eastern Poland by the followers of Sabbatai Zvi in the latter part of the seventeenth century and carried on by Jacob Frank in the first half of the eighteenth century. These messianic movements promised swift redemption and salvation to a population battered by decades of mass violence. Their eventual disintegration, which also led to large-scale conversions, tarnished their reputation; in the collective Jewish memory, their leaders are remembered as false prophets and messiahs, heretics who betrayed Jewish faith, and whose impact was all the more malign for coming from within the fold of Judaism rather than, as was more common and therefore more easily explained, from forces external to Jewish life and religion. For its part, Hasidism came in the wake of, and as a reaction to, these destructive movements, while at the same time deriving much of its momentum and ideas from them. Additionally, while it too was perceived and presented itself as a rebellion against the traditional religious elites, or Mitnaggedim (literally "opponents"), many of its leaders came from the ranks of the Jewish religious establishment. Subsequently, Hasidism's greatest foe from the late eighteenth century and beyond became the Haskalah, secularization, and modernity.[4]

Yet in the first half of the eighteenth century, the extreme revision of traditional Judaism proposed by the Frankists, Jacob Frank's followers, was still influential in Galicia. Frank claimed to be the reincarnation of the self-proclaimed messiah Sabbatai Zvi, who found many followers among Jews devastated by the Cossack massacres but eventually converted to Islam in 1666 along with many of his disciples. But Frank's movement was also a response to the perceived threats of its own time, namely the Haskalah, on the one hand, and Hasidism, on the other.[5] And while Frankism similarly ended up in mass conversion, tales of its indiscretions and transgressions excited the minds of many Jews in eastern Galicia, not least in Buczacz, for many decades thereafter.

Another major influence on mid-eighteenth-century Sabbateans in Buczacz and its environs was the Talmudist and Kabbalist Jonathan Eybeschütz. The head of a yeshiva in Prague and later a rabbi in north Germany, Eybeschütz was suspected of Sabbatean leanings; not only was he said to have issued amulets containing Sabbatean elements, but there were strong indications that he had authored the heretical essay *And I Came this Day unto the Fountain*, recently described by one scholar as "blatantly pornographic," indeed, as "possibly the only truly pornographic text ever written in the rabbinic idiom."[6] The furious controversy that erupted around Eybeschütz in 1751–52 indicated the extent to which Sabbatean ideas and Kabbalistic learning had infiltrated the mainstream of Jewish orthodoxy, been carried over to Hasidism, and become radicalized further in the Frankist movement, to which some of Eybeschütz's descendants belonged. The book *And I Came this Day unto the Fountain* was certainly known by some Jews from Buczacz. At an inquiry conducted by a religious court in the Galician town of Brody in 1752, one witness testified that when he met Mordechai Ben-Moshe of Buczacz, "I indicated [the passages in the book] with my finger to him so that he would learn and understand the heretical interpretations" of this text, "and he conceded what I said and repeatedly expressed regret and confessed his sin, because he had believed in that heresy until that day, and he uttered the following words: 'These things I have learned from Yissachar bar Nathan of Buczacz and these writings are being sent to him by Jonathan of Prague [Eybeschütz].'"[7]

Evidence of a Sabbatean presence in Buczacz and neighboring towns dates back to contacts between a local cell and Haim Mal'ach, a Polish Jew who had joined Sabbatai Zvi in Turkey and then returned to Poland to disseminate his ideas. Additional contacts with Sabbateans in Buczacz were reported throughout the eighteenth century. In 1755 Frank returned to Poland, where he presented himself to Sabbatean leaders from Podolia-Galicia as a kabbalist and an emissary of the Dönme, the Sabbateans of Salonica. The following year he and his followers were discovered conducting an antinomian ritual in the town of Lanckoronie nad Zbruczem (Zarichanka, sixty miles southeast of Buczacz). Alleging that clandestine erotic ceremonies had been held at the "dark house" in the town, the council of rabbis caused the arrest of eight participants by the local Polish authorities. Frank, however, was released the following day as a Turkish subject, and soon after returning to Ottoman territories, he converted to Islam. The other Frankists were subjected to an inquiry by the Jewish court of Satanów (Sataniv, fifty-five miles northeast of Buczacz), which found them and their families guilty of violating a variety of Jewish laws, including adultery and the study of banned Sabbatean books, as well as professing faith in Sabbatai Zvi.[8]

Transcripts of these inquiries provide some insight into how troubling the phenomenon of Frankism must have seemed to Jewish society in Podolia-Galicia at the time:

Shmuel son of our Master Rabbi Shlomo Segal, crying and weeping profusely: "Sirs, first I confess before you that I denied the entire Torah: I did not observe the Sabbath, I smoked tobacco on the day of the Sabbath, I ate non-kosher meat. I did not transgress with a married woman in practice, only contemplated it. I hugged and kissed Haya, the wife of Hershel Shabtis, approximately six times, but did nothing [else] with her. She told me: 'You are not worthy to deal with me, for I believe in Sabbatai Zevi, and my father, also my grandfather, and my uncle, they all believe [in him], [but] you have still not learned much Torah, you do not have this privilege . . . ' Once, her husband Hirsh heard from me that his wife Haya had fornicated with his brother Leibush when they traveled to the fair in Tarnopol. He became furious with her for doing it without his knowledge. He said, 'I would have not chastised her [had she asked me], for you know that this is a mitzvah when there is consent [by the husband].'

Hirsh also told me and his brother-in-law Yosef, that she [Haya] fornicated with his brother-in-law Palnichin from Zborów, but this was at first against her will, then her husband wanted to beat her, until she [eventually] consented.

Hirsh Shabtis himself fornicated with my wife several times in my presence. I am guilty of this, [because] she did not want to do it. Once . . . he told me that . . . he fornicated with his wife's sister Menuha, and I was very pleased. Leibush fornicated with my wife two or three times, also with my knowledge . . . Itzik Meir Bashush Zlachever, who resides in Bunatz [probably Buczacz], also fornicated two or three times with the wife of Leib son of Yeshaya from Zbariza. He brought me writings, the book *And I Came this Day unto the Fountain* and other books . . . The aforementioned Leibush fornicated with an innkeeper, the daughter of Reb Naftali Segal, and he lived with her like a wife. This is what the aforementioned Hirsh told me. He also told me that in Rohatyn [he and] his brother-in-law Leibush fornicated together with the daughter-in-law of Elisha the Elder, the wife of his son Shlomo. Even the Elder Elisha fornicated with her after Frank's arrival."

Shmuel admitted to us all of the above with confessional words and much crying . . . All of the above [transpired] before the aforementioned court.[9]

It was this investigation that led the congress of rabbis in Brody in 1756 to excommunicate Frank and his followers as "impenitent heretics." Initially, the Frankists responded by presenting themselves to the Christian authorities as Contra-Talmudists persecuted by the rabbis; but following two disputations in 1757 and 1759, in the course of which the rabbis were fined and the Talmud was condemned and publicly burned, Frank and thousands of his followers converted to Roman Catholicism. This signaled the beginning of the end of Sabbateanism, at least as an active and recognizable movement rather than a subterranean current in Judaism. Following the Austrian annexation, the remnants of Frankism largely disappeared from Galicia, whether through conversion, departure from the province, or concealment. Frank himself was arrested in 1760 on suspicion of insincere conversion and of wielding a negative influence on other converts. By the time of Frank's death in 1791, his influence had largely dissipated, and his daughter Ewa's attempts to revive the movement also failed. The last remnants of the independent Prague Sabbateans, who had followed the tradition of Jonathan Eybeschütz, were excommunicated in 1800.[10] And yet, as late as 1825, an inquiry into clandestine Sabbatean activists concluded that "a band of these traitorous conspirators, who were in Buczacz, went to Nadwórna" (Nadvirna, sixty miles southwest of Buczacz), where "literally all the heretics believed in Sabbatai Zevi." Among their various transgressions, these Buczacz Sabbateans were said to have "exchanged wives with each other," as had the Frankists two generations earlier.[11]

For Agnon, Jacob Frank's local roots are a source of both fascination and denial. Most historians agree that Frank's hometown was Korolówka (Korolivka, forty miles southeast of Buczacz). Yet Agnon insists that Frank was actually born in Buczacz itself, even as he rejects the notion that Frank might have had any impact whatsoever on the town's Jewish community: "Despite all of the flaws of Buczacz, we have not found even one of its sons who became a follower of Jacob Frank, even though this abominable person came from Buczacz and was born in Buczacz in Kołorówka Street; but because there is a little town called Korolówka, some historians have mistakenly referred to it as Frank's birthplace . . . Frank's apartment after he returned from Turkey was behind the Strypa River . . . During my childhood there was just a ruin at that site, because some malcontents had destroyed the house."[12]

This claim is dismissed by the historian Gelber, who describes it as nothing more than a "popular legend." According to Gelber, Frank was indeed born "in the town Korolówka, where his cousins were still living in 1756." Gelber also contradicts Agnon's attempt to defend his hometown, stating that "how many adherents [Frank] had in Buczacz is unknown, but that there were Frankists there is beyond doubt."[13] But for Agnon, the alleged location of Frank's birth evokes a seemingly unrelated tale, in which love triumphs over the denominational divide, the breaching of which is precisely what gave Frank a bad name. Different versions of this story have come down over the years, but they all exemplify the yearning of youth for liberation from the constraints of ethnicity and religion, even as they simultaneously suggest the dreadful consequences of crossing over to the other side.

In Agnon's interpretation, the name of the street on which Frank was born, Kołorówka, "means 'by the stream' in Polish."[14] It is this brook that acts as the leitmotif in this tale of Jewish-Christian love, as it separates, brings together, conceals, and drowns the two young lovers, or perhaps, ultimately carries them to safety.

> This is the stream that sets out next to the Potocki estate and winds its way through various sites for about a kilometer and then turns right to the Catholic church on Synagogue Street where, prior to the pogroms of 1648, the Great Synagogue had stood and which, because of our many sins, was made by the Christians into their house of worship. It is there that on the first night of Selihot [penitential poems and prayers recited at midnight before the Jewish High Holidays] the lads would light candles, tie them to planks, and send them floating down the stream in order to make light for the slain Jews, who had been thrown by the Gentiles into the river as they made their way to prayer on the nights of Selihot.

The stream, then, initially represents the Jewish-Christian divide, flowing by the church built upon the ruined synagogue, and swallowing the Jewish victims of past outbreaks of violence. Yet it also connects two lovers and becomes the site of a tender, albeit precarious and ultimately, it appears, fatal liaison: "Next to the stream stood a watermill that belonged to the Greek Catholic Church, whose Jewish miller had leased it from the priest. The miller had a beautiful and handsome son. The daughter of the priest saw him, and her heart filled with love for him. She began courting him. Her mother noticed and informed her husband. The priest said: 'If I expel the Jew from the mill, the shameful reason for doing so will be revealed; let me lock the door of the yard so that the girl will not be able to come out.'"

As often happens in such tales, the priest's decision has tragic consequences, while the love of two young pure souls conquers all adversity, even death itself.

> One day the priest and his wife went to a feast. They left the house and forgot to lock the gate of the yard behind them. The daughter saw this. She waited until night fell and then left and went to the mill. She came to the mill and did not find what she was seeking. This was the first night of Selihot, and the boys were preoccupied with tying candles to planks and floating them down the stream, so as to make light for the dead of Israel, who had been drowned in the stream, and who rise from the water on the first night of Selihot and go to the house of prayer for Selihot. The girl stood there and waited for the lad to come. She waited and waited, and he did not come. Overwhelmed by sorrow she threw herself into the stream. Then the lads arrived and with them the one she had waited for, and they were carrying lit candles. And as the one she had waited for swam in the water in order to float the candle, a hand reached out and seized him and took him with her into the stream. The stream was trawled but they were not found.

Was the young Ruthenian girl's love for the Jewish lad a murderous obsession, or did the boy go willingly to his death? Agnon suggests that unbeknownst to anyone, they ended up living happily ever after; or, perhaps, that the Jewish boy had become his lover's captive: "A few years after these events, a vegetable merchant went to the village to buy onions. He came to one of the peasants. The merchant looked at the peasant and said to him, 'Are you not the son of that man who was a miller working in the Greek Catholic priest's watermill?' But before the peasant could respond, the peasant's wife walked in with a fierce dog and set it on the merchant. The merchant picked up and ran off."[15]

Well into the nineteenth century small-town and village Jews on the borderlands lived suspended between the Middle Ages and modernity, collective memories of past trauma and continuing fears and prejudices. The custom of floating candles on the river as a means of bringing back the souls of the dead was likely borrowed from Slavic practices tracing back to pagan fertility rites, such as "Kupala Night," also known as the Feast of Saint John the Baptist. It was reinterpreted as a means of lighting the way for Khmelnytsky's victims to ascend from their watery graves and utter their prayers on Yom Kippur.[16] In the aftermath of the Holocaust, other tales of returning from the dead abounded. One of them concerned Jacob Frank's actual birthplace of Korolówka, although this time it was not an underwater grave that swallowed the Jews but a forbidding underground abode that saved them. On the night of 12 October 1942, the Stermer family—Zaida, Esther, and their six children—accompanied by nearly two dozen Jewish neighbors and relatives, men, women, and children, fled from German-occupied Korolówka to hide in a vast cave some five miles to the north. Descending into the then unexplored "Priest's Grotto," a seventy-seven-mile-long cave that currently ranks as the tenth longest in the world, this remnant of Korolówka's Jewish community lived there for 344 days, surpassing the official record of 205 days for the longest period of time a human has survived underground, set by Frenchman Michel Siffre in 1972 in the "Midnight Cave" in Texas. Siffre's accomplishment was part of a NASA-sponsored experiment on the effects of long-duration spaceflight. For the Stermers and their neighbors, hiding in the bowels of the earth was the only way to survive certain death on the face of the earth, although despite the name of the cave and the town's reputation, rescue involved neither priests nor tzaddiks. The remaining 14,000 Jews of Korolówka, possibly including some distant relatives of Jacob Frank, were mostly murdered.[17]

Magical Rabbis

The tremendous impact of the spiritual-religious movements that swept through Jewish communities on the borderlands suggests that their internal life had a sense and meaning quite incomprehensible to their Christian neighbors and rulers. In such towns as Buczacz, aside from the storm and stress of Sabbateanism and Frankism, what mattered most was the community's own religious leadership, which provided spiritual guidance, oversaw the education of the young, and maintained a complex network of communications with other Jewish communities. Most important, perhaps, this leadership nourished and sustained a sense of historical antiquity and destiny essential to the survival of scattered congregations in the midst of often suspicious, resentful, and at times hostile Christian majorities.[18]

When we observe this world from our current perspective, much of it may seem both quaint and indecipherable. The ancient link that for centuries tied together communities far and wide through a common understanding of faith, fate, and values was broken by modernity and secularization. For most inhabitants of the modern world, it is easier to understand the worship of populist, charismatic, and authoritarian political leaders, and the drive for sheer economic and military power, than to grasp the veneration of erudition and intellect, occasionally intermingled with miraculous tales and supernatural apparitions. The panoply of *ba'alei shem* (masters of the Name of God), *tzaddikim* (Hasidic rabbis—literally "righteous men"), *maggidim* (preachers), and *hozim* (seers) this era prolifically produced indicates the deep faith and ubiquitous superstition among the Jews of Europe's borderlands during the long transition to modernity.

For the economic and political elite, associating with learning could also be translated into social capital; this, in turn, sustained new generations of students. In seeking out young scholars, preferably trained by distinguished teachers, as suitable matches for their daughters, the rich and powerful assured these often wretchedly poor lads of lifelong stipends. In return, the addition of a prodigy (*iluy*) boosted the prestige of the family and was presented as the jewel in its crown. Ideally, when it came to community leadership, economic clout and political sway notwithstanding, prowess was measured by knowledge, not physical strength; perseverance was gauged by interminable study, not accumulation of wealth, and battle was waged not with swords and lances but with erudite interpretations and arguments. The purest love was to be reserved for the Torah, and true devotion to one's master and teacher; glory was not gained through conquest and domination, but by succession to a sage's "throne" or appointment to a rabbinical position held by an esteemed predecessor. Authority, finally, was expressed not by subjecting a community to arbitrary rule, but by articulating for it the right way to live, marry, raise a family, and die.[19]

If the Poles, then, had their immensely rich, sword-wielding, quirky magnates, the Jews had their learned, at times eccentric rabbis, whose powers might transcend the limits of the natural world. Of those, too, Buczacz had its fair share. Agnon, who collected a vast number of stories, legends, and fables on rabbis, cantors, Hasids, and other colorful characters associated with Buczacz, recounts how the town lost its rabbi and set out on a quest to find an appropriate replacement—a tale that symbolizes a community's dependence first and foremost on a spiritual guide. Since the loss that triggers the search is caused by betrayal and denunciation, the quest is extended as a form of atonement for the imperfections of the community. The tale begins in 1740, when the renowned Rabbi Aryeh Leibush Auerbach, who had arrived in Buczacz only a year earlier, is forced to relinquish his position as a result of a vile smear and libel campaign against him, whose content Agnon does not reveal. Although Auerbach subse-

quently serves as the city rabbi in the nearby town of Stanisławów (Stanyslaviv, forty miles southwest of Buczacz), he tragically dies merely a decade after taking up his new post. This premature death is seen as especially
uncanny, because Auerbach's predecessors in that position had all passed
away before their time:

> What happened to those rabbis of Stanisławów, who preceded our
> rabbi, happened to our rabbi, for God took him when he was still
> in his prime. As he was dying he said that he had some more years
> left in this world, long enough for his son David Zvi to grow up
> and marry, but that he had renounced those years, so that one
> would not speak badly of the previous rabbis who had served in
> Stanisławów before him, and had not reigned long. Others offer a
> simple reason for his passing, namely that he was called upon to
> join the Yeshiva on High [*yeshiva shel ma'alah*—the religious col-
> lege in Heaven]. Still others say that the dead of Buczacz buried
> in the cemetery of Stanisławów appointed him as their rabbi.

Why were people from Buczacz buried in Stanisławów? Here the magical tale of the Jews intertwines with the misdeeds of their rulers. "One of
the noblemen of Stanisławów," relates Agnon,

> had some fun and shot a Jew. The Jew fell and died. The owner of
> the city heard of this and was angry with the nobleman. The no-
> bleman said, "Why are you so angry? I'll readily give you ten Jews
> instead of the one I killed." He traveled to Buczacz and caught
> there a cart full of Jews who were going to a wedding celebration
> and took them to the owner of Stanisławów and said to him, "You
> lost one Jew on account of me, and I am giving you instead a cart-
> ful of Jews." The city owner saw that they were all artisans and
> specialists in various crafts, and said, "They are the sort I need."
> He settled them in his town and put them to all manner of hard
> labor. They did not adapt to the place and began dying one after
> the other. The dead knew that their rabbi from Buczacz had be-
> come the rabbi of Stanisławów. Hence they made him their rabbi.[20]

Agnon concedes that Rabbi Auerbach actually died a year before these
Jews were kidnapped; but in his telling, this chronological impediment
does not deprive the story of its own internal reasoning as one of several

plausible explanations for Auerbach's untimely death. Moreover, the crux of the tale is not Auerbach's election as the rabbi of the dead, but rather his return to the world of the living. For even though the rabbi dies before his son has grown and married, he never abandons the boy and diligently caters to his education:

> After his death, our rabbi would return every night to his only son the Gaon David Zvi, and would teach him the Torah, until he became engaged to a woman from Brody, chosen for him by his mother, the rabbi's wife, a good looking and pious girl and the daughter of Brody luminaries. On the night when the conditions [for the marriage] were agreed upon he pronounced an immensely acute and erudite interpretation. They asked him, "Who was your teacher?" He said, "Father, since the day he died he comes to me every night and teaches me the Torah." Once he heard this, our rabbi no longer came, so as not to give a bad name to other tzaddikim.

And yet, even then the dead rabbi did not abandon his learned son:

> Years later he came back to him when the Gaon David Zvi was rabbi in Monasterzyska [Monastyryska, eleven miles west of Buczacz], before he took up his reign in Mogilev, because he had been denounced to the duke with false accusations and the duke had ordered to whip him. Our rabbi came to him and said, "My son, today I was appointed head of yeshiva in the yeshiva of [great fourth- and fifth-century Babylonian] Rabbi Ashi, and it was difficult for me to descend to the Netherworld, but because of my love for you I have come to save you, and you should say this and that to the duke, and the duke will do to the wicked one what the wicked one had plotted that he do to you."

The lives and afterlives of these rabbis are interlaced with miraculous events. The very birth of the soon to be orphaned Gaon David Zvi, later known as Mofet Hador, or "the shining example of the generation," was a miracle. For as it turned out, his father, Rabbi Auerbach, could not have sons. As a great scholar and Hasid, however, he was rescued from his predicament by none other than the Baal Shem Tov himself, on condition that he would be made the boy's godfather. Before agreeing to this arrangement,

Auerbach, who was no novice in matters of the supernatural, queried his master: "'I have looked into all the worlds and nowhere have I seen that Aryeh Leibush [Auerbach] has a son.' The Baal Shem Tov said to him, 'Indeed, that is true, but I am destined to father two sons, and I give you one of them.'"[21]

Yet as Agnon points out, magic and divine intervention can work both ways; if the righteous are recompensed, the wicked must await their punishment. Rabbi Auerbach's removal from Buczacz, which indirectly also caused his early demise, cast a curse upon his denouncers, a curse that wound its path through the generations all the way to the Holocaust. Appropriately, the descendants of the original denouncers were "afflicted by their own sin. Even though that tzaddik had forgiven them, God did not forgive them." And thus, "not a single generation among them was spared this vice . . . And even in the generation that preceded us they were not forgiven for the vice of denunciation. Only that in all past generations they were punished by Jewish denunciations, whereas in our generation they were punished by a Gentile denunciation . . . At the end, only one good-for-nothing was left of that family, who was living with a Gentile woman. At the time of Hitler, the son of that woman denounced his mother's husband to Hitler's boys, and they stabbed him."[22]

Following Auerbach's departure in 1740, the Jews of Buczacz are left without a rabbi. In the quest for a new rabbi, Agnon takes his Argonauts on an intricate journey of tales within tales, ever deeper into a universe of wonder and mystery, traveling across Poland's borderlands just before the forces of reason and secularism enter the scene at the tips of Austrian bayonets. In the course of their travels, the city's representatives reach the town of Żabno, some fifty miles east of Kraków. Their goal is to persuade the venerable local rabbi, Moshe Abraham Abush, to take up the vacant rabbinical post in Buczacz. And although the rabbi of Żabno declines the offer, in the course of their conversations with him, the dignitaries from Buczacz discover that the true diamond in the dust, the ideal man for the job, is none other than Mordechai, a simple tinsmith and lampmaker who has been living all this time in their own town.

As the rabbi of Żabno recounts, he first got to know Mordechai when the latter drove him by cart to a circumcision ceremony in a nearby village. There he encountered a strange, tall, thin man with a comical hat akin to the headgear German Jews were forced to use in the past "so as to make a mockery of them in front of the Gentiles."[23] Soon enough, Rabbi Abush found himself engaged in a learned debate with the stranger, who easily demolished every interpretation he offered. At that point the cart driver intervened, displaying such dazzling erudition that he matched the stranger, who turned out to be none other than the long-dead illustrious Rabbi Meir (Maharam) Schiff. From that day on, for a considerable length of time, the rabbi of Żabno and Mordechai would meet every night for ever deeper and more elevating discussions of the Torah. But each time, as dawn broke, Mordechai would set out on his day job as a much sought-after lampmaker, helping others shed light on the darkness and illuminate the obscure. As for the source of Mordechai's own erudition, it had come to him from his teacher, a sage who was forced to flee from his abusive Polish lord and had similarly concealed his identity as a master of the Torah, taking on only Mordechai, a simple village boy, as his disciple.

By this point, the dignitaries from Buczacz have been persuaded that the tinsmith Mordechai should be appointed to the exalted position of rabbi in the very town where he now resides. And yet, when offered the position, after initially, albeit reluctantly, accepting it, Mordechai abruptly changes his mind and leaves the city, presumably so as to continue his double life as a lampmaker in the daytime and a sage in the dead of night. The reason for Mordechai's sudden change of heart offers a measure of the relationship between the Jews and their Gentile lords. As the dignitaries of Buczacz gather around Mordechai to celebrate his appointment, one of them tries to underline the extensive authority the future rabbi will have over his community: "When it became known in the city that we had all agreed to appoint him Rabbi of Buczacz, the governor of the city summoned the notables and magnates and said to them as follows: 'I agree to the rabbi you are about to take for yourselves and I permit him to judge and instruct, to excommunicate and to ban, and I will not accept any denunciation of him from any informer or denouncer.'"

The Jewish notables are all very pleased with the governor's unmitigated endorsement of their choice, and another one of them chimes in: "No rabbi in Buczacz nor, if memory serves, in any other town, has ever received such a thing." Yet it is precisely at this point, writes Agnon, that "Rabbi Mordechai's face turned as dark as the side of a cauldron." First, he exclaims, "I have never striven to become a rabbi and it has never occurred to me to accept the post of a rabbi, but I did not turn you down because of my respect for the Rabbi of Żabno." But then he explains his decision to decline the offer after all by telling yet another, final tale:

I will tell you what I heard from a rabbi, who heard this from his rabbi, and his rabbi from his rabbi, all the way back to our rabbis the Hasids of Ashkenaz. It once happened that the community of

Cologne appointed a cantor endowed with all the virtues listed by the sages for a prayer leader. The duke heard about this and summoned him and said to him, "I heard that the Jews are appointing you as cantor, and I too agree that you serve as cantor." The cantor then responded to the duke, "Since you are appointing me, I am no longer worthy of the post of being the emissary of the Jews before the face of God." When he returned from the duke he said to the leaders of the community, "I am not worthy of being a cantor, because I appear to have been appointed by a Gentile."

To the astonishment of the joyful dignitaries surrounding him, Rabbi Mordechai then says, "Because you told me that the governor of the city had agreed to my appointment as rabbi of your city, I can no longer serve here as rabbi, and I am declining this post."[24]

Such tales constituted much of the cultural fabric of premodern Jewish life in the borderlands. They reflected the supreme position of learning within the hierarchy of status in these congested, dispersed, but interlinked communities. The sense of common fate and destiny that bound them to each other was akin in some ways to that of the Polish nobility following the disintegration of the Polish state, which helped sustain a national consciousness of sorts for more than a century of foreign occupation. Recovered and reassembled by Agnon, these tales bestowed the highest social value on what would appear to the outsider as the most arcane and esoteric kind of learning, as well as on mastering the art of the *pilpul*, or sophisticated interpretation. Simultaneously, they ascribed magical powers to rabbinic sages that set them apart from the rest of humanity and put them closer to God and in the twilight zone of the supernatural, perhaps as an imaginary counterweight against the overwhelming might of the Gentile authorities.

Indeed, at the core of these tales is the contention that although the Jews lived at the pleasure, and relied on the benevolence, of their Gentile lords, they could not and would not accept Gentile intervention in their internal lives, let alone in evaluating the merits of their sages or delegating power to them. This was, to be sure, largely just another myth, however empowering it appeared, since the noble masters of any city could and did remove Jewish leaders, including rabbis, when they pleased. But it was also true, in the sense that the reputation and renown of a sage depended only on his standing within a universe to which the Polish nobility had no access, just as the intricacies of noble pedigree and status were entirely alien to the Jews. And yet, in the larger sense, the supernatural world of holy men and demons, miracles and wonders, was not infrequently shared, believed, and feared by Jews and Christians alike.

The long quest for a rabbi took the Jewish community of Buczacz to the dawn of the age of reason. Yet magic potions and incantations, extractions of demons and dybbuks, and a whole array of methods and techniques used by wandering *ba'alei shem* and adopted by Hasidic tzaddiks persisted well into the nineteenth century. For its part, Habsburg enlightened absolutism brought with it bureaucratic organization and rational thinking, disdain for mystics, and a perception of those whom the tzaddiks purported to help, heal, or save more as objects of scientific investigation, medical treatment, or psychological observation.[25] This clash of attitudes defined much of the relationship between the new rulers and their subjects, as much as between internal modernizers and their opponents.

CHAPTER SIX

When the Empire Came

The World of Yesterday

IN 1910, JUST FOUR years before the war that put an end to the empire, a remarkable study titled *Galicia: How It Came to Austria,* by the historian and geographer Abraham Jacob Brawer, was published in Vienna. Brawer was in many ways a product of the world created by the annexation. Born in 1884 in the Galician town of Stryj (Stryi, 100 miles west of Buczacz), and raised in Kołomyja (Kolomyya, 45 miles southwest of Buczacz), Brawer acquired only a traditional Jewish education up to age seventeen, followed by three years at a Polish-language state gymnasium, or secondary school. He then enrolled in the University of Vienna and the rabbinical college in the same city, earning a PhD in history and geography, and a rabbinical ordination, in 1909 at the age of twenty-five. After teaching for two years at the state gymnasium in Tarnopol (Ternopil, forty miles northeast of Buczacz), Brawer immigrated to Palestine, where he taught history and geography in Jerusalem. His comprehensive geographical account of Eretz Israel, published in 1928, served as a basic textbook for teachers and students in Palestine/Israel for the next thirty years. Among his numerous other publications is an entry on Buczacz, published in the *Encyclopaedia Judaica* three years after his death in 1975. His son, Moshe Brawer, followed in his footsteps, contributing an essay to the Buczacz memorial book, and publishing numerous editions of a geographical, political, and economic atlas of Israel that every schoolchild in Israel of my generation and several others has studied, a copy of which has been part of my library for the last five decades.[1]

As the elder Brawer's 1910 study notes, when Austrian military forces and administrators entered Galicia in 1772, they knew very little about its demography and economy. The Polish monarchy had never created an administrative apparatus capable of conducting a census, and the Habsburg authorities quickly set about gathering data as the basis for military conscription. They estimated a total population of approximately 2.6 million, which included almost 100,000 nobles, close to 2 million serfs, and more than 300,000 Christian city dwellers. The Jewish population was somewhat more difficult to estimate. Jews unable to pay the new "toleration tax," imposed in 1773, were ruthlessly driven across the border as "beggar-Jews," while married couples that could not afford the new marriage tax of that same year either evaded being registered or were likewise deported, along with their parents. Indeed, Jewish-specific Austrian taxation meant that the predominantly poverty-stricken Jewish masses in Galicia did their best to conceal their existence from the authorities. A much older Jewish tradition against being counted, dating back to biblical and Talmudic prohibitions on head counts, combined with a popular fear of the "evil eye" (*ayyin hara*), which led parents to conceal their children from government officials, also hindered an accurate census. Still, following the initial turmoil, the number of Jews in Galicia is estimated to have stood at 215,000 by 1785, making it close to one-tenth of the overall population of the province and almost one-fifth of the inhabitants of its eastern part.[2]

The difference in Jewish population density between western and eastern Galicia reflected the ownership of the cities and the composition of their inhabitants. In western Galicia, most of the cities and lands were royal property; the nobility had no vast estates there, and the Polish urban population competed fiercely with the Jews. In eastern Galicia, where the majority of the population was Ruthenian, the lion's share of the towns and the vast estates were privately owned by the nobility, and Jews played a vital role both as a major component of the urban population and as estate managers and leaseholders on the land. In fact, while there were parts of western Galicia where Jews were not allowed to reside at all, in eastern Galicia there were Jewish leaseholders in almost every village.

Whereas in the Polish-Lithuanian Commonwealth the Jews were perceived as a separate estate, the Austrians initially made a concerted effort to assimilate them into German culture, as speakers of an essentially German dialect and agents of what they hoped would be the eventual Germanization of the new territories. For this reason, the authorities strove to transform the socioeconomic position of the Jews by moving them from trade and crafts to farming and agriculture. Although this policy, launched in 1784–85, eventually failed, it meanwhile significantly changed the situation of Jews in the rural economy. Because Jews not directly engaged in agriculture were no longer allowed to lease land, mills, inns, taverns, and breweries, about one-third of the Jewish population in Galicia was deprived of its livelihood and forced to move to the ever more crowded Jewish quarters in the towns and cities.

One lasting consequence of Austrian attempts to Germanize Galicia's Jews was their adoption of German family names, made obligatory in 1787. Two years later, as the French National Assembly's Declaration of the Rights of Man and Citizen reverberated around the world, the Austrian government finally issued a comprehensive decree that guaranteed to Jews "the privileges and rights of other subjects." In reality this meant that while Jews were allowed to practice their religion, and restrictions on marriage were lifted, Jewish internal autonomy was greatly limited, and Jews became more generally subjected to the state administration and judiciary, as well as liable for military service. As far as taxation was concerned, however, along with the continuing "toleration tax," the Austrians introduced a series of other, separate taxes for Jews on property, kosher meat, and candles (an essential item for celebrating the Jewish Sabbath and other holidays).[3]

Before 1772, the Polish nobility was the most numerous and powerful anywhere in Europe. But many of the nobles were wretchedly poor, while a very small minority were fabulously rich, owning estates the size of some countries. Yet until the demise of Poland, all nobles, whether rich or poor, had an equal right to vote and, not least, to elect a new king; for this reason they all saw themselves as part of the aristocratic nation of Poland, or the so called nobles' republic.[4] But while the great estate owners had almost unlimited power in their lands, and the lesser nobility developed a relationship of dependency on the magnates akin to that of feudal vassals in the Middle Ages, the numerous impoverished nobles had only their sword, dignity, and vote left over from their former glories, and were often materially no better off than the peasants. Adam Mickiewicz, the great nineteenth-century Polish poet, humorously described these lowly members of the *szlachta* in his masterpiece, *Pan Tadeusz*, published in 1834. "They'd once lived comfortably," he wrote,

At magnates' courts, on forays, on army pay,
At council meets. Now they no longer could:
They had to work to earn their livelihood
Like hired hands! Yet they'd not don homespun gray,
But black-and-white striped cloaks for everyday,
The kontusz on Sundays. The poorest woman there
Instead of a peasant blouse will always wear
Coutil or calico. Taking the cows to graze,
She'll be in slippers, never in bast shoes;
She reaps—weaves too—with gloves on, if you please.[5]

But with the partition of Poland, the petty gentry lost its last raison d'être. The magnates no longer needed its vote since the king was gone. Under the Austrian system, the poor nobles in annexed Galicia often even lost their right to a title, which called for proof of having owned an estate in Poland for the previous 150 years. Many of these nobles had neither possessed such property in the recent past nor could provide documentary proof of their claim to noble heritage. The magnates, for their part, since they were now shut out from the affairs of state, could concentrate on increasing their economic might, expanding their estates at the cost of the middling nobles, whose numbers constantly diminished. As a result of this accelerating concentration of wealth, by 1848 Galicia numbered more than four thousand serf-owning magnates, including not a few German aristocrats, who had come to the crownland as civil servants, as well as landowning city dwellers, among them a not inconsiderable number of baptized Jews.[6]

Although Poland was one of the most Catholic nations in Europe, its clergy was neither numerous nor ascetic. On the eve of the Austrian annexation, priests and nuns made up just over 3 percent of the population. The clergy was known for drinking and feasting with the nobility, from which most priests originated. But the church also had a great influence on social relations and the affairs of state. The power of the church and the religiosity of the nation help to explain the resistance of Poles to efforts of Russification and Germanization after the partitions. And, since the clergy owned vast properties and depended in large part on Jewish credit, occurrences of ritual murder accusations and other manifestations of Jew-hatred were generally not translated into anti-Jewish campaigns by the church.

Roman Catholicism was also closely associated with education, mostly of the nobility, which usually rounded off its studies with training in the law. But the *szlachta* had little interest in intellectual life, and was mostly engaged in politics and social gatherings, in which drinking played a major role, often accompanied by fights and duels. The Austrian regime imposed the death penalty on those engaging in such activities, which appears to have had some impact on the prevalence of violence. But as Brawer puts it, "all the strength that the noble had once expended on the battlefield in honor of the Fatherland and Christendom, he now employed in brawls." The conduct of the *szlachta*, he finds, was akin to that of student fraternities, filled with "the eternal jingling of the sword, the all-too-hasty sense of insult and demand for honorable satisfaction, the competition over gulping down the largest possible quantities of alcohol, the endless frivolity." In Brawer's opinion, "this lack of manly gravity was the fundamental failing from which the Polish nobility suffered as it faced the many catastrophes of the eighteenth and nineteenth centuries." And yet, on the positive side, "what differentiated the *szlachta* from the nobility in the rest of the continent was its proud consciousness of freedom, which gave it the courage not to act with slavish subservience even before the highest and the greatest."[7]

The magnates in pre-partition Poland had a special relationship with the Jews, who leased their lands, as well as manufacturing facilities and services on their properties; served as their court Jews and estate managers; and loaned them money for credit. Polish burghers greatly resented this "silent pact" between the Jews and the magnates, not least because they believed it undermined their own economic interests. Conversely, in the villages the Jews maintained rather good relations with the peasants. August Josef Schultes, professor at the University of Kraków, who traveled in Galicia in 1806–8, commented that those who accused the Jews of exploiting the peasants usually knew only Jewish usurers, not least because they owed them money. In Schultes's opinion, village Jews served a useful purpose. The fact of the matter was that most of Galicia's Jews were poor and were recognized as such by the peasants. As Brawer points out:

> The peasant knew very well that the Jew was only a tool in the hands of the landowner, and that he had to hand over to the noble's court all the money he had made. He saw often enough how the Jew would be mishandled with the whip, and how hounds would be unleashed at him to chase after him whenever he provoked the displeasure of his master. Consequently, the peasant had

no reason to envy the Jew: he appreciated his intelligence and sought his advice in all his important affairs, even if it did not always serve him well.[8]

That being said, the status of the peasants, who constituted the vast majority of the population, was markedly worse than that of the Jews, in that they had no legal personhood and could only be represented in court by their lord, to whom they were also often expected to provide unpaid workdays. Worst of all was the condition of the Ruthenians in eastern Galicia, where they constituted the single largest ethnic group. Because numerous Ruthenian nobles had converted to Roman Catholicism and were subsequently Polonized, the Greek Catholic church received only meager donations, and very little money was available for education and the promotion of Ruthenian culture, the exceptional case of Mikołaj Potocki of Buczacz notwithstanding. Greek Catholic priests could marry and often had many children; consequently, they were poorer and less well trained than the Roman Catholic clergy. Although the Austrians required secondary education and theological training for Greek Catholic priests, they still often had to tend their own plots and received only a limited income, and their sons were likely to revert to peasant status. Far more numerous than the Roman Catholic priests, the Ruthenian clergy was also socially much closer to the population. But there were far fewer Ruthenians in the towns and cities, and they were usually on a lower social rung than the Poles. Nonetheless, the Ruthenian—or Ukrainian, as we now know it—language was on the verge of becoming a literary language and the vehicle of the fledgling Ukrainian national movement in the nineteenth century.[9]

Taking Over

Although Austrian rule gradually dragged its newly acquired province toward modernity, change occurred at the more measured pace of the premodern world. It took many decades for the Jews of Galicia to become intimately bound to the Austrian Empire and the person of its emperor. By then, however, that world, which had come to be seen as normal and as secure as any had ever been, was beginning to show signs of decrepitude. And it was only after its collapse that the empire became a focus of longing and nostalgia, not least in view of the regimes that replaced it.[10]

But for the owners of Buczacz, the imposition of Austrian rule did signal an abrupt and painful end of a centuries-long period of power and privilege. While Mikołaj Potocki could simply not abide living under Habsburg rule, his successor as lord of Buczacz, Jan Potocki, clashed fiercely with his new masters. For their part, the Austrian authorities tried to reorganize and centralize the city's administration, reflecting their attempt to transform the socioeconomic and political landscape of Galicia as a whole, demonstrate the power and reach of the empire, and channel tax revenues to the imperial coffers. Caught between these two forces, the Jewish leadership struggled to maintain control over its "internal" tax collection, used for the purpose of communal expenditure, to protect its religious autonomy, and to limit the extent of the state's intrusion into the lives of community members.

In the early years of Austrian rule, possibly because of his own financial difficulties, Jan Potocki appears to have repeatedly seized the revenues of the "internal" communal taxes collected by the Jewish leadership of the town. Finally, in March 1777, the Austrian district director J. Kolmanhuber ordered Potocki to "entirely cede" these funds "to the free disposition and use of the Buczacz *kehilla* [Jewish community governed by the kahal] without any indemnification whatsoever, and from this time on not to disturb in any manner the *kehilla*'s collection of its revenue or usufruct." Clearly offended by the content and tone of this instruction, Potocki appealed directly to the Austrian governor of Galicia, asserting that the decision had been reached "on the basis of perverse denunciation by the stubborn Jewish people," and reminding the governor that for more than two centuries, a Polish royal statute had determined that the "nobles who have Jews in their towns or villages" could "administer justice to them according to their own will." At this point in time, argued Potocki, it would be wholly unfair to let the Jews, who "possessed numerous tracts of land in the district of the city and outside it," to keep their tax revenues, while the lord of the city was "obligated to turn over a certain portion of his revenue to the Supreme Treasury" of the empire. But unlike such disputes in the past—as when Mikołaj Potocki had threatened the Jewish leadership in 1765 that "if it did not give up [the tax revenues] within twenty-four hours, each and every one of the elders would be tortured and every second elder would be punished by one hundred strokes with the whip"—the Austrians eventually put their foot down. In 1781 the governor addressed Jan Potocki in stern terms. "His Majesty," he wrote, "had deigned to decide and command that, on the subject of the existing controversy between you, Herr von Potocki, and the Jewish community of Buczacz," the tax revenues "be made available and turned over to the *kahal* without any further appeal."[11]

Nonetheless, for the next few years the Jewish community kept complaining about "the cruel oppression by the lord of the manor," even as Potocki, whose finances continued to deteriorate, fretted about losses incurred by his inability to seize the Jewish tax revenues. In a final desperate attempt to avoid bankruptcy, in 1786 Potocki made a "secret arrangement" with the Jews, allowing them to lease properties from him, in violation of the Austrian ban on such practices decreed two years earlier. Upon discovery of this deal, the authorities fined Potocki, disseminated printed versions of his sentence to all local courts as "a warning to rebels," and removed him from office; Buczacz was sequestered and handed over to the canonical priest Imcé Potocki as "plenipotentiary granted full powers." Additionally, in order to prevent future corruption and to provide more rational fiscal management, a purely Polish, four-member city council was appointed, which eventually became a permanent feature of city governance; one of its first tasks was to collect taxes from the "mass of Jan Potocki's creditors."[12]

Yet three years later, Buczacz was still struggling to overcome decades of mismanagement. In September 1789, the Austrian official Leopold Haystorf described the city and its surroundings as still mired in feudal relationships and economic stagnation. Buczacz, he wrote, was a "populous city, suitable as a municipal center due to the considerable number of Christian residents." But because the lord of the city was persisting with the old practice of leasing out toll and tax collection and sharing their revenues with the leaseholders, the town lacked "funds for paying the salaries of individual municipal employees or for police matters" and could not "cover the cost of maintaining the three bridges" over the Strypa River. Even the "very attractive, two-story city hall, erected by Nicolaus Potocki about 36 years ago," wrote Haystorf, where "the city council has been provided with a room in which court hearings are held," could not be kept "in a good state of repair," and the "remaining rooms and vaults on the ground floor are rented out by the lord of the city to other parties," mostly as Jewish shops.[13]

By then, the reforming impulse set into motion by Emperor Joseph II, who became sole ruler of the Habsburg Empire after the death of his mother, Maria Theresa, in 1780, was about to run out of steam. The emperor's tax reform in Galicia, meant to deprive the Polish nobility of the right to impose its own taxes, and his plan for an agrarian reform that would provide peasants with their own plots by confiscating some of the vast tracts of land held by monasteries, were meeting with increasing resistance. Following Joseph's death in 1790, the reforms largely petered out. Yet one consequence of this period was that the majority Ruthenian peasants in eastern Galicia, as well as the majority Polish peasants in western Galicia, came to believe that the empire was on their side, whereas the Polish nobility and clergy felt that Vienna was undermining their privileges. As for the Jews, while they might have initially been glad to be rid of their corrupt and capricious Polish rulers, they soon came to view the empire as threatening their traditional way of life. Only after the 1848 revolution did the Jews gradually come to view the new emperor, Franz Joseph, as their benevolent protector.[14]

In Buczacz, the political and economic uncertainty introduced by the removal of the lord of the city—the traditional enforcer of law and order—led to internal social unrest. In May 1790, a joint meeting of the city council and the *kahal* examined the charges made by the Jew Moszke Berkowicz that students of the Collegium had attacked and robbed him during a riot. The concluding report asserted that "concerning the riots, we know nothing and have heard nothing about a rebellion by students in Buczacz." Nonetheless, the report observed that "such odd behavior would have never been allowed at the time of Governor J. W. Mikołaj Potocki," for even though "there had been student fights" under his rule, "they were pacified without damage to property. As for this riot," the dignitaries ambiguously stated, "none of us knows or has heard about either theft or injury of citizens by the students."[15] Signed by four Poles and two Jews, this is the first known official document that directly refers to, and simultaneously denies, anti-Jewish violence in Buczacz. Reading between the lines, it seems clear that the merry students of the Collegium had set upon the Jewish residents of the town, perhaps during a drunken brawl, but caused only minimal damage. The city's Jewish and Christian elites were unified in their view that Buczacz needed a strong leader in order to prevent the recurrence of such riots. Under the Austrians, order was quickly reestablished, and urban violence became a rarity. One hundred fifty years later, in July 1941, Ukrainian and Jewish community leaders in Buczacz tried again to stop local riots. But at that time, the rioters were equipped with a nationalist rhetoric to legitimize their actions, and the new German occupiers were fully on their side. The result was total mayhem.[16]

Dan and the Noblewoman

One consequence of Austrian economic policies was the proliferation of women abandoned by their husbands. Known in Jewish law as *agunot* (literally, "anchored or tied women"), such forsaken wives cannot remarry before an investigation of their husband's fate provides sufficient grounds to annul their marriage. As Agnon relates, Zvi Hirsch, the first rabbi of Buczacz to remain in this post until his death, in 1813, and known by the title of his posthumous book, *Neta Sha'ashuim*, was deeply preoccupied with helping such women. Agnon, whose own pen name was derived from the title of the first story he published in Palestine in 1908, *Agunot*, writes in his "biography" of Buczacz why the number of forsaken women increased dramatically after 1772:

> Because of the burden of taxes and the lack of work, and the wicked laws that the Kingdom of Austria was enforcing on the Jews after the abolition of the Kingdom of Poland and the takeover of most of the towns of Galicia, the Jews became impoverished, and their situation went from bad to worse. Many of them wandered away from their places of residence in search of work, in the hope that by changing place they would also change their fortune. They left their wives behind and went far away. Some of them died on the way in temples, their bellies swollen from hunger, and some of them went mad from their suffering; collecting testimonies from them by the rabbinical court was difficult, because shame and madness caused them to contradict themselves. The sages of Israel charged with deciding the cases of the daughters of Israel did all they could within the limits of the Torah to liberate the women from the bonds of forsaken marriages.

This, writes Agnon, was a period not only of social and political upheaval, but also of moral chaos, because once Jewish men

> wandered away from their own place to a place where they were not known, they sometimes conducted themselves immorally with the daughters of Israel, so that wherever they came they married women, and then abandoned them, going off to another place and marrying women there, and abandoning them too . . . Our rabbi, when deliberating the question of a forsaken woman, before he consulted books, would consult his own mind, so as to consider whether it was reasonable that the man who had abandoned her was alive, and if he was alive, whether there was reason to think that he would return to his wife. In order to clarify the matter our

rabbi would walk out, where there are no books, because books entice people to ask their opinion.[17]

Thus the Jewish religious leadership in Galicia tried to cope with the disruption of marriage patterns and family structures during the early years of Austrian rule in its own way, allowing women to remarry when it became clear that their husbands had died, abandoned them, or engaged in polygamy. But the new world order was making new demands on the Jews. One of them, perceived as especially onerous, was the conscription of young men, since it was feared that they too would be lost, both as members of their community and as Jews. In Agnon's view, "the hardest" of the many "wicked edicts" that would arrive "each day" from the government "was the decree to seize people, for they would take Jews and make them into soldiers, as had not happened since the destruction of Jerusalem and our exile from our land."

Writing several decades after the state of Israel was established in a bitter and costly war, Agnon, who had been living in Jerusalem since 1924, was not advocating Jewish pacifism. For him, as for many Jews of that era, the recruitment of Jews into the emperor's army was an oppressive measure because it led to "uprooting Jews from their homes and dispersing them among the Gentiles." Individual Orthodox Jews serving with predominantly Gentile soldiers could not "pray publicly, keep the Sabbath and the Holidays, and avoid forbidden food." Consequently, they would "become lax with the precepts [*mitzvot*] first under duress and later out of habit." The problem, then, was not Jews serving as soldiers, but isolated Jewish soldiers serving in a Gentile army.

But conscription also caused great upheaval in Jewish communities throughout Galicia because of the unfair and corrupt practices it entailed in selecting conscripts. According to the Austrian system, each community had to provide a certain quota of conscripts every year, and consequently community leaders would "pay to hire Jewish people and bring them to the emperor's agents." Yet "if there were not enough people who could be bought with money, they would take anyone that the community leaders did not like and forcibly hand him over to the authorities, and at times they took completely innocent lads, who had simply not been able to study the Torah because of their poverty."

In other words, the poor who could neither pay off the *kahal* nor study in a yeshiva were sent off to become soldiers. This was a pattern that would repeat itself one hundred fifty years later under far more murderous circumstances. As a result, "each and every year there was wailing in all the dwellings of the Jews, and they would cry over their families. In one house a mother wept over her son who had been forcibly taken from her, and in another house a woman wept over the husband of her youth who had been taken from her."

Internal debates over the morality of this practice also set a precedent for the future. As had happened before and was to happen again, "the sages of the generation" had different opinions about this matter: "Some justified the ruling, saying it is better to take the ignorant rather than the learned, for it says, 'He who disburdens himself of the Torah must take upon himself the burden of the government'; others summoned heaven and earth, for a clear ruling says, 'One may not redeem one soul with another.'"[18]

Anxieties about the conscription of young men concerned not only loss of members to the community and loss of religion and ethnic identity by the conscripts. Behind the urge to protect the community from encroachment by the outside world lurked a deep, visceral fear of contact with all that was beyond the bounds of Jewish life. This phobia of contamination, whose most overt manifestation was in the realm of sexual relations, had not entirely vanished by the time Agnon was growing up in Buczacz. His story, "The Disappeared," which presumably takes place in the early decades of Austrian rule, combines the themes of internal communal venality, dishonesty, and callousness toward the destitute and the unfortunate, and the horror of losing one's identity and being transformed into something unrecognizable by leaving the perimeters of the town.

Dan, the protagonist of this tale, is an eighteen-year-old tailor's assistant and the single child of a humble widow. Although he is "strong as an oak and taller than anyone his age," Dan is poorly educated and simpleminded. All this makes him into a perfect target for forced conscription when no volunteers can be found, especially after one of the community leaders discovers that his daughter has fallen for this strapping young man, potentially derailing a far better match. Before leaving Buczacz, Dan is given "a surname, one neither he nor his mother nor any of his father's family nor any of his mother's family nor anyone in Buczacz had ever heard of." As Agnon sarcastically comments, "as soon as the town leaders gave him his name, they forgot it. For the time being, it has no significance; later on, its significance will be understood. They called him Hoffmann, which means 'hopeful' in German. But we should say that although by doing so they only intended to improve the quality of their donation, they still gave him a nice name."[19]

Hoffmann spends much of his time as a soldier in a distant town in

Upper Austria; while he is treated well, thanks to his physical strength and humble manner, his isolation from Jewish life gradually erodes his sense of identity. "At times," writes Agnon, "when he finds himself alone, with no one around him, he puts his hand on his forehead, shuts his eyes, and stands there praying, reciting one or two prayers that he knows by heart, for his prayer book, which his father had bought him, and from which he had learned the kaddish [prayer for the dead] that he said after the death of his father, is lost and gone."[20] After four years in uniform, Hoffmann is discharged and decides to return home on foot, so as to make some money on the way by plying his trade as a tailor. But although he writes his mother that he will soon be home, he does not return for another six years; in another sense, he never returns at all.

Dan's location is discovered by mere coincidence. One day a new district director arrives in Buczacz. As he inspects the work being done on his house, the director strikes up a conversation with a Jewish ovenmaker. The man's face is badly bruised, but he is initially too frightened to relate what happened to him. Eventually he relents and recounts that before taking up his current job, he had been asked to install an oven at the home of a local noblewoman. One day, he recalls,

> I inadvertently entered one of my mistress's rooms, which had always been locked but on that day was open. I peeked in and saw something that my mind tells me I could not have seen, even though I plainly know that I did. What did I see? Some kind of human creature that might be male or female, Jew or non-Jew. It looked female because it had long hair like a woman's made up in knots and curls, and it was wearing a blue velvet dress; and it looked male because of the hair that covered its cheeks like a beard, although it might not have been a beard but just the hair of its head hanging over its cheeks; and it looked like a Jew because of the sorrow emanating from its eyes; and that person was tied with an iron chain to the wall.[21]

Just then, relates the ovenmaker, the noblewoman saw him there, slashed his face with her whip, and expelled him from her house with a stern warning not to speak of what he had seen.

Troubled by this uncanny tale, the district director consults his superior, the regional director. Both are aware of the noblewoman's past reputation but stunned by this turn of events. The regional director exclaims:

"Tell me, could you ever imagine that a woman who had turned down noblemen would keep a young man at her home? But why has she chained him to the wall? Is he nothing but a breeding bull? Or is this a matter of a woman's covetousness? What did the Jew tell you? That he thought that young man was a Jew? In the name of all the saints, this is all lies, lies and deceit!" Reminiscing about their own past, the two officials then recall the time when they "were young men, and that noblewoman was a young woman, and many distinguished noblemen courted her, but she turned them all down and remained a spinster." Clearly what they find most disconcerting is that she now keeps a young Jew in her home:

> The regional director said again, "Have we mentioned that the Jew who told you this tale recounted that the man he saw chained to the wall was a Jew? Tell me yourself, how is it possible that of all things she chose a Jew?" The district director said, "I can already see how much rage and jealousy and hatred this will provoke among the nobles when they find that the woman who had turned them down has taken up with a Jew." The regional director said, "When I observe these Jews with their sidelocks and beards I cannot but wonder how a noblewoman would even come close to one of them."[22]

The two officials decide to act swiftly, and dispatch a police squad to the noblewoman's house, where the young Jew, guarded by the lady's mute servant, is soon discovered. All three are then brought to Buczacz, and the town fills with expectant crowds of people who have already heard the rumor. As the carriages enter the town, the young man is spotted in one of them: "He was dressed as a woman and his hair was done as a woman's and his head was uncovered and there was no sign of life in his face and his eyes, and although they had removed his chains, he was still standing as if he were bound."

It has been ten years since Dan left Buczacz; in the meantime his widowed mother has passed away, and he has changed a great deal, and is now wearing woman's clothing. But Bilhah, the young woman who had loved him, and whose father had sent Dan to the army in the hope of finding her a better match, recognizes him right away. She has never married, always waiting for him to return: "When Bilhah saw the boy, she called out loudly, and called again and shrieked, 'Dan!' Dan, the boy who was wearing woman's clothing, looked at her and smiled to her with his eyes and they knew that he was the soldier who had disappeared."

The Jews are now as scandalized by the noblewoman's choice of a young Jew as were the two officials, saying to each other, "May that noblewoman drop dead, aren't there enough noblemen who would have done for her anything she desired, and yet she caught a Hebrew boy to use for her sinful purposes."[23] But Dan himself does not say a word. The Jews of Buczacz shave his hair and dress him as a Jewish man, and feed him, and find him a place to live, and Bilhah visits him and brings him food and clean clothes. But Dan remains mute and seemingly oblivious; within a year, relates Agnon, "he became sick with sorrow and died." As for the noblewoman, she lives for many more years in a convent, leaving behind a diary, whose content proves that Dan "had preserved his righteousness and innocence and committed no transgression. He had suffered greatly at the hands of that Gentile woman, and he had withstood everything and was not tempted by her seductions."[24]

Because Dan is unable to recount what happened to him, Agnon provides us with the noblewoman's version, recorded in her diary, of her fatal infatuation with the handsome youth, who came to her house to make her a dress, but rejected all her advances:

> I sat and watched the young tailor work. His fingers are gentle and all his movements full of grace. I have never seen such gentle fingers or anyone whose movements are so graceful. When it was time to measure the dress again, I washed once more with soap and perfume and came and stood erect before him, and when there was need to bend a little or to turn this way or that, and I found myself somewhat close to him, I saw that he moved back a little. The truth is, I want this affair with the dress to be over, because it is dishonorable for a noble lady to be so absorbed in a Jewish boy.

The noblewoman is herself deeply scarred. When she was a child, her father's mistress had locked her mother in a room where a bear was chained to the wall: "Mother died there of fear and hunger." Now, as she plots to keep the young tailor in her house, yet also tries to take her mind off him, she similarly buys a bear and chains it to the wall. "I did not forget the Jew because of the bear but the bear did me good because my wicked and cruel thoughts grew less intense and were not as cruel and wicked as before." But the bear falls ill and has to be shot, and when the young tailor tries to escape, the noblewoman's servant chains him to the wall where the bear had been, dressed in the dress that he had been making for her. The noble-woman now has him in her grasp:

> I came to him and stroked his face with my hand and said to him,
> "Had I not known that you were a man I would have said that you
> were a girl, because your flesh is soft and gentle as the flesh of a
> virgin girl, and perhaps you are indeed a virgin girl. Sometimes I
> doubt that you are a man." He did not respond, only the sorrow
> in his eyes deepened from week to week. I often thought, how
> long will he stay with me? But I did not have the strength to send
> him away. And I also thought that I would endanger myself if
> I sent him because he would tell everything that I had done to
> him.[25]

This eerie tale reveals much about the perceptions and self-perceptions of Jews and Christians in Europe's premodern borderlands. The erosion of difference—the goal of Enlightenment promoters and maskilim, that is, supporters of the Haskalah, and of later progressives, democrats, and socialists—is perceived here as threatening and aberrant. The Austrian officials, the local gentry, and the Jews all wonder why a noblewoman would prefer a Jew to her own kind. Even more unnerving is this simple Jewish boy's transformation, first from a poor orphan and tailor's assistant into a soldier, and then from a soldier into a terrifying, pathetic, unnatural hybrid, neither male nor female, neither Jew nor Christian, part-human part-bear, mute and subdued, lacking any flicker of life in his eyes.

At a time when the Austrian government was still set on transforming the Jews into agents of Germanization in Galicia, and when the maskilim struggled to drag the Jews out of the ghetto, such stories of deviant mixing and its dire consequences circulating among Jewish communities served as a warning against abandoning the old ways and becoming entangled with their Gentile surroundings. Just as the "forsaken women" epitomized the despair of wives whose husbands had vanished beyond the perimeters of Jewish civilization, so Dan's never completed journey home from the army, his abandoned mother's despair, Bilhah's doomed love and her father's machinations, the community leadership's malfeasance and hypocrisy all expose the malign impact of the modernizing state on traditional Jewish life. If the Haskalah sought to release the Jews from the chains of their atrophied customs as much as to liberate them from the constraints imposed on them by Christian society, those ancient chains still left indel-

The author's parents. His father wears a British army uniform with Jewish Brigade Star of David arm patch. Palestine, 1946. Author's private collection.

ible marks on their bearers, even as they were soon replaced by the new, less visible but perhaps even more restrictive shackles of nationalism.

For Dan's generation, the idea that a Jew could become a soldier seemed alien to Jews and Christians alike. But as the empires and nation-states of the nineteenth century centralized their rule and built up ever larger armies, they increasingly insisted on recruiting all able-bodied young men to military service. For Jews keen to demonstrate loyalty to their state, a military uniform became a potent symbol of patriotism. For the expanding antisemitic movement, in contrast, a uniformed Jew was not just a contradiction in terms but a symbol of the danger from within threatening to betray and topple the state. The stereotype of the effeminate, unmilitary Jew was an important building-block of anti-Jewish policies in Europe. But for the approximately 1.5 million Jews who joined the Red Army, the Western Allies, or the partisans, in World War II, the very fact that they could fight the Nazis and their collaborators as soldiers was a triumph. Some 5,000 of those soldiers, wearing British Army uniforms with a sleeve patch bearing a Star of David, were volunteers from Palestine serving in what was known as the Jewish Brigade Group. One of them was my father.[26] For these young men, taking Wehrmacht soldiers captive, entering Germany as occupation troops, and flaunting their yellow star in German towns was an act of immense personal and collective self-assertion and dignity. Many of them thirsted for revenge, some by assassinating real or suspected perpetrators, others by way of consensual, mercenary, or coerced sex with German women. Yet their most important contribution to the resurrection of the murdered Jewish people was arguably their indispensable role in organizing the illegal immigration of the survivors to British-ruled Mandatory Palestine. They were distant descendants of Dan the tailor's assistant, Hoffmann the soldier, and the noblewoman's wretched, chained plaything. Or perhaps, they were not so distant.

CHAPTER SEVEN

How to Love a Child

The Age of Improvement

PERHAPS THE SINGLE MOST important Austrian attempt in those early years to bring the Jews into the modern world, as it was seen at the time, and to integrate them into the rest of society, was led by the superintendent of all German-Jewish schools in Galicia, Naftali Herz Homberg. A maskil from Bohemia, Homberg was appointed by Joseph II in 1787 to preside over the establishment of a network of 107 "normal" public schools for Jews, including one for girls. This radical educational reform focused on recruiting students from families of lesser means into schools with a grade system based on age and abilities; its ultimate goal was to nurture a new generation of Jews, fluent in German and proper Hebrew grammar, morally cultivated, and effectively trained to take up a productive trade or craft. But the majority of Jews in Galicia were Orthodox, and they vehemently opposed this undertaking, so that once government policies changed, Homberg's school system was abolished. The "normal" school in Buczacz, opened in 1788, lasted less than two decades, closing down in 1806.[1]

Despite its ultimate failure, this educational experiment affected large numbers of Jewish children and youths and created a model for future initiatives. If in its first year the "normal" school in Buczacz enrolled only 28 students, by 1879 the number had risen to 200; in Galicia as a whole, during the same period the number of students rose from close to 6,000, taught by almost 500 instructors, to as many as 28,800, clearly indicating growing enthusiasm among Jewish parents and children.[2] We can only speculate about the long-term effect of this experience on those who attended the schools, and the extent to which this school system might have changed both the nature of Jewish society and its relations with the Christian majority, had it been allowed to remain in place and expand. But it may not be too far-fetched to assume that the fate of the inhabitants of the borderlands would have been quite different had several generations of Jewish children been afforded a more comprehensive education that better prepared them for the onslaught of modernity.

Establishing an integrated system for children of all denominations and ethnicities would have called for reforming Christian institutions as well. One early attempt was made by Empress Maria Theresa, who in 1776 ordered the creation of "normal" schools (*Normalschulen*) in Galicia, mostly in former Jesuit gymnasia, intended largely to train teachers for elementary schools. In 1784, the Basilian monastery's Collegium in Buczacz was converted into such a "normal" school, becoming a decade later a five-grade gymnasium. Yet while it modernized its curriculum, the school remained a Christian institution, the majority of whose 350 students were Greek Catholic, including a fair number of candidates for the priesthood, all taught by priests or clerics of the Basilian Order. As an Austrian report for the school year of 1854–55 stressed, "the teaching staff is appointed by the Basilian priests of the Greek Catholic rite," since "although this is a public school, it is not considered to be governmental, because it originates from a private foundation established by Count Mikołaj Potocki who outfitted it in 1754 and entrusted it to the Basilian monks."

To be sure, the Austrian influence on the school was strongly felt; as the report noted, apart from religion, which was taught in Ruthenian, the language of instruction was German. The curriculum was largely secular, and "teaching materials and collections" included "apparatuses for physics and chemistry," books on history and nature, collections of plants and minerals, geographical wall maps, atlases, globes, and geometrical tables. But it took until the end of the century for a state gymnasium, open to all children and youths, to be established in Buczacz.[3] By then, not least thanks to the segregated schooling, national and ethnic fault lines had solidified, and a much greater effort would have been needed to bring the groups together. Instead, even the new gymnasium reflected, and enhanced, national sentiments in the emerging public sphere on the eve of World War I in Buczacz and Galicia as a whole. What might have been accomplished a century earlier had largely become a chimera by 1914.

But attempts to modernize Jewish education did not end with the demise of Homberg's school system. Whereas the "normal" schools were
established under the auspices of the Austrian authorities, other initiatives
came from within Jewish society itself, mostly as an expression of the
struggle between Hasidism and the Haskalah. Those who pursued reform
often condemned what they perceived as the debilitating effects of traditional schooling. Their stark depictions of children's upbringing provide a
glimpse into Jewish existence throughout much of the nineteenth century.
In their minds, reformers sought what they labeled the improvement, or
Verbesserung, of the Jews, by implementing positive and constructive measures and by radically changing or entirely eliminating past practices. One
reason, for instance, for the vehement opposition to Homberg by the traditional religious elites and many of their followers was that in his capacity
as assistant censor of Jewish books, he had prohibited many kabbalistic and
mystical texts, including the traditional Jewish prayer book.[4]

The Galician maskilim Mendel Lefin—the preeminent figure of the
Haskalah in Poland during and after the partitions—and his disciple, Joseph Perl, best represent the struggle against what they perceived as the
malign influence of Hasidism, which was already well on the way to triumph over the traditional Orthodox Judaism of the Mitnaggedim. But
while the more radical maskilim hoped to bring the Jews into the modern
world by way of progressive secularization and assimilation into European
society, moderates such as Perl proposed to do so by adapting Jewish custom, law, and identity to the changing world around them.[5]

To be sure, although the Haskalah and Hasidism represented two entirely different worldviews, both were revolutionary movements, responding as they did to changing external circumstances, which on the one hand
opened up new opportunities for Jews, but on the other hand imposed severe constraints on them as a religious and ethnic minority in a seculariz-
ing and nationalizing Christian universe. If Hasidism won the struggle in
nineteenth-century Eastern Europe, the assimilationist, nationalist, and
Zionist descendants of the Haskalah came to increasingly dominate Jewish opinion in the twentieth century, all the more so in the wake of the
Holocaust and the establishment of the state of Israel. At the same time,
some of the harsh criticism of traditional Jewish life by the maskilim also
provided grist to the mill of the modern antisemitism that emerged in the
last decades of the nineteenth century.

In 1838, toward the end of his life, after decades of struggle and frus-
tration, Joseph Perl bitterly concluded that "in our country there are no

men who combine Torah and Wisdom." In the traditional elites' view, he asserted, "a Torah scholar must separate himself from the affairs of this world," and if "even a speck" of secular "knowledge is seen in someone, everyone distances himself from that individual and heaps abuse upon him." For them, a Jew who "even begins to learn some kind of Gentile language or writing," or becomes "engaged in any kind of non-Jewish knowledge," is akin to someone who "abandons both the Torah and the commandments." They will therefore "hate and pursue" such people "almost to their deaths."[6]

This assessment of the fierce opposition he faced came at the end of a decades-long modernizing effort focused on a new type of school. As early as 1813, Perl established a so-called Israelite Free School in his hometown of Tarnopol. Within two years enrollments rose from seventeen to thirty-six students, who at that point had moved from Perl's home to a new building that also housed a new synagogue, where services were modeled on Enlightenment principles of quiet prayers and periodic sermons by the regional rabbi. Habsburg Emperor Franz I warmly embraced this school following the return of Tarnopol to Austrian rule at the end of the Napoleonic era. In 1817 the emperor decreed that "as far as its supreme supervision and directorship, teachers and disciplines, this school must be organized on the model of the Christian schools"; but "instead of the Christian religion, the Jewish religion will be taught there, and when necessary, the Jews will be allowed to teach disciplines that are not taught in Christian schools." Yet religious segregation was maintained, and the emperor decreed that "Christian children will not attend the Jewish school."[7]

Perl directed this institution, which came to be known as Eastern Europe's first modern Jewish school, for the rest of his life. Initially the school catered to children of both sexes ranging from age five to thirteen; the curriculum combined Jewish and general subjects in a split-day schedule, with all lessons conducted in "purified German" cleansed of any Yiddish influences. The many subjects offered included Hebrew grammar, Bible, and Talmud studies. But once it was integrated within the Austrian general education system, the school was limited to four years and the study of Hebrew was restricted. Perl's attempt to reform Jewish education in Galicia more generally did not bear fruit, since the Austrian authorities feared that the mass of the Jewish population would perceive such changes as a religious reformation. The proposal by Perl to institute vocational training for Jews was similarly rejected by the increasingly conservative regime.

Perl's outlook on the future of the Jews in the modern world can be gleaned from his response to a police inquiry about the influence of a certain Karl Seyfart, who had urged the Jews to build a Jewish state and renew the rule of Zion. As Perl opined, the Galician Mitnaggedim would oppose such proto-Zionist ideas on theological grounds, while the Hasidim would oppose them on practical grounds; with the Jewish masses torn between these two poles, there clearly was no prospect for Seyfart's plans. As for the small minority of maskilim, such as himself, Perl observed that they did not believe in the Messiah as a personality, but rather as a symbol of salvation and world peace, and they thus looked forward to an era in which "Israel will be liberated from all slavery, will be accepted into the concert of nations, and will have equal rights as other nations."[8]

As a sworn enemy of Hasidism, shortly before his death Perl condemned one last time what he saw as the ignorance, abuse of power, and corruption of the Hasidic establishment, and called upon the authorities to undertake a major reform and to provide support for the maskilim in their struggle against Hasidism, mysticism, and obscurantism. Once again, the Austrians thanked Perl for his efforts and refused to act upon his proposals. When Perl died in 1839, the Hasidim celebrated his demise, while government officials mourned him.[9] In accordance with his testament, his school was taken over by his son, Michael Perl, who had trained as a pharmacist and, in 1832, had opened the very first Jewish pharmacy in Austria by special permission of the emperor. Although Michael was not as active in Jewish affairs as his father, the school continued to function. By 1860 it was called the Jewish Secondary and Girls' School (Israelitische Haupt und Mädchenschule). But the teaching of the Talmud at the school had already been abolished five years earlier and all that remained of Jewish studies were two weekly hours of religion and eleven hours of Hebrew-language instruction. Nonetheless, the school catered to a substantial student body, boasting 656 students and 8 teachers in 1869.[10] From this perspective, we can say that Perl's efforts had not been in vain, in some ways heralding the Hebrew-language Tarbut schools of interwar Poland.

The Altar of Perfection

The jaundiced perception of Hasidism by contemporary maskilim is vividly illuminated in a spirited German-language polemic by the essayist Moriz Bernstein, published in Vienna in 1850.[11] This is an essay written at the crossroads, between the waning of the Haskalah in the face of religious fanaticism and the inertia of Jewish tradition, and the rise of integral nationalism and antisemitism that dashed the high hopes of integration through emancipation and assimilation. Bernstein calls on the Jews to step out of the dark and unhealthy confines of the ghetto toward the rising sun of the Enlightenment; he denounces what he sees as their corrupt and degenerate culture. What he could not know was that, despite the good intentions of Jewish modernizers and the accelerating march out of the shtetl and into the mainstream of European society, these newly liberated Jews would soon be burned by the sun of uncompromising scientific reason and shoved aside to make way for the emerging nations of blood and soil.

The motto of Bernstein's essay, "Our errors become all the more dangerous and incurable when they receive the sanction of religion," is taken from the 1770 treatise, *The System of Nature or the Laws of the Physical and Moral World*, by the French philosopher and encyclopedist Paul Henri Thiry, Baron d'Holbach, who argues that free will is an illusion, since the world is governed only by strict laws that determine the inevitable outcomes of events.[12] This early version of Karl Marx's quip that "religion is the opium of the masses" was scandalous when it was first uttered and continues to scandalize many today; Perl also might have rejected it, but Bernstein appears to have wholeheartedly embraced it.

Bernstein's goal is to depict how, only "a few decades ago," Galician Jews emerged from a state of absolute "dearth of culture," which "they fought tooth and nail to preserve," and "gradually allowed themselves to be led out of their educational poverty and spiritual thirst to the maturity in which one sees them today." For centuries, he contends, "Galician Jewry was unaware of any progress of the human spirit and remained enslaved to the ancient, deeply superstitious ritual of their ancestors." The Jews' "fanaticism" and "dogmatism," expressed in their adherence only to principles "sanctioned and made ethical by time and custom," fueled "their hatred for anything new." They thus turned their backs on "the spirit of the times," and clung to the "absurd principle" that "one must believe, what one cannot grasp." For Bernstein, "belief" of this kind was directly "related to delusion and deception."[13]

One of the main sources for Galician Jews' use of "belief" as a "protective wall against all attacks by logic," argues Bernstein, was the education of their children. Clearly influenced by Jean-Jacques Rousseau's 1762 treatise *Emile, or On Education*, Bernstein asserts that "the historical context in which one sees the light of day, where one is raised and grows up, is of much influence on the manner in which one later views and conceptualizes the world. If, however, this sphere is deprived of knowledge, then the idea and conceptualization of being in the world assumes a one-sided, highly erroneous form." Hence, concludes Bernstein, by examining the education of Galician Jewish children at home and at school, his readers will discover that this was the main cause of "all prejudices and often also all spiritual stunting."[14]

Beginning with homeschooling, Bernstein finds that not only was the image of God provided by the uneducated parents "coarse and material," but also that "in order to give the child a sense of respect and dignity for his religious education," the father presented it as the "wonderful legacy of his ancestors," the culmination of work by "an endless series of forefathers." This, believes Bernstein, was how "the autonomy of the soul was murdered," and "the parents provided the child with a slave mentality and spiritual chains to accompany him into maturity in the wider world." By such a system, he contends, "the freedom of humanity was dragged to the grave." Subjected to this kind of upbringing, "man, who had evolved into a spiritual giant, has now atrophied into a spiritual gnome and everywhere creeps on the earth," while Jewish self-segregation has resulted in a "stark religious partition" that "divides people into enemy neighbors and splits humankind into numerous kinds."[15]

Bernstein's enlightened philosophy perceives humanity as capable of striving for individual and collective good without any religious, ethnic, or national distinction. Yet the conditions he describes draw a line between the long-term psychological effects on children of narrow, repetitive, repressive, and bigoted education, and the devastating social and political impact of dogmatic, fanatic, and intolerant religions on entire groups. The century that followed provided ample proof for the destruction that could be wrought by this lethal combination of wrong-headed pedagogy and exclusionary ideological doctrines.

But Bernstein is especially focused on the situation of Jewish children in Galicia. Once these children were old enough to enter primary school, he continues, things got only worse. The "filth and uncleanliness" of the traditional cheder, where many of these children found themselves, had a "most detrimental effect on the physical condition of the child." The teachers and their assistants were "from the lowest classes," and "lacked any knowledge of religious truth, of nature," and, indeed, had "no perception of life." This kind of education, argues Bernstein, destroyed the children's souls and deprived them of the ability to know, perceive, and enjoy their environment, not least because "the teacher, who lacks any knowledge of psychology, naturally does not grasp" that understanding has to do with the child's "soul-nature" and "inner sense," and can be accomplished only in an "individual manner that is adequate to the developmental ability of each." Instead, these teachers would strive "strenuously to hammer the assigned weekly Biblical chapter into the poor child. Often this exceeded the child's comprehension capacity. Hence the interaction from the side of the teacher was very harsh, rough, indeed often very harsh, and for that reason the children went to school very unwillingly, when not forced to do so."

This elementary school atmosphere was, according to Bernstein, at the root of "all the mental lethargy, all the nonsense and muddled faith, and often all the spiritual ossification, which then accompanied the youth into adult life."[16] The process was exacerbated in the yeshiva, where students studying the Talmud received no preparation for living in the world, resulting in the numerous misfortunes of Jewish marriages, when young men lacking any worldly experience were wedded to largely uneducated young women by arrangement between parents, whose main concerns were social status and material gain.

Bernstein was not describing a distant past. In fact, he notes, this "was the condition of the Jews in Galicia, and so it unfortunately still largely remains at present." Only "an extraordinary miracle" saved the Jews from being "caught unprepared for the call of emancipation of 1848." That miracle, "whose appearance had a powerful and beneficial influence on the reform of religious views, on ideas and ethics, as well as on the current spiritual progress of the Israelite nation in Galicia, was Joseph Perl, the founder of the most laudable and celebrated Israelite school in Tarnopol."

In Bernstein's view, Perl represented all that could be done to liberate Galician Jewry from its traditional chains and to set it on course to spiritual and political freedom:

> If the Jews . . . have already carried a few stones to the construction site of the temple of civilization, it was he who . . . had built the steps to that path and took them forward along it, as teacher and leader. A great moral personality . . . to the Jews of Galicia, Joseph Perl was what the great Moses had once been to the entire people of Israel in Egypt; a true sun, before which the fog of ignorance dissipates, and falsehoods totter to the ground.

With Perl, predicted Bernstein, "an era has come, in which the Israelite population of Galicia begins to reconcile itself with contemporary ideas, with the demands of the spirit of the world and of history."[17]

The genius of Perl's German-Israelite school, as Bernstein sees it, was that it enabled children and youths to open up to the world without thereby threatening to completely alienate them from Jewish tradition. Soon enough, "the school filled up with youths thirsty for knowledge. The sparks of the spirit, which had previously glimmered in the ashes, became a flame of consciousness that seized all layers of society," so that fathers even began sending their daughters to the school in order to acquire foreign languages. As Bernstein optimistically concludes, "the spirit of growth, of striving and marching forward, swiftly made vast strides. And who would have believed that the light of contemporary knowledge, lit in a small model school, would spread so far and would have such astounding consequences?"[18]

Bernstein heaps similar praise on Perl's effort to reform the religious rite of Galicia's Jews and bring it closer to contemporary European standards of order, dignity, and respect. The maskilim felt that the traditional service in the synagogue was undignified and gave them a bad name among their Christian neighbors, and calls for its reform became increasingly prevalent throughout Europe. Secularization and reform of religious cult thus went hand in hand despite their contradictory goals: while the former saw religion as a superstitious leftover of the Middle Ages, the latter hoped to protect religion from disintegrating under the pressure of rationalism and modernity by adapting its practices to contemporary tastes and manners. It is this undertaking by Perl that Bernstein praises, exuding pride in the gradual "uplifting" of Jewish services to a "civilized" level: "One quickly saw religious services being held in worthy ceremony; the pious no longer prayed by swaying perpetually back and forth, disturbing the innocent air with their body and arm movements and plaguing it with irregular noise; [now] the service pulsated with the well-led singing of a choir and was carried up to heaven by delightful, melodious symphonies."

Perl's innovation, reports Bernstein, at first attracted the young and then drew also some of the older generation; soon enough "a large part of the entire Jewish population of Galicia felt a powerful inner urge to pay heed to the demands of the time and to forge forward with its tide."[19] And yet, just like Moses, Perl could only glimpse the Promised Land from the mountaintop, and was barred from seeing his efforts come to fruition and relishing his success. It was only after his premature death that the center of Jewish reform and enlightenment moved from Tarnopol to Lemberg, the largest city of eastern Galicia, where not only was a school established on the model of Perl's Tarnopol German-Israelite institution, but also a new reform synagogue was built. Resistance to these changes was fierce. On 6 September 1848 the Reform rabbi of Lemberg, Abraham Kohn, was murdered by a zealous Orthodox Jew, a rare case of political assassination that reflected the deep rift within the community.[20] And yet, as Bernstein, along with many other maskilim, saw it, Lemberg made a major contribution to the necessary "education in Humanism, Enlightenment, the elevation of morality, and the greater stress on the metaphysical purity and the beauty of ideas of its community members' religious faith." The erection of the magnificent Reform Temple Synagogue, completed in the same year of Rabbi Kohn's murder, symbolized a new, modern brand of Judaism in the heart of the Galician capital for close to a century, until its destruction by the Germans in 1941 signaled the bloody end of that experiment and the triumph of inhumanity and evil.

Bernstein was pleased to see that "Lemberg's spirited, knowledge-thirsty youth are already wearing conventional clothes and manifest a more pleasing external bearing as well as a more graceful social demeanor"; but among the rest of Galician Jews, he complained, "the traditional dress is the reason that the sense of culture has not yet become prevalent, and that a purer and more tasteful tone in word and tact has not pervaded Jewish social circles." The traditional Jew, "marked by his long caftan," he wrote, "finds the circle of his cultivated neighbors almost inaccessible," and because he speaks a "jarring jargon" (that is, Yiddish) at home, the Jew consequently "lacks the conversational skills based on a deeper linguistic knowledge."[21]

There is a certain irony in Bernstein's argument. The revolutions of 1848 were about the rebellion of liberalism against the supporters of the reaction, who tried to turn back the clock to before the French Revolution of 1789, and about the uprising of nationalism against monarchism, of the people against their king, of popular sovereignty against divine right. But if the people were defined by their ethnicity—language, customs, heritage, ancestry—what was one to do with those citizens who belonged to a different ethnicity? Writing in the immediate aftermath of these revolutions, Bernstein has some inkling of this conundrum, though not of the extent to which the nationality question would eventually overshadow much of the Enlightenment's legacy. Many educated Jews, notes Bernstein, not least young women, had taken to studying French as their language of culture. This he finds neither practical nor politically useful:

Instead of French, indeed also instead of German, I would recommend first to teach the language of the land . . . This would allow the Jews of Galicia to feel reconciled with their nationality at home and would facilitate peaceful relations and even friendship with their neighbors, and gradually tear down the partition between them, both morally and as a natural process, because the mighty word Emancipation had already condemned it politically. Therefore, the language of the land should be heartily recommended, the magnificent Polish, with all the expressive dignity, pleasing linguistic contours, and sonorous rhythmic wholeness of its national poetry.[22]

But which was the language of the Jews? Was it the "jarring jargon" Bernstein condemned? Was it the "pure German" or the "grammatical Hebrew" taught at Perl's school, or perhaps the "sonorous" Polish spoken in Galicia (where the majority of the population in fact spoke Ruthenian)?

Bernstein may appear naïve, misguided, hopelessly optimistic, and a terrible prophet. The half-century that came after his essay saw the rise of increasingly violent ideologies that replaced the humanism of the Enlightenment with the rage of self-determination, tolerance with exclusion, universalism with narrow interests, and trust in mankind with a fanatical focus on race, ethnicity, and nation. But he ends his essay on a more somber note. "I will however willingly admit," he writes, "that the Jew, as a tolerated person in a given land, hence as a foreigner, cannot make its sanctuaries into his own and in this sense can have but little taste for any nation, let alone for patriotic interests." The solution to this problem appears clear: "Had all the Jews been offered the gift of emancipation," and "had those of the Christian faith amicably shared with them the entire sphere of human and citizenship rights," then the Jews "would have certainly all marched forward along with them." But, remarks Bernstein, "it is surely sad that even today one must use such a term for human rights," namely, that the Jews were given what they deserved as fellow human beings only as a "gift," a favor or a prize for good behavior. In that sense, he acerbically notes, they were used "as a tasty fruit, whose skin is discarded once its sweet juicy core has been sucked dry."

And, in fact, the emancipation of the Jews in the Austrian Empire in the wake of the 1848 revolution—coming almost half a century after Napoleon emancipated the Jews of France in 1806—was short-lived. With the restoration of the monarchy the tide was reversed, and by 1853 many of the restrictions on Jews, not least in Galicia, were back in place. Full emancipation came only in 1867, following the Habsburgs' defeat in the war against Prussia and the re-creation of the empire as Austria-Hungary. Writing still at the height of the emancipation euphoria, Bernstein stresses that many Jews "already shine brightly . . . in the firmament of European civilization," and therefore "have no more need of this indulgence" of government-sponsored emancipation. And yet he still believes that as a result of emancipation, "the bitter, offensive allegations and vituperative slurs that heartlessly insult" the Jews' "sense of morality and rights" would no longer "injure the Jew within them" but be "directed only against their position" in the economy, into which they were forced by inequality:

> Because it is not the Jew who is a swindler, a usurer, as he is often called; it is but the profit-seeking salesman, and thus also the Christian, or the Turk, as such. Thus the Ancients sensibly represented this unity in one symbol, Mercury, who is both the God of thieves and of trade. These functions appear to be inseparable from each other and are prevalent among the Jews in general because they were forced into this position and because even there they are further pushed down. This is the case for them in most states of Europe, hence also in Galicia.

But now Bernstein can look forward to a better, more just, honest, dignified, and rational future existence, in which Jews would be able to choose their professions without being forced to abandon their faith. For once "the trumpet call of the year 1848 brought down the walls of egoism and narrow-mindedness, there was no longer any need for that magic potion, which was always offered to the Jew with Christian love and enthusiasm, at times even under truly favorable and beneficial conditions, as an expedient universal panacea against his moral and physical crimes."

Accepting this "potion," that is, converting to Christianity, "would make the Jew today worthy of all honorary posts, all awards, all ranks and citizenship rights on the earth, even as yesterday he was still a God-damned, discarded outcast." With emancipation, there is "no longer any need for the authority of the Church . . . in order to go to Heaven." For now, announced Bernstein, "the Jews of Austria have been invited to a celebration of reconciliation with their Christian brothers at the table of emancipation. My dear brothers, all of you, leave behind the fleshpots of Egypt and, worthily, follow the call!"[23]

Unquenchable Holy Childhood

As we know, that was not precisely how things worked out. As late as 1897 the composer Gustav Mahler still felt compelled to convert to Roman Catholicism in order to be appointed director of the Court Opera in Vienna. That was the Vienna of long-term mayor Karl Lueger, who professed his antisemitic sentiments, even as he became known for his characteristically Viennese wisecrack, "as to who is a Jew, I determine that" (*Wer ein Jud ist, das bestimme ich*), an assertion later attributed to Nazi leader Hermann Göring, whose sentiments toward Jews were anything but ambivalent. It was also the Vienna of the populist and violently antisemitic pan-German leader Georg Ritter von Schönerer who, alongside Lueger, was one of the young Adolf Hitler's role models during his years in the Austrian capital before World War I. By then, the German journalist Wilhelm Marr's 1879 pamphlet *The Path to the Victory of Germandom over Judaism*, which argued that the emancipation of the Jews had allowed them to take over finance and industry in the new German Reich, had already popularized the term "antisemitism." This modern concept defined the Jews not merely as adherents of a despised religion, but as a foreign and malign race, against which Germans had to wage a fight to the death in order to preserve their own nation and make it great again. In the same year that Marr's pamphlet was issued, Adolf Stoecker, court chaplain to German emperor Wilhelm II and founder of the blatantly antisemitic Christian Social Party, warned that "if modern Jewry continues to use the power of capital and the power of the press to bring misfortune to the nation, a final catastrophe is unavoidable." Hence, he thundered, "Israel must renounce its ambition to become master of Germany." These were not only slogans handed out by crude rabble rousers and crafty politicians. The prominent German historian Heinrich von Treitschke, a mainstay of the academic establishment, similarly declared that year in a prestigious scholarly journal that "the Jews are our misfortune"; in 1880 he went on to publish a widely sold pamphlet titled "A Word about Our Jews," which greatly popularized this statement, later used as the motto of the Nazi propaganda rag *Der Stürmer.* These men and countless others were responding to the fact and consequences of Jewish emancipation. As the Jews came out of the ghetto and stepped into Christian society, their religion was redefined as a race—an inherent, unchangeable quality—and their attempt to shed the external attributes of Jewish identity, their clothes, beards, and traditional religious cult, came to be seen as a mere façade, behind which lurked their innate and unchanging alien nature.[24]

The crooked path of the Enlightenment and its enemies into the twentieth century, as seen through its attitude to children, is exemplified by the life and death of Henryk Goldszmit, better known under his pen name, Janusz Korczak. Born in Warsaw in 1878 or 1879 into an assimilated family, Korczak was an agnostic, a physician, a pedagogue, the founder of the first orphanage in Warsaw for poor children, and the author of children's books and essays for adults on children's education, with such unconventional titles for the time as *How to Love a Child* and *The Child's Right to Respect*.[25] Korczak believed that children should be helped to develop in their own way, rather than be compelled to follow a path set for them by others, and that they must be respected as fellow human beings. "There are no children," he stated, "there are people."[26] In *How to Love a Child* Korczak writes that "for years I have been observing the quiet sadness of sensitive children and the brazen antics of grownups. The child has a right to be himself, has a right to respect. Before you make revolutions, before you make wars, think first of these proletarians with short legs, think first of the child." He believed that "to reform the world, means to reform the method of bringing up children." He insisted: "Let us demand respect for those clear eyes and smooth temples, that young effort and trust . . . Respect, if not humility, toward the white, bright, and unquenchable holy childhood."[27]

When the Germans forced the Jews into a ghetto in Warsaw, Korczak established there an orphanage for more than two hundred children, where he struggled mightily to maintain his wards' physical and psychological well-being. During the last three months of his life, he also worked on a manuscript he had begun writing after the fall of Warsaw in 1939, now known as his Ghetto Diary. On 15 May 1942, he wrote: "I was carried away by false ambition: to become a doctor and a sculptor of the child's soul. The soul. No more, no less . . . Is this why I struggled, often hungry, through the clinics of three European capitals? Ah, what's the use." Recalling his past ambitions, he added: "One of my frequent daydreams and plans was a trip to China . . . Dostoyevsky says that with time all dreams come true, only in such degenerated form that we don't recognize them. I can now recognize my dream of the prewar years. Not that I went to China. China came to me. Chinese famine. Chinese orphan misery, Chinese mass child mortality."[28]

Two months later he had become increasingly dispirited: "The children moon about. Only the outer appearances are normal. Underneath lurks weariness, discouragement, anger, mutiny, mistrust, resentment, long-

ing. The seriousness of their diaries hurts. In response to their confidences
I share mine with them as an equal. Our common experiences—theirs and
mine. Mine are more diluted, watered down, otherwise the same."[29] On 18
July, the children staged a play, *The Post Office*, by Indian writer and philosopher Rabindranath Tagore, the story of a poor orphan confined to his
room with a severe illness, who is miraculously set free by the king's doctor.
The well-attended, legendary production was remembered many years
later by the few members of the audience who survived the war. That
night Korczak wrote in his diary: "Applause, handshakes, smiles, efforts
at cordial conversation. (The chairwoman looked over the house after the
performance and pronounced that though we are cramped, that genius
Korczak had demonstrated that he could work miracles even in a rat hole.)
This is why others have been allotted palaces."[30]

Another three days passed, and on 21 July Korczak contemplated his
own origins—where he had come from and how he should face death in
that rat hole in the heart of a modern, mid-twentieth-century European
capital:

> Tomorrow I shall be sixty-three or sixty-four years old. For some
> years, my father failed to establish my birth certificate. I suffered
> a few difficult moments over that . . . I was named after my grand-
> father, his name was Hersh (Hirsh). Father had every right to call
> me Henryk: he himself was given the name Józef. And to the rest
> of the children grandfather had given Christian names, too . . . Yet
> he hesitated and procrastinated. I ought to say a good deal about
> my father: I pursue in life that which he strove for and for which
> my grandfather tortured himself for many years . . . It is a difficult
> thing to be born and to learn to live. Ahead of me is a much easier
> task: to die . . . I should like to die consciously, in possession of my
> faculties. I don't know what I should say to the children by way of
> farewell. I should want to make clear to them only this—that the
> road is theirs to choose, freely.[31]

The Great Deportation (*Großaktion*) from the Warsaw Ghetto began
the following day. A few days later Korczak wrote, trying to imagine the
mentality of the perpetrators:

> Jews go East. No bargaining. It is no longer the question of a Jew-
> ish grandmother but of where you are needed most—your hands,

your brain, your time, your life . . . We are Germans. It is not a question of the trademark but of the cost, the destination of the products . . . The Jews have their merits. They have talent, and Moses, and Christ, and are hardworking . . . But besides the Jews, there are other people, and there are other issues . . . There must be some order of procedure, some priorities. It's hard for you. It's not easy for us, either . . . You must listen my friend, to History's program speech about the new chapter.[32]

Everything Korczak had believed in and worked for was being demolished in front of his eyes. On 1 August he wrote: "It's been a long time since I have blessed the world. I tried to tonight. It didn't work . . . What matters is that all this happened. The destitute beggars suspended between prison and hospital. The slave work: not only the effort of the muscles but the honor and virtue of the girl. Debased faith, family, motherhood. The marketing of all spiritual commodities. A stock-exchange quoting the weight of conscience. An unsteady market—like onions and life today."[33] But Korczak remained true to himself. Six days later, on 7 August 1942, he marched, erect and dignified, in front of the children of his orphanage; there were rumors that thanks to his fame, he could have been spared. He showed no signs of hesitation when together with his wards he boarded the train to the Treblinka extermination camp.

The Last Tzaddik

But in such small, provincial towns as Buczacz, the sweeping vistas and high hopes of the Haskalah, let alone its disappointments and disillusionments, remained but a rumor for many decades following the Austrian annexation. After 1790 many of the early economic restrictions were either officially lifted or ignored, and a fair number of Jews could again be found managing taverns and handling much of the trade in grains, cattle, and other agricultural products, as well as working in handicrafts. Indeed, as the economy gradually improved, the community could pay back the debts it had accumulated during the last years of Polish rule.[34]

Ironically, the appointment in 1813 of Abraham David ben Asher (Anshel) Wahrman as the town's rabbi, and his long "reign" of close to three decades, significantly expanded the influence of the Hasidim in Buczacz. Known as the Buczaczer Rabbi or the Tzaddik of Buczacz, Wahrman was a scholar with a powerful and charismatic personality. Typically for his generation, he was a scion of the religious oligarchy in Jewish Galicia and living proof of the argument that Hasidim were not outsiders but very much an outgrowth of the established elites, combining rabbinical *yihus* (pedigree, lineage) with economic prowess.

Born in 1770 in nearby Nadwórna, Abraham David had grandfathers who were rabbis, while his father, known for his learning and wealth as a successful merchant, was said to have earned his new surname Wahrman ("man of truth" in Yiddish-German) thanks to his honesty and integrity. No wonder that the child received an excellent education, which included not only religious studies but also lessons in mathematics, German, and Polish. When the renowned Meshulam Igra, himself the scion of a distinguished rabbinical family from Buczacz, visited Nadwórna in 1780, he predicted the boy's future as yet another sage. This early recognition prompted Rabbi Zvi Hirsch of Buczacz to arrange a marriage between the young prodigy and his own daughter. The young couple lived in Buczacz, where Abraham David also befriended the Hasid and author of *The Well of Living Water,* Rabbi Chaim, the future rabbi of Czernowitz.[35]

In 1790 Wahrman was appointed rabbi of Jazłowiec, near Buczacz, where he continued studying not only the Talmud, but also mathematics and natural sciences, arguing that even the ancient sages of the Talmud had not neglected "the universal sciences and applied knowledge." Yet it was at that point that he came under the influence of several prominent Hasidic leaders. Indeed, "the chief event" of Wahrman's life is said to have been prompted by his visit to the Hasidic rabbi of Berdichev (Berdychiv) in search of a cure for his sick son, even though he "did not believe in the miracles of their rabbis." In this tale of conversion, during the visit Wahrman was persuaded to take up the study of the Kabbalah, but "in trying to reconcile these new views—so utterly antagonistic to those of the extreme Talmudists, which he himself had hitherto held—he nearly became insane." Fortunately, the rabbi of Berdichev "helped him through this struggle and won him over, to the great joy of the Hasidim, who feared his wide Talmudic learning." Still, although Wahrman "adopted the Hasidic mode of living," his decisions in matters of Jewish law, we are told, were "guided, not by cabalistic, but by purely Talmudic, principles."[36]

Perhaps because of his links to both Hasidism and the Talmudic tradition, following his appointment as rabbi of Buczacz upon the death of his father-in-law, Wahrman was said to have brought about a measure of reconciliation between these rival factions in the city. Agnon had good reason to support this claim, since his own upbringing in Buczacz revolved between his father's strong Hasidic inclinations, and his admiration for his maternal grandfather, who was a strict Mitnagged.[37] But eventually, Rabbi Wahrman ended up being a divisive figure, not only because he was opposed by the Talmudists, but also because the growing number of maskilim in Buczacz strongly opposed him. For the latter, Wahrman was nothing more than a "wonder rabbi," and they even lodged a formal complaint against him with the authorities, accusing him and his followers of "acts of trickery," such as healing the sick (presumably by magic), hiding deserters from service in the army, and sheltering smugglers and thieves simply because he took pity on them. When Rabbi Wahrman died in 1840, thousands of Hasids attended his funeral, and the memorial "tent" built over his grave soon became the site of pilgrimage for many of his followers; to this day he is referred to affectionately simply as "the tzaddik."

Yet the passing of the Tzaddik of Buczacz also heralded the demise of Hasidism as a major presence in the town. In August 1841 the Buczacz maskil Joseph Tepper sent the Austrian authorities a memorandum charging the Hasids of the city, and especially their rabbi, Wahrman's son and successor, with deceit and corruption. According to Tepper, the new Hasidic leader was demanding payment for access to his father's grave, which he claimed, allegedly falsely, would support the widow and the Jewish community in Eretz Israel. As Tepper put it, this meant that the young rabbi was using his name Wahrman in vain, merely as a cover for his acts of dishonesty. Tepper not only demanded an inquiry into the finances of the venerable late rabbi's son, but also entreated the authorities to prohibit prayers over the rabbi's grave, where the Hasids were performing what he derisively called "demon-dances." Admittedly, he noted, the entire city might be making a profit from the lively tourism to the tzaddik's gravesite, but it would behoove the authorities to put an end to this pilgrimage and dismantle the "tent" altogether. The domination of Hasidism in Buczacz had gotten so bad, noted Tepper, that he had no choice but to leave the city; the Hasidim there were disdainful of any work and education, and had no intention of becoming useful citizens, while their rabbi promoted only schism and idleness. If only for the sake of the few remaining Buczacz maskilim, something had to be done about this dismal situation, concluded Tepper.[38]

Buczacz did not have a permanent rabbi for another thirteen years. In the intervening time, the 1848 revolutions occurred, and even in this distant borderland town, far from the great capitals of Europe, the Springtime of Nations changed the tempo and nature of life. To be sure, in some other towns in Galicia, such as neighboring Czortków (Chortkiv, twenty-two miles east of Buczacz), Hasidism continued to play an important role well into the twentieth century. In others, such as Tarnopol or Brody, the Haskalah won a prominent place in public and cultural life. In Buczacz, where the Mitnaggedim, or Haredim (literally, "the fearful"), as they were also known, controlled public and administrative life, the growing circles of maskilim nevertheless sought improvements in education and cultural activities for the Jewish community. Most important, both on the municipal and on the regional and state levels, Jewish life after 1848 intersected increasingly with public life more generally, in administration and politics, economic and cultural activity, education, and social organization. The era of mass politics and mobilization was about to begin, and the esoteric preoccupations of magical rabbis, just as much as the burning faith and curious superstitions of their followers, receded to the margins and gradually assumed the status of legend and myth, nostalgic recollections and old people's tales. They were soon replaced by other, no less fervently held beliefs in national destiny and ideological dogmas. But for a moment it seemed as if a bright new future lay ahead, full of promise and opportunity. The paths leading there appeared wide and clear, but each of the different groups inhabiting the borderlands perceived the future differently and set off in another direction. And as time moved on, the paths increasingly diverged, until eventually one group's bright future became another's abyss of despair.

PART III

Where Did We Go?
(*Encounters with Modernity*)

Dworzec kolejowy

The Buczacz train station, in the interwar period. Author's private collection.

CHAPTER EIGHT

The Fiction of History

Emancipation's Discontents

THE GREAT PARADOX OF the period between the Spring of Nations and the outbreak of World War I is that many Europeans experienced it as a time of unprecedented new opportunities for self-realization and collective liberation, and, simultaneously, as a time when individual and collective identities were increasingly constrained within national boundaries. Those living in borderland towns such as Buczacz, perched on the eastern rim of the remote Austrian province of Galicia, could now more easily break free from the restraints of traditional society, travel vast distances on the growing network of railroads, and transform themselves in ways that few could have previously imagined. And yet, as groups and individuals began identifying themselves nationally and ideologically, they also increasingly perceived others through different eyes, distinguishing them not only by religion and ethnicity but also by whether their history gave them the right to continue living where they were and leading their lives as they had previously done. This in turn narrowed the range of individual opportunities, enclosing them within a strictly national-territorial context, and imposed new limitations on those who were redefined as outsiders not belonging to that place. In this manner, personal liberation could be redefined as collective fate, and future aspirations came to be envisioned through the prism of traumatic pasts.

In the wake of the 1848 revolution, the Habsburg Empire abolished serfdom in Galicia. Over the next few decades, a new nation emerged from the Ruthenian (later known as Ukrainian) peasants in the larger, more populous eastern part of the province. It was a long process: most of the former serfs remained wretchedly poor, illiterate, and the target of ruthless exploitation by the landowners. Instilling a "national consciousness" into the rural masses and crafting them into a nation that would eventually claim eastern Galicia for itself was the singular accomplishment of an increasingly radical national movement.[1]

The Jews of Galicia were also transformed into a modern nation in the second half of the nineteenth century. Jewish activists initially focused on civil, rather than political or national, emancipation. Emperor Franz Joseph's "constitution" of 1867 had guaranteed equal rights to all citizens, including the Jews. This fundamentally changed relations between Jews and Christians. As rural Ukrainians were being nationalized, the growing presence and economic role of Jews in the villages created a popular sense of material exploitation and cultural decimation. In the new Ukrainian press, Jews were described as swindling the poor peasants by lending them money at merciless rates, inducing them to alcohol and tobacco addiction, and thereby impeding the development of a healthy Ukrainian nation.[2]

The nationalization of the peasants was thus ironically accompanied by an effort to exclude the Jews. From this perspective, the efforts to realize the Enlightenment's lofty aspiration of liberating the individual from collective feudal constraints ended up unleashing forces that undermined the very core of humanism. There was nothing inevitable about this outcome, but since it did come about, it cast a vast shadow over the entire project of the Enlightenment. In many ways we are still grappling with this conundrum. For the liberation of the serfs, who had been treated for centuries as less than human, indisputably facilitated the emergence of modern society and unleashed the energies and talents of millions of the previously downtrodden. Similarly, the emancipation of the Jews not only lifted the myriad restrictions and altered the mentalities that had separated this religious minority from its neighbors for two millennia, but also allowed Jews to inject tremendous economic, intellectual, and cultural energy and creativity into the mainstream of European society. How such extraordinary accomplishments in human progress could have ended up in so much destruction is one of the central questions of twentieth-century European history.

One answer is that nationalism—for which the integration of the peasants into the nation was a crucial precondition—often became the carrier of ideologies that culminated in mass violence. The emancipation of the Jews—seen as either the precondition for, or the last phase of, Jewish assimilation into European societies—provoked the emergence of a new antisemitic ideology, which presented Jews as the main obstacle to the emergence of the ethnically homogeneous nation state. The path to catastrophe was paved with good intentions, as well as rage and resentment: lifting the downtrodden entailed removing the alien; social justice required eliminating parasites; and love of country was demonstrated through sacrifice and blood.

Your Mother's Soul Be Damned

Nationalism has had a long love affair with exaltation and martyrdom. When the personal sense of longing and passion celebrated by Romanticism was inflated to encompass the millions who made up the new nations, the poetic soul's "storm and stress" was transformed into the blood-soaked struggle of the "awakening" masses. Poets and writers were deeply implicated in this nationalization of emotion. The great Ukrainian bard, Taras Shevchenko, inspired the early Ruthenian populists of the 1860s and many of those who followed them. His powerful works are said to have been "received by young Galician intellectuals as a prophetic revelation"; indeed, the Ukrainian political activist and scholar Ostap Terletskyi described him in 1902, perhaps with a measure of hyperbole, as "the first and greatest peasant poet of all Europe."[3]

Born a serf in Russian-ruled Ukraine in 1814, Shevchenko produced an astonishing quantity of poems, prose, sketches, and paintings by the time he died in 1861, despite having lived a life of much suffering and tribulation. Even as he casts a long shadow on Ukrainian letters, Shevchenko also counts among the few prophets of the modern Ukrainian nation revered by all political orientations, including the communists. An English translation of his works published in the Soviet Union in 1979 describes him as "a great humanist poet," stressing that "Vladimir Ilyich Lenin thought very highly of the Ukrainian bard," and noting that "monuments to Taras Shevchenko have been erected in many cities of the Soviet Union, and also abroad."[4] One such statue is located in Buczacz, prominently placed in front of the city hall.

Shevchenko's brand of humanism may be glimpsed from his 1841 poetic cycle, *Haidamaki*. Titled after the eighteenth-century rebels against

Taras Shevchenko's statue in front of the Buczacz city hall, 2003.
Photo by the author.

Polish rule in Right Bank Ukraine, that is, the part of the country located west of the Dnieper River, the work focuses on the 1768–69 Cossack uprising led by Maksym Zalizniak and Ivan Gonta, which culminated in the sack of the city of Uman, 130 miles south of Kyiv, and the slaughter of several thousand Poles and Jews.[5] "Gonta in Uman," the most harrowing section of the poem, depicts the Cossack leader's fictional murder of his own two children, who were raised as Roman Catholics by his Polish wife. It is a horrifying, yet also deeply moving scene. It has been read by generations of nationalists as a metaphor for the Ukrainian nation's need to tear itself away from the Poles, even at the price of physical and mental mutilation. In World War II, such massacres of family members in mixed Polish and Ukrainian villages were reenacted in Volhynia and Galicia, motivated by the notion that a free Ukraine had to be cleansed of Poles.[6]

In the midst of the slaughter in Uman, Gonta is presented with a horrifying gift:

"Look, Gonta, look!
These youngsters are your sons!
They're Catholics: since you kill all,
Can you leave them alone?" . . .
"My sons are Catholics . . . I vowed
No Catholic to spare . . .
My sons, my sons! Why are you small?
My sons, why aren't you grown?
Why aren't you with us killing Poles?"
"We will, we'll kill them, dad!"
"You never will! You never will!
Your mother's soul be damned,
That thrice-accursed Catholic,
The bitch that gave you birth!" . . .
    He flashed his knife
And the two lads were slain.
They fell to earth, still bubbling words:
"O dad! We are not Poles!
We . . . we . . . " And then they spoke no more,
Their bodies growing cold.

But Gonta's heart is broken. He has done his duty and has kept his oath. But now, in death, his sons have been transformed into Cossacks, and his act has made him into a murderer of his kin. At night, as the city burns, he returns to the scene of the slaughter:

> . . . Then he stoops,
> Two little bodies picks
> And lifts them gently on his back
> And carries them away . . .
> His sons—he bears some place where he
> Can cover them with sod,
> So that the youthful Cossack flesh
> Should not be food for dogs . . .
> The tears then gush like rain:
> "My children! Open up your eyes,
> Look at Ukraine, my boys:
> For her, my sons, you gave your lives
> And I, too, am destroyed . . .
> Forgive me, sons! You I forgive
> That Catholics you died."[7]

Thus the murdered children are sacrificed for Ukraine; God does not intervene to stay the father's hand, and the nation is born from this most unnatural deed. By killing his sons, Gonta cleanses Ukraine of its mongrel outgrowths even as he thereby facilitates their rebirth as thoroughbred Cossacks. This is a scene of biblical, mythical dimensions, filled with the fury of the downtrodden rising up against their oppressors, and wrought in the workshop of overheated Romantic imagery. The emergence of a martyred people from the site of infanticide by its hero has left a powerful stamp on Ukrainian representations and rhetoric of liberation: hacking off one's own limbs for the sake of moral consistency and ethnic purity. The birth of the nation calls for merciless surgery, entailing not only the Poles but also a generous amount of Jewish blood.

The Accumulated Hatred of Centuries

But when *Haidamaki* was published, the masses were still slumbering. It took Ivan Franko, Shevchenko's successor as the next generation's literary icon, to reach out to the people both as writer and as political activist. A remarkably prolific author, poet, and journalist, Franko was born to a peasant family in a small village near the Galician town of Drohobycz (Drohobych, 100 miles west of Buczacz) in 1856, fifteen years after the publication of *Haidamaki*. The numerous statues of him erected throughout the region attest to his stature, especially in West Ukraine. A founding member of the Ukrainian Radicals, with strong socialist and anticlerical leanings, Franko was a key figure in the establishment of the Ukrainian National Democratic Party in 1899. Since he was deeply concerned with the links between social and national oppression, Franko, too, was a favorite of the Soviet Union. In 1962 the Galician city of Stanyslaviv was renamed Ivano-Frankivsk in honor of this region's famous son.[8]

By the time of his premature death in 1916, it was clear that the most important part of Franko's legacy was his essays and fiction, in which he relentlessly defended the rights of the peasants to dignity, identity, and material well-being. At the same time, his familiarity with Galician Jewry, exposure to the peasantry's growing anti-Jewish sentiments, and dedication to radical and socialist agendas combined to produce a series of stark literary representations of Jews as parasites sucking the blood of the Ruthenian nation for their own benefit and in the service of Polish landowner exploitation and oppression. And while some of his early essays and poems contain particularly strong antisemitic tropes and arguments, it is his fiction, widely read in Ukraine then and now, that has been most influential in creating an image of Galician Jewry as a polar opposite of the emerging Ruthenian nation, set within the context of Galician rural and small-town life at the turn of the twentieth century.[9]

Franko's fiction is part of the genre of social realism or naturalism, epitomized perhaps best at the time by the French writer and social critic, Emile Zola. Zola both risked and made his reputation when he exposed the antisemitic roots of the campaign waged against Captain Alfred Dreyfus, in his celebrated 1898 essay *J'accuse*. In contrast, Franko's early novel *Boa Constrictor*, published twenty years earlier, is filled with the very prejudices that Zola so vociferously condemned. As Franko's biographer notes, this work is "quite exceptional for non-Jewish East European literature," since it is "told from the point of view of a Jew." Indeed, as it turns out, "Jews were among the best friends of his childhood, his classmates in the Drohobycz *Gymnasium* and the L'viv universities, and among his colleagues when he participated in the Galician socialist movement."[10] Nonetheless, the novel's protagonist, Hersh Goldkramer, whose name literally means "gold merchant or dealer," exhibits all the traits of the antisemitic imagination.

Goldkramer is something of a Galician hybrid of Shakespeare's Shylock and Dickens's Fagin, mired in his case in the filth, poverty, and promise of vast riches of the fledgling oil industry in the Drohobycz and Borysław (Boryslav) region that Franko knew so well. Goldkramer is raised in utter destitution: his young mother, abandoned by her husband, "had already become fitted, so to speak, to the mold of a type of Jewess so common to our cities, whose development had been affected by unhealthy living conditions, bad upbringing, a complete lack of education, early marriage, slothfulness, and hundreds of other causes." It is this wretched childhood that makes the future millionaire "deaf to the tears and grief of another human being," feeling only "repugnance, not kindness, at the sight of misery."[11]

After his mother dies in the cholera epidemic that swept through Galicia in 1831, Goldkramer is briefly adopted by Itsyk, "a kind-hearted little man," whose "attitude towards Christians" was "the same as any other's: he heaped abuse on some of them while playing up to others, but he cheated and tricked them all as best he could, considering it quite normal to do so." The lesson Goldkramer draws is that "every person of the Jewish faith had, so to speak, two faces: the one that was turned towards the muzhiks [peasants] was always the same—squeamish, sarcastic, threatening, or crafty; the one that was turned towards people of his own faith was exactly the same as all ordinary faces."[12]

Itsyk dies soon thereafter, but once oil is discovered in the region, Goldkramer becomes one of "the first profiteers who flocked to Boryslav like vultures to carrion" and "became rich overnight." Within fifteen years, having changed his first name from Hersh to the more Christian sounding Herman, Goldkramer has become the owner of "a few hundred wells and over a dozen refineries," and has "several thousand workers working for him," bossed "by ruthless, hard-driving idlers and scoundrels," who make "the workers work from morning till night." When Ruthenian workers are sent down into the fume-filled pits to collect the oil, their comrades mutter, "we're lowering a live man into a grave," and call out to them: "Good luck!" and "God bless you." But Goldkramer believes that God is on his side: "Us, naturally. Us, the Goldkramers of the world, who could calmly watch the windlass turning and the cable unraveling and slipping down, who could calmly force these men to work harder, and who could calmly listen to their terrible, gripping farewell: 'Good luck!'" Occasionally, even this hardened Jew may feel pity, as when the rotting corpse of a worker is found in one of the pits, at which point he throws a few coins into the widow's shack. But as Franko stresses, "Herman did not suddenly become a kind man. His kind-hearted gesture . . . had been momentary; the moment passed, and once more he was forced to become what life had made of him—a cold, heartless profiteer who had no time to notice misery, want, or a widow's tears."[13]

If *Boa Constrictor* is an inverted *Bildungsroman*, chronicling the transformation of a Jew into a monster, in Franko's later works Jews are juxtaposed with Ruthenian protagonists whose humble origins only enhance their dedication to the national cause. His 1900 novel *Fateful Crossroads* begins by repeating many of the old, stereotypical depictions and characterizations of Jews, including a memorably tawdry description of a "small, grimy Jewish town," where the streets are "full of potholes," while its center looks "like a collection of stone taverns." In the market, writes Franko, "heaps of garbage" were "scattered here and there," and "Jewish shops faced [it] on all sides." It is not a pretty sight: "Filth, neglect—that was what assaulted the eye and assailed the senses in this town and in this market. Something made it difficult to breathe, eyes grew weary as they wandered over the dismal scene, and thoughts grew gloomy."[14]

At the same time, *Fateful Crossroads* can also be seen as a literary representation of Franko's evolving views on the "Jewish Question," and especially on the relationship of Galician Jews to the emerging Ruthenian nation. The novel introduces two new types of Jews, who are central to the plot, in that they gradually transform into Franko's ideal—sincere supporters of fledgling Ruthenian nationalism and of its local leader, the upright and patriotic Ruthenian defense lawyer, Dr. Yevheniy Rafalovych. Initially, to be sure, these two characters are quite odious in their own particular ways. But over time, recognizing the changing circumstances, they are transformed into much more interesting representatives of the different strands in Jewish society at the time, as seen from Franko's perspective. First, we are introduced to the mayor of the city, Mr. Resselberg, "a medical doctor, a Jew who was a passionate Polish patriot and one of the most prominent proponents of the so-called assimilatory orientation." Resselberg is "one of the few Jews in Halychyna [Galicia] who had taken part in the Polish uprising of 1863" against the Russians. Having also served as a deputy to the Sejm, the Polish Parliament of Galicia, he was eventually elected mayor. Seemingly a man of impeccable reputation, in Franko's view Resselberg typifies the malign Jewish influence on late nineteenth-century Galician towns: "Slowly but effectively, he inaugurated in the city the kind of Jewish power structure that over time became typical of larger cities in Halychyna, a structure that creates a clique of powerful Jews in a city—

tavern owners, purveyors, and other leeches—that embellishes a city with a superficial sheen of culture, introduces sidewalks, gas, and buses, creates parks and promenades, but in return for these good deeds mercilessly sucks dry the population of the city, empties the treasury, drains public sources of revenue, devastates forests, and sells off communally held land."

As Franko sees it, "patriots like Resselberg provide the best possible cover for the management practices of such cliques, especially if their individual reputations remain unblemished, and if they know how to cultivate and maintain good relations with the influential Christians in the city and the district." Indeed, Resselberg "did not spare any costs to sustain that reputation," as a result of which people said behind his back: "Even though he is a Jew, he's a respectable man."[15]

Yevheniy's first encounter with the mayor does not go well. Referring to Galicia's past as part of medieval Kyivan Rus, or Ruthenia, the patriotic lawyer complains that there is "not a single name, not a single inscription to remind people that this city was in Rus and had a Rusyn past." Resselberg responds: "I do not recognize the existence of any kind of Rus! . . . I have heard something about Rusyn patriots, but where are the uprisings for their national rights? Where is the blood spilled for their flag? Where are their martyrs? Where are their prophets? Where are their leaders?" He is clearly calling up demons, as Rafalovych quickly indicates: "As for our uprisings, do not be too keen to experience them, because who knows if you and some of the others would find them very much to your liking." Resselberg gets the hint: "You know that I am a Jew, raised in the Jewish tradition. I experienced much inner turmoil, and it took a lot of effort and hard work to break free of my Jewishness and reforge myself as a Pole. To reforge myself once more, this time as a Rusyn—well, forgive me, Your Honour, but I have neither the strength, nor the time, nor the desire to do so."[16]

This is an interesting moment since, as we find later on, the main complaint by nationalist Ruthenians is that assimilationist Jews are joining the stronger though less numerous Poles rather than the largely still peasant Ruthenians who make up the bulk of the population in eastern Galicia, where the Ruthenian national movement demands autonomy or, eventually, independence. That early conversation plants a seed in the mayor's mind that will sprout toward the end of the novel; it originates in Franko's own thinking about the possible role of the Jews in promoting Ruthenian nationalism and their status in the future Ruthenian state. But the unlikely promoter of the Ruthenian cause in the novel turns out to be the moneylender Wagman, initially also presented as a thoroughly despicable character.

Wagman, who happens to be the owner of the apartment Rafalovych has rented, is described to the young lawyer by the chief justice of the district court as "the worst leech in our county, a usurer, a man who does not shun the most odious ideas." Wagman, he says, "likes to cast his nets for bureaucrats and lawyers in particular," as a result of which three of the "most promising adjuncts have already perished," one of them hanging himself and the other two expelled for "fraud and falsification." To be sure, as we subsequently find out, the three men in question were, in fact, crooks. But this does not prevent the county chief from similarly describing Wagman as "the most dangerous usurer" and "the worst bloodsucker in the county," who has also "cast his nets over all the villages."[17]

Yet when Dr. Rafalovych finally meets his landlord, the man turns out to be more complex. This "tall, lean Jew with a black beard, traditional peysy [sidelocks], and wearing a long coat," confesses right away that "my fellow extortionists consider me to be the worst, the most dangerous usurer," since "I know how to entangle people so skillfully that while they may cry out shrilly in my nets they can never disentangle themselves." But Wagman has been transformed into what he calls "a benefactor of the benefactors," using his skills to hunt down corrupt officials who exploit and deceive peasants and workers. "I divide people into two categories," he explains to Yevheniy: "One category is comprised of those who work, tilling the soil, planing boards, slaughtering, sewing, building. They are the common people." The second category is typified by the lord, who merely "makes sure that his servants and workers do not waste time," and thus "exists only so that others can do things well for him." These people Wagman sarcastically calls benefactors.[18]

In other words, Franko creates a character who is a Hasid and a usurer and, at the same time, has become a progressive, almost a socialist, who believes that his true life's goal is to fleece the rich for the benefit of the poor: Wagman, the human leech, has become a Jewish Robin Hood, fighting for the rights of Ruthenian peasants, not with bow and arrow, but with the same underhanded methods deeply embedded in the antisemitic fantasy. As he says to Rafalovych, "You will not find a single landowner or tenant, you will not find a single functionary who, to a greater or lesser extent, is not in my pocket. And you should know that once someone falls into my clutches, it is only through a miracle of God that he can escape. I have certain means, quiet associates, and advisors, and assistants."[19]

Initially, the upright Rafalovych refuses to do business with Wagman even when he vaguely understands the plan being hatched by the money-lender. It is, so to speak, a scheme that only a Jew could think up, and en-tirely inappropriate for a young, law-abiding, patriotic Ruthenian lawyer. But as Wagman points out to him, "You are a Rusyn, a peasants' lawyer," and for that reason the Polish administrators and landowners "are afraid that you might stir up the peasantry, or expose their nasty secrets and dirty deals." Conversely, since Wagman already knows "the exact circumstances of everyone in the county," he tells Rafalovych, "if you want to promote your politics, to exert your influence, this knowledge might come in handy to you." And so the Jewish parasite and the Ruthenian "peasants' lawyer" forge an alliance against the Polish administrative and landowning elite.[20]

This alliance hardly means that Rafalovych is free of anti-Jewish sen-timents, although they are presented as objective observations of condi-tions on the ground. His goal is to reform and enlighten the peasants—the goal of Franko and the Ruthenian national movement as a whole. At pres-ent, he believes, Ruthenian peasants "are still living at the level of savages in primeval forests: everything that is beyond the borders of my wigwam is hostile, lies in ambush for me, wants to harm me." The Jews, for their part, are seen as profiting from the ignorance of the peasants and the cor-ruption of the lords and administrators, and Rafalovych promises even those peasants who treat him with suspicion that "if some Jew sucks you dry of your money," he would still be willing to help them.[21] Indeed, the under-lying theme of this national project is that the liberation of the peasants can only be accomplished after the removal of the Jews and the Poles from Galicia.

The malign Jewish influence is epitomized by the village tavern. As Rafalovych travels through the Galician landscape, he observes the "drab, impoverished" villages, with "untended orchards, muddy pastures, ragged, grey thatched roofs" and "fallen fences," enveloped in a "gloomy melan-choly." And "there, in the middle of the village, stands the stone tavern with its yawning entrance gate opened wide like a dark, eternally hungry mouth, ready to swallow all that has been earned over an entire year of heavy labour," and "from its windows peers the heavy, bearded face of the tavern keeper." It is, of course, the Jew, who represents "the age-old strug-gle between that dark, voracious, yawning mouth and the village." All that the naïve peasants, in their misfortune, can hope for is that the Austrian emperor will come to their rescue. Gathering in the Jew's tavern, they call out: "If only he'd rein in the Jews. The Jews have taken over the world, the

Jews have made our lives unbearable!" This is the world that Rafalovych, and Franko, have set out to reform and transform.[22]

How, then, can the Jews be reformed? That is not the business of the Ruthenian patriots; but what about the Jews themselves? Here Franko identifies, and expresses a degree of sympathy for, the plight of Galician Jewry, devoting several pages to an encounter between the town's self-hating Jewish assimilationist and Polish patriot mayor Resselberg and Wagman, the county's bloodsucking Hasidic moneylender turned benefactor of Ruthenian peasantry. In pitting these two Jews against each other, Franko attempts to articulate his own position on the "Jewish Question."

What Resselberg and Wagman have in common is their distaste for the manner in which Galician Jews conduct themselves; in this, they are in complete agreement with their creator, Franko. The mayor exclaims, "It is not a very great pleasure to think of oneself as a Jew. All my life I have fought against this feeling, I have forced myself to stifle it within myself, to choke it, to tear it out by its roots, and I still am not able to do it." The reason for his inability to divorce himself from the Jews is not entirely different from Rafalovych's loyalty to the peasants he despises: it is derived from a "feeling of unity and solidarity with the ignorant and filthy Jewish masses." But the mayor feels no further obligation toward these unwashed multitudes and, having removed himself from their company, spends little energy on analyzing their plight. Wagman, for his part, appears more thoughtful. As he sees it, for "our Jews . . . our masses . . . religion takes the place of everything." But "where they live, in which country, among what kind of people" concerns them only to the extent that "it is a field they can harvest without having sown anything." He asks: "Do they feel themselves citizens of that country? Do they care about its welfare, its success, its glory?" "They care nothing about that," he states emphatically. "They feel that they are complete strangers, and they care about the laws, the way the country is run, only insofar as they do not prevent them from being Jews and exploiting the rest of humanity."[23]

For someone who describes himself as having personally "fleeced the peasants and sucked their blood" in the past, and whose religious faith is supposedly at the core of his identity, this appears to be a rather unlikely view. But it clearly reflects Franko's perception of the Jews. More credibly, Wagman also despises assimilationists. As he sees it, assimilation means "casting out of your heart all that was left of the community instinct that once made our nation strong," and instead of "loving your tribe," trying "to find another fatherland, to buy yourself another, alien mother." He thus pitilessly proclaims to Resselberg that for his "adopted mother," namely, Poland, "you will always be foreign," because "in the depths of her soul she hates you, and the more that you try to ingratiate yourself with her, to get into her good graces, the more she will hold you in contempt."[24]

Franko captures here the tragedy of many assimilated Jews, often originating in Europe's borderlands, who tried to assimilate not only in Poland but also in Germany, Austria, Hungary, and many other new nation-states. But for Franko the issue is not so much Jewish fate as Jewish betrayal: by opting for Poland, Galician Jews abandoned and betrayed the just cause of Ruthenians. And it is left to Wagman, whose uncharacteristic empathy for the peasants enables him to realize this conundrum, to spell out Franko's opinion "that the Jews usually assimilate not with those who are closer to them . . . the weaker nations, the oppressed, the wronged, and the indigent . . . but with those who are more powerful," which is why there are "no Slovak Jews, no Rusyn Jews." This is not a statement in favor of assimilation into Ruthenian society: Franko knows that just as the Jews are in no position to merge with the peasants, so too the peasants are unlikely to welcome them. Rather, this is more an expression of resentment against Jews who seem to have completely internalized the perceptions of the ruling Polish elite. As Wagman says, "Polish patriotism here, on Rusyn territory, is not really proper."

What, then, are the alternatives for Galician Jews? According to Wagman, "no Jew can, nor should he be either a Polish or a Rusyn patriot. And he does not need be. Let him be a Jew—that suffices. After all, it is possible to be a Jew and to love the country in which we were born, and to benefit, or at least not harm the people who, even though they are not our kin, are nevertheless closely bound with our lives, with all our memories."[25]

This was, in fact, Franko's position, to which he notably added that the Jews would have to live as second-class citizens within the future Ukrainian nation-state. In his essay "Semitism and Antisemitism in Galicia," Franko advocated that Jews should be recognized as a separate national group. They could then assimilate into the local Ruthenian population—which he obviously found unlikely; remain in Galicia with the legal status of "aliens" deprived of certain important political and civic rights, such as the right to buy land; or they could immigrate to another country where they might live as an independent nation. Franko's "enthusiastic reaction to Theodor Herzl's *Judenstaat*," as his biographer Yaroslav Hrytsak puts it, is consistent with what appears to have been his preferred solution to the "Jewish Question," namely, that they leave Ruthenian lands of their own accord.[26]

As we know from many other instances (such as Polish nationalist calls for Jews to "go to Palestine," and the *Haavara*, or transfer agreement, between the Third Reich and the Jewish leadership of the Yishuv in 1930s Mandatory Palestine), support for Zionism can also be based on antisemitic reasoning, which in this case Franko puts into the mouth of his protagonist Wagman. What he had learned from the pogroms in Russian-ruled Ukraine in the early 1880s, Wagman tells the mayor, is that "when we worked on sucking dry and ruining the Rusyn nation, we, the Jews, were doing much the same thing as the Gypsy who, sitting up in an oak tree, sawed off the branch he was sitting on." His conclusion is ominous: "Living on Rusyn soil, we are bringing down on our heads a conflagration of Rusyn hatred." This is all the more threatening, because "we forget that more than half of all the Jewish tribes now live on Rusyn soil, and that the accumulated hatred of centuries may burst out in such a conflagration, take on such forms that our Polish and Moskal [derisive term for Russians] protectors will not be able to help us in any way." It is for this reason that Wagman finds it "imperative . . . to build a bridge from us to the Rusyn shore as well, to start to do at least something so that the Rusyns would not remember us only for our evil deeds," and "to help them now, when they are still weak, when they are still hunched over and incapable of standing up straight on their own."[27]

This is a worthy proposal, followed by all too few Jews for reasons that are not difficult to figure out: the Jews were hardly in a position to help the Ruthenians, and the peasants were not particularly keen on Jewish help. Among politicians and intellectuals there was a greater likelihood for cooperation; but the "logic of history" was leaning in another direction, since the envisioned Polish and Ukrainian nation-states did not have an ideological space for Jews of any variety, at least as long as they retained some traces of their ethnic and religious identity. In *Fateful Crossroads*, when the assimilationist Jewish mayor actually follows Wagman's advice and helps the peasants, his former Polish colleagues are deeply disappointed. The city architect exclaims, "[W]ho would have expected anything like that! Such a respectable man. Such a patriot!" to which another gentleman responds: "Eh, a Jew is always a Jew!"[28] And when Wagman is brutally murdered by a couple of local crooks, who make off with a great deal of money they find in his safe, his death, initially thought to have been a suicide, elicits little concern. In the words of the county chief, "Wagman was not such a notable figure. There is one bloodsucker less in the county."[29]

Knowing how matters developed in the first half of the twentieth century, one might concede that the dark predictions made by Rafalovych and Wagman were dreadfully accurate. But another way of understanding Franko, and the progressive national movement of which he was an influential member, would be that they were making self-fulfilling prophecies, providing the rationale for excluding, extirpating, and murdering a group repeatedly described as leeches, bloodsuckers, and parasites; alien, foreign, and corrupt; allied with the nation's enemies and incapable of either mixing in or living side by side with the Ruthenian/Ukrainian people. The sanction given by Franko was considerable, both because of his literary, intellectual, and patriotic credentials, and because he in fact wrote so much about real, and even more so about imaginary and fictional, Jews. And as an authority on the subject of Ukrainian nationalism and Galician Jewry, he played a substantial role in preparing the ground for the violence that was to follow, and in persuading its intended targets that they would do well to leave in advance.[30]

Historian of the Podolian Ghetto

In many ways, Franko provides us with splendid reconstructions, based on his own experience and knowledge, of Galicia in the late nineteenth century, and the complex relationship between Poles, Ruthenians, and Jews. His views on ethnicity, social class, and political aspirations reflect the larger reality of the time and combine his literary sensibilities with his political engagement and experience, just as his prejudices are part and parcel of the mindset of the period. As a writer and political activist, Franko had a unique, and a uniquely biased, perspective. So did another eminent writer of his generation, Karl Emil Franzos, born in 1848 (and thus just eight years Franko's senior) near the town of Czortków, 150 miles east of Franko's birthplace and only 20 miles from Buczacz. Because of the very different prism through which Franzos viewed the same world during the same period, his writing greatly enriches our understanding of life on the borderlands in the second half of the nineteenth century, and especially of the challenges facing young Galician Jews at a time of rising nationalism in the decades leading to the war that smashed the old order to pieces.

Most of Franzos's social-realist prose is written from the perspective of the traditional Jewish community in his hometown and of those who sought to leave it, just as Franko's protagonists are men who came out of Ruthenian villages akin to that of his childhood. Like Franko, Franzos left that world as soon as he could and, as he recounts, had never truly belonged to it in the first place. Yet although he lived most of his life in Europe's metropolises, he too drew on those early years in a Jewish-Galician environment for much of his subsequent writing. As the son of a physician, Franzos was given a secular education. Seen as *daytch*, or Germanized, and thus a renegade Jew, by the strictly Hasidic community of Czortków, he was treated as a Jew by his Gentile classmates. This early childhood experience exemplified the fate of those increasingly numerous young Galician Jews of the time, who began moving out of the poverty-stricken, tradition-bound, and God- as well as rabbi-fearing towns of their childhood and youth. This historical moment and its social and psychological burdens became the focus of Franzos's tales.

"My father," he writes, "had always shown himself to be zealously German." But the son, even though he professed that very same "German national feeling," as he put it, "throughout my life," set himself the task of explaining the realities and hardships of small-town Jewish existence in a still largely premodern Galicia to his considerable international readership. As one who succeeded in breaking out of the confines of the shtetl, Franzos always recalled his father's admonition: "Your nationality is not Polish, nor Ruthenian, nor Jewish—you are German"; but "as for your faith, you are a Jew." Such a hybrid identity could not be sustained in a small Galician town; it was meant for the world: "My father brought me up just as his father had brought him up, with the same outlook, indeed with the same goal, that I should not see Galicia but rather the West as my homeland."[31] Yet toward the end of his short life, at a time when assimilated German Jews, who knew little of Judaism, became increasingly suspect as not being truly German, Franzos seems to have realized that such hybridity was coming under increasing threat in that idealized West as well.

As a child, Franzos relates, "I attended the little town's only school, in the Dominican monastery; there I learned Polish and Latin. My father himself taught me German. For Hebrew I had a private tutor." He had little contact with other Jews in town, rarely visited a Jewish home, and never went to synagogue; his playmates were Christian, and his family did not keep kosher: "I grew up as if on an island. I was separated from my fellow students by faith and language, which were precisely what separated me from the Jewish boys. I was a Jew, but of a different kind from them, and I could not quite understand their language."[32]

At the age of ten, after his father's death, Franzos was sent to a gymnasium in the bigger city of Czernowitz, where increasing numbers of Jews were assimilating into German culture. Having emerged from a deeply Hasidic Galician shtetl into the increasingly cosmopolitan capital of Bukovina, Franzos was well on the way to becoming an enlightened, assimilated, German-speaking Jew: "As my father's son, and having also been raised already early in life with a profound sense of duty, it was entirely out of the question that I would ever even think of changing my faith. But I thought just as little that Judaism would play a decisive role in my life."[33]

But play such a role it did. As a Jew, Franzos was denied a government scholarship to study classics at the university: "It was the summer of 1867," he notes wryly, "before the liberal era," which arrived in December that year with the enactment of the Austrian constitution, and Jews could still not expect government stipends. This was a moment of profound crisis for the young man: "Only those who have been in a similar situation can grasp how much pain, how many sleepless nights are contained in these few words." He now realized that his Jewish identity "had brought me harm, the worst that one can suffer, demanding a terrible sacrifice from me: that I give up the profession I chose." Conversion would have removed this obstacle. Instead, Franzos went to law school. He also decided to learn more about Jews. Although he stresses that he "did not become pious," he also insists that his "interest in Judaism," his "feeling of belonging to the impoverished caftan-wearing Jews" of Czernowitz, and eventually of Galicia as a whole, "became incomparably greater than before." In fact, it became the core of his entire oeuvre.[34]

Yet one more rejection, this time by a young woman who refused to associate with a Jew, finally triggered his literary instinct. Franzos summarized his first novella, *The Picture of Christ*, as depicting "the love between a Jew and a Christian woman and how her prejudice is greater than her love."[35] Subsequently he also became concerned with the tyrannical rule of religious leaders in Galician towns over the lives of young men and women, their dismissal of love as a disruptive, Gentile concept, and their insistence that marriage was a matter to be determined by parents, matchmakers, and rabbis. His concern with youthful passion and ambition was similarly reflected in tales about doomed relations between Jews and Gentiles, and the encounter of young Jews who flee the oppression of shtetl life with the myriad forms of exclusion in Christian society. Franzos never practiced law; instead, he began working as a journalist in Vienna and Budapest, and in 1886 moved to Berlin, where he soon established himself as a popular writer.

No wonder that the first English translation of Franzos's stories, published in New York in 1883 under the title *The Jews of Barnow* (his literary name for Czortków), which included "The Picture of Christ," was accompanied by a discussion of the author's presumed Jewish identity. Written by the prominent Jewish journalist Barnet Phillips, the preface noted that "although the high literary art which Franzos possesses . . . is fully admitted by intelligent Jews, the subject matter of his book itself, its *raison d'être*, they have by no means relished." For this reason, according to Phillips, while one New York journal concluded "from internal evidence" that "Franzos must be a Jew," this statement was "directly controverted" by another "Jewish weekly of the highest standing," whereas a third "asserted that the author is or was a Jew." This conclusion was based on the assumption that "no man not born a Jew, perfectly familiar with all the phases of Jewish life in Eastern Galicia, and in sympathy with them, could have created this book." Franzos, writes Phillips, "may have clothed Jews and Jewesses with poetical raiment, given them melodramatic phrasings, but the gabardine, caftan, love-locks, are visible—the whine, the nasal twang audible."[36]

Writing just as the mass immigration of East European Jews to the United States was beginning—bringing no fewer than 2 million Jews by the outbreak of World War I—Phillips, who belonged to an earlier, far smaller, and well-integrated Jewish American community, both understood and to some extent shared the prejudices against the "eastern Jews" so common at the time among their western co-religionists and their Gentile neighbors. "The denial that Franzos was a Jew," wrote Phillips, "though apparently insignificant in itself, and due, perhaps, to a want of acquaintance with the facts, is still peculiarly indicative of a natural *travers* of the Jewish mind," that is, the predilection for self-denial and obfuscation with respect to non-Jews. "Any description of the inner lives of Jews, when written by a Jew, unless it be laudatory, is particularly distasteful to Jews." And while "no race cares to have its failings exposed," what is peculiar to Jews, in Phillips's view, is that "from one of another creed such strictures may be passed over with stolid indifference, but, from one of their own blood, any censure, direct or applied, is considered by Jews in the light of sacrilege." And yet Franzos exposes the life of Jews in the ghettoes of Galicia in all their sordid details, though never lacking in empathy. "What Franzos shows markedly in his *Jews of Barnow*, is that barrier which Jews throw around their household," writes Phillips, and it is precisely "this hiding, of the finest trait the Jew possesses, that love and peace which dwell in his home, that reverence which children have for their parents," that "has tended more than anything else to alienate the Jew from his neighbor. Among the ultra-Orthodox Jews," wherever they dwell, "their doors are inhospitably closed to those of another belief."[37]

Indeed, Franzos writes with love and affection for those wretched of the earth dwelling in the ghettoes of Galicia, and with the moral authority of one who had stepped out of the ghetto and entered the wider world. He is an advocate of education and enlightenment for the Jews, just as Franko calls for the enlightenment of the peasants. He sees the corruption of the Jewish establishment, as well as of the Polish and Austrian rulers, and he senses the simmering, potential violence of the Ruthenian peasants, their addiction to alcohol, and their inability to perceive a way out of their own misery. But what Franzos seeks is not the realization of national aspirations, be they Jewish or Ruthenian, but the kind of mutual understanding that comes from familiarity, and the fulfillment of personal aspirations divorced from ethnic identification. For Franzos the moment of enlightenment is that of Jewish-Gentile contact, through friendship or love, patronage or edification, even if, under the circumstances of the time, such relations and aspirations tend to end up in disillusionment and tragedy. This makes for an interesting, albeit incomplete parallel with Franko. Franko's Jews, too, the assimilated and deracinated mayor and the Orthodox, bloodsucking moneylender, are transformed through an understanding of the Ruthenian peasants' plight. But what they are transformed into, beyond sympathy for the Ruthenian cause, remains unclear and of no great concern to Franko. The peasants will come into their own as a new Ukrainian nation, and the Jews will have to either live next to it as a tolerated minority or else leave, perhaps to create a nation of their own elsewhere.

The novella *Leib Weihnachtskuchen and His Child* is Franzos's most elaborate exploration of Jewish-Christian love. The protagonist, Leib the tavernkeeper, is not a leech and corruptor of peasant morals, but the humble and wretchedly poor father of the beautiful Miriam. The peasants do drink themselves to the floor, but at Leib's expense, since he refuses to cheat them by diluting the vodka; he is also incapable of lying. When the no less brutally honest peasant Janko falls for Miriam, neither Christians nor Jews can accept the prospect of such a union. For Leib, this would be an act "against nature"; similarly, Leib's friend, the local Ruthenian priest, warns Janko against mixing with "that accursed race" and its "Jewish blood," since "they are all vindictive and grasping and dishonest." And yet, what shines through the grime, poverty, hopelessness, and prejudices that pervade the village is Leib's humanity and the growing love between Miriam and Janko; and what must bring about the eventual tragedy is that Christians and Jews alike utterly reject the notion of such interethnic love. Eventually, the two lovers plunge into the raging Dniester River and drown, in a scene reminiscent of Agnon's tale of an earlier event in Buczacz, where such forbidden love finds its eternal tomb in the tamer waters of the Strypa—although Agnon, who eschews the tragic Romanticism of Franko's and Franzos's generation, leaves open the possibility that the lovers of his tale secretly end up living happily ever after.[38]

Franzos's greatest literary achievement is *The Clown of Barnow* (*Der Pojaz*), the tale of a Jewish youth's failed quest for self-emancipation. While the protagonist's father, an itinerant jokester and *schnorrer* (beggar), represents the quintessential "wandering Jew," his son Sender pines to play the role of Shylock, the archetypal Jew of the Christian imagination, on the European theatrical stage. But his quest to shed his Galician Jewish attributes in order to qualify as a proper European actor capable of playing Shakespeare's Jewish character is doomed to failure. For Franzos, Shylock is the ultimate embodiment of two irreconcilable yet complementary perceptions of the world. As the director of a local wandering theater troupe exclaims, *The Merchant of Venice* "is a play for Galicia. It is interesting for Jews and Christians and both can be pleased or angry about it to their hearts' content. Shylock is always a sellout." After all, the play exposes the intimate link between two polar views: Christian audiences see a money-grubbing, parasitical, self-hating, and vengeful Jew, who cares more for money than for his own daughter; whereas Jews see in Shylock a personification of their predicament, eternally dependent on the tender mercies of the Gentiles no matter how much wealth they may have acquired.

Sender never accomplishes his goal. But in the closing pages of the novel, the dying young man sits in the audience as his idol, the legendary, Warsaw-born actor Bogumił Dawison (Davidsohn), performs Shylock's soliloquy in Lemberg: "If you prick us, do we not bleed? If you tickle us, do we not laugh?" At that moment, observes Sender, "this was no longer an actor, but rather a poor, unfortunate man who had long kept his and his brethren's misery bottled up within himself, who had long suffered without complaint, and who had suddenly found words for his terrible pain."[39]

Completed in 1893, *The Clown of Barnow* was only published in 1905, a year after the author's death. It appears that Franzos delayed publication in response to the rise of antisemitism in Central Europe. As a prominent proponent of Jewish integration into the mainstream of European culture, Franzos was shaken by the growing tide against emancipated Jews in the culture and nation he had adopted. Ironically, when the novel was eventually published, and despite its commercial success, German critics greeted it as "too Jewish," and Zionist detractors saw it as "too German." Perhaps Franzos himself had come to think of Sender's predicament, which has to do more with his personal inability to sever himself from his background than with rejection by Christian society, as no longer reflecting the challenges faced by a younger generation of Galician Jews.

When Franko and Franzos set out on their literary journeys, both authors believed that by realistically depicting the ills of the present, they could motivate society to take progressive action. For Franko, the purpose of the historical novel was "to lay bare the human heart, its fervent aspirations and consuming passions, its struggles, triumphs and defeats . . . portrayed against the backdrop of a historical event." Franzos, who referred to himself as "the historian of the Podolian Ghetto," insisted that he had "described this strange and outlandish mode of existence precisely as it appears to me."[40] This, in fact, was the point, because however much they labored to balance empathy with accuracy, these two writers saw the same world through utterly different eyes. Their very insistence on factual accuracy betrayed the gaping fissures between the perceptions of reality by different groups, which eventually widened into unbridgeable chasms and irretrievably shattered that entire universe. And their protagonists, who went out into the world on a mission to change themselves, and thereby to make a change in the world, or at least to make it better understand the plight of the communities they left behind, either entirely failed, or accomplished not at all what they had set out to do.

CHAPTER NINE

Fathers and Sons

A Great and Famous Sage

UNLIKE HIS PROTAGONIST, KARL Emil Franzos had the good fortune of being prepared for life in the "outside world" thanks to his father's insistence on a "German" education. Most Jews of that generation had to chart their own course directly from a traditional Jewish upbringing. Some, such as the future university professor David (Zvi) Heinrich Müller, born in Buczacz in 1846, made subsequent use of the skills they had acquired as children and youths. They also always retained a whiff of foreignness about them, however well they integrated into the European scholarly and intellectual elite; and much as they were admired by the communities they left behind, they were suspected both by the Orthodox and by the emerging Zionists of having abandoned the fold: too Jewish for the Germans, too German for the Jews.

For a man of his generation, Müller was a rare exception. By the time of his death in 1912 he had become a renowned scholar, a university professor, and the holder of a noble title, all without converting to Christianity, as was customary for such official recognition. Müller had excelled in his Jewish learning as a youth and was consequently wedded to the daughter of a wealthy man in nearby Kołomyja. But the young man was already under the influence of the Haskalah, and especially of Peretz Smolenskin, a Russian Jew who was only four years older and became known as the founder and editor of *Hashahar* (*The Dawn*), a Hebrew-language journal published in Vienna that promoted ideas of the Haskalah, a revival of the

Hebrew language, and a return to Zion, as well as providing a platform for radical and socialist essays. Müller had already also made use of his "enlightened" father's bookstore, reading both medieval philosophy and nineteenth-century Hebrew literature. But his father-in-law was much less open-minded, and once he discovered Müller's "profane" tastes in reading, he expelled him from his home.[1]

Many years later, a scathing obituary in the Zionist newspaper *Hatzevi* accused Müller of having abandoned the cause of modern Hebrew. Founded and edited by the Russian-born Eliezer Ben-Yehuda, perhaps the most important figure in the modernization and dissemination of the Hebrew language in Palestine, this paper hosted some well-known writers during its existence from 1884 to 1915, including Arthur Rupin, Max Nordau, and A. D. Gordon. "This Jewish sage," thundered the obituary, "who dedicated his entire life to the field of linguistics and Semitic literature, and whose numerous books were famous in the scholarly world," ended up "worshipping only German literature, which does not need and perhaps also does not want foreign sages."[2]

This was a characteristically unfair allegation, born of nationalist dogmatism. In fact, Müller had sought knowledge anywhere he could find it. Just like Franzos, he first went to Czernowitz, which had already become a haven for many Galician maskilim. One of his friends there recalled that even then Müller "had profound knowledge of the Talmud, the Bible and Hebrew grammar, and in his father's attic he had secretly studied also German, Polish, French, English, Latin and Greek." From there he enrolled at a rabbinical college in Breslau, perhaps still hoping to fulfill his parents' expectations that he become a rabbi.[3] But he left soon thereafter, studied at several important European institutions, and at the age of thirty-one was appointed assistant professor of Semitic philology at the University of Vienna.

In stark contrast to *Hatzevi*, the Berlin-based Jewish monthly *Ost und West* (East and West) published an admiring obituary in 1913, describing Müller as "a sharp-witted grammarian, text critic, decipherer of ancient inscriptions and texts, editor and cultural historian." As a specialist in the languages of southern Arabia, he had published translations and interpretations of inscriptions discovered and brought to Europe at the time. But his greatest and most controversial contributions concerned the links between biblical and Mesopotamian texts. Müller's argument about the literary impact of biblical prophecy on sacred and secular Semitic and European writing provoked theologians, who viewed Bible studies strictly as their own domain, and flew in the face of the convention that the Bible was derivative of earlier Assyrian and Babylonian writings. Moreover, Müller's 1903 German and Hebrew translation of and commentary on the Code of Hammurabi, discovered just two years earlier in Persia, further supported his assertion of the vast differences between Mesopotamian and biblical concepts of law and morality. Simultaneously, Müller engaged directly with Judaism, both as one of the founders of the Jewish Theological Institute in Vienna, where he began teaching in 1893, and in his role in the publication of the Sarajevo Haggadah, one of the oldest illuminated manuscripts of this retelling of the Exodus from Egypt, dating back to fourteenth-century Spain.[4]

Ost und West, which promoted a Jewish literary, artistic, and scholarly renaissance, served as a venue for some of the most influential Jewish intellectuals of the time, such as Martin Buber, Max Nordau, Ludwig Geiger, and Alfred Nossig. For this journal, Müller was a shining example of the enlightened modern Jew: learned in Jewish and secular scholarship, equally comfortable in the company of rabbis and university professors, committed to traditional erudition and to the Haskalah, and publishing in German and in Hebrew. Indeed, Müller wrote essays in Hebrew for *Hashahar*, and maintained a close friendship with Smolenskin; after the latter's early death, he also supported his widow and orphan. As *Ost und West* put it, Müller "strode his path uprightly and faithfully, always devoted to scholarship and to serving the truth, he made no concessions, never denied his convictions and his origin, leaned neither to the right nor to the left, and compelled even his opponents to listen, thanks to his serenity and intellectual superiority."

To be sure, noted the journal, Müller encountered his share of "resentment and envy," especially from "Protestant German colleagues eager to deny a Jew the right to have a word on biblical questions." But at a time when "antisemitism raged at its fiercest in Austria, Müller climbed to the highest levels of honor that can be reached by a scholar," culminating in being "awarded a hereditary noble title by the Emperor Franz Joseph," not "for the profits made from his service" but "for the merits of his accomplishments."[5] In other words, Müller represented the transition from court Jew to an integrated independent member of the elite.

Even *Hatzevi* conceded that "despite his contempt for the Hebrew national idea," Müller—quite differently from Franzos—"never declared that he was German, as was the custom among assimilated professors," and "strongly opposed" the requirement that students at the rabbinical semi-

nary declare that they were not Zionists, saying: "all coercion is villainy."
Nonetheless, the Zionist paper alleged that "the more Müller was honored by the Gentiles, the more his liking for Jewish values evaporated. He
wrote all of his scholarly books in German. He ceased writing Hebrew
altogether," and "was unwilling to lecture on any Hebrew book beyond
the Bible," as well as generally displaying "indifference to the new Hebrew
language." The tragedy of Müller, in *Hatzevi*'s view, was that when his
interpretation of biblical verse was finally accepted, his opponents simply
appropriated it and called it their own. And Müller, who "by nature liked
very much to be respected," was consequently "consumed by rage and his
health was destroyed" by the growing tendency to ignore his contribution,
attribute it to others, take it over, or even claim that Müller had plagia-
rized it. All this "struck his heart, which was already filled with rage," and
before he could respond to these allegations, "death prematurely removed
this old professor from the battlefield. And thus this Jew descended to the
Netherworld in discontent, and his entire intellectual work will be ignored
by the sages of Semitic languages."[6]

It is, however, possible that finding himself between the Scylla of Zionist nationalism and the Charybdis of Christian anti-Jewish resentment,
Müller was most pained by the false rumors spread about him in his hometown of Buczacz. In 1893 he wrote from Vienna to his uncle, reporting
that he had just received a letter from his mother, saying

> that an evil rumor has come to the city of Buczacz, that informers
> have denounced and slandered me, and that she would rather die
> because of this affair. And I honestly have no idea what this all
> means and have no knowledge of any sin I have committed . . . On
> the contrary, I am the strong pillar upon which the house of Judah
> rests, and the whole congregation of Vienna honors me, and the
> Name of God is sanctified through me . . . Who dares speak such
> evil words about me that pain the heart of my dear mother and
> your heart my dear uncle? These are false informers whose only
> intent is to defame my honor out of meanness of spirit.[7]

Buczacz was not a forgiving town. Franzos, who did not spare his criticism of Czortków, compared his hometown favorably to Buczacz. To be
sure, he wrote, Czortków too was "a miserable little Galician Jewish town,"
whose people were "equally uneducated, equally poor and equally un-
heeded, wore the same garb and bowed to the same God." And yet, "the

deepest chasm separated the inhabitants of the two towns," since they served their God "in fundamentally different manners." For while the Jews of Czortków "were Hasidim, bigots and zealots, wild, fantastical fanatics, who fluctuated oddly between atrocious asceticism and exuberant debauchery," Buczacz was populated by the Mitnaggedim, described by Franzos as "tough, sober people, who honored the Bible above all, and the Talmud only insofar as it explained the Bible." These were "practical, cool people," who "lived as best they could by the rules of their faith but held the Ten Commandments to be more important than anything else, explained miracles in the most naturalistic manner possible, and were however averse to any other redundant ruminations."

Czortków, insisted Franzos, was "a place of much fasting, but also of much feasting"; conversely, "in Buczacz life moved in a measured, monotonous rut." In the Hasidic town, "the long days are filled with debates on learned subjects, while work and trade take place only in the pauses in-between; the people of Buczacz devote themselves to craft and trade; their diligence and bourgeois respectability are greater, their esteem for intellectual activity and their willingness for self-sacrifice in poverty and learning are weaker." The people of Czortków "are eccentric and passionate, those of Buczacz are considered hard and calculating." And because it was such a severe and work-oriented town, reported Franzos, Buczacz had the reputation of rarely welcoming strangers: "Whenever a guest was received inhospitably, people said, 'He was received like a *schnorrer* in Buczacz.'" For the town's "sober people detest shiftless vagrants, even when they are very pious and tell amusing tales."[8]

Perhaps for that very reason, as his status in Vienna kept rising to ever greater heights, Müller's reputation in Buczacz also improved over time; he was certainly no *schnorrer*. In May 1908, fifteen years after writing to his uncle, Müller received a visit from the twenty-one-year-old Agnon, who had been instructed by his mother to meet her famous cousin on his way from Buczacz to Palestine. By then, writes Agnon, the Vienna professor was considered "a great and famous sage of whom all Galicia was proud." Perhaps Agnon's mother hoped that the venerable scholar would dissuade her son from this adventure. As Agnon recounts in his autobiographical story "Hemdat," "when his relative heard that he wished to go to the Land of Israel," the professor opined that "settling Eretz Israel is a great deed, but its climate is harsh, and its inhabitants suffer, and you will not be able to withstand the suffering of the land. Better that you settle down in Vienna and prepare yourself for the university and I will support you." But the

young visitor, "whose path had been decided, was not tempted by his relative's words."[9]

We know little more about this meeting. But Agnon's biographer sus-
pects that the young man was rather less decisive than his literary protagonist, depicted almost half a century later, since he apparently stayed for
a while as a guest in the professor's elegant apartment. It is also possible
that they impressed each other, for unlike the libel against him, Müller
was deeply steeped in Hebrew religious and philosophical writing, areas in
which his youthful guest was remarkably well versed. Indeed, Agnon may
have actually been tempted to remain in Vienna under the protection of
his powerful relative. After all, Central Europe—not its Galician borderlands, but the great cities of Vienna and Berlin—certainly had its attractions. Although Agnon eventually opted for Palestine, where he arrived at
some point between May and June 1908, he left once again in 1912, and
spent the next twelve years in Germany, returning to Palestine only in
1924, after a fire in his apartment destroyed much of his library and many
invaluable manuscripts he had been writing. What prompted the move to
Germany was not just the harsh Middle Eastern climate and the nature
of Palestine's inhabitants, but also the attractions of a mature, rich, and
vibrant civilization at a time when Jewish cultural life in Germany was at
its peak. He was not alone, of course. Abraham Jacob Brawer, who immigrated to Palestine in 1911 shortly after earning a PhD from the University of Vienna and publishing his book on Austria's annexation of Galicia,
even as he dedicated himself to the geography of Palestine, was also back
in Europe shortly thereafter, spending six years in Istanbul and Vienna,
where his son was born, and returning to Jerusalem only in 1920.[10]

Had Agnon become a scholar in Vienna, or had he settled down in
Weimar Germany, he would have, in all probability, been swept away by
the events that followed, ending up along with his family in the hands of
the Nazis. Because he returned to Palestine, yet dedicated so much of his
work to the tales of Jewish life on Europe's borderlands, he did his part
in saving that life from oblivion. He also became the mainstay of modern
Hebrew literature, albeit written in his peculiar, immensely rich, and never
easily decipherable language, which no one before or after has wielded in
quite the same way, constituting a literary bridge between the old world
he left behind a few decades before its destruction and the new world he
helped construct. Agnon, Müller, and many others who had left their little
borderland town and gone "out into the world" had this in common, that
even as they discovered new, wide horizons, the town they had left behind

never quite left them, remaining lodged in their memories and hearts to the end of their lives.

Amalia's Race

In certain respects, Müller's story is similar to those of others of his generation: from the enlightened Jewish-German perspective he was the epitome of Jewish success, accomplished through erudition and uncompromising but modern ethnic pride in an admittedly often antisemitic environment; Christian scholars tended to see him as a Jewish interloper, trespassing on their turf; the Zionists, as well as some other educated Polish and Ukrainian nationalists, saw people like him as betrayers of ethnic renewal and sellouts to other nationalities; and the Orthodox suspected him of abandoning traditional Jewish ways. In hindsight, of course, people's opinions changed. In the 1950s, Müller's leap from a Galician shtetl to the heights of Viennese academe and the impact of his seemingly esoteric scholarship were paraded on the pages of the Buczacz memorial book. By 2020 Müller's unique biography and critical scholarly contribution had been rediscovered even in Austria.[11] Success has many fathers, but social and ethnic exclusion tends to produce orphans. In 1942, Bruno Schulz, a Galician Jew who wrote in Polish, was shot like a stray dog by a Gestapo officer on a street corner in his hometown of Drohobycz, where Franko had attended the gymnasium with Jewish fellow students seven decades earlier. Gradually rediscovered after the war and gaining international renown when the murals he painted for a Gestapo officer were accidentally revealed in 2001, Schulz is now celebrated by Polish literati, Israeli Zionists, and West Ukrainians. Once disowned by all, now everyone wants a part of him: the Poles his language and art, the Ukrainians his local color, the Zionists his Jewishness.[12]

At the time of Agnon's visit with Müller, Sigmund Freud was also teaching at the University of Vienna. But although he was later influenced by Freud's theories of the unconscious, Agnon is unlikely to have heard of him at the time, or to know that the inventor of psychoanalysis was also linked to Buczacz.[13] Freud's subsequent fame afforded him a place of honor in the town's memorial book, which claims that both his parents came from there. In fact, his connection to the town was rather less direct. Freud's paternal great-grandfather, Ephraim, and his grandfather, Schlomo, were indeed born in Buczacz, and they may have both been rabbis. Freud's father, Jakob Kalman, was born in 1815 in the town of Tyśmienica (Tysmenitz, Tysmenytsya), thirty-five miles southeast of Buczacz, and later settled in

Freiberg (Příbor) in Moravia. Sigmund, given the Jewish name Schlomo after his paternal grandfather, was born in 1856. His mother, Amalia, who came from the Galician town of Brody, was Jakob's second wife and twenty years younger than her husband. The family moved to Leipzig when Sigmund was three and the following year settled in Vienna, where the boy was raised, having no direct contact with Buczacz.[14]

And yet Freud's Galician origins did leave traces. A century later, in 1958, Freud's sixty-nine-year-old son Martin recalled in his memoir that his grandmother Amalia "came from East Galicia" and was of "Jewish stock." These "Galician Jews," he commented, "were a peculiar race, not only different from any other races inhabiting Europe, but absolutely different from Jews who had lived in the West for some generations." On the one hand, they "had little grace and no manners; and their women were certainly not what we would call 'ladies.' They were highly emotional and easily carried away by their feelings." On the other hand, "although in many respects they would seem to be untamed barbarians to more civilized people, they, alone of all minorities, stood up against the Nazis," and "fought the German army on the ruins of Warsaw." Martin firmly believed that "whenever you hear of Jews showing violence or belligerence, instead of that meekness and what seems poor-spirited acceptance of a hard fate sometimes associated with Jewish people, you may safely suspect the presence of men and women of Amalia's race."[15]

Martin Freud served as an officer in the Austro-Hungarian army in World War I and as a British soldier in World War II. As tall and broad-shouldered as his paternal grandfather, he clearly appreciated physical resistance to one's enemies, and knew very little about Galician Jewry, save for his grandmother. Three generations removed, he thought of his ancestors as an entirely different race yet took pride in what he believed to be their laudable qualities. It did not take very long to transform the *Ostjude* into a civilized European.[16] One can readily imagine that Martin borrowed some of his stereotypical images of eastern Jews from his father, whose own views were poignantly recalled in 1941, just two years after Freud's death, by Dr. Max Grunwald, in an article he published in the newspaper *Haaretz* in Palestine. Known as "one of the great figures of Jewish folklore studies," the seventy-year-old Grunwald, who had served for many years as a rabbi in Hamburg and Vienna, came to Palestine shortly after his arrest by the Austrian authorities in the wake of the Anschluss with Nazi Germany in 1938; as a young man, he had met Freud several times in pre–World War I Vienna.[17]

Their first meeting occurred in 1898, following a lecture by Grunwald on the negative representation of biblical Jewish figures in contemporary Europe. In greeting the speaker, Freud remarked "that he had imagined a Jewish rabbi in the image of John the Baptist, wearing a shaggy coat, with unkempt hair and tormented features," and was "pleasantly surprised" to see him in "an elegant tailcoat." Several years later Grunwald heard a lecture by Freud on the Code of Hammurabi, in which Freud rejected his colleague Müller's views and insisted that the Hebrew Bible and thus Judaism as a whole were indeed derived from ancient Mesopotamian mythology. Raising the issue again at their third and last encounter, Freud asserted "resolutely that the Jews had given nothing to culture" in recent times as well.[18]

One is struck by the irony of Freud's statement, considering his own incalculable impact on modern culture. His discernible influence on Agnon is only one, albeit significant, instance, both in terms of Hebrew literature generally and in linking these two singularly creative offspring of late nineteenth-century Eastern European Jewry to each other. But perhaps Freud himself was being ironic. After all, while he distanced himself from his Galician ancestry, he became increasingly fascinated with ancient Jewish mythology; in this, he had much in common with Müller. These two Jewish men made the most of the opportunities that had opened up to members of their generation, however differently they related to their own heritage, yet their personal fates were the function of changing times and circumstances: Müller, ten years older, died just before World War I as a respected Austrian scholar. Freud fled Vienna as a hunted Jew shortly after the Anschluss and lived just long enough to witness the outbreak of World War II. His four sisters were murdered in the camps. One of his last books was *Moses and Monotheism*.[19]

Radicals in Half-Asia

While Müller and Franzos never returned to their little provincial towns, others of their generation did. Fabius Nacht, Franzos's exact contemporary, was similarly raised speaking German at home in Buczacz, although the family was described as religious. As a Jew, he too was thwarted from realizing his original ambition, which in his case was to study and teach mathematics. Instead, after graduating from the Polish-language gymnasium in Stanisławów, he attended medical school at the University of Vienna, returning in 1879 to Buczacz, where he soon established himself as a respected physician and member of the community thanks to his professional stature and what people perceived as his "higher," German culture.[20]

Between 1891 and his retirement at the age of seventy-seven in 1925, Nacht served as medical director of the new Jewish hospital in Buczacz, which he had helped establish; he kept working as a private doctor until his death in 1937. In its early years, the hospital rented out the first floor as a source of extra funding. When the Baron Hirsch secondary school was opened in Buczacz in 1892—as part of a network of schools established throughout Galicia and Bukovina—it was initially housed in the hospital. The hospital also rented space to the *Folks Kiche* (soup kitchen), which had been providing cheap meals to the poor since 1890, and subsequently served free meals to indigent students at the Baron Hirsch School.[21]

Many years later, people recalled Dr. Nacht's hospital as "the most popular building in the city," an institution that was "respected and loved by all strata of the population," and had become "enmeshed in their lives." It was a modern, "two-story, unadorned white building," with "large windows" and "a low fence on either side, and a few stairs at the center leading to a strong thick door." The "large inscription, *Szpital Izraelicki*," or Israelite Hospital, on its façade was a source of communal pride. The hospital also contained the only public ice cellar in Buczacz, and after 1908 offered a shelter for the elderly on the first floor. Nacht was fortunate to pass away just before the outbreak of World War II. On 27 November 1942, the Germans and their auxiliaries deported the approximately one hundred hospital patients to the Bełżec extermination camp; those too sick to be moved were shot in their beds. Damaged in the fighting in 1944, the hospital was never repaired; all that remains of it today is an empty lot.[22]

Whereas Nacht returned to his provincial borderlands town, two of his sons ended up as radical activists very far from Galicia. Indeed, not unlike Franzos's father, Nacht was among those educated men who prepared the path for the next generation's break with the shtetl and their entry into the brave new world of the twentieth century, where all too many of them were eventually chewed up by war, revolution, and disillusionment. His son Max, whose sometimes acerbic memoir reflects decades of disappointments, broken promises, and shattered hopes, recalled in 1964: "I got my first radical indoctrination from my father, a physician, who was not in love with, and hence not very successful in, his occupation." His father, wrote Max, had "become a socialist in the early 1870s" because of the limitations imposed on him as a Jew by "the reactionary, church-ridden Vienna regime." A somewhat more generous obituary published in 1938 in the Polish Socialist Party's weekly described Nacht as "a socialist out of conviction, a freethinker without hateful intolerance . . . a rationalist filled with deep feelings," and "an internationalist who sympathized with all liberation movements."[23] It was in this home that the doctor's sons were raised.

Only a few years younger than the Nacht boys, Agnon provided his own, no less caustic depiction of the rise of socialism in Buczacz:

> At first Buczacz considered Zionism to be the greatest upheaval in the world, but eventually it saw that there were even greater upheavals. One way or the other, there is a tough war between the Zionists and the socialists in the city . . . Some see this as retribution against Zionism that brought disorder to the world and caused many lads to abandon the Torah. And some bemoan the decline of Israel and find solace in Zionism that came to save the rest of Israel from extinction. Be that as it may, the study houses are emptying . . . Buczacz, which was a capital of the Torah and the Haskalah, has become a capital of socialists that casts its influence on all its surroundings, because the socialists have a great leader from among the inhabitants of Buczacz, who has a following among the Jews and among the Gentiles, and they are willing to do whatever he orders.[24]

While many of the urban workers were Jewish, the peasants were largely Ruthenian, and the estate owners and leasers were Poles and Jews. This made for a combustible overlap of social unrest and nationalist politics, not only internally within the Jewish community between Zionists and socialists, but also between socialists and nationalists, especially among Ruthenian rural laborers and peasants. Socialism, which acquired in this region a nationalist aspect because of the ethnic division of labor, was precisely what men like Franko supported even as they moved from the left to the center of the political arena. Additionally, while it appealed to the Jewish working poor in Buczacz, socialism also caught the passion of youthful Jewish members of the very same bourgeois class they hoped to subvert. One of them was the Buczacz-born leader mentioned by Agnon, Anselm Mosler, who was a close acquaintance of and a major influence on Fabius Nacht's sons.

While Dr. Nacht was an inoffensive, agreeable, and undogmatic social democrat, his sons, who subsequently had a checkered relationship with socialism, went out into the world to blow it up, ending their lives far away in the United States. Max and his older brother Siegfried began using their father's home as a center for political activity in Buczacz, which, under the circumstances of the time, seems to have attracted only Jewish youths. Their childhood, however, was quite different. Whereas Max (officially named Maximilian and known in Buczacz as Monia) was born in Buczacz in 1881, Siegfried was born three years earlier in Vienna, and remained at his grandmother's home in the Jewish quarter of Leopoldstadt, possibly for reasons of ill health. Rejoining his family in Buczacz when he was eight years old, he recalled, was like coming to a foreign land: "I could not communicate with my brothers because they spoke only Polish and Ruthenian, and I only German."[25]

The brothers had early exposure to socialism also outside their home. Siegfried became a member of the social democratic movement already as a schoolboy, and Max, by his own account, considered himself a Marxist before turning fourteen. Because their progressive father would not send them to a cheder, and could not afford private school, they attended the regular public school, where Siegfried quickly acquired Polish and Ruthenian. As a temperamental Jewish-socialist lad he was soon expelled from the secondary school in Buczacz, transferring to the more liberal gymnasium in nearby Brzeżany. But there too he quickly became involved with a conspiratorial Polish group and was expelled again, finally graduating from his father's alma mater in Stanisławów in 1895.[26] At the age of seventeen, Siegfried was already a fairly experienced rebel.

For his part, Max, who was still living at home, joined the newly formed, first-ever workers' educational society in Buczacz, founded by Anselm Mosler. As an indication of the society's focus on class rather than nationality, it was named Bratstvo-Briderlikhkayt ("Fraternity" in Ukrainian and Yiddish). As Max recalled, Mosler was "the only citizen of our town ever to accomplish" the "intellectual feat" of earning two doctorates, in law and in philosophy, from the University of Vienna. He then tried to smuggle illegal literature across the border, was caught, arrested, and spent eighteen months in a Russian prison. Upon returning to Buczacz, Mosler established the Fraternity society, whose membership, according to Max, "was exclusively Jewish, for the Gentile workers, Roman Catholic Poles and Uniate [Greek] Catholic Ukrainians were under the influence of their respective clergymen and would not join such a society." Indeed, Buczacz at the time was just "a small place in the northeasternmost corner of Austria," made up mostly "of Yiddish-speaking Jews," while its Polish and

Ukrainian inhabitants "hated and despised each other even more than they did the Jews."[27]

Since he was one of the better educated members of the Fraternity society, Max was appointed its secretary, second only to Mosler. Soon Mosler began reaching out beyond the city limits to the Ruthenian peasants who were the majority in the district; under his leadership, the society participated in the peasant strikes that engulfed the region in 1902. Max reported enthusiastically about these events in an article he wrote that year for the Berlin-based anarchist-socialist weekly *Neues Leben* (New Life) under the headline "A Letter from Half-Asia." This German-inspired term, suggesting that Galicia constituted a borderland between the civilized West and the primitive and barbaric East, had a long life. A quarter of a century earlier Franzos titled his early collection of stories *From Half-Asia;* and as late as 1961, Hannah Arendt derisively described the Israeli citizens congregating around the Jerusalem courthouse where Adolf Eichmann was being tried as an "oriental mob," reminding her of "Istanbul or some other half-Asiatic country." Here, then, were three generations of acculturated Jews who had internalized a particular German view of the East, part of which was the depiction of Jews, or at least *Ostjuden,* as uncivilized orientals. As the young Max Nacht saw things at the dawn of the twentieth century, he was engaged in a revolutionary civilizing mission, and breathlessly reported how "the strike spread over the entire land." In the Buczacz district, he wrote, "the peasants have seized this weapon in almost all communities." In terms reminiscent of a plot by Ivan Franko, this Jewish doctor's son from provincial Buczacz depicted himself as upholding the rights of Ruthenian peasants against their Polish landlords. At the workers' association meeting, he informed his readers, "during the stormy negotiations between the estate leaser and the peasants, when I called out to the latter, urging them to persist and not to yield, they showered me with well-wishes, as well as asking me to become a minister. An anarchist minister!"[28]

For by then, Max had become an anarchist. His conversion to anarchism prompted a break with his first idol, Mosler, about whom he remained bitter to the end of his life. As he put it in his memoirs six decades later, "the idealism of Dr. Mosler was of a somewhat peculiar nature. He had me expelled from the society as soon as he noticed that, impressed by [Russian writer and activist Peter] Kropotkin's *Memoirs of a Revolutionist,* I had begun to lean toward anarchism and to propagate my creed among the members."[29] The fraternal wars of the left had come to Buczacz. Yet both young men wanted to break out of their shtetl's limits, transitioning from local politics to the world stage; this might have seemed naïve and highly unlikely, as was indeed often the case; but it was also the small beginning of what ended up as a continent-wide upheaval that moved and ultimately also destroyed millions.

True to his new anarchist convictions, Max had become committed to transforming the world by operating from the margins, but with Europe as his playground. Mosler's ambition, as Max described it, similarly "went well beyond cultivating his own garden, with its few scores of Jewish tailors, carpenters, locksmiths, salesmen, butchers, and shoemakers." His goal was "to play a more important role, both in local politics and in the Polish section of the Austrian Socialist party." Unfortunately, as Max notes sarcastically, "his first bid for leadership at one of the party's conventions . . . met with such bitter abuse that [Mosler] resigned from that party and joined the newly organized Jewish Social-Democratic Party, which had been refused recognition by both the central Austrian-Democratic (Socialist) party and its Polish section." In other words, abused as a provincial Jewish activist by Austrian and Polish socialists, Mosler responded by joining Jewish socialists. For Max, this "sudden conversion to Yiddish separatism was utterly ridiculous, particularly in the case of an assimilationist who was unable to speak Yiddish—he always spoke German in addressing the Jewish workers." But it also indicated the predicament of Jewish activists in a rapidly changing world.[30]

Indeed, Mosler's decision to join the Jewish socialist party was clearly the result of the nationalism and antisemitism of the Austrian socialists.[31] But while his conversion might have appeared ludicrous, or at least riddled with contradictions both at the time and subsequently, it was also quite common; many of the Jewish assimilationists ended up as Jewish nationalists, or Zionists, the best example being of course the "inventor" of modern Zionism, Theodor Herzl, who had a vast influence in Galicia both before and after his premature death in 1904.[32] Assimilation largely failed because of the nationalism of those groups the Jews were trying to assimilate into—an increasingly integral, ethnic nationalism that sought to exclude Jews using arguments derived from the new antisemitism that followed Jewish emancipation. What was remarkable about Mosler's conversion, however, was that even as he joined the Jewish socialist party, he also persisted in his attempts to appeal to the much larger Ruthenian population of the Buczacz district.

As Max Nacht describes this period, "at the time of his conversion to

Jewish nationalism," Mosler "was simultaneously carrying on radical propaganda among the Ukrainian peasants of the surrounding countryside.
He spoke to them in a mixture of Polish, Ukrainian, and Russian, and won
their allegiance by his violent attacks against their hated masters—the
Polish landed noblemen. He never tired of painting the bleak future that
the Ukrainian peasants faced, when eventually they would be driven from
their small strip of land and forced 'to carry water for the Jews in the city.'
At the same time he was one of the leaders of the Jewish Socialist Party!"
As Max mockingly observed, Mosler "was actually so popular among the
poor peasants that they simply could not believe their priests when, from
their pulpits, they denounced him as a Jew. For how, they reasoned, could
a Jew talk that way?"[33]

Part of Mosler's success among the peasants, according to Max, was
the result of advice he received from "Father Lototzky, a Ukrainian hunchback monk who was the religious instructor of the Uniate [Greek] Catholic pupils of the elementary school" in Buczacz. That monk, recalls Max,
"was a cynical non-believer who, as a rule, enjoyed my father's company,
for there was no religious antagonism between an atheist monk and an
agnostic Jewish physician." One day, as Mosler reportedly related to Max,
he met the monk in the woods, and "the conversation that ensued" between
the unbelieving Christian and the "brilliant former pupil of his school,"
according to Max, "was quite possibly a milestone in that radical agitator's
life." The monk ridiculed the young lawyer for thinking he was a popular
speaker because in fact, he asserted, "What you keep saying to those benighted hicks has absolutely no effect on them." The reason was the same
that all demagogues quickly learn: "You are telling them far too much—so
they don't remember anything." Instead, the monk recommended, "never
give them more than two or three simple ideas, very simple ones, of course,
and repeat them every five minutes, over and over again. Otherwise you
won't get anywhere with those illiterate yokels." And Max concludes:
"Needless to say, Dr. Mosler religiously followed the irreligious monk's
advice, with the result that he became one of the most popular peasant
agitators in eastern Galicia."[34]

Of Peasants and Herrings

In fact, there was much more to Mosler's popularity. As it turns out, in 1905
he launched, edited, and largely wrote a local bilingual Polish-Ukrainian
monthly newsletter titled *Służba dworska* (The Manor Service), of which

five issues were published. Describing itself as "a periodical for farm laborers of the Buczacz district and other districts of Podolia," the newsletter demanded social justice for workers and servants on manorial estates.
The largely illiterate peasants had no health or retirement benefits, were
ignorant of their rights and vulnerable to all manner of exploitation, while
the estate owners used the state's fear of peasant uprisings to demand suppression of protests with armed police and military units. As part of its
self-designated task of enlightening the peasants, Mosler's newsletter also
published their own accounts of conditions in the countryside.[35]

Trying to allay the farm laborers' fear that they would be punished for
possessing his newsletter, Mosler promised that "the editorial office will
notify the military police headquarters and the military court" of confis-
cations of the newsletter and would "take to court" any landowner who
"threatens a farm worker." He then called upon "whoever was harmed or
has learned about someone else's grievance" to "write about it to the editorial staff," and vowed to "print everything, except for the writer's name,
so that no one would be afraid of retribution."[36]

Mosler's aim was to publicize all such cases in which the manor workers were subjected to arbitrary "justice without established proceedings,"
were "beaten and insulted with impunity," received no assistance, and were
"left to perish like a dog" when they fell ill or were injured at work, even
as their "lords go abroad to health resorts, to waste the money you have
worked so hard for." For instance, the twenty-one-year-old Łuć Baran had
choked to death while cleaning a container in Mr. Serwatowski's alcohol
distillery near the town of Monasterzyska, but since the state attorney
found no grounds for prosecuting the owner, the widow received no compensation. Wasyl Hnydka, also aged twenty-one, who was kicked by a horse
and severely injured, was simply expelled by the owner "from the farm,
without calling a doctor or giving him money for medication or for living
expenses." The twenty-two-year-old Wasyl Kordowski died of severe burns
in Srulek Stein's distillery, described as "a real death-trap," since he was the
fifth such victim, yet no one was punished. "Do we live among wild beasts?"
exclaimed Mosler. "Aren't there any laws applying to what the lords and
the owners can do?" From this perspective, he remarked, it made no difference "whether this is a leaseholder with sidelocks, a nobleman with a
long aristocratic pedigree, or a newly-made lord—none of them abides by
the law and no one punishes them." Here reigned an equality of impunity:
"When Srulko Stein washes himself, puts on his fur coat and goes to the
rabbi—the miracle-maker of Czortków—or when Władysław Serwatowski
rides his four-horse carriage to the industrial exhibition, no one sees the

Ilko Szesterniak, from *Służba dworska*,
no. 2, 1905, p. 2. This local, bilingual
Polish-Ukrainian monthly newsletter,
whose title translates as The Manor Service,
published only five issues. Library of the
Polish Parliament.

blood of the dead farmhands on their gold coins or the tears and despair of the unfortunate widows and orphans."[37]

The ultimately wretched fate of such activist idealists as Mosler should not take away from the role they played in awakening the consciousness of the downtrodden of Galicia, and perhaps also in stirring the conscience of some of those who were keeping them down. Just as Nathan Hanover expressed sympathy for the serfs who rose up against their tormentors in the mid-seventeenth century, Mosler's newsletter sought to give a face to the invisible multitudes of suffering peasants and farmhands in the last years of the Austro-Hungarian Empire, create a sense of solidarity among them, and provide them with some tools to fight for their interests. In this he was not unlike Franko, although he is no longer remembered in Galicia and not a single photograph of him is known to have survived.

We do, however, have a photograph of one farm laborer, whose identity and fate Mosler rescued from among the faceless, nameless, browbeaten, and forgotten masses. Why, asks Mosler rhetorically, is he featured on the second page of the newsletter? Was he a king, who feasted while his people starved, or perhaps a general, whose soldiers bled on the battlefield while he basked in glory? No, he answers, "Ilko Szesterniak—the son of Kieryła," is "an ordinary peasant—a manor laborer" from Kościelniki (Kostilnyky, fourteen miles south of Buczacz) on the Dniester. So why was he photographed? The photo had been taken "to commemorate his fifty years of service on the same farm," half a century of work "from dawn to night . . . on weekdays and holidays," often "beaten with whips and fists," unable to feed his family sufficiently or to educate his children. This man, writes Mosler, had "lived the same life as thousands of other people in Ruthenia and in Masuria." Yet shortly after the photo was taken, he "was expelled from the manor." Now "Ilko is dying of hunger. He will die without leaving anything to his children and grandchildren who will share his fate: Kseńka, his 13-year-old granddaughter already works as a servant at the manor."[38]

There were many more such stories of abuse and exploitation in Mosler's newsletter, including some from the village of Kośmierzyn (Kosmyryn), where my mother was born two decades later.[39] Many laborers were clearly grateful to the young lawyer who fought for their cause. A blacksmith from the village of Zarudzie (Zaruddya) in the Buczacz district wrote to the newsletter, "I can see that it is dedicated to people like me," manor laborers "forced to obey some people who are not worth a single finger of an honest, hardworking man." The people he had in mind were the local leaseholder and former tavernkeeper, the Jew Arnold Fried, who treated the peasants badly; his wife, who "resembles a Jewish cook"; and his daughter, an insolent "little Jewish girl." Helping them maintain their tyrannical rule was the steward Tomek Szpunar, "notorious in this area" as "the manor's beater and executioner." A ditty written and sent to the newsletter by the blacksmith about Szpunar's exploits and his masters' greed was said to be "sung by boys everywhere":

In Szpunar's old hut,
The chimney's collapsed.
His wife's run away,
Because Szpunar is nuts.

At the lord's manor house,
Szpunar serves and attends,
And from morning to night,
Blows and curses he rains . . .

When summer arrives,
There is peace on the farm,
Szpunar's gone to the field.
And the hamlet is calm . . .

But when leading your cow,
To the master's domain,
Madly Szpunar springs up,
And approaches again.

He drives off your cow,
And he drives off your heifer.
As a pledge he will take,
Both your sheepskin and jacket.

In the morning comes Szpunar
To his lord with the loot:
"Get up, Your Honor,
I have earned my reward."

When his lordship awakens,
Upon seeing the plunder,
His joy is so great,
That his mind goes asunder.

"Hand me some brandy,
Hand him one too."
"Chaim—Szpunar!"—"Szulim—my lord!"
What excellent servants I have at my door.

Her ladyship too,
Is thrilled to the core.
For breakfast she hands out
Smelly herrings galore.[40]

Mosler was fanning socialism; but the sense of injustice and resentment among the peasants often translated into rage at the Jews. His career as an agitator did not last long after the demise of his newsletter, and his life came to an early end in Vienna during World War I, when he succumbed to the tuberculosis he had contracted in the Russian prison as a newly minted agitator.

The World Is Becoming Ever Uglier

But Mosler did make one last, ghostly appearance in Agnon's novel *A Guest for the Night*, published two decades after his death, under the evocative name Knabenhut, which can be read as "boys' guardian" in German. Based on Agnon's last visit to his hometown in 1930, the novel depicts his protagonist's encounter with a character bearing a striking resemblance to Max Nacht in Szybusz, the name Agnon gave to Buczacz in his fiction.

> A man came up to me, stopped me, looked at me for a while, and said, "Tell me, aren't you so-and-so, my friend?" He stretched out both hands and greeted me. I greeted him back and said to him, "You are Aharon Schützling, what are you doing here? Don't you live in America?" He said to me, "And what are you doing here? I thought you were living over there in Eretz Israel." I said to him, "It appears that both of us were mistaken about the other." Aharon nodded and said, "Yes, my friend, both of us were mistaken about the other. I am not living in America. And you, if I may judge by what I see, are not living in Eretz Israel. Not only that, when I observe us, it appears to me that there is no America or Eretz Israel in the world, but only Szybusz. Or perhaps even Szybusz doesn't exist, and only its name exists."

Both the narrator and Schützling have been away from their hometown for many years and are keenly aware of how profoundly both the city and their own outlooks have changed since their departure. "We were about seventeen or eighteen," recalls Agnon's protagonist, and "although we differed in our opinions, for I was a Zionist and he an anarchist, we were glad to talk to each other." Neither man's hopes have been realized. At the time, he remembers, Schützling

> would often tease me and call me a bourgeois of the next world, because I studied the Torah and preached for Zion. And I would enrage him by conceding some of his arguments and saying that

there is no need for kings, since the King Messiah is destined to reign over the entire world. So many years have passed since that time. So many kings have toppled from their thrones, and still the Son of David has not come . . . But that man returned and is in Szybusz. And he is like a bridegroom who went to marry a woman, only to find her sorrowful and ill, and so he returned home, wearing all his finery, but he has no pleasure in it, for dejection has dried his bones and his clothes are too opulent. He tries to put on his old clothes, but cannot find them, for he had already discarded them.

This is the condition of the exile, who can never find what he was looking for in his new land yet can never return to the same home he left behind. This is the condition of those who abandon their hometowns around the world and, having changed in the process, also find their towns unrecognizably transformed when they come for a visit, both because of circumstances and because they no longer see them with the same eyes. This was all the more the condition of those who, like Agnon, looked in on their towns after the devastation of World War I, and, most radically, of those few who survived the Holocaust and returned, however briefly, to their former homes, seeing them inhabited by people they had never known, and being perceived by these new owners as a threatening reminder of a crime for which few were punished in a court of law and many were rewarded with material gains.

The two friends decide to have a drink together and mull over their respective exiles and their temporary return to their common hometown:

My friend said to me, "Meanwhile you have been in the great world." "And you?" "So have I." "And we returned from there." "In the past, when we used to stroll in the streets of Szybusz, it never occurred to us that we would travel to far-off lands." "And when we were in far-off lands, it never occurred to us that we would come back here." He said, "Perhaps it never occurred to you that you would come back, but I always wanted to return here." Why was he drawn to this place? Because he was not drawn to America. I said to him, "And now that you are back, you don't live in Szybusz." He smiled and said, "In this world nothing is perfect. And if you wish, I'll tell you, the tragedy of my life is that I do not live in Szybusz." I said to him, "You like Szybusz that much?" Schützling said, "When you realize that you don't like any place in the world, you fool yourself and say that you like your own town. And you, do you like Szybusz?" "I? I have still not thought it over." My friend took my hand and said, "In that case I'll tell you; all your love for Eretz Israel comes to you from Szybusz. Because you love your town, you love Eretz Israel." "How do you know that I love Szybusz?" "You need evidence? Had you not loved Szybusz, would you have been preoccupied with it your entire life, would you have been digging up tombstones to find its secrets?"

Before they part for the night, the narrator asks Schützling about his children. Schützling's response gives a measure of his sense of dislocation, loss, and missed opportunities, and the tragic fate of his own offspring:

He began counting on his fingers, "Two boys that my first wife brought with her from her first husband, and one from her second husband, and three girls that she had with me, and one boy that I had with the American, and my first boy who was born of the brunette seamstress. Do you remember that charming brunette? She forgave me before she died. From this son I have contentment. From the day his mother died he sends me money and clothes. And even now I have come with his money to see whether I can open a bakery here. My father's son has grown tired of acting as a sales agent of all kinds of nonsense and wishes to take up his father's trade. But this is a vain hope. One cannot say that Szybusz needs no bread, but there is no one to pay the baker."

Schützling's other children appear to have trodden the same path as he did, with little hope of success or long-term survival:

"My youngest daughter was arrested for communist activity, and her older sister was arrested with her, although she was completely innocent, and the middle one escaped so as not to be arrested, since she was the one who started it all. Gone are the good times when one could express one's opinion without being punished for it. This republic [Poland] is stricter than the emperor. You would think that it would not care much if a high school student bows before Lenin; did my friends and I cause any harm as anarchists? The two girls have been in prison now for eight months and I doubt they'll be released any time soon. If you like, I have already somewhat come to terms with this, but I am sorry about my youngest boy, the child I have from the American. Perhaps you can suggest some way for me to save him from ruin, so that he will not follow his sisters' path? Should I send him to Eretz Israel? But there, too, there is trouble and suffering, riots, and communists." I said, "The fathers gathered the kindling, and the sons started the fire."

Schützling finally asks the narrator about his life in Palestine:

"What have I done? I have still not done anything." "You are being modest, my friend." "I am not modest, but when you see that most of your time has gone by and you are still at the beginning of your work, you cannot say that you have done anything. As it is said in the Gemara [the interpretive portion of the Talmud], 'He who has not seen the Temple built in his lifetime, it is as if it was destroyed in his lifetime.' I refer not to the Temple, but as a metaphor for all our deeds in Eretz Israel."

Thinking back about all their hopes as young men of changing the world and altering the course of history, Schützling comes to his own conclusion about the parallel inefficacy of Zionism and anarchism: "You will not build just as we have not destroyed. What are we and who are we in this great and terrible world?" Curiously, this thought, and the significant amount of brandy he has already drunk at this point, takes Schützling back to his first love and the mother of his firstborn: "Do you remember that song the charming brunette used to sing? Let's drink to her memory and sing her song:

My years have passed in pain and wrath,
I've known no joy or blessing.
I spent my days in futile grief,
Sleep now, sleep now my baby."[41]

The following evening the two meet again. As they stroll in the town under a moonlit sky, the two friends recall Knabenhut, the character based on Mosler. His name brings back a host of memories from the heady days of their youth. Knabenhut, says Schützling, "is dead and gone. It was through him that I got to know her at the time of the tailors' strike. Those were the days. Such days will never return. Strikes during the day and wild parties at night. Knabenhut did not take part in the parties and did not dance with the girls and was not jealous of whoever was lucky and found himself a pretty girl."

Then Schützling recalls his last meeting with Knabenhut, his first mentor and hero:

> During the war I made my way to Vienna and found him standing on a bridge over the Danube, gazing at the passersby. I wanted to walk by him silently, so as not to awaken his early rage at me, when he was angry with me for becoming an anarchist, and some speculated that he had denounced me to the authorities, and I had to flee to America. He beckoned to me, and I walked over to him. He said to me, "Don't come close, I am gravely ill." I stood at some distance from him. He began lecturing about the war and the destruction that is in store for us and the entire world. His voice was weak, but his words were bold and eloquent. And again, I was standing before him as in the early days, when he had taken me in from my father's hearth and opened my eyes with his words. Finally, he whispered to me, "This generation that is about to come will be worse than all the generations that preceded us. And I will tell you one more thing, the world is becoming ever uglier, more than either I or you had sought to make it."

With this, the two friends arrive back at the narrator's hotel. As they part, the narrator watches his friend walk on down the street, humming to himself: "I spent my days in futile grief / Sleep now, sleep now my baby."

Max Nacht himself never visited Vienna during World War I; by then he was living in the United States. But Knabenhut's words were as prophetic as Mosler's actions at the turn of that century were noble. As Schützling walks off into the moonlit night, Agnon's protagonist ruminates:

> It had been years since I thought of Knabenhut, although I should have remembered him, for there had been no one in Szybusz before the war who was talked about as much as Knabenhut, and we had never had a time in which he had not excited the city, for he would call public meetings and preach to the socialists, whom he had created and established, and he had organized the first tailors' strike,

and had gathered ten thousand reapers during the harvest, calling them not to return to work unless their demands were met and their pay was raised, since more than they depended on their masters, their masters depended on them, and he kept them from working for three days, until the government dispatched a battalion of policemen to send them back to work, and Knabenhut had taught them that no regime could coerce them to do that. And when the policemen mounted their bayonets, Knabenhut drew them with words, until the bayonets faltered in their hands, and they came close to joining their striking brethren. There have been some people from Szybusz, who acquired fame in the world and acquired fame in Szybusz, but we did not feel their presence as we did Knabenhut's, because while they added to what we knew, Knabenhut taught us things of which we had never heard before.[42]

As the narrator sees it, "at the beginning, when the world was based on the Torah, Buczacz produced rabbis. After that it produced sages. After that it produced activists, and they gave us only a whiff of actions, but when Knabenhut became engaged in public affairs, he poured actions upon us, as one would pour out of a barrel." In recalling Knabenhut's efforts to ease the plight of the downtrodden in Buczacz and its environs, without distinguishing between ethnicity and creed, his attempts to raise them from the dust and help them stand up for themselves, before he, too, was swept by fate, the narrator laments his long forgotten contemporary, whose star shone for a while and was then extinguished by the circumstances of the time and Knabenhut's own nature.

Knabenhut's actions were meant well; the actions of others, those who followed him or his ideas, were not always meant well, at least not for everyone. They wanted power, control, and the realization of a utopia, whereas Knabenhut wanted to lift up the lowly, the marginalized, and the ignorant:

There were wretched lads in the city, poor boys of poor families, shop assistants and laborers, who were treated like beasts, tyrannized day and night by their masters. Then Knabenhut came along, gathered them together, rented them a room, and lectured to them on the natural sciences and social theory, until they straightened their backs and lifted up their heads. Some of them followed him for the rest of their lives and were willing to go through fire and water for him, and some of them betrayed him and falsified his teachings. And when they reached the position of their masters and stood on their own, they behaved just as their masters had previously done.

Knabenhut, recalls the narrator, "did not take to heart those who betrayed him and when the opportunity came, he did not pay them back." One of his disciples was Schützling, who "initially was devoted to his teacher more than all the others," for which reason his subsequent betrayal hurt more than all the others. The cause of this betrayal was Sigmund Winter—Siegfried Nacht's literary persona. It was Winter who persuaded Schützling that their master Knabenhut "was deluded, since he wanted to repair the world through socialism whereas the world can only be repaired through eradication." This Winter, the narrator tells us, was "the son of a doctor," who was "distinguished from his friends by his black hair and beautiful eyes, which he would fix on the girls," but "he was not distinguished in his studies and would move from one gymnasium to another." Eventually, Winter went to university, and for many years was not heard of, until "one day a rumor spread in the town that he had been arrested in Gibraltar for something that the mind cannot grasp, which, had it not been reported in the newspapers, no one would have believed, that he was suspected of attempting to assassinate a king who was passing through that state." Adding to the town's astonishment, the Austrian government intervened on behalf of its citizen and Winter was released. Not long thereafter he was back in Buczacz, walking down the street "as if all of Szybusz belonged to him," accompanied by "beautiful maidens from the best families, and all the officials making way for him," in a scene resembling Mordecai the Jew's triumphant march through the city of Shushan following his victory over Haman the Agagite.[43]

Agnon's narrator has a jaundiced view of such young revolutionaries. "Why did Winter return to Szybusz? If he really wanted to assassinate a king, Szybusz has no kings. And in any case, what harm have the kings done to him that he wants to irritate them? And if he is an anarchist, what of it? People have all kinds of opinions, one more peculiar than the other, and if everyone acted on them, what would the world look like?" But Knabenhut, the narrator believes, was something different.

I was not attracted to Knabenhut or to his opinions, but I thought about him a great deal. Power is a great virtue; renunciation is even greater. When both inhabit the same person, we admire him. These two virtues distinguished Knabenhut. He demonstrated the power of his deeds and renounced himself. At times his means were false, and his goal was righteous, at times his means were righteous, and his goal was false; but in neither case did we ever hear that he looked after his own interests . . . When they tried to bribe him with a good post, he rejected their offer. Moreover, he abandoned the study of philosophy and such matters and studied the law, and did not make it into an instrument of profit, but helped the needy even without compensation, and would take loans on credit so as to finance the strikes . . . Knabenhut did not chase women, and did not strive to become a deputy in parliament, and did not seek any other honors for himself. This is not to say that Szybusz lacked idealists, but to be frank, how much did it cost them? . . . Whereas Knabenhut rented and furnished a house for his comrades and brought them books and magazines and learned to speak Yiddish, so that he could speak with his comrades in their tongue. Which is not the case with most of our leaders, who are too lazy even to acquire the Hebrew alphabet.

Like many true idealists, Knabenhut ended up badly. After breaking with his increasingly radicalized disciples, his life gradually fell apart. The woman he loved married another, and the woman he married, he did not love. Since he practiced law to help the poor, he lived on his wife's dowry until it ran out. As Schützling relates to the narrator in their last meeting, at that point Knabenhut "went back to the love of his youth, namely philosophy, and abandoned his mistress, the practice of the law. As for real women, he did the opposite: he abandoned his wife in favor of his mistresses." And so he spent his days "lying in bed reading Sophocles or spending time with women," until his wife left him. And when the war came, he ended up in Vienna, where "his old friends did not recognize him, and he did not make new ones." Eventually he locked himself in and "did not leave his room, until the one against whom no door is locked came and took him from the world. This world that is growing even uglier than Knabenhut and his comrades had wished to make it."[44]

CHAPTER TEN

Wild Sheep

Wandering Anarchists

THE LIVES OF THE historical Nacht brothers extended beyond the scope of Agnon's 1939 novel. By the time Agnon and Max Nacht died, just three years apart, their early ideological differences had been largely eroded by the historical events that separated them from their youth; one can imagine them taking one final stroll on a moonlit night in Jerusalem, or perhaps even New York, and resuming the conversation their literary personas had struck up midway between the world wars.

Whether or not it was in fact Siegfried Nacht who broke up Mosler's fraternity by persuading his younger brother of the superior qualities of anarchism, once he graduated from the gymnasium in Stanisławów, Siegfried left Galicia to study electrical engineering at the technical university in Vienna. But because he was a Jew, a socialist activist, and the founder of an electricians' trade union, the degree he acquired did not help him find employment in his profession; forced to work as an assistant fitter, a physically challenging and poorly paid job, he found it hard to keep body and soul together. These circumstances may have further radicalized him, and while he grew closer to Austrian social democracy, he became a severe critic of all national movements, not least of Zionism, and in 1897 he officially severed his links with the Jewish community of Vienna. Yet within a year, Siegfried became just as disenchanted with what he perceived as the nationalism, parliamentary orientation, and increasingly antisemitic rhetoric of Vienna's social democracy, left the party, and moved to Berlin.[1]

That same year Max arrived in Vienna. His choice of profession was clearly influenced by his grudging admiration for his first idol, Mosler. Looking back, he was struck by the irony of that decision, made by a then newly minted anarchist, for "while professing a philosophy which rejected all laws as tyrannical and unnecessary restrictions of personal liberty, I studied law at the university of Vienna." In part, this was a practical move, because while he was apparently more interested in "philosophy, or any other branch of the humanities," such disciplines "offered no prospects to a non-Christian in the semi-medieval Habsburg Empire." In that sense, he was still operating under the same constraints as his father decades earlier.

But these contradictions were quickly resolved with the abrupt termination of Max's law studies. As a committed activist, soon after coming to Vienna he joined forces with another student, the young Ukrainian poet, journalist, political agitator, and fellow anarchist Mikhailo Lozynsky. Together, they established "the first anarchist periodical in the Polish language"—a curious linguistic choice for this Ukrainian-Jewish pair, necessitated by the fact that "Polish at that time was the lingua franca of all Galicians, Poles, Ukrainians, and Jews." They managed to publish just one issue before being charged by the authorities with high treason, leading to Lozynsky's arrest.

Max, for his part, managed to escape, ending up in Switzerland, where he remained until 1907. Along with his brother Siegfried, he worked as editor and writer for the militant anarchist journal *Der Weckruf* (The Wake-up Call), living first in Zurich and then in Geneva. His hurried departure from Vienna, as Max later remarked, not only changed the course of his professional life, but also saved him from the fate that awaited the residents of the Austrian capital, especially its Jews, over the following half-century: "I sometimes shudder," he wrote, "when I reflect what my life—and my death—might have been like if Mikhailo Lozynsky had not crossed my path. For in that case I most likely would have remained in Austria to die for my Emperor during World War I, or, in case of survival, to be gassed by Eichmann during World War II."[2]

As for Lozynsky, his fate epitomized the tragedy of young Ukrainian activists of that generation. While Max became an itinerant anarchist and subsequently a critic of European radicalism and totalitarianism from the shores of America, Lozynsky became a Ukrainian nationalist, a Soviet supporter, and, like so many other names mentioned in Max's memoir, one of

Stalin's innumerable victims. Lozynsky's anarchism, writes Max, was "the rabid expression of a nationalist intellectual's protest against the Austro-Polish landed nobility who—with Vienna's approval—were oppressing four million Ukrainian peasants in that godforsaken corner of the Habsburg monarchy," namely, Galicia. To his mind, "Lozynsky's 'negation' of the state, in abstracto, for his great-great-grandchildren, as it were, did not prevent him from dreaming of a democratic Ukrainian Republic in a less distant future, one that would embrace all the Ukrainian-speaking subjects of Russia, Austria, and Hungary. He had in mind a republic that would be ruled by men like himself, men of peasant stock who at the same time were poets, public speakers, and fluent writers." These men included members of the older generation, such as Ivan Franko, but also the younger Stepan Bandera, born in the village of Uhrynów Stary (Strayi Uhryniv, sixty miles west of Buczacz) in 1909. Bandera, who emerged as a radical nationalist leader in the interwar period, was neither a democrat nor a writer, but rather a new type of integral nationalist, with strong fascist sympathies and a penchant for indiscriminate violence.[3]

To be sure, as Max observes, Lozynsky "was certainly not aware of his subconscious cravings, nor was I conscious of what it was that made me tick." But years later, Max heard from a fellow Ukrainian in New York that "Lozynsky had taken part in the armed struggle for Ukrainian independence after the resurrection of Poland at the end of World War I," and that "after the collapse of the short-lived Western Ukrainian Republic," he "had fled to the once-tsarist Eastern Ukraine, which was fighting for its own independence against the newly established Russian Bolshevik regime." Once that effort also collapsed, "Lozynsky, along with most Ukrainian intellectuals, capitulated to Moscow, taking a job with one of the Ukrainian scientific institutions in Kiev, but refusing to join the Communist Party." Finally, "during the great purges of 1936–1938 Lozynsky, then the head of the Ukrainian Sociological Institute, was shot along with all the other well-known Ukrainian intellectuals who had ever shown any Ukrainian nationalist inclination."[4]

The subsequent history of the Nacht brothers in the years leading to World War I is a patchwork of great expectations, increasing disillusionments, and mediocre accomplishments, in the course of lives lived mostly on the move, often with very limited material resources. The real Siegfried, just like his literary embodiment Winter, was indeed arrested upon entering Gibraltar in April 1903 on suspicion of plotting to assassinate King Edward VII during his planned visit to the British territory. Upon receiving the news, Max immediately organized a protest "assembly of Ruthenian socialist workers" in Vienna, while additional protests were made by Polish political activists in Paris, and a committee formed for this purpose in London, with such eminent members as Peter Kropotkin and the philosopher Herbert Spencer.

Thanks to the new miracle of the telegraph, news of Siegfried's release on 5 May for lack of evidence reached Buczacz that same day, prompting "hundreds" of well-wishers to converge on Fabius Nacht's house to bring him the good tidings. Previously known in his hometown as "the locksmith"—on account of people's vague understanding of electrical engineering—Siegfried was propelled to local fame by coverage of the event in the Polish press. As Max snickered, "it was written, black on white, that he was an engineer, an author, and whatever else, and that a former minister, a real countess, [and] an actual prince had come out in his support." All of a sudden, "the relatives and friends of the freed man were besieged from all sides with questions, when would 'he' be coming to Buczacz, since all were already curious to have a glimpse of this eighth wonder of the world, who had fortunately eluded the gallows."[5]

Agnon also recalled Siegfried's moment of fame, depicted in his humorous account of the anarchist's literary persona, Winter. Shortly after the local hero's visit to his hometown, he writes,

> newspapers arrived in Szybusz with pictures of Kropotkin, [Russian revolutionary and anarchist ideologue Mikhail] Bakunin, and [French geographer, writer, and anarchist Jacques Élisée] Reclus, and among them was also a picture of Sigmund Winter. My Lord, my Lord, never before had Szybusz merited a young man to have his picture published, let alone with such world-renowned figures. The truth be told, we had no idea who were Kropotkin, Bakunin, and Reclus, but we could tell that they were great people, since otherwise their pictures would not have been published in the newspapers. And the fact is that we were not wrong, because those in the know related that the first two were princes and sons of princes, and the third, Élisée Reclus, was a professor at the university.[6]

But shortly thereafter, Siegfried slipped back into obscurity. In 1912 he immigrated to the United States, where he changed his name to Stephen Naft; he was joined there by his brother, who appropriately changed his name to Max Nomad, the following year. The two lived for the rest of their lives in New York City. Siegfried's most lasting claim to fame to this day appears to be the anarchist pamphlet "The Social General Strike," published in German under his name in London in 1902, and reissued under the pseudonym Arnold Roller in 1905; it can still be found under that name in English translation on the Internet.[7] He died aged seventy-eight in 1956. The brief obituary in the *New York Times* described Stephen Naft as "an electrical engineer in Vienna, London, Berlin, Paris, and other cities in his youth and a speaker and writer in many parts of Europe for syndicalism, a movement advocating the control of industry by councils of workers. The workers would take over by means of general strikes. He tramped on foot across the Alps and Pyrenees and through Spain and North Africa in the interests of his political beliefs." As the *Times* concluded, after coming to the United States, Naft "was much less active politically," working "for ten years as head of the translation bureau—he spoke six languages," and later employed by "foreign-language news services."[8] The young rebel, it seems, had been finally tamed by age and circumstances.

In trying to understand the lure of radicalism during their youth, Max Nacht commented that "of all the various ideologies that, at the turn of the century, were attracting young intellectuals or semi-intellectuals," men such as himself and his older brother "embraced anarchism which, for all its utopianism, expressed most violently the educated underdog's resentment."[9] These two "wild sheep" from Buczacz, as their biographer calls them, went far, though one might also say that they got nowhere. Yet unlike his older brother, Max did achieve a certain notoriety also in American radical circles as the author of several books and many essays, and as a lecturer at a number of universities in New York. One of his best known books, *Aspects of Revolt*, published in 1961 under his American name, has, among other things, the distinction of including an introductory essay by none other than the eminent critic Edmund Wilson, whose own book, *To the Finland Station*, I admired in my own more socialist youth.[10] Wilson writes about the author:

> What, then, is the fascination that revolution exerts for Max Nomad? What has made him a connoisseur of radicals? In order to understand Nomad's point of view, you must know that he was born in Poland and that, as he tells us in the preface to this latest book, he was "a Socialist in my high-school days, an Anarchist as a college student, a Syndicalist sui generis during the years of my romantic and not-so-romantic vagabondage, and finally a Soviet

sympathizer some forty years ago when Lenin and Trotsky were still glorious legends, between 1917 and 1920."

As Wilson observes, when comparing *Aspects of Revolt* with the books Nomad published during the interwar period, such as *Rebels and Renegades* and *Apostles of Revolution*, "one sees that before the last war Max Nomad, though quite non-utopian, still retained a little more of his original radical faith. At the end of the second of these [books], he expressed the hope that 'out of this bloody welter may emerge a European Union of Democratic Socialist Republics, equally remote from the jungle of capitalist chaos and from the graveyard of Fascist or "Communist" totalitarianism.'"

But that modest optimism waned in the wake of World War II, remarks Wilson, who notably makes no mention of the Holocaust. Still, even at this sober moment, Nomad "has not allowed himself to become a cynic. In the preface to *Aspects of Revolt*, which is, I suppose, his real testament, 'I have no use,' he says, 'for those snobs, whether Nietzscheans or plain Babbitts, who look down with contempt upon the crowd; yet I cannot help realizing that the masses are hopelessly benighted and gullible, ready to submit to any form of servitude, either sanctioned by tradition or ushered in by demagogues and adventurers after the long overdue collapse of the old regime.'"

Father Lototzky, that long-dead Ukrainian hunchback monk, who trained Anselm Mosler to propagate socialism in the countryside at the beginning of the twentieth century, would have heartily agreed with Nomad's views about the ignorance of the masses and their susceptibility to demagogy and authoritarianism. But whereas the monk was speaking about illiterate Ruthenian peasants, Nomad applies this insight to people everywhere. Perhaps, as Wilson suggests, Nomad had not become entirely cynical, but there is little doubt that by this point in his life he had acquired a rather dim view of humankind. Still, Wilson insists on a more optimistic interpretation; as he elegantly puts it, "although also 'disenchanted,'" *Aspects of Revolt* "is the most impressive example [Nomad] has given us of his good will and his fundamental humanity as well as his immense multilingual learning and his inquiring comprehensive intelligence."[11]

Nomad's final statement on the matter came three years later, at the age of eighty-three, with the publication of his memoir, tellingly titled *Dreamers Dynamiters and Demagogues*. In it, he offered what he called a "merciless analysis of the author by the author himself," tracing his beginnings to his father's choice to become a physician, and wondering, "did my father also infect me with his 'mania of smallness'?" By this he means both Fabius Nacht's "feeling of inadequacy" in the profession he was compelled to take up as a Jew in an antisemitic empire all those decades ago, and possibly also the father's decision to go back to his provincial hometown. In hindsight, Nomad proposes that "perhaps as a compensation for my shyness and physical weakness, I greedily absorbed all the radical and modern ideas both in politics and literature. This gave me an edge on my stronger and smarter, but more 'normal,' i.e., less civilized, schoolmates." But this final psychological explanation must also be placed within a social and political context. For this sense of inadequacy had just as much to do with where one came from and how one was categorized; being a Jew from a Galician shtetl, or a Ruthenian peasant from a wretched village, when not entirely debilitating as was so often the case, could provide an impetus to radical action in compensation for such "objective" circumstances, or what we might term today systemic marginalization.

To his credit, over the long arc of his life, from the heady days of strikes in the daytime and wild parties at night in turn-of-the century Buczacz, to old age in Washington Heights, where he passed away aged ninety-two in 1973, Nomad had retained his belief in the need to struggle for justice, even as he had grown disillusioned about the prospects of success. His view of humanity in his eighties was bleaker than ever; and we might concede that some of his insights are as true today, almost six decades later, as they were when he wrote his final observations. But while he abandoned "the illusions and contradictions of anarcho-syndicalism," and then gave up those "optimistic hopes for a 'final revolution' that could put an end to all oppression and exploitation," he did come up with his own "conception of the 'permanent revolution'—permanent in the sense of a never-ending struggle of the eternal underdog for 'more and more now' against the ever-recurring elites ruling the majority of the human race." It was from his position as a perpetual outsider that he could state: "I have never learned to shed my indignation at those injustices and at the backsliding and the opportunism of those erstwhile rebels who have accepted the role of either partners of the beneficiaries of the status quo, or of office-holding and managerial inheritors of the eliminated capitalists."

That indignation was, as Nomad put it, "a remnant of the utopian enthusiasm of my youth," and of his refusal "to accept this 'natural' scheme of things with equanimity." This, finally, was the cause of his "utter pessimism or 'despair,'" which, to use a phrase of Bernard Shaw's, is 'the lot of man who sees life truly and thinks about it romantically.'"

That despair was deepened by Nomad's conclusion, based on observing the events of the twentieth century, that "aside from occasional saints, the common man's concept of justice, fair play, and human kindness is as a rule on the same level as—and often below—that of his cruel masters." Hence, he believed, "those who claim that the masses can be 'redeemed'" are either naïve or hypocritical. But this did not lead him to remain "indifferent to the plight of the poor for all their gullibility, servility, and bestiality." Rather, he supported "the greatest possible extension of welfare state measures and similar incursions into the pocketbooks of the rich," if only because this "alone can prevent the recurrence of situations that would enable totalitarian demagogues of any hue to seize power by pandering to the resentments of the hungry and therefore bloodthirsty mob of unemployed or underpaid manual or white-collar workers."[12] How true this rings in our time!

The twentieth century did not pan out as Siegfried and Max had hoped when they first set out from Buczacz. In some ways it is remarkable that precisely these two men, who were, so to speak, looking for trouble from the very beginning, survived it for so long, coming out on the other side of Nazism and Stalinism and two world wars relatively unscathed. But of course, it was precisely their radicalism that made them seek shelter in the United States, that haven of capitalism that they and their father had always disparaged. No wonder that toward the end of his life, Max Nacht, or Nomad, who never forgot his origins, wrote such a scathing critique of everything and everyone he had believed in. And yet, like many of his generation—like many people in general—he was not as honest as he would have liked us to believe, not just because he might have been unfair to the many friends and colleagues, co-conspirators, and fellow revolutionaries he had associated with over a long and busy life, but also because he had a skeleton in his closet that I happened upon quite by accident.

My Years Have Passed in Pain and Wrath

History has a strange way of returning, resurfacing long after the protagonists, heroes and villains alike, are long dead, infusing new meanings into our retrospective understanding of their lives, ones they themselves might have denied or never really known. On 22 March 2010, I received a letter from Dr. Alain Kanfer, a retired physician living in Paris. As it turned out, Kanfer was Dr. Fabius Nacht's great-grandson, though he was unaware at the time of his ancestry. Perhaps the medical profession was in the family genes after all, and not just a product of Habsburg antisemitism. In December of that year, we met at a Parisian café near the Jardin du Luxembourg: untypically, the city was covered with a substantial layer of snow, which was rapidly turning from powdery white to a brownish slush.

Kanfer had written me after reading my book *Erased: Vanishing Traces of Jewish Galicia in Present-Day Ukraine*, published three years earlier, which contains a brief account of Buczacz before, during, and after the Holocaust. "The history of Buczacz touches me more personally," he wrote:

> My grandmother on my father's side, named Sara (and at times Sabina, I don't know why) Kanfer, daughter of Markus Kanfer and Civje Herman, was born in Buczacz in 1880. She left Buczacz in 1912 and arrived in Paris in August 1912, pregnant and unmarried. She lived in Paris, where she worked as a teacher of Polish, until her death in 1936, four years before my birth. She converted to Catholicism in 1931. My father, Julien, was born in March 1913. Apparently my grandmother never said a word about my grandfather, who remained entirely unknown. My father (died in 2008) married my mother (non-Jewish) in 1939. I was born in November 1940 and was raised entirely by my maternal grandparents after my mother died in 1942 and my father joined a group of the Résistance in 1943.[13]

Having recently retired, Alain was hoping to finally shed some light on "my family and its probable tragic fate during the Shoah (my father never talked about that)." But there was more to it, as he explained in his letter:

> Using the Internet, I have recently discovered that in around 1900 a journalist (an anarchist and a Zionist) named Moshe Kanfer was living in Buczacz, whose father was Mordechai Kanfer, a teacher in the synagogue of Shmuel Agnon. Having cross-checked a few old photographs, I think that Mordechai was the brother of Markus (Sara's father). Irma (Irène) Kanfer (died 2002), Moshe's daughter, lived in France near Paris where she was known as a poet both in French and Yiddish; unfortunately, I met her on only a few occasions in my teens and (the blame is mine) never afterward.[14]

Could I, wrote Dr. Kanfer, provide him with "some further information about the Jewish branch of my ancestry?" Enclosed with the letter were several other items, including a copy of Sara Kanfer's certificate of residence, completed in Buczacz in 1912 and confirming that she was born in 1880, was employed as a private tutor, and was single. Another copied document was a certificate issued by the police prefect in Paris in May 1915, according to which Sara Kanfer, an Austrian citizen born in Buczacz (Galicia) to Markus and Civje Herman Kanfer, single and employed as a teacher, had arrived in Paris in August 1912.

It took some time to unravel this mystery. As it turned out, Markus and Mordechai Kanfer were the same person (the latter being his Jewish name). Markus was employed as a teacher at the Baron Hirsch School—where Agnon studied German and some Polish with him—and wrote for Hebrew-language magazines. His children included Sara and Moshe. Moshe had first attended cheder, in accordance with his mother's more traditional views, but went on to study in a general elementary school, presumably his father's institution, and was then admitted to the gymnasium in Brzeżany. However, at age seventeen he was expelled from the gymnasium for having joined an anarchist group and organizing a peasant strike on an estate where he had worked as a tutor during the summer vacation. This was the same gymnasium that Siegfried Nacht had also briefly attended before similarly being expelled for political activity. Indeed, it was during those years that Moshe got to know both Agnon and the two Nacht brothers, and one may safely assume that this was also how his sister Sara met Max.

Moshe, subsequently known as Mojżesz Kanfer, went on to have an illustrious career. In 1908 he received a doctorate in law from the university of Lemberg; two years later he married Gizela Waleria Stern, a teacher, librarian, translator, and one of the directors of the women's Zionist society called Rachela. Mojżesz clerked at the court in Vienna, but then became engaged in journalism, traveling throughout Europe and publishing articles in Polish and German. In World War I he served as an officer in the Austro-Hungarian army, and participated in efforts to assist Jewish refugees from Galicia. After the war he veered politically toward socialist Zionism, was active in the Poalei Zion Party, and began writing for the Polish-language Zionist daily press as well as for Polish Jewish and Yiddish literary and scholarly journals. The family moved to Kraków in 1923, where Kanfer worked for the literary section of *Nowy Dziennik*—the first Zionist Polish-language magazine—until the outbreak of World War II. Kanfer also became an active member of the Jewish Theater Society and was involved in establishing a permanent Yiddish scene in the city. Additionally, he worked for the Central Yiddish School Organization and the Safrus publishing house, which published his Polish translation of Sholem Asch's 1919 novel *The Mother*. At the same time Kanfer was active in Polish cultural circles, worked for Polish Radio, and co-chaired the Union of Polish Journalists of western Galicia for many years. During the German occupation he was a member of the Judenrat in Lwów and was murdered in Bełżec in 1942 along with his wife.[15]

But the couple's two children survived the Holocaust; their son Julian became a lawyer, economist, and journalist in France; he passed away in 1978. Their daughter Irma, later known as Irène, born in 1920, was the poet and translator mentioned in Alain Kanfer's letter; they were, in fact, his cousins. Her daughter is named after her mother, Gizela.[16] But what happened to Alain's grandmother, Sara? In fact, it appears that Sara left Buczacz long before the residence permit that made Alain think she had lived there until 1912. Although Max Nacht never mentions her by name in his memoir, and her surviving documents describe her as single, it appears that she and Max had been living together, at least since he escaped a police raid on anarchist cells in Zurich in late 1905 and moved in with her in Geneva, where he assumed her last name and presented himself as her husband. As a resident of this French-speaking city's colony of Russian émigrés, Max also took the time to acquire both French and Russian. In a letter he sent from Paris to his friend in Zurich, the Swiss physician, writer, socialist activist, and anarchist sympathizer Fritz Brupbacher, in June 1906, Max wrote: "On the way to Paris my wife (S. Kanfer) will step off the train in Zurich for two days and use the opportunity to call on you." In other communications that year he referred to her either as "a friend" or as "Frau Nacht." Indeed, a letter sent from Paris to Brupbacher in May 1908, signed Max and Sabina Nacht, reported that the couple had married in London earlier that year.[17]

This is all we hear about Sara, who by then was using her Christian name, Sabina. In 1910 the couple may have been living in Paris, since we know that Max returned there after serving a three-month prison term in Lwów for illegal political activity. The following year he was already working as a copyeditor in Rome, where Sabina apparently joined him, as indicated by her surviving admission card to the 1911 Rome international exhibition. But in 1912 Max was compelled to leave Italy after participating in a general strike, and traveled to Constantinople; as we know, Sabina went to Paris, likely pregnant with his baby. Since Max immigrated to the United States shortly thereafter, they may never have met again.[18]

But Max did journey to Europe in 1930 and may well have met Agnon in Buczacz as related in *A Guest for the Night;* and if Agnon is to be believed, Max, in the person of Schützling, did know about his son Julien, born the same year his father went to the United States. Perhaps, then, Sabina was that "charming brunette" Schützling so longingly recalls, the woman he left with his child, and who, as he says, "forgave me before her death" in 1936, when Agnon was writing the novel. Did Max hear her sing one more time the same song, which tragically came to represent her life, that he was humming to himself on that moonlit night in Buczacz?

My years have passed in pain and wrath,
I've known no joy or blessing.
I spent my days in futile grief,
Sleep now, sleep now my baby.

Whether Max abandoned Sabina, or she left him before he departed for the United States, and whether they had officially married, or divorced, is not known. From his obituary we learn that Max left behind his wife, "the former Rae Trotzky"; no children are mentioned. Because Sabina had not spoken to her son about Max, and because Julien never mentioned any of this to his son, Alain, this entire history receded into oblivion. It would appear that Max was not proud of this episode in his life, since he makes no mention of it in his writings. Only in the person of Schützling, beset by melancholy and after several brandies, does he hint at this murky part of his past, real or fictional. Just as the histories of these men and women, their dreams and their works, have been largely forgotten, so too their few surviving descendants went on to build new lives with very little knowledge, if any, of all that had gone before. They might well have known the main outlines of the past, the history taught in schools and commemorated in official events; but they generally remained oblivious of their own intimate links, often unexpected and filled with coincidences, as most personal lives are, to those momentous events, and of how improbable and miraculous was the very fact that they had somehow emerged, seemingly unscathed, on the other side of the abyss. And so it took Alain Kanfer seven decades before he found that, just like him, his great-grandfather had also been a physician, a progressive, essentially optimistic man in a distant little town on the eastern fringe of Europe, who sent his two sons out into the world to make it better. No one could have known how things would eventually turn out.

Apparatchik

The borderlands also produced professional revolutionaries, men of a rather different temperament from such dilettantes as Anselm Mosler and the Nacht brothers. An outstanding example from Buczacz is Adolf Langer, born in 1892, and thus eleven years younger than Max Nacht. Described by communist colleagues after his death as having been raised "in an atmosphere of patriotism and democratic ideals," he was in fact the son of Joachim Langer, director of the Baron Hirsch School, who also taught extracurricular classes of Jewish religion at the Buczacz gymnasium, from which Adolf graduated in 1912.[19] Shortly after the outbreak of World War I Adolf enrolled as a student of philosophy at the University of Vienna. Already active in the left wing of the Polish Social Democratic Party's youth group, by 1916 Adolf was reportedly so "deeply moved by the tragedy of the imperialist war" that he could no longer "resign himself to the opportunism of Social Democracy's right-wing leaders," and "unequivocally joined the revolutionary left wing grouped around Lenin." As Langer subsequently recalled, "my later political ideas were decisively derived from a number of Lenin's articles published in Switzerland in the *Vorbote*," a short-lived magazine of the antimilitarist socialists.[20]

In 1917 Langer was called up for military service in the Austro-Hungarian army. Since he was politically suspect as an antiwar activist, he never received the officer rank to which he was entitled by his education and was sent to serve in far-off Albania. Once the war ended, he returned to Vienna to complete his studies, and in 1919 acquired a diploma that entitled him to teach at a gymnasium. By then the Austro-Hungarian Empire no longer existed, and Langer began working at a private Polish school. Yet clearly, he did not perceive this to be his vocation. The previous year he had been one of the founders of the Communist Party in Austria, and soon thereafter was appointed leader of its Polish section, as well as editor of the Polish communist daily *Świt* (Dawn); at the same time, Langer played a leading role in the establishment of the Communist Party of eastern Galicia in 1919.

A crucial moment early on in Langer's career occurred when he chaired the Galician faction at the Communist Party's national conference in Lwów in 1921. Coming in the wake of the defeat of the West Ukrainian People's Republic (ZUNR) by the Polish military and the annexation of eastern Galicia to the newly independent Poland, the meeting saw a clash between the mostly Ukrainian Galician communists, who wanted to retain their autonomy, and the Polish representatives, who insisted on strict central party control. Ironically, it was the twenty-nine-year-old Jewish communist Langer, now known by the more Ukrainian- and Polish-sounding name Ostap Długski and serving as editor of the party's Ukrainian-language organ, *Nasha pravda* (Our Truth), who attempted to resolve this largely ethnonational crisis within the new Communist Party.[21]

As a loyal communist, Długski agreed to subordinate the Galicians to the Polish party; but he expressed strong misgivings about the manner in which this was done. Referring to the "brutal suppression of the Ukrainian nation" by Poland in 1919, he stressed that not only nationalists, but even Polish communists "came to us not with a vehement, all-inclusive protest against the horrors which had been committed, but rather with the slogan 'Polish Soviet Republic,' which to us was incomprehensible, alien, and aroused suspicion." Yet charges by Galician communists of Polish "imperialism and great-power chauvinism" were answered by Polish communist accusations of Ukrainian "nationalism and separatism." Indeed, critics of the Galician party alleged that its position reflected an internal struggle "between the Ukrainians and the Polish and Jewish elements over the Ukrainian character and supremacy of the party." In fact, three-quarters of the Galician communists were Ukrainian.[22]

Ultimately, the main issue was that the majority Ukrainian population of eastern Galicia was strongly anti-Polish, a fact that the local communists could ignore only at their peril, because, from the perspective of their economic condition, the Ukrainians were their natural supporters. The communists believed that the struggle between large landowners and land-hungry peasants had produced a revolutionary potential. But since the former were mostly Poles, the peasants were unlikely to support a Polish Communist Party that was striving to subject the Galician branch to its authority.[23] Four decades later, Długski recalled that at the time he "had a poor prognosis for the conference," and had asked the Polish delegation to consider "the Leninist view of national self-determination without secession," but to no avail. Długski understood that when the Polish communists "said that this was one state," the "simple Ukrainian . . . interpreted this in simple terms to mean: 'You are nationalists, you are exactly like the other bourgeois parties.'" Długski agreed: "The Polish revolutionary movement had been transformed from a party of an oppressed nation into the party of a nation engaged in oppressing other nations." Consequently, "many good Ukrainians did not join our movement," because "we pushed them into the arms of nationalist parties." Długski's own position was to strike a compromise: "In respect to national independence—self-determination without separation; in respect to organization—organizational unity of the communist party in the whole territory of Poland, provided, however, that the Communist Party of West Ukraine [eastern Galicia] is autonomous with its own Central Committee, etc." It was, as Długski wryly commented, therefore "not accidental that I was unanimously appointed as the chairman of the commission to the conference."[24]

The vehement debates between the two sides came to an abrupt end when the Polish authorities arrested the delegates. During the trial that followed, Długski unflinchingly professed his belief that "only communism can eliminate the oppression, poverty, and misery of humanity," and that Soviet Russia marked "a new beginning in the progress of humankind."[25] But writing many years later, he noted that "in assessing what happened in our party we cannot disregard and neglect to evaluate what happened around it. In that period Ukrainians were exposed to great terror. We were imprisoned; but they kept some Ukrainian generals on the floor, on stone tiles, without any bedding. In our prison yard, bourgeois nationalist followers of the independence movement were shot." Długski also recalled the affinity between the imprisoned Galician communists and nationalists, commenting that even during the trial he had exclaimed: "While we are debating here, bullets are being fired at the heads of those who are fighting for their country's freedom and independence, albeit with false methods." Prisoner solidarity crossed the ideological divide, he stressed: "we [Galician communists] sat in separate cells from Ukrainian nationalists," but "we played chess together, and when we fought, they defended us, and when they fought, we defended them. Although we opposed each other."

As Długski suggested, while the Galician communists had hoped to profit from the link between nationalist sentiment and socioeconomic conditions in eastern Galicia, they ended up riding the tiger's back. "One should distinguish the peasant masses from the party leaders," he noted. "We as the party did not organize any acts of sabotage. We applied different methods of fighting. The peasant masses which set off to burn the manor houses of the gentry and seize their forests, etc., were solving these problems not according to programmatic declarations by party radicals but in their own way." Many of the communist leaders arrested in 1921, he recalled, "were Polish and Jewish comrades," along with "a few workers," while rank-and-file support came mainly from "railway men, printers, metalworkers and bakers." But Ukrainian peasants were conspicuously absent from the party's ranks; many of them "marched under the banners of the nationalist parties" and "absolutely did not want to hear about Poland," not least because "at that time terror was raging in Ukraine" and "prisons were filled with Ukrainians." In retrospect, Dłuski believed that "had we had a fair attitude from the very beginning," the party might have won over "those Ukrainian peasants, most of whom were very poor." But clearly, this failure also resulted from the fact that the Polish Communist Party itself included "some nationalists."[26]

One cannot but admire Dłuski's support for the Ukrainian faction of the Polish Communist Party, as well as his incisive analysis of why the party failed to appeal to the Ukrainian peasants of eastern Galicia—a situation that persisted throughout the interwar period, leaving a void that was eventually filled by Ukrainian nationalist radicals such as Bandera's supporters. But following his release from prison in 1923, Dłuski increasingly toed the party line. As deputy member of the Polish Communist Party (KPP) Central Committee, as well as member of the Central Committee of its Galician branch, now renamed the Communist Party of West Ukraine (KPZU), Dłuski was repeatedly arrested by the Polish authorities, prompting him to leave for the Soviet Union in 1929. Returning to Poland in 1934, he became head of the Central Editorial Office of the KPP. He happened to have been in Germany when Hitler was appointed chancellor in 1933, and upon returning to Poland the following year was elected member and then head of the National Secretariat of the KPP's Central Committee. In 1936 he was sent to France to liaise with the French Communist Party, during which time he also wrote profusely for Comintern publications in Paris and Basel.[27]

When the Polish government dissolved the Communist Party in 1938, the forty-six-year-old Dłuski was removed from political activities in France and earned his keep as a porter. But following Germany's attack on the Soviet Union in June 1941, Dłuski resumed his political activities, working with Polish and French communists in German-occupied France. In 1942, with the French police hot on his heels, he went into hiding in a shack owned by none other than Dr. Edgar Longuet, Karl Marx's grandson and mayor of Alfortville, located just outside Paris.

Completely isolated, with no running water or heating, the indefatigable Dłuski applied himself to composing a lengthy German-language indictment of Nazism, whose title, "Germany: A Horror Tale," alludes to Heinrich Heine's scathing satirical attack on German militarism, reactionism, and chauvinism, in his famous 1844 poem, "Germany: A Winter's Tale." Writing under the pseudonym Oswald Ostende, Dłuski exhibits re-

markable erudition, knowledge of and love for German culture, and un-
bending ideological dogmatism. He does not seem to have been swayed by
Stalin's betrayal of European communism with the signing of the Molotov-
Ribbentrop pact in 1939, which sealed the fate of Poland and facilitated
Germany's entry into World War II, let alone the collectivization campaign of the early 1930s that cost the lives of millions of Soviet citizens;
instead, he asserts that "on the battlefield, Soviet peasants have demonstrated to the entire world what *they* owed to the agrarian policies of the
Soviet government and *how* determined they are to defend their revolutionary achievements."[28]

One aspect of the war, however, seems to rattle Dłuski more than any
other, despite the generally triumphal communist tone of the essay as a
whole. Writing in January 1943, Dłuski initially rejects Hitler's claim that
many of his "prophesies" have already come true.[29] But then he qualifies his
statement, referring to the Führer's notorious speech on 30 January 1939,
in which he unambiguously threatened to murder European Jewry:

> I have very often in my lifetime been a prophet and have been
> mostly derided. At the time of my struggle for power it was in the
> first instance the Jewish people who only greeted with laughter
> my prophecies that I would someday take over the leadership of
> the state and of the entire people of Germany and then, among
> other things, also bring the Jewish problem to its solution. I be-
> lieve that this hollow laughter of Jewry in Germany has already
> stuck in its throat. I want today to be a prophet again: if inter-
> national finance Jewry inside and outside Europe should succeed
> in plunging the nations once more into a world war, the result will
> be not the Bolshevization of the earth and thereby the victory of
> Jewry, but the annihilation of the Jewish race in Europe.[30]

This "prophecy" by Hitler, exclaims Dłuski, "has indeed been realized":

> In order to accomplish this glorious task, he sent his bloodhounds
> to drag millions of unarmed Jews in all occupied lands out of their
> houses, to bring them to Poland, and to heinously slaughter them
> there in slaughterhouses built especially for this purpose, among
> them hundreds of thousands of Jewish children . . . This valiant
> warrior then boasted about his deed to the German nation. But
> this was also the only battle he won; the only prophesy that came

true. This heroic deed disgraced the name of Germany, but it could not help in realizing the other "prophesies."[31]

This was one of Dłuski's rare references to the fate of the Jews, perhaps the product of enforced solitude. The essay, of which hundreds of copies were distributed, was to have included additional chapters. But shortly after writing it, Dłuski was called back into action, working with the French Communist Party, organizing a Ukrainian underground in France, editing the Ukrainian-language magazine *Batkivshchyna* (Fatherland), and writing articles in French aimed at justifying Stalin's takeover and reordering of Eastern Europe. Poland, asserted Dłuski, "will be able to conquer and establish its independence only in alliance with the Red Army," while "the territories of Ukraine and Belarus" previously under its rule "were voluntarily returned to the bosom of the free Soviet Republics of Ukraine and Belarus." Proclaiming without a trace of irony that "a nation that oppresses another people cannot be free," he insisted that the Soviet Union "had made the principle of liberty and independence of peoples into the basis of its *raison d'état* and of its foreign policy." Speaking in liberated Paris in 1945, Dłuski depicted the Polish uprising of the previous year, when the Red Army stood by as the Wehrmacht crushed the rebels and destroyed the city, as a "premature insurrection," in which "the heroic people of Warsaw fell victim" to "the egoistical politics" of those who "wanted to drive a wedge into the Allies' front."[32] Tellingly, he made no reference to the Warsaw Ghetto uprising of 1943 or to the extermination camps recently overrun by the Soviets.

Did anything remain of the young man of 1921, who had defended the right of Ukrainians to an autonomous position within the Polish Communist Party, and, as he recalled many years later, could feel empathy for Ukrainian nationalists oppressed by Polish rule even as a communist of Jewish origins? For that matter, did anything remain of the lad from Buczacz who, before setting out into the world, had grown up in a Jewish community he must have known had been wiped out, but to which he seems never to have referred publicly? Perhaps there was one such moment, in which he showed uncharacteristic courage with respect to the dogma—he obviously never lacked personal courage—a moment that he must have experienced, like so many others, as one of both collective and personal crisis.

In 1946 the fifty-four-year-old Dłuski was back in Poland as member of the Central Committee of the Polish Workers' Party. On 4 July that year the bloodiest postwar pogrom in Europe took place in the Polish town of Kielce; more than forty Jewish survivors of the Holocaust were killed. Altogether between 500 and 1,500 Jews were murdered in Poland in the immediate aftermath of the war, which had witnessed the slaughter of 90 percent of Polish Jewry. Possibly shaken by these events, on 29 July Dłuski proposed at the conclusion of a Central Committee Secretariat meeting "that an institution be established which would facilitate departure of the Jews from Poland, so that they could join their families"; additionally, he took note of the disappointment of the Jewish community with the lack of democracy in Poland, and its dismay that despite the widespread pogroms, Władysław Gomułka—at the time deputy prime minister but de facto ruler of Poland—had not addressed the situation of the Jews in a recent five-hour speech to the Communist Party. Two decades later, in 1968, the same Gomułka, now leader of the renamed Polish United Workers' Party, expelled the remaining Jews from the country.[33]

Dłuski's brief engagement with antisemitism in Poland, also reflected in his role as editor of the party's main organ, *Głos Ludu* (The People's Voice) in 1945–48, may have been merely part of the communists' attempt to accuse their enemies at home and abroad of inciting such sentiments.[34] But even if there was a more personal edge to it, Dłuski did not return to the issue, and became subsequently absorbed in what were billed as humanitarian activities, as organizer of congresses for peace in Wrocław in 1948 and Warsaw in 1950, as president of the Polish Committee on Peace, and as member of the World Peace Council (WPC).[35] In truth, most of this activity was nothing more than a communist propaganda tool.

Dłuski also seems never to have repeated his observation regarding Hitler's realization of his "prophecy" about the extermination of the Jews; this was not at all in line with communist rhetoric in the postwar period. When given the opportunity to speak publicly about Nazi crimes, such as on the occasion of Wolfgang von Goethe's two-hundredth anniversary in 1949, Dłuski's German-language speech refrained from any mention of the genocide of the Jews. Instead, speaking as a Polish patriot, a communist ideologue, a lover of German culture, and a self-described supporter of humanism and enlightenment, he called upon his German audience to follow "the path of coexistence and fraternal cooperation with the democratic camp, at whose forefront stands the mighty Soviet Union under the leadership of the great friend of humanity, the genius Stalin. Your task," he declared, "in the name of the ideals of Lessing, Goethe, and Heine, in the name of the immortal legacy of Marx and Engels, is to lead the German people in the fight for a united, democratic, freedom-loving Germany against the forces of reaction and of vengeance, against the American and British imperialist warmongers, who want to make West Germany, supported by capitalist war criminals and former Nazis, into a forward attack base against the free and independent peoples, against Poles, against our border on the Oder and Neisse."

By that point, Dłuski had become a propagator of the postwar Orwellian-Stalinist view of history, not as a record of the past but as an instrument of ideological manipulation: "Who does not know today," he thundered, "that Hitler's quest for the suppression of the revolutionary movement in Germany, his quest for the destruction of the Soviet Union, were actively supported and supplied by the imperialists in France, England, and America?"[36]

Stalin died in 1953, soon after he had unleashed an anti-Jewish campaign throughout his vast empire. As "in Moscow people were smothered in the mob desperate to say goodbye," Dłuski composed a panegyric for this butcher of millions. This lifelong resister and professional revolutionary now exposed himself as a wretched party hack, speaking of Stalin's memory as "eternally alive, warm and sincere," praising the Bolshevik Party for representing "the highest achievements of advanced human thought," and highlighting the Polish people's "relationship of friendship, equality and mutual co-operation with the great Russian, Ukrainian and Belarusian nations."[37] To be sure, this was just one of innumerable such professions of deep sorrow upon the setting of the "sun of nations." But as in so many other cases, one is tempted to ask, did Dłuski believe the verbiage he spouted?

What a vast difference between Dłuski and the Nacht brothers. He had become a man of influence, locked in an ideological dogma and a Stalinist frame of mind; the Nacht brothers had been in constant ideological and political flux, ending up on the margins of the left, with Max in particular becoming its vehement critic, though never joining the ranks of the right. He always retained a sense of humanism and a belief, naïve perhaps, but deeply felt and at times eloquently articulated, in people's potential for good, even as he lost his faith in the "masses." He was, of course, far from perfect, and buried the skeleton of his marriage and abandoned child deep in his closet. We know even less about Dłuski's private life; these were men for whom the public trumped the private, the collective reigned supreme, and the personal was maligned as egotistic. But it appears clear that Dłuski, trapped within the rhetoric of triumphant communism and possibly enjoying the trappings of late and all-too-fleeting power, became increasingly jaded and formulaic in his pronouncements on humanity, and chronically, maybe even spitefully, forgetful of where he had come from and what had happened to the world he had left behind. Perhaps he was in denial; but then Dłuski was not given to introspection, sentimentalism, or nostalgia. Still, I wonder, did he ever think of his hometown?

Dłuski's long career was capped with the Lenin Prize, awarded for "strengthening peace among nations" in 1961. Following his death at the age of seventy-two, he was described as "an activist of outstanding measure," a man "characterized by wide-ranging views, unconventionality, great experience and practical wisdom," as well as "a good, decent person who believed in his fellow man and exhibited a high degree of optimism"; these qualities were "the source of the trust and great fondness bestowed upon him by all those who knew him." In brief, "he was a model communist."[38] That he certainly was. He also had impeccable timing; four years later he would have likely been "unmasked" as the crypto-Jew Adolf Langer and expelled from Poland as a "fifth column" Zionist.

Dłuski might have erased Buczacz from his mental landscape, but he remained within the Polish sphere on whose periphery he was raised. Agnon, for his part, spent a lifetime writing about Galicia, yet made his home in the very different environs of Jerusalem. Max Nacht, who ended up in far-off New York, ultimately acknowledged that his worldview was forged in Buczacz. As for Zvi-Heinrich Müller, even as he reached the pinnacle of accomplishment in the imperial capital of Vienna, he drew greatly on his upbringing and remained committed to his community. Linked in so many ways to the world they had left behind, in their own particular ways, these men were also all trailblazers: coming from the margin, they struggled to make themselves known to the world, and in the process became part of its remaking.

CHAPTER ELEVEN

Bringing Light to the World

Terra Incognita

PEOPLE LEFT THE BORDERLANDS for many reasons, personal, ideological, and, not least, economic. But they also went away because they were unwanted and hoped to transform the circumstances that made for that rejection, or to find a new place where they would be welcomed.

In 1847 the Polish poet, artist, and traveler Maciej Bogusz Stęczyński depicted how a tourist riding through the "sprawling, seemingly endless plain" of Galicia suddenly spots "woods of beech and hornbeam" descending "into a valley surrounded by hills." There he is "astonished to behold the small town of Buczacz, picturesquely dotted on the slopes of the ravine . . . separated into two parts by the Strypa River flowing through the town center." Buczacz boasts "many towers: that of the stone-built town hall, that of the parish church, and that of the Basilian monastery, as well as the ruins of the old castle," all evoking "many memories, both sad and joyful: our entire past seems to emerge from them." This is the Polish past of an "ancient town . . . the hearth of the famous Buczacki family," whose "many brave men" were "celebrated for their heroic lives and deaths for their homeland"; its townspeople were "festive and joyful," and even its horses "were famous all over Poland." Here King Sobieski himself "pitched his camp," and Mikołaj Potocki built the monastery and the town hall, "that most beautiful building of its kind anywhere in Galicia." But those days are over; the good citizens of Buczacz, lamented Stęczyński, "once rich and commercially active," had "become impoverished," for now the town was "full of Jews, mud, and stones."[1]

Sobieski was actually venerated by Galician Jews as their liberator from the Turks. As an often despised minority they never forgot their dependence on the powers that be. Under Habsburg rule, public expressions of loyalty and gratitude to the emperor became increasingly common. Following the assassination attempt on Emperor Franz Joseph in 1853, the head of the Jewish community in Buczacz, Zadek Reich, delivered a sermon at the Great Synagogue, later published as a brochure, praising God for having protected the emperor and professing boundless fidelity to the young ruler.[2] But Jewish expressions of allegiance to the Austrian emperor only further aggravated Polish nationalist perceptions of Galician Jewry as being inimical to the goal of regaining independence.

In his book *Galicia and Kraków under Austrian Rule*, published anonymously in Paris in the same year as Stęczyński's account of Galicia, Father Waleryan Kalinka shares Stęczyński's view that "the small towns in Galicia look sad . . . dirty, and sparsely paved," because they "are swarming with Jews." In their marketplaces "the young livestock" brought by the peasants "remains in Jewish hands," while the local burgher "drinks willingly" and is consequently "indebted to a Jew," even as he "wistfully recalls the Polish times and hates today's government." It is thanks to the "wicked system" imposed by Austria that "the Jews predominate in the towns and are the cause of their decline and disarray" throughout the "eastern, and even the central districts" of the land, while "close to the border" they "support corruption by embezzlement."

For Poles, notes Kalinka, the Jews are "terra incognita," even though they constitute "three million people who were born in Poland, live with and on us, and go to the grave with us." Poles know Jews for "their greed, which we find offensive, and their mobility, which reconciles us with them." Especially "the Polish Jew" presents a contradictory "mixture of good and evil," combining "high virtues" with "moral filth"; exhibiting "profound religiosity, yet almost no sense of dignity"; belonging to "the greediest nation in the world," yet also being "the most merciful to the poor." Jews are "the only capitalists in Poland, and yet the only proletariat"; "the toughest people" and "the easiest to humiliate"; they "dislike hard work, but toil more tenaciously than the strongest worker"; they are "cautious and apprehensive, yet courageous to the point of recklessness"; being "the very embodiment of materialism and practicality, they bury themselves in mysticism to the point of frenzy."

This breathtaking mid-nineteenth-century depiction of "the Polish Jew" proved to have tremendous staying power, lasting well past World War II and the Holocaust. With all its ambiguity, resentment, and envy, its underlying logic was that Jews were anathema: unwelcome strangers who refuse to go away. Kalinka's antisemitism *avant la lettre* makes the usual association between moral character and external appearance. "Let us look at the Polish Jew," he proposes: "A pale, oval, sickly-looking face, a hooked nose, bulging, restless eyes, his beard and sidelocks in disarray, his rarely combed hair visible under his dirty skullcap . . . His figure crooked, unshapely. No fresh underwear can be detected; there is dirt and repugnant filth everywhere"; his "long coat" is "greyish or black with age, stained and full of holes," his "dirty stockings drop onto worn-out shoes." In brief, the Polish Jew's entire figure betrays "slyness, trickery, and knavery."

The moral degeneracy of the Jew is reflected also in the way he lives, inhabiting "a dark, narrow room" that houses "three, four or more families," naturally filled with "dirt, stuffy air, filthy and half-naked screaming children," and surrounded by "walls of imperceptible color" and "doors smeared with grease or chalk." His food never includes "any warm, liquid meal"; his resulting physical condition means that "three Jews are needed to lift what one Polish peasant can easily pick up." He drinks only water, unless he is offered a drink, which "he will drink willingly, because it's free." His work is mostly "brokerage, pandering, smuggling, usury, exchange transactions, huckstering and the sale of liquor," and he is so "devoured by the fever of profit" that all trades end up "in Jewish hands." Yet this "nation within a nation," this "Jewish phalanx," with its "separate laws, separate language, separate customs, separate courts and separate businesses," is "bound by a chain of solidarity" and shielded from "criminal law, police or recruitment regulations," perpetuating its existence as a "separate camp" that "does not contribute in any way to improving the lot of the general population." Hence, its "history is separate and will never join the national history."[3]

This diatribe was likely read by far more people when it was reissued in Kraków in 1898, both because its sentiments had become more widespread, and because more people had access to it thanks to growing literacy, promoted not only by the empire but also by nationalists. If the empire categorized spoken language as an indicator of nationality, the nationalists linked language to national identity much more rigorously, perceiving it as a crucial tool in the formation of group identity. Literacy enabled people to learn what group identity meant beyond the confines of

their village or town. It also helped to identify all those others who differed from "our own."

There were of course such Jews as Anselm Mosler, the Nacht brothers, and Adolf Langer/Ostap Długski who, within the fold of radical politics, socialism, anarchism, and communism, were no longer thought of as
Jews. But sooner or later, they too were, or would have been, "unmasked,"
be it when they encountered pre-1914 Austrian and Polish socialist nationalism and antisemitism, or in the national communist anti-Zionist campaign of 1968. Moreover, as the cunning of history would have it, the very
radical politics that had facilitated Jewish self-transformation came to be
seen by the nationalists as a Jewish conspiracy, and communist crimes were
increasingly attributed to the Jews, as indicated by such terms as *żydoko-
muna*, or Judeo-Bolshevism, which have not entirely vanished from the
scene to this day and may actually be enjoying a revival of sorts.

As for the majority of Jews living in the borderlands who did not turn
to radical activities, by the late nineteenth century they became the object
of more scientific inquiries into moral degeneracy and criminal inclinations. The Polish criminologist Piotr Stebelski, for instance, argued in
1892 that Jewish delinquency and rate of incarceration in Galicia were
proportionately higher than those of any other group, reflecting what he
termed the Jewish "criminal physiognomy," whose "characteristic feature"
was "the greed that drives them" to perpetrate such "despicable crimes."
While he could not determine whether the Jewish population's "negative
and yet characteristic morals" were the consequence of "a historical-racial
development," or of "the properties of its national character," they clearly
provided unambiguous proof of the baseness of the Jewish character.[4]

The growing participation of Jewish nationalists in public life, for its
part, made for their perception as disloyal to the Polish nation. Edward
Dubanowicz, who subsequently became professor of law at Lwów University and member of Parliament for the antisemitic National Democratic
Party (Endecja), was incensed by the collaboration between Jewish and
Ukrainian parties in the 1907 national elections, precisely the kind of
cooperation Ivan Franko had been hoping for. "What could balance out
the discrepancies and create friendship" between Jews and Ruthenians,
he asked, "when on the one side, among the unenlightened masses of the
rural population, smoldered not just suspicion and hidden resentment but
overt hatred, written in blood," toward the Jews, "while on the other side,
there was a sense of cultural superiority and a feeling of barely concealed
contempt" with respect to the Ruthenians? To his mind, the Jews "simply

relied on the ignorance and economic ineptitude" of the Ruthenians, yet the two groups' "attachment to religious, racial, and traditional differences, as well as differences of character and temperament," were bound to create "antagonism between the organism being exploited," namely, the Ruthenians, "and the organism which lived on that exploitation," that is, the Jewish parasites.[5]

Born in 1881, the same year as Max Nacht, Dubanowicz withdrew from politics after Marshal Józef Piłsudki's takeover of Poland in 1926 but was removed from his chair of constitutional law at the University of Lwów in 1934. In 1940, following the Soviet occupation of Galicia, Dubanowicz was deported to Kazakhstan, where he eventually served as a delegate of the Polish embassy. He moved to London in 1942, where he died the following year.[6] His was very much a Polish life of that generation. As for the Galician Jews he had denounced as disloyal to Poland, most of them were far more concerned at the time with making ends meet than with politics. As another Polish scholar, Stanisław Gruiński, argued in a meticulous study of Galician Jewry published in 1910, this "ignorant, superstitious population, residing mostly in small provincial towns," which constituted close to two-thirds of Austria's overall Jewish population of 1 million, was still mostly living in congested ghettoes with increasingly scarce economic resources and extremely limited access to modern education and training. Consequently, immigration overseas played a crucial role in addressing widespread poverty. Especially the Jewish Colonization Association (Ika) in Galicia constituted one of "the largest and most important Jewish institutions aiming to raise the material and moral level of the Jews" by settling them "as farmers in extra-European countries." These included, most prominently, Argentina, whose "oldest colony has existed there for sixteen years," but also Canada, Cyprus, Palestine, Asia Minor, and Brazil, as well as North America, where no fewer than 10,000 Jews were living exclusively on agricultural work, especially in New Jersey.[7]

Some Polish observers were concerned by the effects of Jewish emigration. In his widely read 1888 study, *Galician Poverty in Numbers*, the oil magnate and international entrepreneur Stanisław Szczepanowski, for instance, found it galling that "abroad, in England and America, our kikes [*nasi żydkowie*] usually describe themselves as Poles, even though they typically can't understand a word of Polish," with the result that "the English and American common folk identify the Poles as Jews." Since these characters were "only known" to them "from police reports," where they "are habitually named Moses or Salomon," and described as "petty thieves and

swindlers," they gave real Poles a bad name. At the same time, Szczepanowski insisted that the creation of a modern Polish nation required the integration of the Jews and bemoaned the fact that "too few Jews admit their
Polishness." That had to change, "because we cannot tolerate an enemy
in our own house." Yet he also believed that it would be "psychologically
absurd to require . . . sincere and profound patriotism" from the Jews,
since "nationality and patriotism" were not "convictions that one can voluntarily adopt or reject"; rather, they require "traditions sucked with one's
mother's milk," which eventually form "an unconscious instinct" that "drives
one to sacrifice his life for the homeland." Acquiring this instinct would
take the Jews "at least a few generations," a process that apparently called
on them to first be unmade as Jews and only then to be remade as Poles.
As Franzos's protagonist Sender learned, and indeed possibly Franzos himself, there was no assurance of success to this kind of metamorphosis.[8]

Indeed, for both objective and subjective reasons, this never quite happened. Szczepanowski had envisioned a modernized greater Poland, where
all ethnic groups, especially those large minorities living on the borderlands, would eventually meld into a useful, responsible, and patriotic Polish citizenship. This was an inclusive, liberal-Romantic vision, with a substantial dose of melting-pot ideology. It was not only far from the economic
and mental reality of Galicia on the eve of World War I, it also increasingly
contradicted most of its inhabitants' aspirations. From this perspective, all
assertions of rational analysis notwithstanding, this was a utopian vision.
In Buczacz, as in much of the rest of Galicia, there were promoters of
Polish hegemony, makers of Ruthenian identity, defenders of Jewish tradition, and pioneers of Zionism, socialism, and anarchism; but the notion
of an all-inclusive new Polish citizenship does not seem to have had much
purchase. The "wild sheep" who abandoned the scene to remake themselves elsewhere remained always linked to their place of origin; but that
place, and that origin, was not the sort of all-inclusive national identity
Szczepanowski had hope for.[9]

Un bel dì, vedremo

In 1905, a certain Rajmund Scholz published a little "theatrical fairytale"
in Buczacz called "Princess Spring." In this allegory of youthful hope ver-
sus aged disenchantment, the princess is carried off from the court of her
father, King Winter, to a lonely mountainous retreat. Visited by a young
singer filled with contempt for humdrum humanity, she admonishes him

for his youthful ignorance: "Have you even looked into a single human heart . . . and peered into its very bottom?" Next an old singer arrives, overcome with "remorse for a life squandered by its own blindness," and haunted by a bleak image of descent from hope to despair: "Dreaming of a victorious, proud procession—and under your feet—pile up heaps of rubble!" But the princess appeals to him not to abandon his faith in humanity, "for the bell in the soul that chimes to the future . . . is as great and sincere as life itself!" Finally, the young singer returns: He has seen mankind, with all its "tedium, drudgery and toil," but he has also learned to love "the poverty of that gloomy world." Having "looked into the bottom of the innermost heart," he yearns to "reach out to the souls of men" and bring forth that "great rebirth" that only youth can accomplish; from now on, he will follow the princess's injunction: "Believe in the boundless power of the heart, and the dominion of the great, full life."[10]

Beyond the fact that he was born in 1882 and was therefore a contemporary of the Nacht brothers and Agnon, and that he died aged fifty-seven in 1939, little is known about Scholz, not even his ethnic and religious background. This naïve little play, written when he was twenty-one, may well be all that he ever published. But its main theme suggests that echoes of the new cult of youth, which engulfed Europe at the turn of the century, had reached even its distant borderlands. The high point of this movement was reached with the publication in 1912, by two young French intellectuals, Henri Massis and Alfred de Tarde, under the collective pseudonym "Agathon," of a series of articles, later issued as a book titled *Les jeunes gens d'aujourd'hui*. Ostensibly on the basis of a scientific survey of student opinion at the elite schools of Paris, Agathon claimed that French youth was rebelling against the older generation's political liberalism, philosophical "scientism," and reasoned pacifism. These "young men of today" yearned for active, virile, and antirationalist nationalism. Responding to the positivism and anticlericalism of their elders, the youth were returning to a deep Roman Catholic faith.[11] This was more than a fringe phenomenon among French elites; what became the "generation of 1914" encompassed a vast number of youths throughout Europe, many of whom would be dead by the end of the "great" war they had so enthusiastically embraced.[12] Their spring swiftly turned into winter, their youthful exhilaration transformed into endless despair. For some, this was the beginning of a path that led to a new kind of ruthless fanaticism aimed at rebirth through total annihilation.

Many young Poles, Ukrainians, and Jews from Buczacz served in the

Austro-Hungarian army, some quite bravely, even if their loyalties shifted dramatically in the course of a war that reordered the continent and top-pled the great empires straddling its eastern rim. But others were more skeptical about the prospects of fighting and dying for distant rulers or in the service of ethnocentric expansionist policies. Siegfried and Max Nacht got out of Europe just in time; Adolf Langer was tucked away in Albania as a political suspect, before transforming into Ostap Dłuski; Agnon, who moved to Germany shortly before the war, successfully avoided the draft he had dreaded and continued doing what he did best.[13] He firmly be-lieved that his life's mission was his writing, and little could distract him from this self-imposed task, not even his family. His stories immortalized a world of Galician-Podolian Jewry that had begun to disintegrate even before much of it was shattered in the ferocious fighting and deliberate acts of destruction of World War I. For Agnon there was neither glory nor sense in that titanic struggle, only ruin and devastation. What interested him was the fate of the Jews, and he eventually came to see Palestine/Israel as the place where that fate would find its future.

The internationally renowned Ukrainian soprano Solomiya Krushel-nytska was also passionately dedicated to her art and linked it increasingly to the fate of her people and culture; not unlike Agnon, she found beauty and love rather than violence and hate in that devotion. Born in the village of Bielawińce (Bilyavyntsi, eight miles north of Buczacz) in 1872, and best known for her leading role in the triumphal relaunch of Giacomo Puc-cini's *Madama Butterfly* in 1904, she performed at famous opera houses around the world, brandishing an astonishing repertoire of more than sixty works. The Italian critic Rinaldo Cortopassi wrote that during her time, she "was the only female singer to have attained" the fame of such reign-ing male singers as Enrico Caruso and Fedor Chaliapin.

But while she spent much of her active operatic career living in Italy, Krushelnytska retained close ties to Ukraine, and was known as a fervent promoter of Ukrainian songs and musical works. Her father, Amvrozyi de Krushelnytsky, supported her in launching her career, and visited his cel-ebrated daughter several times in the capitals of Europe. A Greek Catholic priest of noble origins and a member of Prosvita, the Ukrainian Enlight-enment Society, de Krushelnytsky was popular with the peasants, whom he urged to send their children to school. He is also known to have been sympathetic to such radicals as Ivan Franko.

Clearly influenced by her religious and patriotic upbringing, and despite her brilliant international career, Krushelnytska ended her life in

Ukraine. In August 1939, following the death of her Italian husband, she went to visit her sister in Lviv. Shortly thereafter the Soviets took over the city and nationalized her house; she was never again to leave the country. Krushelnytska died in 1952 in Lviv and is buried next to Ivan Franko in the beautiful Lychakiv cemetery. Listening to a scratchy recording of her singing "Un bel dì, vedremo" as Cio-Cio San, one can only imagine the impact she had on pre-1914 audiences and lament the tragedies she was compelled to witness in the last years of her life.[14]

There were others who brought their talent for art and beauty from the borderlands to the world during those years preceding the great catastrophe of 1914. Joseph Knebel, born in Buczacz in 1854, a member of the generation of Müller, Franzos, Freud, and Franko, subsequently became one of the most renowned Russian publishers and booksellers before the revolution. We know that his great-grandfather, of the same name, was already living in Buczacz in 1789, and that his father, Nikolai (Mikołaj, Nicolaus), was a well-to-do merchant and probably a maskil, who had a liking for design and architecture, as can be seen from the three-story family home he built in Buczacz, quite unusual for the time, and still standing there. But while the family seems to have spoken German at home as a symbol of its cultivated status, the father also reportedly had a violent temper, as a result of which his three children left home as soon as they could.

Joseph abandoned his family at the age of thirteen in 1867, with nothing more than a loaf of bread in his backpack. He made his way to Vienna, where he spent the next thirteen years working his way into the university (where he studied either medicine or philology) and, after graduating in 1876, studying for another two years at the Vienna Academy of Commerce. He moved to Russia in 1880, and subsequently founded the very first Russian publishing house specializing in art, eventually producing more than four hundred richly illustrated books on art, as well as children's stories and fables.[15] His daughter, Maria Osipovna Knebel, born in Moscow in 1898, studied with the founders of the Moscow Art Theater, Vladimir Nemirovich-Danchenko and Konstantin Stanislavsky (the latter's famous "method" had a major impact on such American actors as Marlon Brando, Al Pacino, and Robert De Niro). She also worked with the acclaimed actor Michael Chekhov, Anton Chekhov's nephew, and played, among other roles, in *The Cherry Orchard* in Moscow, as well as directing a legendary production of the play at the Abbey Theater in Dublin in 1968, an event recalled by the actors in 2014 as one of the greatest moments of

The Knebel house in Buczacz, 2003. Photo by the author.

their professional lives. Known for the "Knebel Technique" of acting, she was belatedly recognized in the West as "arguably the most important theatrical voice of Russia's Soviet era."[16] And so, just like Krushelnytska, little Joseph, escaping his violent father and the constraints of a small provincial town, and his immensely gifted daughter brought out to the world light and beauty and passion that have outlasted not only their own lives but the rage and hate and destruction that put an end to Europe's forgotten borderlands.

For the generations born on the borderlands between the Spring of Nations and World War I, new, unprecedented opportunities opened up.

To be sure, as invariably happens, most people stayed where they were and changed as little as they could. But those who left were filled with hopes of self-realization and self-transformation, and at times also aspired to change the world. And change they did, as did the world, though not necessarily as they had wished. Those of them who lived past the Great War, let alone the younger generations that survived into the post-1945 period, experienced upheavals on a scale that none of them could have imagined; some of them took part in bringing about those events, others recorded them, others still sought to reestablish, if only in memory and representation, the world as it had been before, that very same world they had abandoned with such determination in their youth. And then there were those who never gave up, and despite all the darkness and horror that came to rule the world, persisted in seeking out and creating beauty, love, and compassion. In doing so, I believe, they had no choice but to fall back on the past, to draw from it whatever moments of grace and fleeting recollections of goodness and splendor they could conjure, and mold them into the stuff from which their own creations were crafted. If we look hard enough, we may find traces of that vanished world, in all its complexity and ambivalence, poverty and ambition, tall tales and fabulous fables, in ourselves; for we all are descendants of those who once left the borderlands behind and went out into the world. In doing so, we will give a lease of life to what had once been before everything was erased and forgotten. I came to understand this relatively late in life, not surprisingly, perhaps, thanks to my mother. We often learn about love and compassion from our mothers; but in my case, my mother was also the last, and most direct, link to that world of yesterday. It was the story of her childhood, and of her transition to the new and foreign land where I was born, that set me off on my own journey.

PART IV

The Final Journey
(*My Mother*)

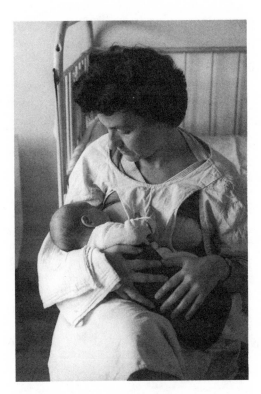

The author and his mother. Israel, 1954.
Author's private collection.

CHAPTER TWELVE

Galician Childhood

Two Worlds, Two People

> I was born in Kośmierzyn, a little village on the banks of the
> Dniester River in Polish Podolia, which now actually belongs to
> Ukraine. All the inhabitants of the village were Ukrainian, and
> they spoke Ukrainian even at the time. I was born there because
> my father's father managed the estate of Potocki's widow . . . and
> actually lived in a house on the estate in what was called "der
> Neuhof" [the new farmyard]. Later I remember that he had a sep-
> arate house of his own somewhere else in the village.

I N THE SUMMER OF 1995, a friend told me that if I ever wanted my
mother to tell me about growing up in Europe, I had to produce a tape
recorder: "That's what I did," she added, referring to an interview she
had conducted with her otherwise taciturn father who, like many of
my friends' parents, was a Holocaust survivor. At the time, members of my
generation in Israel, then in their forties, began realizing that they knew
practically nothing about the world their parents had come from; they
never asked, and their parents did not tell. And so, late one Friday morning, I came into my mother's kitchen, put my six-month-old daughter in
her chair by the table, told my seven-year-old son to play in the living
room, pressed the recording button on the tape recorder, and asked my
mother to tell me about her childhood. Mostly standing by the counter,
chopping carrots and cutting onions for chicken soup in the growing heat

of an Israeli summer day, she spoke, guided by a few questions, for about an hour and a half; it was as if she had been waiting all these years just to be asked.

At that point, I had only a vague idea of the geography and history of the region my mother had come from. I spent the next couple of decades studying it. These lands, whose borders and rulers had changed time and again, were dotted with towns and villages with strange, often unpro-nounceable names, some of which I had heard in my childhood without being able to locate them on the map; they were populated by different groups of several faiths, who spoke multiple, overlapping, and at times antagonistic languages. As I learned about that world, I also realized that it had been irretrievably lost. Listening to my mother recount her long-ago childhood, in that humid kitchen on the seventh floor of a Tel Aviv high-rise, I began thinking for the first time about the process that led to the transformation of such borderland regions from a rich, creative, and vola-tile mix of humanity into what I subsequently discovered were today's drab and uniform spaces, afflicted by an acute case of collective amnesia, not unlike the malady that had taken hold of my own, Israel-born generation.

At the time of that interview, I not only was ignorant of my mother's past, but also had no inkling that this would be the last opportunity to hear her tell it. Listening again to that interview now, after another quarter of a century has elapsed, I also realize that the story of my mother's child-hood was not only about that far-off corner of Eastern Europe, but also about her journey from there to Palestine, and her transformation into the person I thought I knew. In a sense, what she told was a story of two worlds, and two people: how radically different they were from each other, and how intimately linked. Ultimately, for me, it was the story of my own beginning, which I had never known, and had never cared to find out about, until that day.

I Might Have Called It Home

"Do you remember the estate?"

"I can't always distinguish between the stories that my father told me and what I remember."

"What do you remember, or think you remember?"

"What I think I remember is that there was a rather large house there. I don't know how old I was at the time, perhaps four or five, so to me it looked big. It was a two-story house, and the countess, as she was called, lived there, along with the count's sister and his sons. One son was even good friends with my father's younger brother, Mendel, who came to Israel before us. They even met here; he visited Father and Mendel when he came with the Anders people. I didn't see him, I was then already studying in Jerusalem, but I heard about it from them. I don't know how it happened, how he found them, or they found him. I remember they called him 'Tuszko' but that must have been a nickname."

As related in earlier chapters, the noble Potocki clan had been one of the most powerful and richest families in Poland, going back to the glory days of the Polish-Lithuanian Commonwealth in the sixteenth and seventeenth centuries. One historical seat of the clan was the town of Potok Złoty, located less than eight miles east of Kośmierzyn, where they built an impressive palace, which now lies in ruins, still preserving the romantic air of faded splendor and long-forgotten power. Like so many other former Polish palaces, fortresses, and Roman Catholic churches in this land now ruled by independent Ukraine, it could well carry the sign "Omnia Vanitas."[1]

Tuszko, or rather Toszko, is the Polish diminutive for Theodor. Karol Potocki, born in Kośmierzyn on 16 October 1910, and possibly Theodor's brother, might have also briefly joined the Anders Army, or the "Anders people," as my mother called them. On 17 September 1939, the Red Army invaded Poland from the east, in agreement with Nazi Germany, which had attacked Poland from the west just over two weeks earlier. The Soviets took numerous Polish prisoners of war and deported many more Polish citizens to gulags and to Central Asia; members of the old aristocracy were a favorite target. But following Nazi Germany's surprise attack on the Soviet Union in June 1941, Joseph Stalin agreed to release tens of thousands of Polish prisoners in order to conscript them into newly established military units under command of Polish general Władysław Anders. The formation was subordinated directly to the Polish government in exile, headed in London by General Władysław Sikorski. In 1942 the so-called Anders Army was transferred to British command and traveled through Iran and Iraq to Palestine. Most of the formation's Jewish volunteers deserted it at this point and joined the Yishuv—the prestate Jewish population living there at the time under British Mandatory rule. The best known of these deserters was Menachem Begin, who became the leader of the Jewish underground known to the British as the Irgun, and decades later was elected prime minister of Israel.[2]

I try to imagine that meeting in Palestine between the scion of the

Potocki clan, my communist great-uncle, and my Zionist grandfather, the three of them drinking vodka, reminiscing about playing together in Kośmierzyn, and wondering how the world of their childhood on the banks of the Dniester had descended into such mayhem; perhaps Tuszko, as my mother referred to him, told them about the mass murder of the Jews. Soon thereafter, he must have departed with what became the II Corps of the Polish Armed Forces to fight in the bloody Battle of Monte Cassino in Italy. But Karol never made it out of the Soviet Union. Like many other Potockis, he was arrested by the NKVD, the Soviet secret police, in 1939, and is reported to have died on 16 June 1942, in Kermine (Navoi), located at the time in the southern Soviet Union and now in southeastern Uzbekistan. He may have died while still in the hands of the NKVD or following his conscription.[3]

"There was a house there, with a huge courtyard, and there were stables and cowsheds and other structures, and a large barn. They lived in the two-story house, and I think that my grandfather, if I can visualize it, lived in a one-story house, a long structure, that was perpendicular to the other house, like an arm. I remember more clearly the house that Grandfather owned later on, no longer in the courtyard, so I don't know if he stopped being the manager of the estate and stayed in the village, or just built his own house."

"So how many family members were there?"

"Ours? First of all, Grandfather and Grandmother, and their sons, but that's all I remember; in fact, we didn't live there anymore. I was born in the village, but we already lived in a little town nearby called Potok Złoty. Potok means 'stream' or 'brook,' so the name means 'golden brook.' I was still very young then, too; I don't think that I even began attending school there."

I visited Potok Złoty and Buczacz for the first time in 2003. My mother and I had begun planning a trip together not long after we spoke about her childhood. That conversation must have evoked deeply suppressed memories in her. In part, perhaps, this was because she had never talked about the world that she came from in quite the same manner as she had done with me, her son, who had finally asked and, as a total stranger to that world, needed her guidance. This was a very different conversation from those she must have had with her mother about their hometown, to which I was never privy (and were conducted in a language I did not understand). But the reason that I had not asked her for all those years, aside from my brash Israeli reluctance to acknowledge that I too had roots

stretching not that far back to the shtetls of Eastern Europe, was also related, I think, to my mother's own ambivalence about her lost childhood.
To be sure, we all own and relate to a lost childhood. But in my mother's
case, as in the case of many of her generation, this was not only a matter
of recalling a childhood experienced a long time ago in a distant land, or
of realizing the unavoidable fact that life after leaving that land was so radically different as to appear utterly unconnected to those fleeting memories of childhood. It also had to do with the stark knowledge that return to
that land was completely impossible: not just because we can never return
to our childhood, which is generally true; nor because a single lifetime
lived in the twentieth century could have encompassed more dramatic
changes than scores of generations in earlier times. It was impossible to
return because that land had been entirely emptied of the people and culture into which my mother was born. The manor houses and courtyards,
the cowsheds and stables, the barns and the dirt roads, are still there, as are
the hills and meadows, forests and rivers; but the Jews, who were an inherent component of that world, are gone forever.

We did not go to Potok Złoty and Buczacz together because my mother
died of colon cancer in 1998. That disease, too, is a legacy of Eastern Europe. Ashkenazi Jews have an unusually high incidence of it, and no less than
80 percent of all Jews in the world today hail back to the Polish-Lithuanian
Commonwealth of the eighteenth century.[4] Genes are far more difficult to
shake off than cultural and social norms; hence, I also carry that particular
legacy. I do think that my mother's original instincts were right. Going
back would only have caused her pain and sorrow. But as she reached into
herself during our ninety-minute conversation, rather than brutally tear-
ing out fragments of memories, she gently and affectionately pulled little
strands of recollections and wove them, perhaps for the first time, into her
own fabric of a childhood, both very private and personal, and, as I know
now, similar to that of many other Jewish children of that time and place.

Still, I sometimes wish she had been with me on that first journey. As
I stood in the farm courtyard across the now paved road from the derelict
palace of Potok Złoty, I could not resist imagining that it might have been
the very same place that she had recalled. It was not huge, but then she was
a little girl; it was not in Kośmierzyn, but she had seemed unclear as to
whether she spent her early years in the village or the little town. And
ultimately, of course, it didn't matter, since this was an unremarkable spot
like many others. But in another world, had history turned out slightly
differently, I, too, might have called it home.

As I listen now to the tape, recorded twenty-five years ago, I keep hearing my mother chopping carrots for the soup. Occasionally my son's voice can be heard. Twenty-five years is a long time in an individual life. He has since served in the Israeli Defense Forces and earned a law degree; my daughter, gurgling in her little seat, has graduated from college and now works in New York.

"Then they moved to Buczacz, which was a town."

"Your parents?"

"Our parents. And then also Grandfather. What I remember is that we lived in one house with Grandfather, so he must have also moved, probably for another business, because he had a flour mill in some place called Rukomysz [Rukomysh, three miles north of Buczacz] and, I don't know, he was always traveling, he would go to Stanisławów, to Lemberg—to Lvov. But I know that they used to say that I was born there, in that village. So, whether they still lived there, or Mother came there just to give birth, I really don't know."

Kośmierzyn is now known by its Ukrainian name, Kosmyryn, a village of about one thousand inhabitants. Different people will have different memories. Stefan Hnatkiwskyj related his own story in 2005 as part of a reminiscence project celebrating the history of the Ukrainian community in Gloucester, England, and subsequently included in the BBC Archive of World War Memories:

> I was born in Selo [Village] Kosmyryn, Buchach [District], Ternopil [Region], Ukraine. I don't have any happy memories of my early life, only despair. I had two brothers, two stepbrothers and two stepsisters. We earned our living off the land. We had a small-holding with two horses, two cows, a sow, two pigs, 24 sheep, a ram, 24 hens and a cockerel. On the arable land we grew crops. I started school at the age of 8 and attended for 4 hours a day. I left school when I was 12 years old and worked on the smallholding until the Germans came. I was sent by the Germans to work on a collective farm. After the war I had no other choice of country to go to but England. I was sent to a transit camp in Malvern and then on to Elmbridge Court in Gloucester. From there I was sent out to work on different farms in Gloucestershire.[5]

In the borderlands, the experiences of Ukrainians, Poles, and Jews differed substantially, especially, as is invariably the case, in times of crisis, war, and internecine conflict. Potok Złoty is now known as Zolotyi Potik. In 1919 it was inhabited by 1,450 Ukrainians, 1,050 Jews, and 1,000 Poles.[6] The name changes are not merely political or cosmetic. While some of the buildings that my mother might have seen there before World War II are still standing, the population has drastically changed. The inhabitants are almost exclusively Ukrainian. The only remaining sign of former Jewish life in Potok Złoty is the cemetery, although most of its sturdier tombstones have been carted off to be used for other purposes. This sweeping demographic transformation has also determined how people remember the past and define who they are in the present.

On the tape I can again hear my mother chopping something on the cutting board. She had left Buczacz sixty years earlier, and the recipe for her chicken soup likely went back many generations before that. But the setting had changed dramatically. In Poland, eating a hot lunch at 1:30 p.m. was perfectly reasonable; doing so in the Middle East, long before air-conditioners were introduced to Israeli homes, was not; yet old habits die hard. We take the food we eat at home for granted. When I eventually went to Poland, I was initially surprised to find that the borscht did not resemble my maternal grandmother's dish. It was only in West Ukraine that I discovered her version, made with sour cream rather than with meatballs; it reminded me of my childhood in Tel Aviv.

A Love for German

"So what do you know about the family from before?"

"From before?"

"How far back do you know anything about the family?"

"I just know about Grandfather on Father's side, and Grandfather on Mother's side."

"Whose Grandfather was in Buczacz?"

"That's my father's parents. He had two brothers and a sister. My mother's parents were also from a village called Rożnów, which was in the Carpathians, and was considered very far away. Today that would probably not be thought of as a great distance. We would go in a cart the whole day to visit them. We went in the summer, Mother and the children."

"Grandmother told me about a grandfather who passed away at a very old age."

"That was her grandfather. My mother was orphaned when she lost her father at age six or seven. I still remember her mother, my grandmother.

She was left with six or seven children, when she was only thirty-two years old, as Mother told me, and they were raised by their grandfather, her mother's father, my grandmother's father. He died when we were already in Israel. He was ninety-six or ninety-seven years old. I remember him too a little; he used to sit outside the house and ruminate, and we would always giggle because he would make this gesture with his hand," she shakes her hand to demonstrate, "and say, '*arop fon mark!*' [Yiddish: 'enough with that!'] when he was done with a thought. By then he no longer worked. Grandmother lived with one of my uncles, one of Mother's brothers. One brother lived in Kosov, and another brother lived in the same place, in Rożnów, but he had a big house, which at the time seemed huge to me."

Rożnów, now known as Rozhniv, is located sixty miles south of Buczacz, close to the Czeremosz (Cheremosh) River. In 1921 Rożnów had a population of close to 6,500 people, the vast majority of whom were Ukrainians, with just over 400 Jews. The Ukrainians were mostly peasants, and the Jews constituted the urban commercial and artisanal element.[7] Kosów, called Kosov by the Jews and now known as Kosiv, is situated just a few miles to the west of Rożnów, on the eastern slopes of the Carpathian mountain range. A Polish guide published in 1919 describes it as "a very dirty provincial town," whose population was made up of 200 Poles, 400 Ukrainians, and 2,500 Jews.[8]

Today's Kosiv, a pretty town that serves as a base for hikers and skiers, houses a museum dedicated to the heroes of the Ukrainian resistance against the Red Army's return to the region following the withdrawal of the Wehrmacht in 1944. One such hero was Dmytro Bilinchuk, nom de guerre "Khmara," or "Cloud," who kept fighting the Soviets until his capture in 1952; he was executed in Kyiv the following year. The museum is located in the house of the town's prewar rabbi. The few Jews still alive in the region perceived the arriving Red Army troops as liberators; the Ukrainian resisters, who had collaborated with the Germans in murdering Jews, saw the Soviets as occupiers. This polar perspective of events makes for split memories, as well as denials and obfuscations, to this day. It is not impossible that Stefan Hnatkiwskyj, the peasant from my mother's birth-village of Kosmyryn, actually ended up in the United Kingdom, like many other Ukrainians at the time, because he had escaped the Soviets as a member of the collaborationist Ukrainian underground.

"So, were there no stories about the family from before?"

"Maybe there were, but I don't know any, and my father didn't tell me. He didn't talk about 'before.' What I know is that during the war, World

War I, when my mother herself was still a girl, they were always afraid when the Russians marched in. They were always glad when the Germans or the Austrians arrived. And in fact, they grew up in the Austro-Hungarian Empire, and that's why she knew German. They were *Flüchtlinge*, she always said, they were refugees in Czechia."

"In World War I?"

"In World War I they were evacuated as refugees to Czechoslovakia, and her brother studied music there. He had a violin, and sometimes, on family occasions, he would play."

"Grandmother Rina's brother?"

"Yes, Shimon, Shimen."

"And he perished?"

"He perished, with his wife and children, they all perished there, not one of them survived. What's tragic is that in fact, until the very end [of her life], despite everything, she admired the Germans more, you know, German culture, and she loved to read and speak German. What there was before them, I really don't know. I don't know."

During most of our recorded conversation my mother's voice is even. She had a good, strong voice, and articulated every word very clearly. She had been a teacher for decades and loved the Hebrew language, which she knew better than any of us, with all its ancient historical layers of meanings and allusions. But she never lost her slightly foreign accent; her *r* would roll from the tongue as in Polish and never went deeper into the throat as in the more guttural Hebrew pronunciation. Even my own name sounded slightly foreign when she called me. When I began going to Poland, I was startled to find that people pronounced my name just as my mother had. Yet when she speaks about the murder of Uncle Shimen (or Szymen in Polish), his wife, and his children, her voice trails off for a moment, as if the thought that this family, a family of which she had only faint memories, had simply been wiped out, along with every other member of her extended clan, save for the few who left Poland before the war, is so inconceivable that one can simply not articulate it in any appropriate manner. And when she speaks of her mother's love of German, which I found out just a few years before her death in 1980, her voice becomes harder, tinged with subdued exasperation.

The two of them, my mother and her mother, were very close. For many years they would spend several hours together every week, as Grandmother Rina would dye my mother's hair with henna and they would talk and talk, about family, I assume, about the men who always provided good reasons for complaints, and about the children and grandchildren, who were a regular cause of worry and admiration. But I don't really know what they spoke about and am only certain of the strong link between my mother, an educated, well-read, and well-traveled person, and her mother, who had no chance to study after her stint at the German gymnasium in Prague, and never traveled anywhere after arriving in Palestine in her mid-thirties, and that my mother tended to follow her mother's advice on most important matters. But my mother could not quite understand, perhaps not even forgive, her mother for that stubborn love of German culture, despite everything.

I realized then, as I do even more clearly now, how late I was in setting out on this inquiry about my family. The people who could remember beyond my mother's memory, such as my grandparents, all born around 1900 and themselves possessing memories of family stories dating far back into the nineteenth century, were all gone. My mother remembered only fragments of that past, just as she knew only bits and pieces of the languages they all spoke—Polish, Ukrainian, Russian, German, Yiddish. With the sole exception of one document, my family has left, it seems, no traces in the archives. The few remaining family photographs largely contain people whose names and relationships to each other I will never know. At times I can identify a family resemblance and make educated guesses. Some photos are inscribed and dated on the back. But the moment to tap into the memories of those who knew the people in the photos and in most cases mourned their murder long thereafter, has passed.

On the tape, my son is asking for something, and I stop the recording for a moment. Listening to it now, so many years later, I regret not having left the tape recorder on, so that I could still hear my son's seven-year-old voice, before it acquired the booming male baritone I used to hear on the telephone every week, before we switched over to live video chats. The millions of people who immigrated across continents and oceans in the nineteenth and twentieth centuries had to reconcile themselves to never again seeing or speaking with the loved ones they had left behind; instead, when they could, they sent photographs, for which they often put on their finest clothes and went to a photographic studio, to demonstrate how well they were doing, even if they were not, and to show due decorum to the camera, for which, of course, they never smiled.

Ten years after the interview, I asked my son to transcribe the tape for me. He was very attached to his grandmother, who died far too early, when he was only ten years old. He used to call her every day when he came back from school and just chat with her. If my father answered the phone, he would say, "Hi Grandpa, where is Grandma?" This was the sort of intimate connection that exists, sometimes, only between grandchildren and grandparents. But when he transcribed the tape, he showed only moderate interest in its content and little nostalgia for his grandmother. At the time he was already one of those young men who don't say more than they think is necessary. I probably spoke more as a boy and a young man, and still do so today. I also have distinct memories of my grandparents, and perhaps now, well into middle age, I am more willing to recall and share them. And my son, now in his thirties, has also taken to speaking more. Perhaps, if we synchronize our lives between his maturity and my old age, we will find the right moment to speak with each other about my mother.

When I visited the former Jewish neighborhood of Kazimierz in Kraków, Poland, for the first time, I was struck by the so-called Jewish restaurants run by Catholic Poles in the main square of this quarter—a manifestation of what has been called virtual Jews that prevails in some postcommunist East European towns. Having rediscovered their Jewish past as well as its current commercial value, they fill the void created by the murder of the Jews with often well-meaning but occasionally grotesque virtually Jewish replacements of the "real thing."[9] The traditional Jewish *kugel* I ordered was not as good as the one I remembered from my childhood. Every time I came to visit my maternal grandmother, she would set about making me her own special *lokshen kugel*, consisting of egg noodles and raisins, and fried in a pan rather than baked in the oven. This was hardly light fare, but I was young and always hungry. I can still recall the smell that filled the tiny kitchen, the crunchy burned noodles on the outside, the moist raisins on the inside, and the feeling of warmth and security, of being welcomed in a way that I would never experience anywhere again. My mother never made this dish.

In my generation, having two full sets of grandparents was uncommon. Few people had extended families, and various distant "aunts" and "uncles" were brought into the family fold to fill the void of closer kin murdered in the Holocaust. But I don't recall ever asking my grandparents about the world they came from, and now I am left with a gaping abyss between photos I cannot decipher and documents that provide historical context but lack any direct mention of the family I never knew. I could blame the Zionist education of the 1950s and 1960s in Israel that told us to look forward to the future and to shed the dead skin of the past, to make ourselves into "new Jews" and to expel from our psyches the haunting and debilitating Diaspora figures still represented by our few surviving older relatives. But I could have just asked, and now it's too late.

When the Russians marched into Austrian Galicia at the outbreak of World War I in 1914, thousands of Jews fled to the west from the marauding Russian soldiers and the numerous pogroms that erupted in their towns and cities. Even as the Russian authorities were deporting Jews who came under their control deep into the Tsarist Empire, Jewish refugees ran as far as Vienna, Budapest, and Prague.[10] "Czechia" was the Czech part of Czechoslovakia, the state established after the fall of the Austro-Hungarian Empire at the end of World War I, and since the fall of communism divided into the Czech Republic and Slovakia. Under Austrian rule, Prague was in the province of Bohemia, and while the rural population was mostly Czech, the city of Prague had a large German and German-speaking Jewish population.[11] Which is why Grandmother Rina would have learned German in the heart of what would soon become an independent Slavic country.

My grandmother's love for German culture and language was hardly unique. Many educated Jews in Eastern Europe, most of whom had never been to Germany or to the German-speaking parts of the Austro-Hungarian Empire, saw German as the main vehicle to reach the best of what European culture had to offer.[12] This admiration for German *Kultur,* along with fear of the Russian military and loathing for the repressive, reactionary, and officially antisemitic Tsarist Empire, was perfectly rational in 1914–18. And, indeed, German and Austrian conduct toward Jews in World War I was far better than that of the Russians.[13] But the memory of these events had tragic consequences for the millions of Jews still living in these areas when the Germans invaded the Soviet Union in June 1941. Personal or transmitted memories of the previous world war persuaded many Jews to reject rumors and fragments of information about German Nazi atrocities. Having experienced the often arbitrary and violent rule of the Bolsheviks, most Jews chose to stay where they were rather than flee with the retreating Red Army, and almost all of them were subsequently murdered by the new carriers of German *Kultur.*

Rochaleh's Return

"Where did the family come from?"

"Ah, the family is from there, from Poland. Probably they were there for centuries."

"That's in . . . Ukraine?"

"There, yes. See, this was first the Austro-Hungarian Empire, and after World War I it became part of Poland, it was called Polish Podolia. And that's why the city came to be named Lvov [officially Lwów] and not Lemberg like before."

"And the population was Ukrainian?"

"But the population was Ukrainian, and in Buczacz there was a Ukrainian gymnasium, both Polish and Ukrainian [in fact, it was a Polish school, though Ukrainian was taught there as a second language], and if I am not mistaken, my mother had a cousin, Zelig, who also studied at some Ukrainian [likely Polish] university. I am not completely certain, but I think I remember such a story. The village population spoke Ukrainian. By the way, one day Rochaleh called me and said, 'You should watch, there's a program about Buczacz on television.' I turned it on and watched, but I didn't recognize anything, although I think I remember exactly the house, our house; but everyone in the film spoke Ukrainian."

Rochaleh is my mother's cousin, the daughter of her father's brother Mendel and his wife Tsila (Cyla in Polish). Mendel, who was a communist, and believed that the Polish authorities were on his track, managed to acquire an immigration certificate to Palestine and came there a couple of years before his older brother Yisrael, my grandfather. Tsila, a young woman from Buczacz, who wanted to get out of Poland but had no immigration certificate, persuaded Mendel to marry her fictitiously, so as to be able to go with him as his wife. On the ship he fell in love with her. But it was not a happy marriage, and they divorced. Their daughter Rochaleh was born in Palestine and raised in a kibbutz (communal settlement). My father recalled that one day, about fifteen years ago, she called him up and announced that she was returning to Buczacz. She had in fact been to Galicia only once, as a child, shortly before the war, and had entirely repressed the fact that the Buczacz of that childhood visit, on the eve of the catastrophe, no longer existed; that even then, before the destruction, it was far from the ideal town she imagined; and that today's Buchach (as one should transliterate its Ukrainian name) would hardly be a welcoming place for an elderly Jewish woman who had lived her entire life in Israel. Rochaleh was raised in a harsh environment on sweet memories of an idyllic site that had never actually existed. It was there that she wanted to return, to the childhood that she never had. But, of course, there was no going back, and she did not actually go.

Having been to Buczacz several times since recording this conversation with my mother, I wonder whether, had she come with me, we would have been able to find the family home. All I know about where it was and what it looked like comes from my mother's rather vague description. But while the town was damaged in the fighting in World War II, especially between March and July 1944, most of the residential houses seem to have remained, and the damage was in fact less severe than in the previous world war. And yet Buczacz has changed a great deal. At the turn of the previous century, it was a lovely little town with some remarkable buildings and an enchanting setting. Since then, while the setting has not changed, the destruction wrought by two major wars, the effects of several regimes seemingly dedicated to shabby and ugly architectural designs, and the poverty and ignorance of a post-1945 population that moved in from the villages lacking any prior experience of urban living, have finally transformed the town into a hideous mishmash of structures piled together in a beautiful valley and straining to hide both the magnificent scenery and the few remains of once elegant buildings. During my mother's childhood, more than half of the town's population spoke Yiddish, and most of the rest spoke Polish. It is hardly surprising that she could not quite recognize Buczacz in the film her cousin Rochaleh had recommended.[14]

The extraordinary painter Samuel Bak, whom I have known for many years, once told me about visiting his hometown of Vilna (Wilno, Vilnius), where he was born in 1933, and where he survived the Holocaust.[15] Sam is fluent in many languages: Polish and Yiddish, Hebrew and Italian, French and English, and probably others, too. His town looked in some ways just as he remembered it. There was only one major difference: he could not understand the language spoken on the street. This is the experience of many of those who lived in prewar Eastern Europe and were lucky enough to survive the catastrophe that engulfed it in their childhood.

Before the war, Wilno had a majority Polish and Jewish population, and the main languages spoken there were Polish and Yiddish. In 1897, when the city was still under Russian rule, Yiddish was spoken by 40 percent of the inhabitants, Polish by around 30 percent, Russian by about 20 percent, Belarusian by just over 4 percent, and Lithuanian by barely more than 2 percent of the population.[16] According to the Polish census of 1931, the Polish-ruled Wilno Voivodeship, or province, had a population of more than 1.27 million people, of whom just under 200,000 lived in the city of Wilno. No fewer than two-thirds of the inhabitants of the province claimed Polish as their native tongue, followed by slightly over one-fifth claiming Belarusian and somewhat under one-tenth claiming Yiddish. Lithuanian came in fourth place with 5.5 percent, higher only than Russian with 3.4 percent.[17] After World War II, when Vilnius became part of Lithuania, these proportions changed dramatically, as was the case elsewhere in Eastern Europe. According to the 2011 census, the city's population of more than half a million inhabitants was made up of more than 60 percent Lithuanians, 16.5 percent Poles, 12 percent Russians, 3.5 percent Belarusians, 1 percent Ukrainians, and less than 4 percent "Others."[18]

I recall Bak remarking that the only way to tell what the official language had been in the past was to examine the cast-iron sewer covers, which are rarely replaced and tend to be highly durable, resisting even wars and fires. In Vilnius many still had Polish inscriptions. I tried this out in Chernivtsi, known in the past as Czernowitz (Chernovtsy in Russian, Cernăuți in Romanian), when I visited there in 2004. According to the Ukrainian population census of 2001, of the 250,000 or so inhabitants, close to 80 percent were Ukrainian, and more than 11 percent Russian, with the rest of the population being made up of Romanians, Moldavians, Poles, and others. Jews constitute just over half of one percent. In 1930, Jews made up almost one-third of the city's 100,000 inhabitants, with the second largest group being Romanian, followed by Germans and Ukrainians. The German and Romanian inscriptions of the sewer covers still bear witness to the city's past as part of the Austro-Hungarian Empire before World War I and of Romania in the interwar period; but the vast majority of the population there today speaks Ukrainian and Russian.[19]

There is a measure of irony in the fact that the layers of an urban center's identity can be revealed by observing the covers of its sewers. It is somewhat akin to an archaeological excavation: the deeper you dig, the further you go back in time. Sewers played a prominent role in World War II Europe and its aftermath. In the Warsaw Ghetto they served as an underground lifeline to an imprisoned population that eventually vanished from the city, and as a last resort for the fighters of an uprising that ended in a German attempt to raze every material trace of that "Jewish city" even after its inhabitants had been murdered. All that is left now of those Jews and the ghetto they had lived in are these hidden sewers. Yet the sewers of Warsaw became a site of contestation over historical memories. As postwar Poland strove to monopolize wartime heroism and victimhood, the underground tunnels used in the Polish uprising that erupted a year after the ghetto was wiped out came to symbolize resistance to German rule as a whole, thereby obliterating the memory of the ghetto's last stand and the shame and horror associated with it, when one-third of the city's population was massacred while its Christian inhabitants stood by. Polish director Andrzej Wajda's celebrated film *Kanał* (Sewer, 1957) accomplished this act of simultaneous remembrance and erasure most poignantly. Half a century later, his disciple Agnieszka Holland created her own version of heroic resistance and survival underground in her film *W ciemności* (*In Darkness*, 2011), which depicts the rescue of a group of Jews in the sewage canals of German-occupied Lwów/Lemberg by a Polish Catholic worker.[20]

But sewers were also sites where crimes could be perpetrated and hidden. Carol Reed's *The Third Man* (1949), with a script by Graham Greene and starring Trevor Howard and Orson Welles, takes place in a postwar Vienna suspended in the twilight zone between West and East, glorious past and sordid present; it ends with an unforgettable chase through the city's extensive sewage system. As the Iron Curtain severs the empire's mutilated body from its inflated head, the sewers underneath the ruins of this once splendid imperial metropolis are still teeming with crime and deceit, and invisible rivers of filth wash away the sins of its past. Only the cast-iron covers on the streets offer passersby cryptic clues about the city's erased and forgotten former inhabitants, even as they also provide the perpetrators hiding in the dark an escape hatch through which they can reemerge into the sunlight as respectable citizens.[21]

Wild Strawberries

"So, in the years before you went to Palestine, you lived in Buczacz itself?"

"In Buczacz, in Buczacz itself. I remember it was a house with two sections; we lived in one section, on the right, and Grandfather and Grandmother lived in the left section, along with my father's sister, who later married, still before we left. And I remember the street—it led to the train station. The house was on a hill and from the street level there was a stone staircase that led to our house. To the left was the house of a Polish father and son who were always referred to at home as Endeks. The Endeks, you know, were the nationalist party, I don't precisely know what that meant, probably NDK or something, I don't know what, but they were called the Endeks. This was a derogatory name because they were big antisemites, living right next to us. And why do I remember that? Because I recall that once I was coming back with Mother from someplace and we were going up to our house, and that house on the left was very close—I suppose the houses were not large, you know as a child they would appear to you as such; they were one-story houses, that's for sure—and the old man was dead. He was laid out on what they called 'katofelek,' you know, when they lay them out like that, and I looked through the window and I saw something terribly scary, it frightened me horribly, and that's why I remember that house until now as some kind of childhood trauma."

Listening to the recording now, I realize how this first and frightening confrontation with death became associated in my mother's mind with her fear of the "Endeks" and merged into a childhood trauma that helped her remember where she had lived. The menacing, antisemitic Pole living next door was lying on a "katofelek," or rather, as the Polish would have it, on a *katafalk*, or catafalque, the wooden framework that supports the coffin when the body is lying in state or is carried during a funeral. The "enemy" was dead, but somehow that death became associated with fear and foreboding. Perhaps, despite her generally pleasant memories of childhood, at a deeper layer of my mother's consciousness lurked some dark terror that she never quite articulated. As I analyze my mother's words, uttered a quarter of a century ago, it occurs to me that, ironically, I am engaging in precisely the kind of interpretation she would so often propose, to my intense irritation, of my own actions and words, always seeking their deeper psychological causes and motivations. My mother taught child psychology for many decades and was a great admirer of Sigmund Freud, and at times I found her analyses of dreams, impulses, unconscious drives, and the rest of it too rigidly based on the psychoanalytical model, allowing the individual, especially me, insufficient room for thought and action unlinked to a predetermined, and as I saw it, oppressive framework. I was probably unfair to her. And yet now I was indulging in the same exercise. As my mother used to say, "Oedipus or no Oedipus, he certainly loves his mother."

That Freud himself had family roots in Buczacz—which I am not sure my mother knew—is just another one of those twists of fate, or coincidences, that first-person histories so abundantly contain. From his perch in Vienna, Freud was, of course, himself in an excellent position to delve into the psychology of political and popular antisemitism in Europe between the late nineteenth century and the eve of the Holocaust. As for my mother, her personal trauma surrounding the death of the neighbor next door reflected Polish Jewry's general fear of the Endeks, the name commonly used for members of the National Democracy (ND) movement, or *Endecja*, founded by Roman Dmowski in 1897, which promoted the idea that Jews were Poland's main internal enemy.[22]

A final, even more sinister historical twist to my mother's tale of the dead old antisemitic Pole concerns the location of the event. For the family's home, as she describes it, was located on Kolejowa (Railroad) Street, which led from the town center to the Buczacz train station. Seven years after she and her family left the town, thousands of Jews were led along this street, humiliated and beaten and shot as they made their way to the train station, where they were shoved into inhumanly crowded cattle cars and sent on a slow and hellish journey to the extermination camp of Bełżec, from which no one returned. Was the traumatic memory of that dead old man a premonition of things to come, or more likely, did my mother remember it so vividly precisely because of the horrors that engulfed her hometown soon thereafter, but which she and her nuclear family were spared? Did she remember this single death of an "enemy" because she was unconsciously haunted by the innumerable deaths of her kin she had never witnessed?

"But," and my mother moves back to happier topics, leaving that moment of fear behind, "we would spend every summer with the grandfathers and grandmothers, half a summer in each village. No, not after Grandfather lived with us, no, but when I was very little we would go to our paternal grandfather [in Kośmierzyn] in the summer and then we would go to the grandmother and uncles in the other village [Rożnów]."

My son calls to me again. "Just a moment," I say.

"And what was Grandfather Yisrael's occupation at the time?"

"What did he do? That's also interesting, as if I would know. I don't know what he did. Er hot gehandelt. Wos hot er gehandelt, weys ikh nisht."

When she speaks about her father, my Grandfather Yisrael, she switches suddenly to Yiddish. We never spoke Yiddish with each other. In fact, I can't speak Yiddish. Unlike my parents, who could understand a fair amount of German because they spoke Yiddish at home, I can understand and read Yiddish because I studied German. It occurs to me that my family has a strange relationship with that language, going back at least to my maternal grandmother's love of German since her days as a child refugee at the gymnasium in Prague, and, even earlier, to the Germanizing effects on my paternal Grandfather Simcha and his annual pre–World War I summertime visits to his family in Prussia, just across the Warta River from his hometown of Pyzdry.

"He traded. What he traded I have no idea," my mother says in Yiddish. Then she continues in Hebrew: "I know that Grandfather had properties, so perhaps he [her father] worked with Grandfather, I don't know."

My son has not given up and is calling again. I say, "Come, listen, it's interesting." He says, "Grandma, did you buy me a present?" "No, you told me, and I forgot," she replies. "I'll buy you one tomorrow," I promise him. He groans unhappily. My mother runs water in the sink.

"Maybe he worked with Grandfather. Perhaps this was his rebellion, leaving, I don't know. What I know is that Grandfather had a big flour mill in some other village. My aunt married a university graduate, which was quite rare; she only wanted an intellectual, an educated man, not that she was, she never went to secondary school. But he couldn't find a job, you know, at the time they would not let Jews teach, even at a Polish high school. So her husband managed the mill, however well he could, and my aunt moved in with him; he arranged a house for them, and she lived with him there. What other properties did Grandfather have? I know he had properties and was considered wealthy—I don't know how wealthy—but apparently quite wealthy."

"So what do you remember as a girl?"

"What I vividly remember and loved very much was when we went in the summer, when we went to Grandfather in Kośmierzyn; we used to go to the forest and gather wild berries, and we would go to the Dniester, to the river, to bathe. It seemed to me huge at the time, the other bank looked so far. And there we would spend our time and it was interesting to watch, because they would cut down the trees and float the logs down the river and would stop them at various points along the riverbanks. I also remember that I used to play with the *shiksalakh*. Across from Grandfather's house lived a Ukrainian family, they had, I don't know what it was, a garden, or an orchard, and I would go to play with the goy's daughters. In Buczacz I remember that I had a very good friend who was not Jewish, Irka [or Irenka, diminutive of Irena], whose aunt was a teacher in the same school. She was in the first or second grade."

I try to envision my mother as a little girl gathering wild berries in the forest by the Dniester, which is still a wide and beautiful river, across which I have driven several times since that conversation. I am reminded of Ingmar Bergman's film, *Wild Strawberries*, which moved me deeply already as a teenager, even though I did not quite understand it at the time. I have subsequently watched it again over the years, and each time my own age coincided with that of different characters. In the film, an elderly professor is driving with his daughter and son-in-law to receive a prestigious prize; on the way, they stop for a picnic in the forest. The professor falls asleep, and in his dream he is playing with other children in the woods; but he has not changed, remaining the old, decrepit man he has become, even as he grotesquely tries to mix in with the characters of his childhood, cutting a ridiculous, pathetic, and touching figure all at once.

My mother's incongruence is different. It is of a Jewish girl playing with *shiksalakh*, the derogatory Yiddish word for Gentile girls and young women. Like other Jews of that time, she does not intend it at all to be demeaning; it simply means, in the context of her recollection, a non-Jewish girl. But this memory reflects both the fact that children could and did have friendships free of any prejudice, fear, and hate in that lost world of distant childhood, and that once they grew out of childhood, things often changed, and the walls of separation rose between them. Bergman's old professor recalls his childhood as he faces his approaching mortality; his life was not all that it should or could have been, and the honors he receives are no substitute for lack of love and nagging regrets. But he is old, and death will come to him as it comes to all. Over my mother's recollections of gathering wild berries hangs a darker, more ominous cloud; only a few years later, one group of people, not infrequently made up of the now grown children who had played together in the past, denounced, robbed, hunted down, and killed members of the other group, or, in rarer cases, rescued them from foreign murderers and their local accomplices. Natural death from old age became the exception; violent, premature, often gratuitously cruel death became the rule; the normal order of things turned upside-down.

Photographs from that period are more staged than those we take today. This had to do both with the photographic equipment, which necessitated standing still and posing for the picture, and with the fact that such photos, especially of a group in a provincial setting, entailed a ceremony, often celebrating or commemorating an event, and were meant to represent something beyond the features of the individuals captured on film and printed on paper. In one such photo, taken in Buczacz in 1936, the year after my mother left, a group of children, properly dressed in local Ukrainian ethnic attire, along with their priest, are arranged next to their church. As my mother was ten years old when she left Buczacz, these children are just a few years younger. In another photo, also taken in Buczacz in the 1930s, Ukrainian youths, similarly dressed in their ethnic costumes, are posing with an older man who appears to be their teacher; they are just a little older than my mother.

In a third photo, taken in Palestine in 1920, several young members of the Jewish-socialist youth movement Hashomer Hatza'ir (the Young Guard) from Buczacz are engaged in redefining and reframing their identity. Mostly

Ukrainian schoolchildren in Buczacz, 1930s. Author's private collection.

Ukrainian youths in Buczacz, 1930s. Author's private collection.

wearing what were called at the time "Russian shirts," these youths have shed all traditional Eastern European attributes of Jewishness, and look much more like the Narodniks they admired, those Russian members of the intelligentsia who "went to the people" to spread the message of socialism and reform in the 1870s. They are also reminiscent of Mosler's Fraternity society, those shtetl Jewish youths who sought to whip up strikes among the rural masses of the Buczacz district in 1902. Similarly to those precedents, the youths in this photo are as much about transforming themselves as about transforming others. They appear extraordinarily young, determined, and somewhat drained. In one sense, they are the forerunners of an entirely new society. In another, having shed the traditional markers that would identify them ethnically and religiously, they have joined the European mainstream by internalizing and performing abstract European ideologies as secular, socialist, and nationalist Jews. Yet this assimilation simultaneously means separation, because it can be completed only by leaving Europe and moving to a territory that they claim to be their historical patrimony even before landing on its shores, where they will eventually establish a Jewish state.

"Did you go to a non-Jewish school?"

"Not Jewish, no. I didn't know Hebrew. My mother studied Hebrew when she was a child; she knew Hebrew, and Father knew Hebrew from the cheder . . . "

"And there was no Jewish school there?"

"There was a Tarbut school . . . "

"But you didn't attend it?"

"No. I attended the state school."

"And neither did your brothers?"

"No. Why? I don't know. Because my father was such a Zionist and activist, but I didn't know Hebrew, not a word of it. My father knew it from the Siddur . . . "

"So what did you speak at home? Yiddish?"

"What did we speak at home? We spoke Polish and Yiddish. Although when we came to Israel and there were many Poles here, I discovered that my parents weren't such great Polish speakers. My father knew Ukrainian better, and my mother spoke . . . "

My son is whining. He wants us to come out of the kitchen, where we have been standing and talking now for a while, and move to the living room, so we can play with him and keep him company. My mother seems to be done with preparing the soup. She had just run some more water in

Hashomer Hatza'ir members from Buczacz. Palestine, 1920.

the sink, and now there is no longer any noise associated with cooking and cleaning up. Listening to this exchange, I am annoyed at my own impatience. I cut my mother off at some crucial points and ask another question without letting her complete the previous answer. I know now that my grandfather studied Hebrew at the cheder, the traditional elementary education in Judaism and Hebrew language, usually only for boys, conducted by a "melamed," or teacher—a system that persisted in much of Eastern Europe until the Holocaust—and I know that he read Hebrew from the "Siddur," the Jewish prayer book that contains a set order of the daily prayers. But my mother also makes a fleeting mention of the Tarbut (literally "culture") school in Buczacz, which was part of the network of secular Zionist, Hebrew-language educational institutions, including libraries and a publishing house, founded in Poland in 1922. By 1939 there were some 270 Tarbut schools in Poland, enrolling almost one-tenth of the country's Jewish student population, with a higher proportion in elementary schools and a lower, and declining, ratio in secondary education. But in Galicia, as many as 95 percent of all Jewish children attended state schools in 1937, not least because most of the Jews there were poor and state education was free, whereas Jewish schools charged tuition.[23] I wonder whether my mother would have been able to tell me more about that Tarbut school in Buczacz had I let her speak. But the opportunity was lost. And then, just as she is about to say what language my grandmother most commonly spoke, my son interrupts and I never receive an answer, although I believe it was Yiddish, quite apart, of course, from that "higher language," my grandmother's *Lieblingssprache*, or beloved language, German. Now again I hear my mother moving some pots and pans around. So we must still be in the kitchen.

"But with the girls you spoke Ukrainian?"

"You're asking me? I assume, what do I know, after all, I also had to speak Polish in school."

"In school Polish was spoken?"

"Actually, in school I studied Polish, but I also studied Ukrainian, so that I learned how to write and how to read also Ukrainian. It's a pity that here, when I reached fourth grade . . . Just a moment . . . when it boils I have to lower the flame; it needs to simmer . . . "

So my mother is still cooking something after all. She does not make much of it, but that fleeting expression of pity suggests that she regrets having lost most of that language she had studied for three years in school. She could still understand some Ukrainian and would translate for me the lyrics of Russian songs, but for a moment I sense that she laments how the circumstances of the time made it impossible to embrace a new language and country without erasing the links to another. Perhaps it was inevitable, as with most immigrants, but the major difference in her case was that not long thereafter the language she had begun learning turned out to be the language of those who turned against her family and community, the neighbors who at times moved into the homes of the murdered and took over their property.

My mother, I think, retained a certain sentimental attachment to Ukrainian, the language she had spoken with her girlfriends, just as several elderly Ukrainians from Buczacz and other towns whom I got to know over the years preserved some sentimental attachment to the Yiddish they heard in their childhood. Roman Voronka, a retired professor of mathematics in the United States, who was raised in 1930s Buczacz, would often sign off his emails to me with the Yiddish term *zay gezunt*, or be well. He wished his hometown had not erased the Jews from its memory. But for many Jews, Ukrainians are associated with antisemitism, pogroms, and collaboration with the Nazis during the Holocaust; and for not a few Ukrainians, especially nationalists, Jews are associated with exploitation, greed, and collaboration with the Soviets. I cannot say that my mother was free of such views; but she did not associate them with her memories of childhood. For by the time the natural innocence and trust of the children she knew might have been eroded by age and circumstances, and the events of the Holocaust unfolded according to their own murderous logic in Buczacz, my mother was far away, removed from a physical to a spiritual homeland by a father who had embraced Zionism and sought better opportunities elsewhere. All of which made my own birth possible, a most unlikely event had the family remained just a little while longer where it may well have lived for the previous four centuries.

"So, did you have girlfriends?"

"Yes, I had girlfriends, also in the village. When we would visit Mother's family—they lived there on a kind of hill—we would go down to the river. But it wasn't the Dniester, it was the Czeremosz, or maybe the Dnieper? The Czeremosz, I think. We were together with the *shiksalakh* and the *shkotzim*, and we used to fish with a bottle. We would take a bottle, seal it, make a hole in the bottom, and fill it with a bit of mamaliga. In that place in the Carpathians, they ate mamaliga every day for lunch, with meat or with fish. This was probably not far from the Romanian border. I know that Erika Beisky always said that my mother reminded her of her own mother, she spoke like her . . . I think she came from Czernowitz, Erika, so maybe this was close to Czernowitz."

The Czeremosz River, which runs next to my grandmother's family home in the Carpathian village of Rożnów, demarcated at the time the border between Poland and Romania. Nowadays both banks of the river belong to Ukraine, encompassing the former Austro-Hungarian provinces of Galicia to the north and Bukovina to the south. The Czeremosz flows into the larger Prut River, which then winds its way south, marking out the border between Romania and Moldova, and then flows into the Danube, which reaches the Black Sea along the Romanian-Ukrainian border. Across the Czeremosz and forty miles east of Rożnów lies the city of Chernivtsi, formerly known as Czernowitz. At the outbreak of World War II, the Czeremosz became a crucial crossing point for the remnants of the Polish army and government, which fled south to Romania when the invasion of the Red Army from the east dealt the coup de grâce to the Polish state already reeling from the massive German invasion two weeks earlier. Throughout the war, Jews fleeing the Germans also tried to cross over to what they believed, erroneously for most of the time, was a safer Romania. And following the liberation of Galicia by the Red Army in summer 1944,

Jewish survivors again fled across the river to Czernowitz from violence by Ukrainian nationalist groups fighting the Soviets in the hopes of establishing the long-sought-for, Jew-free and Pole-free, independent Ukraine. But in my mother's childhood memories the banks of the Czeremosz were a site of carefree summers with her family and local Ukrainian friends.

CHAPTER THIRTEEN

Gate of Hope

Grandfather Yisrael's Deceit

THE LITTLE TOWNS ON both sides of the Czeremosz, once heavily populated by Jews, have erased all memory and most material traces of their former inhabitants. All that is left today of Kosów's Jewish community is a cemetery that is gradually being sucked into the fertile soil of the region. The nearby town of Kuty (Kitev in Yiddish) had a population in 1919 of 1,300 Poles, 1,900 Ukrainians, 3,300 Jews, and 500 Armenians. It still retains an abandoned, overgrown cemetery, with many quite astonishingly elaborate tombstones dating back to the early eighteenth century.[1] The local goats seem to have taken a liking to it. This borderland of cultures and civilizations once had a colorful mix of traditions, languages, religions, and cuisines. No wonder that, being so close to concentrations of Romanian populations, the regional dish of mamaliga—made of yellow maize and similar to the Italian polenta—was regularly consumed.

Here were also some of the most interesting and varied Jewish communities, ranging from the Hasidic stronghold of Vizhnitz (now known as the Ukrainian town of Vyzhnytsia) to the Germanized Jewish intelligentsia of Czernowitz. One of the city's most famous sons was the poet Paul Celan. Although he never lived in Germany, barely survived the Holocaust in Romania, and resided in Paris after the war until his suicide in 1970, Celan wrote poetry in German. Initially rejected by the new postwar German literary elite, Celan is now considered one of Germany's most important modern poets. The Austrian Ministry of Culture has put up a plaque commemorating him on the front of his family home in Chernivtsi, even though by the time he was born in 1920, the city no longer belonged to the Austro-Hungarian Empire. But the local Ukrainian population of the city appears little aware of its rich past and the complex legacy of such figures as Celan.

Erika Beisky's reference to her mother's and my grandmother's similar manner of speaking reveals the intricate web of links and associations reaching back to that multifaceted past, now largely forgotten or flattened out and simplified into a caricature of itself, a site of touristic nostalgia and virtual Jews. Whereas these two women came from the border area between Bukovina and Galicia, Erika's husband, Moshe Beisky, was born in 1921 in Działoszyce, near Kraków, in western Galicia. Beisky testified during the Eichmann trial about his incarceration in the notorious forced labor camp of Kraków-Płaszów, which features prominently in Steven Spielberg's film *Schindler's List* (1993). At the trial, the Israeli state attorney Gideon Hausner repeatedly asked Beisky why the prisoners in the camp did not rebel against their Nazi guards, implying that they were cowards.[2] Hausner's inability to understand the reality of the time reflected the attitude of much of the rest of the public in early 1960s Israel. Beisky was among the 1,100 Jews saved by Schindler. He subsequently had a distinguished legal career in Israel, capped by twelve years as a Supreme Court justice. After the film was made, he was asked for an interview by a German journalist. Initially he declined. The journalist then wrote him to say that he was the son of Hans Frank, the brutal Nazi governor of the German-occupied General Government in Poland, and detailed his struggle to come to terms with the horrors perpetrated by his father. It was then that Beisky relented and granted the interview.[3]

One of the people who taught me most about the folly of making such quick and facile moral judgments as Hausner's was another survivor of the Płaszów concentration camp, the writer Ilona Karmel, whose autobiographical novels are among the most truthful and devastating accounts of the Holocaust I have read.[4] Karmel had similarly little patience for stereotyping people by ethnicity and religion. But she came from an upper-class, rather assimilated, and quite wealthy Jewish family in Kraków. My mother, who was just a year older, was raised in a more traditional setting, and retained a somewhat ambivalent attitude toward non-Jews. Karmel would never have used such terms as *shiksalakh* and *shkotzim*, derived from the Hebrew word *sheketz*, "abomination." For Jewish men, the image of the *shikse* could also be associated with sexual fantasies—attractive yet forbidden, hence all the more desirable, but simultaneously threatening and dangerous, as they appear in many of the Galician artist Bruno Schulz's works. Similarly, *shegetz* could imply a rascal or a hooligan, but might also describe someone capable of tempting and defiling Jewish women. The ambivalence of employing these terms is obvious from my mother's accounts, and even more so from numerous survivor testimonies, where Jews might speak with profound gratitude, even awe and admiration, about this or that Christian rescuer, all the while referring to them as a *shikse* or a *shegetz*, seemingly unaware of the irony of using a derogatory term to express these feelings.

"Did you also have Jewish friends?"

"Well, we were all small children; we didn't really go anywhere on our own to have friends. There were children in the family; on Mother's side the uncle who lived in Rożnów had two daughters. The uncle in Kosov was childless; he and his wife had no offspring. On Father's side, Mendel was the youngest brother, and he went to Palestine a couple of years before us to escape imprisonment, because he was suspected of communism. There was terrible persecution of communists there, that's what was said in the family . . . not that I understood anything about it at the time. My father went as a Zionist, he was in the General Zionists, very active, still here in Israel, too. He told me that he went once to Tel Aviv to help with the elections and so forth, and refused to be paid for his work. He even slept on the beach so as not to waste the money of the General Zionists.

"But how did we go to Israel? I remember that there was something called the 'Tsitkov Aliya.' I don't really know; it must be known in the history of the Yishuv. There was apparently a citrus grower called Tsitkov. And here, you know, there was a struggle with the Jewish Agency over working conditions, and they used Arabs as cheap labor. But perhaps they decided also to bring immigrants, you know, to work for them. So he went to Poland, this Tsitkov or his agents, I think to Stanisławów or somewhere there, and he interviewed people who wanted to go to Palestine. I don't know how he could have done that because this was still the time of British rule and one needed some kind of permission, but perhaps there was permission, and maybe he received certificates for labor, for workers. And I remember my father saying: 'I must make a good impression.' He put on a leather coat and boots, so as to look like a worker, a manual laborer, not like some *soicher*. I remember that well because he came back on the train probably very early in the morning and when he walked in we woke up; it was still dawn. I remember that he seemed very strange to me, because he was wearing some kind of leather coat, with fur, and boots. He was then a young man and was handsome. Of course they took him, he made a good impression, and so there was a whole ship of Tsitkov people, a ship called 'Polonia.'"

My mother slightly mispronounced the name, but the basic details of her story were accurate. In the mid-1930s the citrus grower Yissachar Sidkov from the town of Rehovot in Mandatory Palestine, assisted by the Farmers' Association of the Yishuv, arranged for the emigration of a group of Jews from rural areas in Poland and Galicia, in order to boost the number of Jews with agricultural experience. A second motivation may well have been to provide cheap Jewish labor in response to demands by local Jewish workers for better conditions and in pursuance of the Zionist slogan of "conquering labor," which meant competition with local Arab workers. Sidkov was also one of the members of the Parity Committee established in Palestine in 1931, which functioned as the direct executive body of the Haganah, the Jewish defense organization, considered illegal by the British but widely recognized as legitimate by the Yishuv.[5]

Whether my grandfather had any of the required agricultural experience is doubtful. But he dressed like a peasant for the occasion and was a big, strong man who had dealings with Ukrainian villagers and spoke their language. Looking like the wheeler-and-dealer type suggested by the term *soicher*, literally "merchant" in Yiddish, would not have helped this father of three in his mid-thirties to acquire an immigration certificate into a country that sought sturdy young manual laborers and farmers. But the Jewish *soicher* was also no longer wanted in Galicia, since he was increasingly represented as a parasite by both intellectual antisemites and much of the local population; such men faced diminishing opportunities for making a decent living, as the Ukrainians organized their own cooperatives and the Polish government increasingly discriminated against Jews.[6]

This rare act of deceit by my grandfather, a simple, honest, and straightforward man, succeeded in providing him with that highly sought-after "certificate," the permit to immigrate to Palestine recognized by the Mandatory authorities. An activist in the General Zionists—a centrist, liberal, middle-class Zionist party established in 1931—he likely never expected that by immigrating to Palestine he would be transformed into precisely the kind of manual laborer he had pretended to be; in that sense, he ended up not fooling anyone, or perhaps simply being fooled in return. In March 1935 the permission was granted. By some extraordinary coincidence, while working in the archives in Lviv in the early 2000s, I found the very note stating that permission to immigrate to Palestine had been granted to three men from Buczacz; one of them, who appears there as Izrael Szimer, was my maternal grandfather.

The *Polonia* was originally launched in Glasgow in 1910 and sailed under the name *Kursk* in the Russian merchant navy, with a capacity of 800 passengers. In 1921 it was sold to the Polish Baltic-America Line and renamed *Polonia*. The ship was then sold in 1930 to the Polish Gdynia-America Line, and used to transport immigrants from Europe to North and South America. In 1935 it began carrying passengers from the port of Constanţa (Constanza) in Romania, via Istanbul, to Palestine. This line operated until 1938, during which time the *Polonia* transported tens of thousands of Jews from Europe to Palestine. In her autobiographical account, Dvora Rogovin Helberg recalls arriving at Tel Aviv Harbor on 12 October 1938, after a three-day trip on the *Polonia*. To her the ship appeared as a "newly built" vessel. In fact, the *Polonia* was on its last legs, and was sold to be scrapped the following year.[7]

"Do you remember the journey?"

"I remember the first essay I wrote in Hebrew, it's a pity my parents didn't keep it because I remember that the teacher really liked it. I wrote: 'It's a hot day, the train rolls and rolls.' This was the first sentence, my first Hebrew essay. I think we went to Lvov, or to Stanisławów; I think it was to Lvov, and from there we went by train to Constanţa, and in Constanţa we got on—in Hebrew one should say we went down to—the ship, the ship 'Polonia.' I even have a photo here with all of us standing, all these immigrants and also Father and Mother and me and my two brothers, still children, it must be here somewhere . . . "

"In 1935?"

"This was in early '35, we came here in early May '35."

For many years I thought my mother was born in 1925, because she was said to be a year older than my father, born in Palestine in 1926. Only when she was ill in the hospital did I see that the tag on her wrist gave her date of birth as 5 November 1924. I guess that admitting to being two years older than her husband was too much of a concession. In the photo my mother is with a group of men, women, and children, including her parents and two brothers, Ovadia and Zvi, about to board the ship in spring 1935. She is wearing a fashionable though slightly oversized coat and an elegant cap. I recall my father saying that the cap had to go not long thereafter since it made her look too European in the class-conscious and grubby atmosphere of Petah Tikva, the town in which the family set up home and where she met my father in school. Petah Tikva, "Gate of Hope" in Hebrew, was founded in 1878 as the first modern Jewish agricultural settlement in what was then an Ottoman province, and for that reason is also still referred to as "the mother of the settlements." Located just east of Tel Aviv near the source of the Yarkon River, by the 1930s it had evolved into a little town with an agricultural school and some industry.[8]

I am not entirely sure about the identity of the other people in the photo. My mother is standing apart from my grandmother and uncles, perhaps because she wanted to assert her individuality. My grandfather is in the back, wearing a cap. He was a religious and a shy man despite being physically robust (as were both his sons). I must have discovered the photo only after my mother's death, which is why the identification of the other people is uncertain.[9] The essay she mentions disappeared long ago. I find it somewhat curious, as I listen to her speak about what must have been a radical transition from one world to another, that in answer to my question about her impressions from the journey she speaks instead about her first Hebrew-language essay. Language was the main obstacle in this transition, especially for my mother, for whom linguistic expression was paramount. The sentence she recalls has a different, punchier, yet more archaic flavor in the original Hebrew יום חם, הרכבת רצה רצה, literally, "hot day, the train runs, runs." Just seven years later, in October and November 1942, several thousand Jewish residents of Buczacz boarded two trains heading in the opposite direction, approximately 150 miles northwest of Buczacz, where they were gassed in the Bełżec extermination camp.

Jackals

"What do you remember about the arrival?"

"I remember that we got to Jaffa. From the journey I don't remember much. We arrived at Jaffa, and ships at that time could not enter the port; they would come with boats and bring you to the shore. I remember my parents standing there, and everyone with their luggage, and us children, and then they were coming with the boats, and I saw a huge man, black, with these pants which people don't wear any longer, tight in one place and wide in another, taking children like that, grabbing me and boom, straight into the boat, grabbing another child and hop, into the boat, this was really scary."

Listening now to my mother's account of arriving in Jaffa, I cannot help recalling the testimonies I have read meanwhile of children grabbed from their parents' arms and crushed into walls or torn apart in German-occupied Buczacz, just a few years later. My mother was eighteen years old when the mass killing began in Buczacz, the same age as several survivors who witnessed these events and testified about them after the war. It appears inconceivable that she would have been subjected to the same fate had it not been for her father's decision to emigrate. But what made reading, listening to, or watching these testimonies at times entirely unbearable was the thought of my daughter, the child growing up in my home, being caught up in the unspeakable events described by women who were her age when they experienced them.

"So we got to the harbor, and my uncle Mendel was supposed to welcome us, but there was some misunderstanding. By chance we met there the husband of Tsila's cousin—the cousin of Mendel's wife Tsila—and he took us. He brought us to the bus, and we all went to Petah Tikva, to the uncle. My uncle Mendel already had a house, because Tsila's parents had bought a plot of land, and her uncle had already come to Israel, I don't know when, and bought lands here and built a house. So when Tsila and Mendel came, they were given the plot of land and had a house. It was a house, oh, I don't remember, with three rooms, but they lived in one room and rented out the rest, you know, that was some kind of income. There was also a large space behind the house. Mendel worked in construction, he was a mason or maybe a scaffold worker."

She stops for a moment and calls my son over to taste what she has made. "Come, try this, like yesterday." But I no longer remember what she made for him that day.

"We came to them, that I remember very well, they had a double bed, or two beds in that room. So they gave the bed to my parents and they slept on the floor and so did we, the children. It was summer; in May it's already hot here. And I remember that they went for a walk in the evening, and we stayed in to sleep, and it was terribly scary because there were *shakals*, you know, jackals. And at the time it must have been quite empty in that neighborhood, and they would come very close to the house and howl, and that was frightening, I remember, a kind of very, very bright night, a moonlit night, and these howls which were like the cries of children; I knew they were not children because they told me, but it was very scary."

My mother uses first the German and Slavic word for jackals, before reverting to the Hebrew *tanim*. There is something eerie in her description of that first night, a sort of retrospective premonition, though this must have more to do with my own foreknowledge than hers. She has just arrived in a new, strange, and forbidding land, and is terrified by what appear to be the cries of children in the night; yet the children turn out to be jackals, and the jackals are harmless, more scared of humans than humans need be frightened of them. The cries of children in her hometown were not those of jackals and were silenced only when the children were murdered in their thousands. I also remember those jackals in my childhood, two decades after my mother's arrival in Palestine, though they were far less numerous and soon vanished altogether. For me they remained a remnant of a past I had not experienced, just as for my mother they were an introduction to a new and threatening future and a clear sign that her other homeland had been left forever across the sea.

As far as I can recall, neither my mother nor I was familiar at the time with Franz Kafka's story "Jackals and Arabs" ("Schakale und Araber"), published in 1917 in the journal *Der Jude* (The Jew), described by Dimitry Shumsky, who analyzed this tale, as "the intellectual organ of German-speaking Zionism founded and edited by Martin Buber." The story appeared together with a better-known Kafka tale, "A Report to an Academy," in which an ape explains his difficult and somewhat incomplete transformation into a human being, often interpreted as an allegory of the limits of Jewish assimilation. But as Shumsky argues, the jackals in "Jackals and Arabs" represent both the unsettled Jews within the multiethnic context of Eastern Europe, especially in Kafka's Bohemia, and the Zionist settlers in Palestine. Like the Jews, Kafka's jackals keep to themselves, preserve the rites and rituals that differentiate them from their surroundings, and wander from place to place. Conversely, the Arabs represent the local population, physically and spiritually rooted in the land. Tellingly, Buber suggested to Kafka to put his two stories, the one about the ape and the one about the jackals, under the common heading "Parables." But, as Shumsky comments, Kafka resisted this idea, writing back: "May I ask you not to call the pieces parables; they are not really parables. If they are to have any overall title at all, the best might be: 'Two Animal Stories.'" The ape, Kafka insists, was really an ape, and the jackals were real jackals; and so, one may assume, the Palestinian Arabs were real as well—those people whose land was actually being settled by Jews from Europe, such as my mother and her family. Neither the jackals nor the Arabs managed to scare them off and prevent them from inheriting the land.[10]

"Did you miss home?"

"I missed it very much, because suddenly I didn't know the language or anyone and there were no grandfathers or grandmothers. There we had lived in the same house with Grandfather and Grandmother. Here we lived at my uncle's for about a month or so, until my father found work. His first job was in the quarries of Migdal Tzedek [five miles east of Petah Tikva], in the quarry."

"Was this actually the first time that he did manual labor?"

"Real manual labor, yes."

"Didn't he do any manual labor before?"

"Look, in the village perhaps . . . "

"He was about thirty-five years old then?"

"He was, how old was he? He was actually quite young, certainly not older, yes, he was born in 1900 or perhaps even 1901, I think the latter. Yes, he would come back—this I remember throughout my childhood, even many years later—that they would hang up his undervest to dry, and he would drink a *jarrah*, there were no refrigerators, you would put an earthenware jar full of water on the floor and it would really get cooler, because you would cover it with a sort of tulle. There were also smaller *jarrahs*, he would take with him one such small *jarrah* and when he came back, he would drink down a whole vessel of water; he worked very hard the whole time."

This account signals the change in culture, climate, and language. *Jarrah* is the Arabic word for "vessel" or "jar"; in fact, the English word is derived from the Arabic. When I was a child, we still used that word. When my son transcribed the taped interview with my mother, he wrote a question mark next to the word. Some of the terminology my mother had to learn when she came to Palestine, words borrowed from Arabic, has meanwhile vanished. The jar, she says, was covered with a tulle (she says *tool*), meaning woven cloth; that word too is no longer understood by many young Hebrew speakers. The most drastic change my mother's family experienced was a precipitous decline in social status. In Poland my grandfather was a respectable middle-class citizen—though also an increasingly despised Jew. In Palestine he became a manual laborer—the Zionist ideal, to be sure, but in reality a hard-working and poorly paid laborer—as well as a Jewish settler living on land in Petah Tikva that had been bought from the Arabic village of Mulabbis (or Mlabbes). He did not own any land of his own until many years later.

"Then we moved and lived in the 'hotzer,' Goldberg's backyard. Old Goldberg had a 'hotzer,' a large backyard, with many 'hushot,' and she would rent them out. We lived in a house that shared a wall with hers.

The author's mother with her parents and brothers. Palestine, late 1930s.
Author's private collection.

There were open, wooden porches. Then there was another slightly bigger house in which her son Pinchas lived. He was considered wealthy because he was a driver in the Regev Union, a bus service between Petah
Tikva and Tel Aviv; this was thought of as a very good job. And they actually treated me very nicely. His wife Sonia—they were Russian, and very
kind—she had a long blond braid, and I really loved her . . . And from
there I began to go to school."

My mother says "hotzer" with a touch of irony; it is the Yiddish pronunciation of the Hebrew word *hatzer*, which means "yard." In this Yiddish-

named yard there were "hushot," derived from the Arabic word for "shack." These words, too, have vanished from the modern Hebrew vocabulary, but were then part of my mother's process of socialization into the prestate Jewish community in Mandatory Palestine. The family lived in very humble circumstances there. Yet what my mother remembers most distinctly is not the poor living conditions, but the kindness of their neighbor, Sonia.

"So you were nine when you went to Israel?"

"Yes, nine. I turned ten in November."

"So you had already spent three years in school in Poland?"

"I did, yes, three, or four, no, four years; here I went to fifth grade."

Neither my mother nor I was ever very good in arithmetic. But now I know that 5 November 1935 was my mother's eleventh birthday. Which explains why she entered fifth grade. I fancy that by the time she told me about this, she had become used to thinking of herself being a year younger than she actually was, even if that did not quite fit her memory of school in Israel. After all, she rarely, in fact, never, spoke in any detail about her childhood in Poland, at least not with me.

"Do you remember anything like antisemitism in Poland, a sense of fear . . . ?"

"I'll tell you where. In Buczacz no, I don't know about that. But when we went to Rożnów, Mother's village, I remember that at night, there were these wooden shutters, like what you see in France, full shutters, not just panels, and they would close them and check twenty times to make sure that everything was shut and locked. And that made you feel anxious, which means that they were fearful. There was also a goy who would come there, very well dressed, he would visit them, and they always said that he hated Jews, that he came only to sniff around."

"You didn't have any direct contact?"

"Direct contact in the sense of attacks, no. Of the kind that Israel Levin speaks about, that when he would go home from school the goyim would beat up the Jewish kids, no."

Israel Levin was an old friend of my parents. Born in the same year as my mother in Zamość, western Galicia, he came to Palestine a year before her and had a long career as a professor of literature specializing in Hebrew-language poetry from medieval Spain and its links to contemporary Arabic verse.

"You went to a non-Jewish school?"

"I went to school . . . Where was the school in Buczacz? Good heavens . . . "

"Do you remember teachers, what you studied there?"

"I do remember, in fact, yes, I remember. I remember the teacher of Ukrainian, of all things, I don't know why, and the songs they taught us, I remember the classroom. In each classroom there was a big picture with many small pictures around it, and above it was written 'Poczet królów polskich,' something like 'the succession of Polish kings,' and all kinds of names, for instance, [King] August Poniatowski suddenly comes to mind . . . [King] Władysław Łokietek, I remember; why was he called Łokietek? Because he was short, short as an arm, Łokietek must mean arm [it means "elbow"; he was known as Władysław the Short or "elbow-high"]. All kinds of names. Kazimierz the Great, I remember how he became king; all sorts of things like that. But the school itself, how we studied . . . that's strange, because my going to Israel was such a huge transformation, the climate, the change in family life, that I must have suffered from some kind of amnesia. It somehow erased everything in some manner, you know . . . I know that my brothers didn't even know a single word of Polish; I don't think they know any. I still knew a little. I also knew some perhaps because other immigrants would come to us for lengthy periods, you know, new immigrants would stay at home with us. I keep thinking, did we live in some other place or just these two, Goldberg and then Cohen's yard? From Cohen's yard I already ran away . . . "

Dr. Nussbaum's Shikse

Growing up in Israel, I had no real idea of what antisemitism meant, and certainly no direct experience of the kind I was questioning my mother about. But when I was twelve years old, my family moved to London for two years, and I was enrolled at the Jewish Free School in Camden Town. My parents thought that the adjustment would be easier for me if I attended a Jewish school, since I did not speak English and was unfamiliar with the culture. The school itself turned out to be a rough place, filled with Jewish boys and girls from the East End who spoke incomprehensible cockney and were always itching for a fight, and teachers who had adopted the English public school ethos of humiliating the students and keeping control by having the older kids beat up the younger ones. I hated the place, but it toughened me up at least as much as service in the Israeli army six years later. The school had another disadvantage. In Britain one had to wear distinctive school uniforms, and mine showed clearly that I was attending a Jewish school. Not long after the school year began, as I was making my way from school to Camden Town tube station, a couple of kids from another school walked up to me, looked at my uniform (mine was blue; theirs was black), spit at me, and called out, "You filthy Jew!"

Obviously, I was not prepared for this and simply froze in astonishment. Nothing much happened after that, and I made it home safely. I never told my parents about this humiliating experience. But some months later, after several attacks on other students in the school, the few scores of Israeli students in the upper grades decided to go out on a punitive raid and beat up some of the kids in black uniforms from the nearby school. The following day, at the morning school assembly, our headmaster, Dr. Conway, berated the students who had acted in such an aggressive manner, and called for the rest of us to turn the other cheek. This was in 1966 or early 1967. Shortly thereafter the Six Day War transformed Israel into a country that punches back, often as disproportionately as it deems fit. It has never quite recovered from that victory and the occupation that came in its wake, gradually acquiring all the traits of a bully who knows he can get away with it. But to the kids in the black uniforms this response must have made perfect sense. And for me it was a useful lesson in antisemitism and the possible responses to it; it also taught me something about the relationship between circumstances and events, location and prejudice.

The names of kings my mother could still remember six decades after leaving Poland as a child were also a product of circumstances. Public schools in Galicia of the 1920s and 1930s trained students in Polish patriotism. At the time, this seemed to be the only possible educational course; but, of course, after World War II the curriculum was determined by communist principles, and since 1991 it has been based on a Ukrainian nationalist perspective. The succession of Polish kings seems as irrelevant to Ukrainian teachers and students today as the succession of British kings and queens, taught in the Hong Kong school that my wife attended in the 1970s, appears to teachers and students there today. But for my mother, a Jewish girl growing up in a religious family in Buczacz, learning about Polish kings and other national heroes appeared perfectly normal, and she retained their names into her seventies, however unrelated they were to any experience she had had since the age of eleven.

"So the family stayed in the 'hotzer' until you went to high school?"

"So it was like this. We lived there, and in the summer, just after we arrived, there were preparatory classes for new immigrants, for children. I used to go almost every morning, I remember, to the 'PICA School,' where I later also studied. There was a teacher there who prepared us for school, he taught us Hebrew; they really taught us. And children learn quickly, because in this 'hotzer' many families were living, people spoke Hebrew, so the children picked it up quickly. I don't remember having any problems as far as the language was concerned. I don't remember any such difficulty, even though I knew no Hebrew at the beginning; it seems that for children this is not such a big issue. I entered fifth grade, and my classroom teacher was Kadishman. He remained my classroom teacher all the way to eighth grade, and that was my great good fortune. He really loved me dearly. At the time you needed to pay tuition for studying at the elementary school, because this school belonged to the National Council."

The National Council was the executive branch of the Jewish representative assembly during the British Mandate in Palestine, a kind of shadow government in anticipation of the future Jewish state. My mother's transition from a Jewish girl in eastern Poland to a young Zionist being prepared to be a member of what seemed at the time a very distant independent state was facilitated by very basic, yet crucial instruments provided by the Yishuv. The "PICA" school she attended had in fact been established in 1885 with funds provided by Baron Edmond James de Rothschild, known in Israeli lore simply as "the Baron Rothschild," "the Famous Philanthropist," or "the Father of the Yishuv." As of 1905 the school was open to boys and girls and became committed to providing a national Zionist and liberal education. The "PICA" school is still active today and prides itself on promoting an "open, tolerant, and respectful democratic atmosphere." Its name is derived from the Palestine Jewish Colonization Association, founded by Baron Rothschild in 1924.[11] No irony was intended by the incongruity between the school's name and its stated mission.

This was how my mother, at age eleven, became a product of the Zionist undertaking. The dimensions of this ambitious project were at best modest. The Jewish population of Palestine was minute by any standard— a British census undertaken in 1931 counted 175,138 Jews. But the numbers were rising fast; it is estimated that there were some 450,000 Jews in Palestine in 1939, thanks primarily to emigration from Europe in the wake of the so-called Nazi seizure of power and increasingly antisemitic policies adopted by many other European countries. And despite severe restrictions on immigration by the British authorities during World War II, the total Jewish population of 553,600 in 1945 constituted 31 percent of the entire population in the land, as opposed to merely 17 percent just fourteen years earlier.[12] In other words, as the Jews of Europe were being murdered—as the bulk of my own family was slaughtered in Buczacz and other Galician towns, or in extermination camps—the Jewish population of Palestine, and later Israel, was expanding at a significant rate, even if it still represented only a small part of world Jewry. My mother, her parents, and her brothers had barely escaped in time; she was rapidly transformed into an Israeli, fought in the 1948 War, and raised a family. Had her father waited a little longer in Buczacz, she would most likely have been dead by the age of twenty.

"Was Father in that school, too?"

"Father? No, Father didn't study at the 'PICA' School. Father studied first at some religious school and then Grandfather transferred him to the gymnasium, to fifth grade."

"So you met at the gymnasium."

"In ninth grade, at the gymnasium, that's when we met."

"And didn't you feel different at school?"

"When I came at the beginning, I looked for those who were like me. So first of all, I had a girlfriend who came with us together on the same ship, Sara Weinstein, you've never heard her name. So we were very close, because we were different [from the others]. You know, despite the conditions, we used to do our homework together. One night she would sleep over at my place, the following night I would sleep at her place, on the piled-up drums. She even followed me later to the Teachers' College in Beit Hakerem. She died a couple of years ago. Later we drifted apart. She still used to visit me in the kibbutz, but as girls, now when I think about it, we were attached to each other because of that feeling of being different. Then there was another girl, she too is no longer living, Rachel Weisbrod. They came a little before us, they were wealthier—her father had a store for clothing materials in Petah Tikva. And her mother, she was an educated woman, by the way, she used to help us with our homework. I still remember studying a chapter in the Bible, and it had the word 'pregnant,' 'became pregnant,' and I had no idea what it meant, and she would explain everything to us. She knew things, she was an educated woman."

It's interesting to me, as I listen to this recording, how only a few questions change the initial impression of a smooth transition into a new land and culture, and allow my mother to delve deeper into the implications of that passage from Poland to Palestine. First, she denies any major difficulties with the language; for children, she says, it was not such a problem. She also says nothing of her own accord about any feeling of otherness, or alienation, though she came as a child who spoke not a word of Hebrew into a classroom where the vast majority of the students spoke only Hebrew. Then she gradually recalls that indeed there was a feeling of otherness, which was why she and the other new immigrant girls clung to each other, did their homework together, slept overnight at each other's crowded homes. They may have had difficulties not only with the language; they were also lonely, socially isolated. They were living in difficult circumstances, and their parents had little time for them, since they had to work long hours, and could provide little help, because they too were strangers to this new land and for the most part had received only the most rudimentary education themselves. Which is why my mother repeats several times that her friend Rachel's mother was an educated woman who could help them with their homework and explain the meaning of difficult Hebrew words—as well as what it actually means to be pregnant, which my grandmother might have been uncomfortable explaining even had she not been dog-tired when she came back from work every night.

Eventually, my mother went on to become an "educated woman" herself, probably much better educated than the mother who remained etched in her memory as the person who explained to her the word "pregnant" in Hebrew. She studied at the Teachers' College in Beit Hakerem in Jerusalem, established in 1913 as one of the first colleges in Palestine that emphasized the use of the Hebrew language.[13] She later studied at the Hebrew University with such teachers as Gershom Scholem, Martin Buber, and Ben-Zion Dinur, although her studies were interrupted by the war of 1948. In the early 1950s she went with my father and sister to Kibbutz Ein Hahoresh, a communal settlement founded in 1931 by members of Hashomer Hatza'ir from Poland and Belgium. The poet Abba Kovner, who urged the Jews of Vilna not to "go like sheep to slaughter" in January 1942, and led the partisans in the area, joined the kibbutz in 1946.[14] I was born there in 1954.

"But life was very tough . . . for instance, I never had any school textbooks."

"And there, in Buczacz, were you affluent, or at least had a comfortable existence?"

"We lived, what do I know, we were not considered poor; I don't know if they were rich."

"Did anyone speak about that at home, when you were already in Petah Tikva?"

"No. My father, never."

"I mean, because you declined socially from merchants to blue collar."

"My father never spoke and never complained, and he also did not want to hear about this."

"And Grandmother?"

"For Grandmother it was hard; Grandmother was different. My father was a silent man; he never spoke much anyway. Mother, first of all, she right away also tried to find work, she was an energetic woman, and she began working as domestic help."

"She had not worked until then, in Poland, did she?"

"Certainly not, what are you thinking? It was not proper for a Jewish woman to work, don't you know? So she arranged domestic work for herself, I'll never forget that, with Doctor . . . How could I have forgotten his name? It'll come back to me. They emigrated from Germany, that family. He was a doctor, and they had a nice large house . . . Nussbaum! Doctor Nussbaum. And Mother worked from . . . Father would go to work very early, and she would go, I don't know, at 8 a.m., when we went to school, and she would come back at 2:00 or 2:30 p.m. For many months Father didn't even know that she was working."

"She worked there as what?"

"Domestic work. Simply as a domestic worker."

"Cleaning lady?"

"Simply domestic worker, yes."

"Did she have a cleaning lady in Poland?"

"In every house there was a shikse, this was nothing special, and it wasn't very expensive."

"So she became Dr. Nussbaum's 'shikse'?"

"So she was at the doctor's . . . and what she used to tell me—because, after all, she knew also German and, as you know, she was a nice woman and so the children loved her, that family had a son and a daughter—she would tell me that the doctor's wife was such a 'lady,' that whenever she saw that it was 1:45 p.m. she would find my mother something extra to do that would take half an hour, because she was supposed to leave at 2 p.m. So the girl, who loved Mother very much, would say to her mother: 'Mama, Frau Szimer also has children who come back from school, let her go home.' She never finished work precisely at 2:00, always later, and these people were so nasty that they demanded that she also come on the Sabbath just to make their beds, you know, not full cleaning. So when Father would go to the synagogue, she would run there, for a bit, you know, so as to be back before Father returned from the synagogue. So that he would not know, because for him it was shameful that his wife . . . "

Ek Velt

It is difficult to grasp the meaning of immigration, of transition from one place to another, without perceiving the personal, intimate aspects of this transformation. My mother belonged to the last generation that had some knowledge and memory of prewar Jewish life in what the Jews called the shtetl. Looking back at my family's act of self-transplantation, the move to Palestine literally saved their lives. But from their own perspective in the 1930s, things looked rather different, and it was that experience which stamped itself on their minds and perceptions for the rest of their lives, despite the knowledge of the horror that had meanwhile engulfed the communities they left behind. My mother speaks ironically about the norm that a proper Jewish woman—meaning a middle-class, married woman—could never go to work. Work outside the home would cast shame on her husband, whereas domestic work—much harder at a time when labor-saving devices were almost unheard of—was performed by a maid, which, for East European bourgeois Jewish families, almost invariably meant a "shikse."

Immigration to Palestine often led to an abrupt decline in social status. My grandfather worked as a manual laborer until he was felled by a heart attack. My grandmother became the equivalent of a "shikse" for another, wealthier family. That this was a Jewish-German family just adds to the irony of it all, considering my grandmother's love and admiration for everything German. The Nussbaums belonged to a much more elevated social class, since the man of the house was a doctor, and they came, reputedly, from a higher cultural milieu. Many of the Jews who emigrated from Germany in the 1930s, the so-called "Yekes," belonged to, and arguably were key to the making of, the Central European *Bildungsbürgertum* (educated bourgeoisie), which in turn served as a model for such middle-class *Ostjuden* as my grandmother. None of that helped them much after the Nazis came to power, and they were kicked out of Germany as unwanted foreigners, often to the delight of their Aryan colleagues, who swiftly moved in to replace them. The less fortunate among them, those who stayed behind, were packed off to ghettoes, killing sites, and extermination camps in the "East." Yet even as they were hunted down by the Nazi regime, as we can see from the extraordinary published diaries of Victor Klemperer, a professor of Romance languages and a convert married to an "Aryan" woman, they kept believing that they were true Germans—indeed, they sometimes believed that they were in fact the last true Germans in a land taken over by Hitler's goons and millions of fellow-travelers.[15]

As for those who came to Palestine, they still often perceived themselves as culturally superior both to the indigenous "Orientals" and to the less refined local *Ostjuden*. Perhaps the most striking portrait of the German-Jewish academics, who played a major role in creating the Hebrew University in Jerusalem, and of their ambivalent relationship to German scholarship, which they continued to admire even after fleeing from their homeland by the skin of their teeth, as well as to Palestine, perceived by them as their indisputable new homeland but also as a site of exile from the true fount of culture, is drawn in Agnon's magnificent novel *Shira*. The novel's protagonist is Manfred Herbst, who was born, raised, and educated in Germany, and now works as a lecturer at the Hebrew University. The realization of this inner contradiction, of the unreciprocated love for Germany that blinded its Jews to the ubiquitous prejudice among colleagues and acquaintances, dawns on Herbst only during World War II, when he returns to reading German literature. It was only then, writes Agnon, that he

> saw and recognized that even Germany's best bards were not free of that malice, so much so that they lyricized it and made it into a virtue, so that all manner of cruelty to the Jews became acceptable ... It should be mentioned here that many books ringing out with malice and cruelty came to Herbst as presents given to him by Jews for his Bar Mitzvah. The Jewish spirit had become enslaved to such an extent to Germany that they did not perceive the hatred of Jews lyricized by these books. But what the Jews did not feel the Germans did feel.[16]

Unlike Manfred Herbst, my grandfather, as my mother stressed, never complained. I remember him, many years later, when he was (or seemed to me at the time) very old, after his heart attack and shortly before his death, leafing through the pages of the Buczacz memorial book, his still thick silver hair long and silky to the touch, his rough face covered with a two-day stubble. I never heard him speak with any bitterness about his own life, nor with any anger about the destruction of the world he had left behind along with his entire family. He was, in the most conventional sense, a large, tough, and silent man; whatever conversations about fate and injustice he might have conducted, he did so with his Maker, and since he regularly performed the daily Jewish rituals, just as he had done in Galicia, he had plenty of opportunity for such communication. I think he had a rather simple spirit, but he also had a strong will and a mind of his own. He was neither given to accepting what he did not like nor to complaining about it. When he found the Ashkenazi synagogue in the neighborhood to which they moved shortly before his death not to his liking, he changed over to the Sephardic synagogue, with whose congregation he got along much better.

When he died at the age of sixty-nine or seventy, just a couple of years older than I am now, I was sixteen years old, and although I was as secular then as I am now, I would come to their little two-room apartment every morning before school and join the minyan, the required quorum of ten men, to recite the prayers during the seven-day period of mourning, or *shiva*. That was the only time in my life so far that I wore the *tefillin* (phylacteries) and a *tallit* (prayer shawl), with the exception of my bar mitzvah three years earlier and my son's bar mitzvah, thirty-one years later, which was also conducted at a Sephardic synagogue of his choosing in Ashkelon, Israel; my mother was no longer there. Over the years, the town where my son was raised has been regularly subjected to rocket and missile attacks from the Gaza strip, located only a few miles to the south, and Israeli warplanes, artillery, and tanks have just as regularly pounded Palestinian neighborhoods and refugee camps across the line. As a seven-year-old child, my son's maternal grandfather had jumped off a train heading from Hungary to Auschwitz, walked back to his parents in Budapest, and was holding his father's hand when a local fascist Arrow Cross militant shot the father in the head on the street. My son's maternal grandmother survived in a subway station in Berlin during the war with her mother and sister; they all had "Aryan" looks. But the father, who looked Jewish, was left to die on the pavement when he was wounded in an Allied bombing raid while trying to find food for his family.

The German Jewish sociologist Erich Fromm, who escaped from Nazi Germany and settled in the United States, famously argued that at the root of fascism was people's urge to "escape from freedom" into a false sense of security under a "strong" leader, who would in turn deprive them both of their rights and of their security. In the case of Israel, the escape from fascism in Europe provided its citizens at best with only the most tenuous sense of security, and there have been growing indications in the last few years of the Israeli public's urge to escape, once more, from freedom. This return to a politics of fear and resentment has become an increasingly common feature in many other countries across the globe, not least in those that once contained large Jewish populations, such as Poland and Hungary, as well as in the land across the Atlantic that took in so many of them, and only recently has found itself mired in the new rhetoric of "American carnage."

"You see," my mother explains, responding to my suggestion that her father was ashamed of his wife's work as a maid for their German neighbors, "she also did not like this job too much, and after a year she decided to leave it and began working in the orange grove. To her, this was more dignified. It meant of course long working hours. She would leave in the dark and return in the dark, because they had to go on foot to the *hamra*, or whatever they called it there, to the orange groves in *ek velt*, where the new municipal cemetery of Tel Aviv is now located, on the way to Hod Hasharon . . . to all kinds of places where there were once orange groves; and they would walk there on foot. So they would leave at 5:00 a.m., and by the time they came back it was dark—and sometimes they still had to run off to the labor office—and we children grew up on our own. We would prepare ourselves for school, go to school, come back from school. No wonder that I say that at age twelve I was already a homemaker. I don't remember ever having time to play or that I went anywhere to have fun . . . "

My mother did not become a homemaker in the sense of not working outside the home. One thing she learned from her mother was that she wanted to have her own profession and independence. She did make a home and care for her husband and children. But she always worked and would occasionally say to me, "I have my own bank account, just in case." But here she was actually speaking, without acknowledging it, about the end of her childhood. Within a year of coming from Poland to Palestine, from Buczacz to Petah Tikva, she had not merely adjusted to the language and culture of her new country—without really being liberated from that sense of otherness, which I am not sure she ever entirely lost—but also became a grownup, having to care for her two younger brothers and run the household, as well as prepare herself for a life that would raise her above the conditions of poverty and ignorance into which she had been plunged. The word "hamra" takes me back to my own childhood; I have not heard it for many years. The name of this fertile soil, enriched by iron oxides that give it a reddish brown hue, is derived from the Arabic word for "red"; I remember playing in it as a child.

Today, both the word and the soil have largely vanished, along with the orange groves. The entire area my mother recalled is covered with endless towns and suburbs, roads and streets, such as the neighborhood of Hod Hasharon she refers to. Tel Aviv and Petah Tikva, once separated from each other by miles of fragrant orange trees, are now fused together into

Grandmother Rina in an orange packing house. Palestine, late 1930s.
Author's private collection.

one great urban monster. For people living in Tel Aviv in the 1930s, Petah Tikva itself was almost *ek velt*, a Yiddish term that literally means "the corner of the world," that is, the end of nowhere. In a certain sense, my mother had come from one *ek velt* to another; her abbreviated childhood was quickly transformed into a struggle to overcome the transition from a remote town in Europe's eastern borderlands to a provincial settlement in Mandatory Palestine. Yet by pulling herself up by her own bootstraps, she did find her way out into the world.

The orange groves in which my grandmother worked were all a long distance away by foot, though today, were it possible to identify their precise locations, it would only be a few minutes' drive. In a photo, taken probably in 1937, my grandmother is standing at the orange grove's packing plant. She looks by far the oldest person there, though she is only in her late thirties. She was a short, roundish person, and later in life suffered from rheumatism and diabetes. But in this picture, she looks not only healthy, but also strong, vigorous, and confident, even in that group of younger men and women, standing at the center with one arm over the packing cardboard boxes and another on her hip. She had made compromises, and her life was not easy; but despite her short stature and diminished social status she had a presence and an inner strength. As my family always agreed—and this was a family that eventually filled with people who all read too many books and had too many opinions—she was definitely wiser than the lot of us.

"Didn't she complain?"

"She never complained. She missed the family very much. In truth, she said that she had been cut off already at the time of her marriage, because my father and his family lived far away, well, about as far as Haifa is from Tel Aviv. But then, I remember, we used to go in the summer; we would travel the whole day, in a horse-drawn cart. Father would hitch two horses to the cart and take us there. This was a long journey. We would cross the Dniester in a *peron*, a kind of raft, with the cart: you would drive onto it and then continue on the other side. We would pass through endless villages. I remember those trips, that sometimes I would get scared when the forest got a little dark, and all the stories they would tell about what comes out of the forest. Once we even spent the night at a peasant's home because it got dark on the way. And this was quite frightening. It would rain in the middle and that was, you know, a big deal. So she, she was always waiting for this, to go on this annual trip to her family. So she already felt lonely, even there, and here she was totally alone."

A certain measure of time and distance, of strangeness and familiarity, emerges from this story that can easily be lost in the larger narrative of immigration, let alone that of the Holocaust and Zionism. Perhaps it is best encapsulated in the picture of that *peron*, literally "platform" in Polish and Ukrainian, which was used for many centuries as a wooden raft to transport wagons and people from one bank of the river to another: the *peron* across the Dniester, and the *Polonia* from the Black Sea across the Mediterranean. My grandmother, born around 1900, already missed her family and the scenes and sights of her village following her marriage in the early 1920s. Although the distance was not great and the culture not much different, that day-long journey from one town to another could be undertaken only once a year.

My grandmother, like so many of her generation, had an arranged marriage. That too gives a measure of the immense transformation experienced by people within a single lifespan. My mother would never have contemplated such an option, whereas her mother saw it simply as the way of the world. She loved and respected her husband, my grandfather, and was proud of the home and family she had with him. But she was lonely. And the only way to overcome such loneliness, apart from that annual journey, was to have one's own family. And so family became for such women the center, and core, and meaning of life. Yet leaving Poland for Palestine severed that entire network of ties and not only plunged one economically down the social scale but also deprived the immigrants of those familial bonds that made life meaningful and bearable. The distances and means of communication were such that one hardly expected to see the family again. And then the Holocaust put an end to any lingering hope of reunion. People had moved to a new collectivity, to the state of the Jews, but those Jews that constituted their home, their family, were gone forever.

My grandparents left Poland because my grandfather decided to go. I don't know how much he discussed this with my grandmother, although I expect that he did. I also feel relatively certain that, left to her own devices, she would have stayed in Poland, to be closer to her family and to lead a more respectable life than what she could reasonably expect in Palestine— and, as it turned out, life was much worse than she probably anticipated. Once they came to Palestine, she never complained, never looked back. It was not in her nature to be angry or resentful or to refuse to accept a new reality. But only now do I realize how lonely she was in that new, alienating world. And yet, as we know, my grandfather was right. Within seven years the entire family would have been murdered. And that too was never spoken about in such terms. No one ever said, had we stayed there such and such would have happened, we were right to go just in the nick of time . . . Perhaps this was because so many family members did not leave and speaking in this manner would have put the blame on them for making the wrong decision, assuming that they actually had the choice of leaving. But of course, neither those who left nor those who stayed behind could have known what the future held for them. Decisions were justified or proven catastrophic only in retrospect, which renders the entire notion of making the right decision absurd. Who could have known?

That men made decisions for their wives and children was hardly uncommon at the time. This was why my father's family came from its little village of Pyzdry in western Poland in 1925. My paternal grandmother never adjusted to Israel, and until her dying day, having spent most of her long life there, she always missed Poland and her family, and never quite acknowledged that they had all been murdered. Being more inclined toward bitterness and resentment, she never quite forgave her husband for dragging her against her will to this arid and inhospitable place on the rim of the Middle East. The thought that staying in Poland would most probably have resulted in the killing of her children simply refused to enter her mind.

Unlike my grandmothers, my mother had great professional ambitions. She did very well at the Hebrew University just before and after the 1948 War—in which many of my parents' friends were killed. She went to the kibbutz largely because my father had decided that it was their turn to do what was called at the time "realization," or *hagshama*, which meant realizing the Zionist-socialist dream of communal agricultural life based on social equality and justice for all. Since the nuclear family ostensibly obstructed the path to the ideal collective, children were separated from their parents, whom they were taught to call by their names, and raised together in children's homes. The fundamental principle of this new society was that in the collective people would work as much as they could and be given as much as they needed. Of course, since the "collective," guided by its most influential and charismatic leaders, determined the abilities and needs of individual kibbutz members, things were not always fair or equal. My mother went along with much of this, and became an enthusiastic teacher, who was still remembered by her students many years after she left the kibbutz, indeed, even after her death. But the arrangement with the children was not to her liking, and she never allowed my sister and me to address our parents as anything but Mother and Father. And because of those years in the kibbutz, my mother never had the career she could and should have had.

Much less accepting of the vicissitudes of fate than her mother, my mother resented this outcome for the rest of her life. She had married for love, not through a *shiddukh*, or matchmaking. But love brings with it higher expectations, which cannot always be met. Left to her own devices, she might still have made up for the loss of time. In the late 1950s she received a scholarship to study in the United States and completed master's degrees in psychology both at UCLA and Columbia. This was her last chance to launch the academic career she yearned for, since she was already in her mid-thirties. For a mother of two children, studying in her third language, this was a major achievement. After she died, I found the transcripts of her grades from both institutions; as I expected, she had straight A's. But my father, who had launched his career as a writer during our years in the kibbutz, wanted to return to Israel, and so we did.

Perhaps this was not mere ambition; perhaps my mother's apparent willingness to make a new career for herself in America had to do with the fact that she had already left one world and exchanged it for another. Some people leave only once, and never look back. Such were my grandparents, who never left Palestine/Israel for the rest of their lives (but my paternal grandmother did look back). My mother had sweet memories of childhood in Poland. Perhaps she, like me, was one of those people who, once they leave, will always be leaving, in practice or in their thoughts, who will always contemplate alternative lives for themselves, not because the lives they lead are necessarily unpleasant, but because they cannot get used to the idea that their present existence is the only option, a permanent, unchanging condition. This is, I think, the state of mind of an exile.

CHAPTER FOURTEEN

We'll Never See the World
We Came From

Ethics of the Fathers

"**D**IDN'T GRANDMOTHER HAVE ANY friends?"

"They had some. At the beginning there were contacts, I remember, with those who came with them on the same ship, you know, the Tsitkov people. After that some other contacts were formed, what do I know? Some contacts at work, and then there were my uncle and my aunt, as long as they lived together; and that's it. After all, they worked and, on the Sabbath, you know, they rested. They worked like dogs; such were their lives . . . That's why I was so sorry that when we were in London, I could not bring them there, just to show them something else. But my father was already sick."

She is silent for a moment. You can feel in her voice the regret and the pain. She had made it out of the muck, and she felt that she had never been able to pay her parents back. The closest, most intimate link she ever had, I think, was with her mother. But no one ever loved her as much as her father. She was the jewel in the crown. He thought his sons were fine, they worked, had families, raised children. They were big, strong working men who never complained, never had much of an education, and hard as they were, they also broke easily at times of adversity. My mother was different. She was the first person in her family to have received an academic education (apart perhaps from that Cousin Zelig who reputedly attended

a Ukrainian, or most likely a Polish, university before that world came
crashing down and he was swallowed up in the catastrophe). She was very
well read and kept reading and learning until almost the last day of her
life. Just months before she died, she published a lengthy essay on the
Italian author Elsa Morante, whose book *History: A Novel*, one of the mas-
terpieces of postwar European literature, tells the story of wartime Italy
from the perspective of its most marginal and forgotten protagonists, a
half-Jewish Italian woman raped by a German soldier and the angelic and
doomed child that issues from that act of violence. I read it in 1988 on a
flight to the United States that resulted in my move there from Israel, and
cried for much of the time, not least because my own first child had been
born only months earlier.

A man with almost no formal education, my grandfather looked up to
his daughter as the embodiment of his ideal of leading a life that combined
honest work and human decency with ongoing study and learning. Since
he was a man of few words, it was hard for him to express his love for his
daughter. I remember him coming in the afternoon, drenched in sweat, carrying a huge watermelon he had picked up at the market—not the nearby
supermarket he detested, but the much more distant open market, of the
kind he must have remembered from Buczacz—assuring her that this was
the absolute best watermelon, completely red inside, as he could establish
by tapping on it with his rough fingers, and indeed it always was.

My parents were usually away somewhere when their parents died:
traveling in Ireland on one occasion, vacationing in Austria on another.
They were nearby only when my father's mother died, but she was blind
and senile, and in that sense was completely isolated from her immediate
family, though she may have finally found some peace with the family she
had lost in Poland decades earlier. When my maternal grandmother died,
just eighteen years before my mother's death, my parents were visiting me
in Oxford to celebrate Passover together in my dismal little rented room
looking out to a backyard with a dead tree. We received the news the next
day in London, where we had planned to spend the second night of Passover with friends. Instead, I sat up all night with my mother on the second
floor of our friends' house in Hampton Court, and we read together passages
from a book I had happened to find there, *Pirkei Avot*, or *Masekhet Avot*
(Chapters or Tractate of the Fathers, also known as *Ethics of the Fathers*).

Unlike other tractates in the *Mishna*, that vast collection of oral laws
that served as the basis for the Talmud, *Pirkei Avot* does not set down laws
but provides basic principles for human behavior, some of which have be-

The author and his mother in Oxford, Passover 1980.
Author's private collection.

come so much part of Jewish culture and Hebrew-language usage that people will recite them at more or less appropriate moments without necessarily feeling obliged to follow them: "Silence is the enclosure of wisdom" (סייג לחוכמה שתיקה); "say little and do much" (אמור מעט ועשה הרבה); "if I do not stand for myself, who will stand for me?" (אם אין אני לי מי לי?); and finally, "may your friend's dignity be as dear to you as your own" (יהי כבוד חברך חביב עליך כשלך).

When I was writing my book on the life and death of my mother's hometown of Buczacz, I thought back to that moment and wondered which of these injunctions was most appropriate to telling that tale of a shared existence ending up in fraternal slaughter. I was certain that the story had to be told but was far less sure what one could learn from it. I wanted to tell the story at length, because I believed that the devil was in the details, and that in the wake of catastrophe one's first duty is to tell what happened with as much accuracy and honesty as possible. I thought of it as a story of self-reliance, because it entailed so much abandonment and betrayal, but also as a story of trusting others, of courage, altruism, and selflessness, for the rescue of fellow human beings sheds light on the shards of goodness that shine all the brighter in the darkest of times. But finally, perhaps more than anything else, I thought of it as a story of human decency, the first step of which is to recognize the other's essential dignity, and with that, to realize that our own humanity derives from acknowledging the value of other people's lives, for otherwise we are all doomed to eternally dwell in a Hobbesian world of "homo homini lupus," where people prey upon people.

It was by mere chance that I found an edition of that extraordinary text at our friends' London home. But it was a fitting book to read aloud with my mother for much of the night in remembrance of her parents. Yet what I remember most distinctly is that when she heard the news of her mother's death, my mother, who was then fifty-six years old, more than a decade younger than I am at the moment, and who had a husband, children, and grandchildren, said with the kind of complete honesty and lack of irony that she must have inherited from her father: "Now I am all alone in the world."

"Okay, that was life," my mother continues, "that was it. So Mother worked in the orange grove. Then she worked in a factory together with Father, where the war industry was; the British were producing here, you know, for the army. And they worked together. She worked in three shifts: one from early morning until noon more or less; another in the afternoon; and a third which was a night shift, every other week . . . "

"That's what Father writes . . . "

"That's what he describes in the book, yes, that's correct . . . "

My baby daughter is crying in the background. She must have woken up from her nap. My son is getting impatient again. "When are we going?" he asks. My mother continues, "She would come early in the morning, and I remember . . . " Then she stops, worried about the grandchildren. "Why don't they go out a bit? She can't be shut indoors all day. Does she need to eat or drink something?" My daughter makes a happy sound. Maybe I am feeding her. But I want to go on with the interview, afraid that we will run out of momentum as everyday life begins making its demands on the recollections of the past. My father has written several novels intimately concerned with life in Mandatory Palestine and Israel, a sort of quasi-fictional autobiographical narrative that makes it occasionally difficult for us all to distinguish fact from fiction.[1] At times I think that we are all seeing our family's past through his writer's eye. But my mother, though she loves literature, is quite relentless in pointing out what is correct and what is false—

The author's mother with his children. Israel, 1995. Photo by the author.

or fictionalized. At the start of my conversation with her, I ask my father to "go and write something" in his study, so as not to impose on her story his own views, memories, and opinions, which he cannot help but do when present. But time is running out, between my children's demands and my father's expected return to the kitchen. He cannot be kept away too long, knowing what we are speaking about.

My father had to leave school when he was fifteen, because there was no money at home, and he began working in the diamond industry. That was in 1941, and the economy was booming, since Britain came to rely on Palestine as its main supply and production center in the Middle East. Factories were indeed working in three shifts, as my mother recalled, providing the British army with food, clothing, ammunition, and other products for the military.[2] In one of the many ironies of that era, while European Jews were being massacred in their millions in Europe, Jews in Palestine were emerging from a long economic recession thanks to the war. In Europe Jews were being worked to death as forced labor in camps and ghettoes, producing goods for the Wehrmacht in the hope of somehow being spared; most were eventually murdered. In Palestine Jews were producing goods for the British army, seeing the first signs of prosperity in what had until then been a relatively poor community, and creating the modern industrial infrastructure that would facilitate the creation of a Jewish state only a few years later. Even in the seemingly unrelated diamond industry, as my father loved to boast decades later, he made three or four times more money than his father. But following a strike by the diamond workers, and perhaps also because he wanted to contribute more directly to the war effort, my father found a job producing jerry cans for the British army at a plant in Kiryat Aryeh, an industrial area established in the 1920s in Petah Tikva and greatly expanded in the 1930s.

And so, in 1942 my father found himself working in the same factory as my grandmother. She operated a steel press, and he worked as a welder. Jerry cans were a British copy of the German steel containers known as *Wehrmachteinheitskanister* used to provide mobile units with extra supplies of gasoline and renamed by the British and Americans after the derogatory name for Germans. The British army eventually produced vast numbers of these jerry cans, and President Franklin Roosevelt commented in a November 1944 report to Congress that "without these cans it would have been impossible for our armies to cut their way across France at a lightning pace which exceeded the German Blitz of 1940."[3] But a year later, when he turned seventeen, my father forged his ID card to make him appear a year older and joined the British army. He subsequently served in the Jewish Brigade, satisfying both his urge to fight the Germans and his desire to escape the narrow confines of his own poor, religious, and what he felt to be claustrophobic home. After some fighting in Italy, he was active along with the rest of his formation in the Briha, known also as "Aliya B," the organization for illegal immigration of Holocaust survivors to Pal-

Wedding of the author's parents. Palestine, 1946. Author's private collection.

estine. Many of the new arrivals, who had hardly recovered from their or-
deal in the war and often knew no Hebrew, were swiftly recruited into the
fledgling Israeli military, and sent to battle in the 1948 War.[4]

But my father returned from Europe already in 1946 and married my
mother that same year. The two of them spent just one semester at the
Hebrew University before the fighting in Palestine broke out, and then
joined the volunteer students' companies. The 1948 War had a profound
impact on them, but they never spoke much about it. While my father

wrote a well-received novel on his experience in the Jewish Brigade, the brutal fighting in Palestine appears only in his late writings, and even there it is never the heart of the story. If the war against the Germans was clear-cut, the war that made for the creation of the Jewish state, and simultaneously put an end to the Arab majority in the country, left not only scars and mourning but also a lingering and never quite articulated sense of guilt. Like many others of their generation, my parents took their memories of brutality and horror closely associated with the birth of the state to their graves.

But There Were Only Us

"And so she worked. When I got married, she was still working, and even when Gillat was born, I remember that I came to visit her, since I went to the kibbutz when Gillat was about six months old or a little older, because I actually completed my exams just before she was born."

Gillat is my sister; she is three years older. As I listen to my mother speaking, I hear my own six-month-old daughter cooing near the microphone. My son gives me something to eat. "Okay, I'll take just one," I say.

"I still remember coming there and putting Gillat in the stroller in the yard and cleaning the whole house and everything. And when I was a child, who do you think would prepare everything? Who went shopping, and who cooked? I would clean the house and before Passover I would do the Passover cleaning all on my own. I still remember to this day that I would whitewash the walls, and after that when I washed up, I had, you know, such holes in my fingers from the whitewash and the water, because I didn't know that one had to wait for it to dry . . ."

"And in Poland, how were the Holidays there? Did you celebrate the Jewish Holidays?"

"Yes, very, very traditional."

"Was it done with the whole family, everyone together?"

"Yes, very much so. Together with Grandfather. With Grandfather from Father's side, all together. I told you, in Buczacz we even lived in the same house, so it was very much a family affair. But here, you should also know that my parents kept a traditional home. On Thursday Mother would come back from work, maybe she would also do some shopping; I know that I went shopping and that they would write it up. People paid when they received their salary, and in the meantime they would write it up in a little book of debts, you know. She would tell me what to buy. In the evening on Thursday, she'd go into the kitchen, and she would cook for the Sabbath until almost daybreak, just as it was always done: fish and soup and meat and cake. We would put the cake on top of the closet, I remember, because there was no other place, and she would wash and go to work on Friday. This was the arrangement. The Sabbath was the Sabbath."

"And it included just you?"

"But there were only us. Sometimes on the Holidays we'd be together with the uncle. But they were far away, they lived way down on Rothschild Street—I should go over there one of these days to see what it looks like, I have not been there for thirty years at least, maybe more, yes more. And at the beginning we lived at Goldberg's, I told you. When I graduated from eighth grade we moved to Cohen."

"Did your parents stay there after you left home?"

"They were . . . Yes. By the time they finished building the house, none of the children was home any longer. Because they built a house, do you remember it? So it was like this, at Goldberg's there were still just two tiny rooms, in one of which we the children slept and in the other the parents. What was it like? Full of beds, and I made myself a bookshelf from a box of oranges, and Mother had a kind of Ukrainian kerchief, so I made it into a curtain over the bookcase, so that it would look nice, and that was it. Then we moved to Cohen, and at Cohen's we had one room, a big room but just one with a kind of small 'foyer' and a rather large kitchen, almost as large as ours here."

"And you were all in the same room?"

"No, when they moved there . . . let me see . . . when they moved there I was . . . Ovadia had left, he went to Geva, to the kibbutz, he probably got fed up, he went to Hevrat Hano'ar, you know, he was in the kibbutz."

"All three of you were still born in Poland?"

"All of us, yes, yes. Zvi began first grade in Israel. And Ovadia was one grade below me, that's all the difference of age between us. A year, a year and a half. He was one grade below me, because he went to fourth grade, and I went to fifth."

The Youth Societies, or Hevrot Hano'ar, were established in the 1930s in collaboration between the Youth Aliya (Immigration), or Aliyat Hano'ar in Hebrew, and the kibbutz movements, to bring Jewish youths from Europe to Palestine following the establishment of the Nazi regime in Germany in 1933. The ages of their members ranged between ten and seventeen, and each society numbered from twenty-five to seventy boys and girls. Hevrot Hano'ar became part of the kibbutzim, and their members were given a formal education as well as becoming part of the work force. They also had adoptive families in the kibbutzim. In 1945–49 alone, close to 80 percent of the children accepted by Youth Aliya were Holocaust survivors, and about two-thirds of them went to Hevrot Hano'ar in kibbutzim; of the 11,500 children and youths who joined the kibbutzim in this period, 9,000 were survivors. Eventually eleven new kibbutzim were established by graduates of this program. Altogether, some 55,000 youths went through Youth Aliya from the time it was first created. Although prior to the establishment of the state of Israel most of the youths came directly from Europe, others, such as my uncle Ovadia, joined the Youth Societies either after having already lived in Palestine for several years or as native-born youths from poor or broken homes seeking a different way of life.[5]

One prominent representative of these youths is the celebrated Israeli actress Gila Almagor, born in Petah Tikva in 1939. Almagor's father was killed before she was born, and her mother became mentally ill. She joined a youth group in a kibbutz when she was thirteen years old and describes her experiences and those of the other youths in her group, mostly child survivors of the Holocaust, in two autobiographical books, which were also made into remarkable films: *Aviya's Summer* (1988) and *Under the Domim Tree* (1994). In her acceptance speech upon receiving the prestigious Israel Prize in 2004, she said:

> I came into the world at point zero. My parents had escaped from burning Europe, young, almost children, met here, fell in love, and married. All my mother's family, a tribe of 147 souls, was wiped out in the Holocaust. I did not know my father. He was murdered four months before my birth by an Arab sniper. He never held my hand and never said to me, "my girl." I raised myself without hatred and without a will for revenge. I always thought that there must never be children who lose their fathers because of hatred and war. I grew up in a home in which there was very little, and I strove to distinguish between good and evil, I learned to struggle and to fail and sometimes also to win. This moment is a victory.[6]

"Tell me, so what happened when the war broke out? How did people speak about it at home? Did they speak at all?"

"Of course they talked, they talked a lot. But I will never forget one thing: Rosh Hashanah and Yom Kippur in 1939 [just two and three weeks after the outbreak of war]. So it was like that: our parents would of course go to the synagogue, Grandmother too, on the Holidays. Now they knew about the Germans, what they had done up to 1939, and then in September they invaded Poland, so there was tremendous anxiety, and in the synagogue, I remember, everyone was crying and covering themselves up with their prayer shawls, there was real weeping and lamentation. Everyone was very worried. No one imagined, no one could imagine what would happen. I told you, my mother would always relate that in World War I they wanted the Austrians and the Germans to reoccupy them over there rather than the rough and ready Russians, because apparently the front, the region, changed hands several times, and they preferred, you know, the Germans. So, indeed, until 1939 they already knew enough about Hitler, right? There were already the racial laws there, and in 1938 *Kristallnacht* occurred and all that, but I don't think they realized; it's true that they were very worried, and I remember from the stories, and a little also from the newspapers. But I will never forget that event, and to this day I don't understand how it happened. Perhaps they spoke about it also in school, or at home? I remember that I came back from school, and it was raining terribly so Mother didn't go to work, because one could not work picking oranges on a rainy day. I always prayed for rain, so that I would come home and find Mother there, otherwise we would come home and there was no one. I came home, it was warm in the kitchen, and Mother gave me steaming hot food, I still remember it, there in the kitchen, because we would eat in the kitchen, there was a large table there, and I was thinking the whole time, you know, and I looked out of the kitchen window, it was overcast, and suddenly, I couldn't understand, the window grew smaller and smaller, it became darker, and I lost consciousness, what with the imagination that children have and all their fears, I fainted. And Mother told me, you know, that they called a doctor because I simply passed out, just like that. And that was, I must have been in ninth grade, because in 1939 we went to high school, we were already living at Cohen's. This was already in winter 1939."

My baby daughter is making noises in the background. I still remember that moment very well. My mother coos back at her. "Let her go out a bit, the little one," she says. Then she turns to my son: "Take one of these prunes, they are wonderful." I cannot imagine how my daughter would have responded to that terrible autumn and winter of 1939. The thought of her faced with such a cataclysm is unbearable; I must chase it away from my mind to be able to write, yet I want her to know this, I want her to hear my mother's tale, the story of the grandmother she lost when she was merely three years old and of whom she has practically no memory.

"And when did the news begin to arrive?"

"So, news, that took a long time. We never got any news. Each time someone arrived, they would try . . . "

"But in October they already knew that Poland was occupied and that was that."

"Yes, but there was no one to get any news from. What I remember is a story, which is a bit Kafkaesque or mystical. I was already studying in Jerusalem, and I came home on vacation, and they told me this story: One day the door opened, over there at Cohen's, you know, in those 'hushot,' and an old man was standing there, as Mother related this, asking for alms. It was hot, so Mother let him in, gave him water, and began speaking with him about this and that, and it turned out that this Jew knew them, they probably got to know each other in World War I when they were refugees in Czechia or somewhere, I don't know, they had been either his neighbors or he had taken care of them, or something. That's when Mother was a child. So Mother was very moved and, you know, she asked him where he had been, in what . . . they were in some kind of camp for immigrants. And he had come to Petah Tikva, who knows how, and had no money to go back to the camp. So he just walked from door to door asking for money for the fare."

"When was this?"

"That was during the war, I think, or just after, I really don't remember."

"So he was a refugee, or a survivor?"

"No . . . later Mother lost track of him. And she looked for him . . . Maybe with the technology today she would have been able to find him. She could not find him."

So here was the only faint contact my grandmother ever had with her own childhood. When she first met this man as a refugee in World War I, she was the same age as my mother was when she fainted from anxiety in 1939, more than a decade younger than my daughter is today. A man walked into their "husha," their shack at the Cohens' place, and evoked a memory of childhood in my grandmother, a childhood not simply lost as all childhoods inevitably are, but a childhood from which all human and physical trace had been erased, as if it had never happened, without a single voice, object, text, familiar landmark, simply nothing. This old man was the only link; most probably a Holocaust survivor, he came for a moment, and then he too vanished without a trace, and the curtain fell for the last time.

What did people in Palestine know, what did they make of the information that did filter through, what did they repress? On 30 June 1942, the Hebrew-language Palestine daily *Haaretz* published an item that reported in great detail the mass murder of East European Jewry. The article cited a British newspaper, the *Daily Telegraph*, whose own information came from a report sent to the Polish government in exile by the Bund, the Jewish workers' party in Poland. Although the facts were not entirely accurate, the general outline closely reflected reality on the ground. To me it is still striking to read the names of numerous towns in Galicia mentioned specifically in the report:

> Among other things, this report [in the *Daily Telegraph*] related that the extermination of the Jewish people began with the outbreak of the war between Germany and Russia, in summer 1941 in the territory of eastern Galicia. In every site similar events occurred: all the men aged 16–60 were assembled in the city square or the cemetery and were murdered there with machine guns or bombs. Prior to that they were forced to dig their own graves. Vast numbers of children in orphanages, the elderly in old people's homes, and the sick in the hospitals were murdered, and women were executed by gunfire on the cities' streets.
>
> In Lwów, 30,000 Jews were murdered in this manner, in Stanisławów 15,000 people, in Tarnopol 5,080, in Złoczów 2,000, in Brzeżany 4,000 (that town numbered 18,000 Jews and today has 700); the same murder operations took place in Zborów, Zbararz, Sambor, Stryj, Drohobycz, Kołomyja, Przemyślany, Kuty, Sniatyn, Brody, Przemyśl. They were repeated a second and a third time in Lwów . . .
>
> In Równe [in nearby Volhynia] the slaughter began in early October. For three days and nights some 15,000 men women and children were executed. In Hancewicz near Baranowicze [in present-day Belarus] 6,000 were executed . . . In November the Nazis began killing the Jews with poison fumes. They did so in Chełmno . . . For that purpose they used a special installation into which they crammed 90 people at a time. They then burned the poisoned people in the forests.
>
> Every day they poisoned 1,600 people . . . Then in February

1942 the extermination of the Jews in the General Government began from Tarnów to Radom. For that purpose Gestapo men arrived there every day and perpetrated murder in full daylight in the houses, streets and yards.[7]

I don't know whether my grandparents read this specific news item or not; but I am sure that this and other such news items, which reached the Yishuv in 1942 and later, were known to them. After all, as early as winter 1939 my fifteen-year-old mother had heard enough to faint from fear and anxiety. But what was there to say? There was nothing they could do about the horrors unfolding in Europe but pray that the news was exaggerated and that at least their own families would somehow be spared. Yet this was not to be.

The Chudak and the Jewel in the Crown

"In any case, no member of the family survived. Only one of Father's cousins arrived, also a Szimer. You may have met him; he used to come to us occasionally with his wife. He had a characteristic Szimer look, rather handsome. He did all kinds of business here, made money. Father was ambivalent about him. I don't know where he heard this, because he didn't like to gossip or to blame others—that somehow there was something not straight about his cousin. But because he was the only one who survived from the entire family, it was indecent not to stay in touch with him. But Father was always, [reticent] with him, you know . . . whereas his wife and Grandmother became quite friendly, the wife was from Romania, she also spoke German. Father was, so . . . he behaved politely with him, but nothing beyond that, no, although he was the only cousin. He must have heard something, and he wanted, you know, neither to harm him, nor to . . . I don't know. It was impossible to get it out of Father, whether the cousin was some kind of . . . "

My mother, just like her father, actually cannot come out and say directly what she means and goes around and around without ever articulating her father's suspicions. But clearly, what she is speaking about, considering that he was the only one who survived, is that the cousin had been a collaborator, a Kapo, a Jewish policeman, or perhaps a member of a *Judenrat*; in any case, that there was, as my mother puts it, something not entirely kosher about him. Later I check on this with my father, who confirms my suspicion. The cousin's name was Heynkh, or Hanoch in Hebrew, the same as my father's. "He was a Kapo," says my father. "How do you know?" I ask. "Everyone knew." But of course, it was just a rumor; no one produced any evidence. "One way to know that he felt guilty," argues my father, "is that when he eventually became wealthy, he donated a great deal of money to charity. So he must have had a great deal on his conscience." That may be the case. But it may also just reflect the warped logic of that time. None of the perpetrators ever donated money to Jewish charities because of pangs of conscience. The German government paid restitution, but individual killers never even bothered to say sorry.

In periods of extreme and ubiquitous violence, people are often forced to make impossible moral choices; recognizing this should prevent us from turning to simplistic explanations, allegations, or apologetics. But precisely because of the horrifying and fraught nature of the event, observers tend to insist on just such simple answers, pointing accusatory fingers at others without stopping to consider how they might have behaved under similar circumstances. Even some of those who came from "there" have at times been keener to level harsh criticism at others rather than subject themselves to the same scrutiny. Heynkh was the only survivor of the Szimer family. Still a relatively young, handsome man, how did he survive? Suspicion may have been fed by rumor; it may also have been based on the conjecture that for a man like him, survival must have entailed collaboration. In fact, because many of the survivors were young men and women, since children and older people died in far larger numbers, they were often suspected, rarely with any factual basis, of having collaborated with the Germans or, in the case of women, of having literally slept with the enemy.

For men such as my grandfather, who left his town shortly before the disaster, and whose entire family was wiped out while he faced no greater danger than that of a hard day's work, feelings of guilt were often also involved. In a certain sense, he had left them all in the lurch and was not there to help when they were slaughtered. And then again, he could say to himself, had they followed in my footsteps, had they been willing to share the hardship of immigration and the loss of social status, rather than staying and refusing to read the writing on the wall, they would also have survived.[8] I cannot attribute any of this reasoning to my grandfather, who never complained about his lot, never expressed any self-righteous attitude of "I told you so," and rarely suspected others of base motives. But in the immediate aftermath of the Holocaust, these were widespread attitudes in Israel.[9] I do not know what my grandfather's cousin did or did not do during the Holocaust. But I can imagine the horror of having survived hell only to be suspected of having come out alive by consigning others to the flames; and, even worse, if there actually was a measure of truth to that suspicion, of having to live with that guilt for the rest of one's life.

"But you never found out what happened to the rest of the family?"

"So that's it, nothing was found out. Someone told Mother that her brother was caught and shot during the roundups, and that his wife and two daughters were shot even earlier in Kosov. As for Father's only sister, who was, so to speak, the jewel in the crown, because she married a man with an academic education, they escaped to Kośmierzyn, to their village, and hid there with a goy. They had one son, I have a picture, Rochaleh gave it to me, I should return it to her . . . "

As my mother speaks, I can hear my two children giggling right next to the microphone, but she keeps on talking.

"Tsila and Rochaleh visited them in 1938 or so, and they photographed the two of them as little children. The goy demanded from her that she get rid of the child, because a child cries and would give them away. But she refused, and apparently, they denounced her, and that's how they perished. Grandfather died a year before the war, I told you, of a heart attack."

And so it turns out that my grandfather's only sister had a son, who was the same age as Rochaleh, his brother Mendel and Tsila's only daughter. The two children were photographed together during Rochaleh's visit to Galicia. Tsila and Rochaleh must have returned to Palestine more or less at the last moment. Four or five years later the boy was murdered. But in her late middle age, Rochaleh wanted to return to that far-off place she had once visited as a little girl, so utterly different from the land where she was born and lived an unhappy life—she wanted to move back to Buczacz, the Buczacz that no longer existed. Perhaps her mother, who had once been so desperate to leave Buczacz that she married my great-uncle Mendel, subsequently instilled that longing in her daughter. But my grandfather's sister, who stayed, had chosen death rather than sacrificing her son. This appears to us as a heroic act. But at the time, if she was in hiding with other Jews, it might have been perceived as a selfish, even immoral decision, since it condemned others to death: the child threatened everyone, hence the child had to go.

Testimonies of the Holocaust are replete with such stories. In many cases they unfold somewhat differently. A group of Jews is hiding in a bunker. A baby begins to cry. The mother covers it with a pillow. When the roundup is over, the baby is discovered to have been smothered to death. Rarely, the baby miraculously survives; in some cases, the mother goes insane with guilt and grief. And yet, many of these testimonies are by people who were then children, and survived only because their mothers, and in some cases their fathers, struggled to the very last moment to save them, or because the Gentiles into whose hands they were entrusted protected them. Innumerable other children were abandoned, exploited, abused, and murdered.[10]

I do not have the photo that my mother mentioned. Perhaps she returned it to Rochaleh, and now it's too late to ask her for it. It occurs to me that had she had the money, my grandmother, too, might have taken my mother to visit her family in Galicia. Had they made that journey, they could have been stranded there when the war broke out. My mother might have after all ended up in the hands of the Germans and their local collaborators. From this perspective, even as her safety in Palestine was tenuous, poverty there actually played in her favor.

"How many siblings did Grandfather Yisrael have?"

"He had the brother who was here, and another brother, and this sister. As for that other brother, Hersh, we also don't know anything about him, we know nothing. I told you about him, he was a kind of *chudak*, he would just sit and read; he separated from two women and lived with Grandfather and just read all day: newspapers, books, and that's all. It appears that he had other ambitions in life that were never realized, but he was the screwed-up member of the family."

Hersh was a *chudak*, meaning a "crank" or an "oddball" in Ukrainian. To me he appears a little like Anton Chekhov's Konstantin Gavrilovich Treplyov in *The Seagull*, or any number of other characters in Chekhov's plays, who have great aspirations but can never find the energy and drive to make the first move to realize them. My mother, who loved Chekhov, showed little sympathy for Hersh, who just read all day and did nothing, whether because his ambitions were too great to be pursued or because he simply had none. Unlike her uncle, who must have still been sitting and reading when the Germans came to take him away, my mother went to Palestine, where action was everything and lazy intellectuals were dismissed as Diaspora types standing in the way of collective "realization": building roads, draining swamps, settling the land. Hersh was obviously not made for that. Mendel, the youngest sibling, was an idealist, a communist; he had great dreams and tried to realize them, having accidentally ended up in Palestine because he had to flee the Polish authorities. But nothing much came of his idealism either. He died of mouth cancer, and I still remember the horror of meeting him as a child, each time with more

Grandfather Yisrael's family with author's grandmother and mother.
Galicia, mid-1920s. Author's private collection.

of his mouth cut out in an attempt to halt the spread of the tumor. As for my grandfather Yisrael, I don't believe he was much given to either idealism or intellectual pursuits. He turned more to religion as years went by, and he worshipped my mother, both as a father loves his daughter and as a man of little education admires a child who has gained knowledge and recognition. In old age he became increasingly nostalgic about the world he had left behind, the world that no longer existed. But he hardly ever spoke about it and never complained.

The only photo I have of my grandfather's side of the family must have been taken in Buczacz, if not even earlier in Potok Złoty, around 1926. At the center of the front row is my great-grandfather, my grandfather Yisrael's father. To his right is his wife; to his left is my grandmother, Rina, and next to her is my mother. That is the earliest photo I have of my mother. In the middle of the second row is my grandfather's sister, that "jewel in the crown," who was denounced and murdered for refusing to give up her son. At the time the photograph was taken, that son had not yet been born. Behind my mother stands my grandfather Yisrael. The other young man is likely my great-uncle Mendel, who was younger and appears somewhat socially rebellious in his less formal attire. People used to dress up for such special occasions as having their picture taken. Hersh the *chudak* may have refused to come; perhaps he was engrossed in reading his newspaper or contemplating the great career he would never live to have.

The back of the photo was apparently used for practicing calligraphy. But the address line prominently carries the name Regina Bergman. Only years after my grandmother Rina's death did I discover that her maiden name was Bergman (distinguished from the German spelling by having only one *n*), and her Christian first name was Regina. The old Jewish tradition in Galicia not to officially register marriages meant that married women often kept their maiden names. Many Galician Jews also felt that while they might still be speaking Yiddish with each other, the language of correspondence should be the more dignified German, even if they had not always fully mastered it, and that while using it, they should also address each other by their Christian names. Yet especially in the interwar period, Polish became a strong competitor for the status of linguistic respectability; hence my grandfather's name was spelled Szimer, as in Polish, rather than Schimmer, the German spelling and the obvious origin of the name.[11]

"How many siblings did Grandmother have?"

"Grandmother Rina had Shimon and Yosef. We have a photo here. Shimon and Yosef and, I think he was called Yehoshua, no, he even visited us, he is Hebe's father, who went to South America, although he wanted to go to the United States."

I wish I could examine the photograph again with my mother, but it's too late. It was probably taken in Rożnów, my grandmother's village, sometime in the 1920s. At the center of the front row is my great-great-grandfather Bergman. All I have of him is this single photo and the phrase he used to utter, "enough with that," brushing away a thought with his hand as one would an irritating fly. Born in the early 1840s, this was a man who had seen vast transformations of society, culture, and politics in his time. But to his great fortune, the traditional Jewish blessing, "May you live to 120!" did not come true, and his death on the eve of World War II spared him the last twist of fate under Soviet and Nazi occupation. The world came out of joint, and few people lived to be old. Even brutal deportations by the Soviet authorities, mourned and lamented at the time, turned out in retrospect to have been a blessing in disguise. God was working in

Grandmother Rina's family. Galicia, mid-1920s. Author's private collection.

mysterious ways during those years, as my paternal grandfather used to say in response to my youthful assertion that the Holocaust proved either God's utter indifference or His evident nonexistence.

To the patriarch's left is his daughter, my great-grandmother, who was not as fortunate and was most likely murdered during the Holocaust. I have no information about the circumstances of her death. In the case of my family, as with numberless others, the biblical story of Korah and his clan was reenacted in historical time, as "the earth opened her mouth, and swallowed them up."[12] On the other side is my grandmother Rina, still very young and already a little roundish, as she remained for the rest of her eighty years. Because my mother is not in the picture, I assume the photo was taken before her birth in 1924. Behind are the three brothers. The one on the left, standing behind my grandmother, is probably Yehoshua, as my mother called him, or rather Eliezer, as I believe he was actually called. The other two are Shimon and Yosef. Shimon is the brother

Grandmother Rina and her siblings with Grandfather
Yisrael and his sister and brother. Galicia, late 1920s
or early 1930s. Author's private collection.

who learned to play the violin in Prague during World War I and used to
entertain the family with his music on special occasions. Everyone is dressed
for the occasion and looks appropriately solemn.

My son is complaining. He wants this interview to be over already and
to get some attention. Did he cut himself? My mother says, "You need a
Band-Aid, I'll get you one." I turn off the tape-recorder. Then we resume.

"So again, how many did she have, grandmother?"

"She had three brothers. She actually had more, but one of them died
in childhood and the other died later. During the war she had three living
brothers. Two brothers were there and one who wanted to go to the United
States and got stuck in Uruguay, Hebe's father. And the two who stayed
were also gone. No one was left."

One other surviving photo shows only the young people; it was probably taken later, in a studio with fake and painted scenery. I believe my
three maternal great-uncles are all there. Eliezer, it appears, is on the left
in the second row, next to his sister, my grandmother. One of his brothers
is in front of him, the other is standing in the back. My grandfather is in

Eliezer and Rivka Bergman. Uruguay, 1939. Author's private collection.

the front row on the right, and his sister, the "jewel in the crown," is next to him. Behind him, I think, is his brother Mendel, possibly with Tsila, whom he took to Palestine with him shortly after the photo was taken. If I am correct in identifying them, this was a fortunate group; of the eight people in the photo, five left Poland before the war and consequently survived. On 27 February 1939, Eliezer sent a postcard, apparently from Uruguay, to Palestine, of himself and his wife. On the back it says, uncharacteristically in Hebrew, "In eternal memory from Eliezer and Rivka."

"So one survived?"

"This one, yes, he also visited us here. He came from Uruguay and visited us."

Oscar (Eliezer) Bergman. Uruguay, postwar.
Author's private collection.

"Didn't she have any sisters?"

"No, she was the only sister. This was generally the case in the family, I am the only girl, and my mother was the only girl. Most were boys."

Some years later, perhaps after the war, Eliezer sent another postcard to his sister. This time he wrote in a mix of German and Yiddish in Roman script, on the back of the card: "In remembrance from your brother who has never forgotten, Oscar Bergman. The picture is for my dear sister Renczi." The card was sent from Salto in Uruguay, where Eliezer, who had now become Oscar, had set up his home. His daughter Hebe eventually came to Israel with her family. They always spoke Hebrew with an unmistakable Latin American accent. Renczi was the diminutive form of Rina, in Polish spelling. Oscar looks like a well-to-do, middle-class citizen who never got out of the habit of dressing up for a photograph. He has also not acquired the custom of smiling for the camera.

The Kosów memorial book ends with 35 pages containing approximately 2,300 names, spelled in Yiddish, under the heading "A List of the Holy and Pure People of Kosov and Its Surroundings." The list includes Yosef and Gitel Bergman, as well as Shimon and Gitel Bergman, along with their two children. This is the only mention of my maternal great-uncles and their families that I have been able to find. In the copy I inherited from my parents' library, someone, probably Grandfather Yisrael, drew a line under those names. He spent his last years looking through such books. The volume also contains a harrowing essay on how Jews tried to survive in underground shelters and among the local population after most of the Jewish population had already been murdered and the town declared *Judenrein*. Although there is no mention there of my relatives, one quickly grasps under what conditions they lived and how slim their chances of survival were.[13]

"And at home, during the war, did people speak?"

"Yes, they spoke, they spoke, people spoke all the time: 'Who knows what's happening with them?' Yes, they spoke, but the point is, I should also say, that at the time mother was working in the factory, life was really very hard."

My son is putting on his shoes and getting ready finally to leave the house. My daughter is crying in the other room. "It's terrible that she is locked up there," my mother says. The baby must be in her crib. "Don't worry, she is happy there," I say. "That's true, she is not locked up," my son comes to my rescue.

"Then at home did people not really talk? Grandmother must have talked, didn't she, about life over there?"

"Yes, and Father would also tell us."

"I remember Grandfather sitting and going through picture albums. But that was when he was already sick . . . "

"He loved to tell tales . . . "

"And I remember him telling us lots of legends, probably Ukrainian, I remember there were silkworms there, I remember there were kings, there were forests, all kinds of things . . . "

"Yes, sure, he liked to tell stories about hunting wild boars in the forest . . . "

"But what the legends were about I don't remember. Did he tell you any of that, or was this only for the grandchildren?"

"No, only for the grandchildren, I don't remember . . . "

I Cut Myself Off Completely

The earliest stories I remember being told as a child are associated with my maternal grandfather. My sister and I used to lie in our grandparents' double bed, which seemed very large at the time, and Grandfather would tell us forest legends. Our parents used to go to Europe quite often, or at least we felt they did, sampling the treasures of Western culture in Paris or London or Amsterdam or Rome, and they would leave us with our grandparents. This was a big treat, especially in those few years when they lived in their own house. I don't know how my grandparents managed to save enough money to build a house. It obviously was not a good deal, because the house stood in a little, mosquito-infested valley surrounded by citrus trees and connected to the main road by a narrow, unpaved path. My father's ancient Citroën would always sink into the dirt whenever he parked it next to the house, and we would have to push it out, or start the motor with the crank, though that probably had more to do with the condition of the car than the location of the house. My mother said that her father, who was a trusting, naïve man, had been tricked into buying this plot. By now, of course, this land is worth a fortune; the orange trees have all been uprooted, and in their place rows upon rows of ugly tenements for the country's growing population have been planted. But my grandfather sold it off long before its value went up. The house is gone. But at the time, in the 1960s, when it stood there, with a red-tiled roof and fruit trees in the yard, it looked just like the kind of house children draw even if they have never seen one; or maybe I just remember it that way.

Thinking back, I realize that in his own silent fashion, my grandfather missed the land in which he had spent his first thirty-five years. Living in a "husha" in somebody's backyard, unable to grow anything or to have any contact with nature, must have been very hard for him. His dream was to have a house of his own, however small, with fruit trees in the yard. And he actually realized that dream. But he had worked so hard to be able to afford it that his health deteriorated. The house was a few miles away from the nearest bus stop, so he had to walk there every morning and walk back every evening. When his heart failed him, it was clear that they would have to move. My parents helped them find a small apartment next to where we lived, in a neighborhood built north of Tel Aviv for Jews expelled from Poland by Władysław Gomułka's antisemitic communist regime. But although that ensured that my grandfather would be close to his beloved daughter, he must have lost all hope of leading the life he had hoped for. Unable to work, without a house and trees of his own, locked in a tiny apartment, he retreated into his memories of the past, turning the pages of memorial books and picture albums, looking at the faces of those who never had a chance to grow old.

But during the few years that my grandparents lived in that house, it was a source of legends and adventures, as well as substantial amounts of loquat fruit, whose orange-yellow skin, sweet-and-sour flesh, and shiny dark pits have lodged themselves firmly in my childhood memories. Nowadays this fruit is known in Israel as *shesek*, but at the time we called it by its Arabic or Turkish name, *eskidinia* or *askadinia*. My grandfather would dig a trench around each tree, so as to hold the water and direct it to the roots. Then my sister and I would water the trees with a long rubber hose. The fruit was covered with brown paper bags to protect it from birds. The area was teeming with life. Every once in a while, a colony of ants would decide to move house straight through Grandmother's sitting room, under the dinner table, over which hung a reproduction of Vincent van Gogh's still life, *Vase with Twelve Sunflowers*, and she would try to block their path by pouring kerosine on them, which was otherwise used in winter in the little oil heater that every family in Israel had in those years. In the kitchen there was a bucket filled with water and yesterday's bread for the old German shepherd, Lassie, who had lost most of her teeth and could no longer eat anything solid. One day she disappeared and was found dead at the edge of the orange grove a couple of days later. She had gone to die on her own, my grandmother said. We were very sad. My grandfather buried her. And my sister and I reenacted her funeral by carrying a doll on my toy fire engine through the yard and ceremoniously burying it under a fruit tree.

But what I remember most fondly is the two of us tucked into bed with Grandfather as he told us those stories of silkworms and dwarves, kings and giants, witches and wizards, bears and wolves (but I don't recall any wild boar hunts). Yet even though I remember very vividly the context in which the stories were told, I cannot remember any of their plots. These were, I assume, tales from the vast borderlands of Ukraine, and while my grandfather was an observant Jew, his stories must have come to him from the local folklore. Jews had lived in those regions for centuries, and many, like his own father and grandfather, had worked with the peasants, and traveled by wagon from village to village; they spoke the language of the people, and knew their customs. They may have not shared their vodka and food for dietary reasons, but they internalized much of the peasant culture of the region and blended it with their own Jewish traditions. Growing up, as I did, in my minuscule, dusty homeland, where any bunch of trees was designated a forest, where the widest river could be crossed in moments, where snow was but a rumor and wildlife was banished to the desert with the last of the jackals, only to be replaced by hordes of street cats, I could not hear enough about that imaginary land, as far in time as in space, a land of titanic rivers, primeval forests, deep snows, giant bears, and howling wolves.

Perhaps my memories of these tales were one unconscious reason for finally going to Ukraine for the first time in March 2003. It did not look precisely as in my grandfather's tales. But the snow and ice, the forests and hills, the cows led by little girls and old men, the chickens in the yards and the mother geese crossing the potholed roads at the head of their goslings, the rolling hills and the horse-drawn plows, the onion-domed churches and the little houses with vegetable gardens and fruit trees: all these things were still there, as if rising from a dream of my childhood. It was a beautiful, melancholy region, where the people were poor and the land was rich; it also felt as if it was covering up a great absence, as if the marrow had been sucked out of its bones, now filling the unmarked mass graves surrounding each and every town. It was shrouded in a blanket of silence that smothered the voices of the past.

"I remember that we used to receive letters. Until the war broke out letters would still come. They would write in Roman script using a kind of Germanized Yiddish."

"But do we have any of these letters?"

"I don't know. No, there are none. Father found some at Grandfather's, which he keeps."

"At Grandfather Simcha's?"

"Yes, yes, he found some, yes. But I haven't, I don't know, I haven't seen any."

"But was there ever a time when you thought about that world, or did you entirely cut yourself off from it?"

"When I came here, as a child? I cut myself off completely. Totally cut off."

"Was that conscious?"

The author's mother and her aunts. Buczacz, late 1920s.
Author's private collection.

"No, I don't think it was conscious. It's simply . . . I don't know if this generally happens to children or what. Perhaps there was a strong urge to enter into this world, because it was clear we'd never again see the world we came from."

In one early photograph, my mother seems perfectly happy in that other world, sitting on a sled with what I was told at some point were two "aunts." Who were these aunts? "Aunt" and "uncle" were often used as generic terms even in my childhood for any relative and even just for someone close to the family. This may have had to do with the scarcity of real family members after the Holocaust. But it was also a habit brought from Eastern Europe. Yet as I examine the photo more closely, I realize that one of the women on the sled is my great-aunt, my grandfather's sister, the "jewel in the crown." The photo was most probably taken in Buczacz in the late 1920s, since the aunt was living in the same house with my mother's family and her paternal grandfather. They are all dressed well, with fashionable hats and furs. They look content, and even allow themselves a faint smile. This was home: the snow and the sled and the fur coat and the aunts and the wooden fence behind them, the slope, the hill, the forest. And then it was no longer home, and the memory of it was deleted. As in doctored photographs of the communist regimes, where figures of purged functionaries were removed, one can imagine this photo also being altered to fit the postwar reality at the site: the background remains, the fence, the snow, the sled; but the people have been rubbed out.

"It's true that Mother would say every once in a while, 'If we have the money, we'll go to visit the family.' But you know, ten pounds sterling, or thereabouts, was considered a huge amount of money at the time. Mother made three pounds per month and Father six, and that was just enough to make ends meet, with difficulty. Did I think about it? . . . At the beginning I felt, you know, a kind of oddness, and a kind of loneliness. It was fortunate that we had an uncle here in whose house, as I told you, we lived together at the beginning. But later there was a very strong urge to fit in, and I think that the hardships of life, all the demands made on us, you know, we were always under some kind of pressure . . . There was no time to sit back or to think or . . . "

My mother stops for a moment, asking, "What's this?" I can hear my father's voice in the background. So he has finally come to the kitchen. My mother says, "Tomorrow I'll go to buy a cake, today there was nothing worthy of the name there." Then she continues:

"For me it was very . . . I'll tell you, I also think that there, in the yard, the first place where I lived, those who helped me a great deal were the families that lived there, and especially the family of Pinchas Goldberg, that Sonia, who took care of us, you know, I always tell the same story . . . "

My father intervenes and tells his own story about meeting Avigail, Sonia Goldberg's daughter, now an elderly woman, a few days earlier when he went to the doctor. My mother comments, "She was younger than me." My father goes on to say how Avigail sang my mother's praises, "What a girl she was!" I want to get back to my mother's story.

"So this Sonia Goldberg was . . . ?"

"The wife of Pinchas, the driver. He was the son of the owner . . . "

"Were they Yekes?"

"No, Russians."

"They were among the founders of Petah Tikva . . . " My father interjects. I now know that we are heading away from story to History.

"Their father," says my mother.

"They were several brothers; there was Meishke . . . " My father is getting into his stride.

I try to stop this digression. It is as I feared, the struggle between my mother telling her story and my father telling the Story, of the Yishuv, of Zionism, of other people . . .

"Let's not speak about the general history," I say, "I am interested in the private history."

I can hear my son meanwhile chattering in the background. He is happier when everyone is in the kitchen speaking all at once. My mother continues:

"She, Sonia, helped me a great deal, because Mother was out of the home all day long. She taught me how to do the dishes and everything. But the most beautiful thing was, in the morning—now, my hair is, you know—but then I had curly and very thick and long hair. At that time people didn't wear their hair loose, you had to gather it in a braid or tie it together with a band. So she would—you had to get to school all fixed up, the nurse used to check your nails and your scalp—she would do my hair every morning, and in order not to make me feel second best she would first comb my hair and only then comb her daughter Avigail's hair. She was a wonderful woman. She used to take her children to the beach; she also didn't have to pay the bus fare. My parents worked; the beach was out of the question. Who would have thought of going to the sea in the summer? So my brothers actually never went to the beach. I was lucky, because they loved me there, so Sonia would take me with her children in the bus. I didn't have to pay, and I went with her to the beach in Tel Aviv two–three times a week. And everywhere she went—they used to go places just to have a good time—she would take me along too. And she would always sing my praises, not those of her children . . . She was a very special woman, Sonia."

"Were they born in Israel?"

"She, Sonia, no, she was not born in . . . Her maiden name was San-dalon, her parents . . . "

"They came from Russia?"

"They were Russian, yes. And his parents, her husband's, were among the founders of Petah Tikva."

"But you mentioned her because we discussed whether anyone talked about 'there.'"

"Ah, the Goldbergs didn't talk much about 'there.' At home, when those who came with us on the ship were visiting, then they would talk about 'there.' But the Goldbergs did not talk about 'there,' they were from here."

"I was asking also because the war broke out merely four years after you came here."

"That's true, come to think of it, it was only four years . . . "

"But do you remember if something changed, how they spoke about that world after the war broke out? After all, the whole family was there . . . Was there some feeling that they had done the right thing and that this somehow justified the difficulties and poverty?"

"No, they didn't talk about that. No, they didn't talk about that."

"After all, your parents really declined economically . . . "

"But they didn't know that it would be the end there."

"But at least the war, they knew that . . . They had recollections from World War I . . . "

"Yes, but they did not think . . . No, no, they never said how fortunate it was that they had come here. No, they never talked about that."

"Not even after the war?"

"After the war they thought that . . . How stupid they were over there, because when Father left, he said that he was going to Palestine, and they said to him, we have a Palestine right here. He always used to tell that story, you know, that they made fun of him in this manner, what was he looking for in Palestine. But that was after the war. I don't think that they even imagined that . . . Look, the letters stopped arriving and all that . . . "

"Do you know why he decided . . . ? I assume it was Grandfather who decided . . . "

"Yes. Yes, of course."

" . . . to go to Palestine? It wasn't Grandmother?"

"No, no, no, it was my father, my father."

"Do you know why?"

"So look, first of all, he was . . . "

"I know he was a Zionist, there were many Zionists . . . "

"He was a Zionist. It's also possible . . . Now I'm psychologizing . . . "

My daughter is crying in the other room. My son walks in to show my mother something. I push on:

"Apart from being a Zionist . . . "

"It's possible that I am psychologizing now, because they never spoke about it . . . "

My son interferes. "What, what are you asking?" "I'm just asking something," I reply. My mother continues speaking: "But I think that the link to Grandfather and the dependence on him were a factor. He was the eldest son, and in fact he was always with Grandfather, and the big boss was Grandfather, I remember him, he had a beard . . . I even have a photo of him."

"Was he an authoritarian man?"

"He was authoritarian, yes. Perhaps, beyond everything else . . . he certainly decided about everything . . . "

"Decided about what?"

"That they would live in the same house in Buczacz. This was Grandfather's house."

"And then there was one brother who only read books . . . "

"And one brother who left two years earlier. He completely dropped out. He had no interest whatsoever in the family."

"Where did he go, the third one? What did he do?"

"Mendel, here?"

"Ah, Mendel came here, of course . . . "

"He came here, but not out of Zionism, he escaped from . . . "

"So in fact they all escaped from that father . . . "

"He got hold of an immigration certificate . . . Look, he had all kinds of aspirations."

My son finally loses it. "Let's go!" he demands. I say to my mother, "Now I have to go."

The Stories We Tell

What am I left with after this conversation with my mother? Her story is the tale of an end and a beginning, a departure from one world just before it blew up, and the construction of another, whose future was then and perhaps still is not entirely certain. It is not a tale of triumph, of making the right decision, or of foresight, let alone of schadenfreude. At the heart of this story, I think, is the recognition that we all are a product of where we came from, just as much as of where we ended up, and that, hard as we try to sever the links to the past, to look only forward, we can never separate ourselves from that original part of us that is at the core of our being. This is true on a personal level, in that we can only deny our childhood at our peril, and collectively, in that what gives meaning to our lives as human beings is more than the sum of our individual biographical experiences: it includes the stories we were told, and the stories we tell ourselves and our children, about where we came from, how we became who we are, and where we eventually ended up or are still headed. Most people know, I think, that stories of the past give meaning to the present. But it is also true that the place where we were born and raised acquires a different meaning when we leave it, just as the landscapes of our childhood instill meaning into all those future sites where we may eventually build and end our lives.

Like all other stories, my mother's tale is both conventional within its own historical and cultural context, and unique, as all individuals and their lives invariably are. This is true about the Szimer and Bergman families, as it is more generally true about that last generation of those who came from Europe's eastern borderlands. Many more family strands of this story could be told if I still had access to those who remembered them, but they are all gone. If much of my mother's story is about the end of one world and the beginning of another, it is also a tale that breathes life into the last moments of that now vanished world, extending that life beyond its erasure in the memories and emotions of those who came out on the other side.

In speaking with my mother, I realized that I knew practically nothing about how my own family members had lived and perished. Unlike some people, who can cite precise figures of the number of relatives they lost in the Holocaust, I have no idea how many they were and can only assume that, like all families at the time in those regions, mine too was large. What I have told in this book are the tales of the borderlands that no longer exist, at least not in the form they did before the catastrophe; my family was part of that history and those tales. In that sense, this book is also a family story, the story of families that even today are linked in intricate and invisible ways to that lost world they have never visited and know almost nothing about. For who we are, what we remember, how we raise our children, what we say and believe and cherish and despise are all also a result of chance, as well as of decisions, deliberate and thoughtless, made for good reasons and bad, by us and by our ancestors, and by others who may not have given us and our families a single thought. If I have learned anything from the tales of the borderlands, as much as from the story of my family, it is that we are all who we are not only because of the stuff we are made of but, at least as much, because of the haphazard yet relentless unfolding of events.

For me, the end of this journey is encapsulated in a photograph taken in Israel in 1979. Looking at it now, I am struck by the precarious balance it reveals between human will and aspiration, and the grim logic of history and biology. At the center is my grandmother Rina Szimer, or Regina Bergman. To the left of her is my mother, holding my baby niece. To the right is my sister, the baby's mother. In the first row are my brother-in-law, with my nephew on his shoulders, and me, just before I left Israel and set

Four generations of the author's family. Israel, 1979.
Author's private collection.

out on my own private journey. Four generations, each with very different life stories, from childhood to old age, sharing some memories, separated by many others. All four intersected in the world for just a little while, because my grandmother died the following year. Our lives have been guided, or misguided, by happenstance and coincidence, hope and determination. But like so many others, we still carry deep within us a fragment of memory, transmitted from one generation to the next, of those long centuries lived, for better or for worse, in that *ek velt*, that corner of the world, like the fading echoes of a lost yet never entirely forgotten childhood.

Acknowledgments

THIS BOOK COULD NOT have been written without the support of many institutions and the assistance of a cast of researchers, colleagues, and friends in the United States, Europe, and Israel. I especially thank my home institution, Brown University, for providing me with the time and resources to undertake sustained research over the years, as well as my colleagues and students who have enriched my understanding and served as a constant and reliable sounding board as I sought to articulate what I was actually trying to do. Fellowships and other financial support at Brown University were provided by the Cogut Institute for the Humanities, the History Department, the Pembroke Center, and the Watson Institute for International and Public Affairs. I am grateful for additional critical support from the National Endowment for the Humanities, the Radcliffe Institute for Advanced Study at Harvard University, the John Simon Guggenheim Foundation, the Internationales Forschungszentrum Kulturwissenschaften in Vienna, the American Academy in Berlin, the Center for Advanced Holocaust Studies of the United States Holocaust Memorial Museum in Washington, DC, the International Institute for Holocaust Research at Yad Vashem, Israel, and the Israel Institute for Advanced Studies at the Hebrew University of Jerusalem.

Of the numerous research assistants, translators, colleagues, and friends who helped and inspired me along the way I especially thank Natalia Aleksiun, Israel Bartal, Alon Confino, Havi Dreyfus, Saul Friedländer, Ziva Galili, Amos Goldberg, Jan Grabowski, Jan Tomasz Gross, Atina Grossmann, Irit Halavy, Dagmar Herzog, Ariel Hirschfeld, Anna Michalska, Joanna Michlic, Yoel Rappel, Shimon Redlich, Naama Shik, Roman Voronka, Thomas Weiss, Larry Wolff, and Yael Zerubavel. Special thanks for introducing me to Galicia and its archives go to Sofia Grachova and Frank Grelka, without whom this book would have been neither conceived nor written. Eric D. Weitz, who passed away far too soon just as this book was going into production, set out with me on our first excursions into the borderlands. I will always miss his friendship and wisdom.

My wife, Wai-yee Li, whose scholarship on Chinese literature is surpassed by none, somehow found the time to carefully read and provide a final stamp of approval on every word in this book, for which I am eternally grateful, even as I accept responsibility for any infelicities and errors that have remained in the text. I dedicate this book to Alan Mintz, who became a friend in what unfortunately turned out to be the last years of his life: a wonderful scholar and a true mensch, who taught me a great deal and whom I dearly miss; and to Esti Amit (Eichenwald), who was my dear friend for most of my life and was snatched away by fate so suddenly that I will never quite accept her absence.

Notes

Introduction: Out into the World

1. S. Zweig, *The World of Yesterday*, trans. B. W. Huebsch and H. Ripperger (Lincoln, NE, 1964 [1942]).
2. O. Bartov and E. D. Weitz, eds., *Shatterzone of Empires* (Bloomington, IN, 2013).
3. L. Wolff, *The Idea of Galicia* (Stanford, 2010).
4. P. R. Magocsi, *The Roots of Ukrainian Nationalism* (Toronto, 2002).
5. B. Porter, *When Nationalism Began to Hate* (New York, 2000).
6. I. Bartal, *The Jews of Eastern Europe, 1772–1881*, trans. C. Naor (Philadelphia, 2002).
7. J. Shanes, *Diaspora Nationalism and Jewish Identity in Habsburg Galicia* (New York, 2012).
8. Y. Slezkine, *The Jewish Century* (Princeton, 2004).
9. O. Bartov, *Erased* (Princeton, 2007).
10. A. Mintz, "'I Am Building a City,'" in S. Y. Agnon, *A City in Its Fullness*, multiple translators, ed. A. Mintz and J. Saks (New Milford, CT), xx.
11. O. Bartov, *Anatomy of a Genocide* (New York, 2018).
12. O. Bartov, ed., *Voices on War and Genocide* (New York, 2020).

Chapter One. Origins

1. A. Zamoyski, *The Polish Way* (New York, 2001), 185; D. Stone, *The Polish-Lithuanian State, 1386–1795* (Seattle, 2001), 235–36.
2. M. Miławicki Op, "'Świat ode mnie zawsze rzeczy nadzwyczajnych wymagał, a ponadto niesłusznie.' O. Sadok Wincenty Barącz OP (1814–1892) w świetle źródeł," *Lehahayer* 2, no. 2 (2013): 153–98.
3. S. Barącz, *Pamiątki Buczackie* (Lwów, 1882), 9n1.
4. C. Miłosz, *The History of Polish Literature*, 2nd ed. (Berkeley, 1983), 65.
5. Y. Cohen, ed., *Sefer Buczacz* (Tel Aviv, 1956; Hebrew and Yiddish), 44, 64n1;

H. Sienkiewicz, *With Fire and Sword,* trans. W. S. Kuniczak (New York, 1991 [1884]), 11–12. Prince Władysław Dominik Zasławski-Ostrogski (c. 1616–56) was a powerful Polish magnate at that time.

6. J. R. Krzyzanowski, "Introduction," in Sienkiewicz, *With Fire and Sword,* xii–xiii.

7. Barącz, *Pamiątki Buczackie,* 3–4.

8. Stone, *The Polish-Lithuanian State,* 3–20, 36–66, 136–48; P. R. Magocsi, *Historical Atlas of East Central Europe* (Seattle, 1993), 48–52, 59; P. R. Magocsi, *A History of Ukraine* (Seattle, 1996), 175–92.

9. I. Babel, *Red Cavalry and Other Stories,* trans. D. McDuff (London, 2005).

10. H. Abramson, *A Prayer for the Government* (Cambridge, MA, 1999).

11. Y. Maor, "The Anti-Semitic Proclamation of the Narodnaya Volya," *Zion* 15 (1950): 153 (Hebrew); Bartal, *The Jews of Eastern Europe,* 165.

12. *New York Times,* 13 April 2009, A6.

13. Y. Stotskyi, *The Basilian Monastery* (Lviv, 1997; Ukrainian), 36–37.

14. Barącz, *Pamiątki Buczackie,* 4–5; S. J. Kowalski, *Powiat Buczacki i jego zabytki* (Biały Dunajec, 2005), 32–34, 49–50.

15. I. Kladochnyi, *Brief Sketch of Buczacz* (Canada, 1990; Ukrainian), 1.

16. Kowalski, *Powiat Buczacki,* 35–36.

17. Kladochnyi, *Brief Sketch of Buczacz,* 1–2. O. Hnatiuk, *Courage and Fear,* trans. E. Siwak (Boston, 2020), 468.

18. Kladochnyi, *Brief Sketch of Buczacz,* 2.

19. Stotskyi, *Basilian Monastery,* 37.

20. Stotskyi, *Basilian Monastery,* 48–49, citing two versions of the clan's takeover of Buczacz; O. Klymenko and B. Khavarivskyi, *Heraldry of Cities and Towns in the Ternopil Region* (Ternopil, 2003; Ukrainian), 176, inferring an earlier date; Kowalski, *Powiat Buczacki,* 25–26, for yet another version.

21. See also A. Teller, *Rescue the Surviving Souls* (Princeton, NJ, 2020).

22. Barącz, *Pamiątki Buczackie,* 49–52.

23. Barącz, *Pamiątki Buczackie,* 6.

24. Urban Media Archive, Lviv Center for Urban History, http://www.lvivcenter .org/en/uid/picture/?pictureid=2577.

25. Kowalski, *Powiat Buczacki,* 42–43.

26. Stotskyi, *Basilian Monastery,* 39.

27. J. Tokarski, *Ilustrowany przewodnik po zabytkach kultury na Ukrainie,* vol. 2 (Warsaw, 2000), 37; Kowalski, *Powiat Buczacki,* 43.

28. *Sefer Buczacz,* 43.

29. Kladochnyi, *Brief Sketch of Buczacz,* 2–3.

30. Barącz, *Pamiątki Buczackie,* 6–7; Stotskyi, *Basilian Monastery,* 39.

31. Generally, see D. Laor, *S. Y. Agnon* (Tel Aviv, 1998; Hebrew).

32. S. Y. Agnon, *Ir u-melo'ah* (Tel Aviv, 1973; Hebrew), epigraph (this and all subsequent translations of Agnon are my own—O.B.); Mintz and Saks, *A City in Its Fullness,* epigraph.

33. Agnon, *Ir u-melo'ah,* 14. The allusion is to Psalms 125. See also his story "Vehaya he'akov lemishor," in S. Y. Agnon, *Elu ve-elu* (Tel Aviv, 1998 [1912]);

Hebrew), 47–103; *And the Crooked Shall Be Made Straight*, trans. M. P. Kramer (New Milford, CT, 2017).

34. A. Lipsker, "The Founding of Buczacz," in his *Reflections on S. Y. Agnon*, vol. 1 (Ramat Gan, 2015; Hebrew), 171.

35. S. D. Ezrahi, "The Shtetl and Its Afterlife," *Association for Jewish Studies Review* 41, no. 1 (2017): 133–54.

36. S. D. Kassow, *Who Will Write Our History* (Bloomington, IN, 2007), 49–89; A. Teller, "Polish-Jewish Relations," *Studia Judaica* 15, nos. 29–30 (2012): 27–48.

37. B. D. Weinryb, *The Jews of Poland* (Philadelphia, 1972), 25, 27; M. J. Rosman, *The Lord's Jews* (Cambridge, MA, 1991), 39–40.

38. G. D. Hundert, *Jews in Poland-Lithuania in the Eighteenth Century* (Berkeley, 2004), 6; Bartal, *The Jews of Eastern Europe*, 14–15.

39. Rosman, *The Lord's Jews*, 39; Bartal, *The Jews of Eastern Europe*, 17; Hundert, *Jews in Poland-Lithuania*, 14–15.

40. I. Schipper, *Studja nad stosunkami Żydów w Polsce* (Lwów, 1911), 155, cited in *Sefer Buczacz*, 64n2; M. Nosonovsky, *Hebrew Epitaphs and Inscriptions from Ukraine and Former Soviet Union* (Washington, DC, 2006), 25, 107; A. J. Brawer, "Buczacz," *Encyclopaedia Judaica*, vol. 4 (Jerusalem, 1978), 1037, https://www.jewishvirtuallibrary.org/buchach.

41. Agnon, *Ir u-melo'ah*, 9; *A City in Its Fullness*, 31.

42. See also Lipsker, *Reflections on S. Y. Agnon*, 159–75.

43. Agnon, *Ir u-melo'ah*, 9–13; *A City in Its Fullness*, 31–37.

44. S. Y. Agnon, "Kedumot," in his *Elu ve-elu*, 287. A slightly different version was published in 1919. See *Polin*, vol. 12: *Focusing on Galicia*, ed. I. Bartal and A. Polonsky (London, 1999), ix–x.

45. S. Y. Agnon, *Ore'ah nata lalun*, rev. ed. (Tel Aviv, 1998 [1939]; Hebrew); *A Guest for the Night*, trans. M. Louvish (Madison, WI, 1968).

46. "Autobiography of Stanisław J. Kowalski," unpublished; S. J. Kowalski, *Archiwum Wschodnie*, II/1339.

47. Further in P. Brock et al., eds., *Nation and History* (Toronto, 2006), 8, 386; P. R. Magocsi, *Galicia* (Toronto, 1983), 78; J. Raba, *Between Remembrance and Denial* (New York, 1995), 333n1418.

48. Kowalski, *Powiat Buczacki*, 5–9.

49. Kowalski, *Powiat Buczacki*, 54–55.

50. N. M. Gelber, "History of the Jews in Buczacz," in *Sefer Buczacz*, 45; Kladochnyi, *Brief Sketch of Buczacz*, 3.

51. See, e.g., E. Apperly, "'Stumbling Stones,'" *The Guardian*, 18 February 2019.

52. Agnon, *Ir u-melo'ah*, 149.

Chapter Two. Massacres

1. N. N. Hanover, *Yeven metsulah* (Tel Aviv, 1944–45; Hebrew); *Abyss of Despair*, trans. A. J. Mesch (New Brunswick, NJ, 1983 [1950]). See also Raba, *Between Remembrance and Denial*, 38n128.

2. S. Y. Borovi, "The Ukrainian People's War of National Liberation against Polish Rule and the Jewish Population of Ukraine," *Istoricheskie zapiski* 9 (1940): 81–124 (Russian); F. P. Shevchenko, "The Participation of Representatives of Different Nationalities in the 1648–1655 War of Liberation in Ukraine," *Ukraiinskyi Istorychnyi Zhurnal* 11 (1978): 10–22 (Ukrainian); A. Teller, "Jewish Literary Responses to the Events of 1648–1649 and the Creation of a Polish-Jewish Consciousness," in *Culture Front*, ed. B. Nathans and G. Safran (Philadelphia, 2007), 17–45; Magocsi, *A History of Ukraine*, 199; F. E. Sysyn, "Ukrainian-Polish Relations in the Seventeenth Century," in *Poland and Ukraine, Past and Present*, ed. P. J. Potichnyi (Edmonton, AB, 1980), 55–82; F. E. Sysyn, "The Jewish Factor in the Khmelnytsky Uprising," in *Ukrainian-Jewish Relations in Historical Perspective*, ed. P. J. Potichnyi and H. Aster (Edmonton, AB, 1988), 43–54; Raba, *Between Remembrance and Denial*, 411–34.

3. N. Hanover, *Yeven metsulah* (Berlin, 1923; Hebrew); Abramson, *A Prayer for the Government*, 109–40; J. Veidlinger, *In the Midst of Civilized Europe* (New York, 2021).

4. M. Krüger, "Buchproduktion im Exil," in *Juden in Kreuzberg*, Berliner Geschichtswerkstatt (Berlin, 1991), 421–26.

5. A. Holtzman, *Hayim Nahman Bialik*, trans. O. Scharf (New Haven, 2017), 11, 223–26.

6. H. Belloc, "The War by Land," *Country Gentleman and Land & Water* 63, no. 2731 (12 September 1914): 2.

7. *Davar*, 17 July 1934 (Hebrew). Bialik died in Vienna on 4 July, and was buried in Palestine on 16 July. Holtzman, *Bialik*, 227.

8. Cited in I. Zangwill, *The Voice of Jerusalem* (London, 1920), 183.

9. "Jewish Massacre Denounced," *New York Times*, 28 April 1903, 6; S. Lambroza, "The Pogroms of 1903–1906," in *Pogroms*, ed. J. D. Klier and S. Lambroza (Cambridge, 2004), 200. S. J. Zipperstein (*Pogrom* [New York, 2018], cover flap, xiv, 73) mentions 49 dead, 40 rapes, and 600 casualties altogether. The *Jewish Encyclopedia* 1906 edition notes that "47 Jews were killed, and 92 severely, and 500 slightly, injured . . . 700 houses were destroyed; 600 stores were pillaged; 2,000 families were utterly ruined"; http://www.jewishency clopedia.com/articles/9350-kishinef-kishinev.

10. H. Rogger, "Conclusion and Overview"; Lambroza, "The Pogroms of 1903–1906"; and P. Kenez, "Pogroms and White Ideology in the Russian Civil War," in *Pogroms*, ed. Klier and Lambroza, 328, 228, 293, and 302; Veidlinger, *In the Midst of Civilized Europe*; H. Abramson, "Russian Civil War," *The YIVO Encyclopedia of Jews in Eastern Europe* (2010), https://yivoencyclopedia.org/article.aspx/Russian_Civil_War.

11. For background and analysis, see Zipperstein, *Pogrom*, 114–19, 124–33, 137–43.

12. Zipperstein, *Pogrom*, 138–39, 142–43.

13. B. Harshav, *Hebrew Renaissance Poetry* (Tel Aviv, 2000; Hebrew), 137–47 (my

translation—O.B.); Project Ben Yehuda, H. N. Bialik, "In the City of Slaughter" (Hebrew), https://benyehuda.org/read/1784.

14. Y. Fichman, "On 'Yeven Metsulah,'" in Hanover, *Yeven metsulah* (this and all subsequent citations are from the 1944–45 edition), 5–6.

15. Fichman, "On 'Yeven Metsulah,'" in Hanover, *Yeven metsulah*, 11. The historian Emanuel Ringelblum, born in Buczacz in 1900, and head of the Oneg Shabbat Archive of the Warsaw Ghetto, similarly insisted on objective, dispassionate testimony. Kassow, *Who Will Write Our History*, 308.

16. Fichman, "On 'Yeven Metsulah,'" 10.

17. Fichman, "On 'Yeven Metsulah,'" 13–14.

18. "The Life and Work of Nathan Hanover," *Abyss of Despair*, 13–22.

19. Magocsi, *A History of Ukraine*, 195–96; "Introduction," *Abyss of Despair*, 1–12; Raba, *Between Remembrance and Denial*, 367–434.

20. Magocsi, *A History of Ukraine*, 192, 196–200.

21. Weinryb, *The Jews of Poland*, 115–16, 151–52, 318; Raba, *Between Remembrance and Denial*, 398–403; Magocsi, *A History of Ukraine*, 200–202. J. Pelenski, "The Cossack Insurrections in Jewish-Ukrainian Relations," in *Ukrainian-Jewish Relations*, ed. Potichnyi and Aster, 35, argues that no more than 14,000 Jews were massacred.

22. F. E. Sysyn, "The Problem of Nobilities in the Ukrainian Past," in *Rethinking Ukrainian History*, ed. I. L. Rudnytsky (Edmonton, AB, 1981), 61.

23. O. Subtelny, *Ukraine*, 3rd ed. (Toronto, 2000), 124, 127.

24. Magocsi, *A History of Ukraine*, 202.

25. Magocsi, *A History of Ukraine*, 202–28; Magocsi, *Historical Atlas*, 59–61; J. Lukowski and H. Zawadzki, *A Concise History of Poland* (New York, 2001), 75–83.

26. Hanover, *Yeven metsulah*, 31–2 (this and all subsequent citations translated by me, OB); *Abyss of Despair*, 42–44.

27. B. Lukin, "Nemyriv," trans. I. M. Aronson, *The YIVO Encyclopedia of Jews in Eastern Europe* (2010), https://yivoencyclopedia.org/article.aspx/Nemyriv.

28. Hanover, *Yeven metsulah*, 37–38; *Abyss of Despair*, 50–51.

29. Hanover, *Yeven metsulah*, 39; *Abyss of Despair*, 53.

30. Hanover, *Yeven metsulah*, 39; *Abyss of Despair*, 53.

31. O. Bartov, "Kitsch and Sadism in Ka-Tzetnik's Other Planet," *Jewish Social Studies* 3, no. 2 (1997): 42–76.

32. Hanover, *Yeven metsulah*, 40; *Abyss of Despair*, 54.

33. Hanover, *Yeven metsulah*, 41–42; *Abyss of Despair*, 55–56.

34. Hanover, *Yeven metsulah*, 41–42; *Abyss of Despair*, 56–57.

35. Y. Arad et al., eds. and trans., *Documents on the Holocaust: Selected Sources on the Destruction of the Jews of Germany and Austria, Poland, and the Soviet Union* (Lincoln, NE, 1999), 283.

36. G. J. Horwitz, *Ghettostadt* (Cambridge, MA, 2008), 294–95, 322.

37. *Documents on the Holocaust*, 402–3.

38. *Documents on the Holocaust*, 453–55.
39. *Documents on the Holocaust*, 440–44.
40. J. Noakes and G. Pridham, eds., *Nazism, 1919–1945* (Exeter, UK, 1988–2001), vol. 3: *Foreign Policy, War and Racial Extermination*, 1199–1200.
41. B. Harshav, "Introduction," in H. Kruk, *The Last Days of the Jerusalem of Lithuania*, ed. and trans. B. Harshav (New Haven, 2002), xxvii, xlvi–xlvii.
42. E. Fram, "Creating a Tale of Martyrdom in Tulczyn, 1648," in *Jewish History and Jewish Memory*, ed. E. Carlebach et al. (Hanover, NH, 1998), 96.
43. See, e.g., M. Głowiński, *The Black Seasons*, trans. M. Shore (Evanston, IL, 2005); S. Friedländer, *When Memory Comes*, trans. H. R. Lane (New York, 1979).
44. *Documents on the Holocaust*, 404.
45. Fram, "Tale of Martyrdom," 89–112; Raba, *Between Remembrance and Denial*, 75, 98–99, 108.
46. Hanover, *Yeven metsulah*, 42–43; *Abyss of Despair*, 57–58.

Chapter Three. Divine Justice

1. Hanover, *Yeven metsulah*, 52, 56–57, 63; *Abyss of Despair*, 68–69, 76–77, 86.
2. Agnon, *Ir u-melo'ah*, 16; *Sefer Buczacz*, 46.
3. Barącz, *Pamiątki Buczackie*, 6–7; Kladochnyi, *Brief Sketch of Buczacz*, 3; Kowalski, *Powiat Buczacki*, 37.
4. *Sefer Buczacz*, 46.
5. *Das Reisejournal des Ulrich von Werdum (1670–1677)*, ed. S. Cramer (Frankfurt am Main, 1990), 210–13; *Sefer Buczacz*, 46.
6. Z. E. Kohut, "The Khmelnytsky Uprising, the Image of Jews, and the Shaping of Ukrainian Historical Memory," *Jewish History* 17 (2003): 141–63.
7. R. B. Pikulyk, "Introduction," in P. Kulish, *The Black Council (Chorna rada)*, trans. G. S. N. Luckyj and M. Luckyj (Littleton, CO, 1973), vii–xxii.
8. Pikulyk, "Introduction" to Kulish, *The Black Council*, xxi–xxii.
9. Kulish, *The Black Council*, 3–4.
10. Kulish, *The Black Council*, 5, 14.
11. Kulish, *The Black Council*, 119.
12. "Biographical Note," and "Translator's Preface," in N. Gogol, *Taras Bulba*, trans. P. Constantine (New York, 2003), v–vii, xvii–xxi.
13. Gogol, *Taras Bulba*, 29.
14. Gogol, *Taras Bulba*, 39.
15. Gogol, *Taras Bulba*, 42.
16. Gogol, *Taras Bulba*, 43–45.
17. Gogol, *Taras Bulba*, 47–48.
18. On the massacre, see Hanover, *Yeven metsulah*, 59–60; *Abyss of Despair*, 81. Y. Adini, ed., *Dubno Memorial Book* (Tel Aviv, 1966; Hebrew and Yiddish), 41; B. Lukin, "Dubno," trans. I. M. Aronson, *The YIVO Encyclopedia of Jews in Eastern Europe* (2010), https://yivoencyclopedia.org/article.aspx/Dubno.

19. Gogol, *Taras Bulba*, 79–80.
20. Gogol, *Taras Bulba*, 117–18.
21. Gogol, *Taras Bulba*, 118.
22. Gogol, *Taras Bulba*, 118–19.
23. Gogol, *Taras Bulba*, 119.
24. Gogol, *Taras Bulba*, 119–20.
25. Gogol, *Taras Bulba*, 121–22.
26. Gogol, *Taras Bulba*, 138.
27. For a sustained and nuanced discussion of the writers mentioned here and many others, see M. Shkandrij, *Jews in Ukrainian Literature* (New Haven, 2009). See also G. Grabowicz, "The Jewish Theme in Nineteenth and Early Twentieth-Century Ukrainian Literature"; and for views in Jewish literature, I. Bartal, "On Top of a Volcano," in Potichnyi and Aster, *Ukrainian-Jewish Relations*, 327–42, 309–26, respectively. For Ukrainian writers of Jewish origin, see Y. Petrovsky-Shtern, *The Anti-Imperial Choice* (New Haven, 2009).
28. F.-P. Dalairac, *Les Anecdotes de Pologne ou Mémoires secrets du Règne de Jean Sobieski* (Paris, 1699), 231; cited in Barącz, *Pamiątki Buczackie*, 11–12. Published also as *Polish Manuscripts, or The Secret History of the Reign of John Sobieski, the III. of that Name, K. of Poland* (London, 1700).
29. Kowalski, *Powiat Buczacki*, 26.
30. *Sefer Buczacz*, 46, citing *Akta grodzkie i ziemskie*, vol. 24 (Lwów, 1931), 380, no. 198, §§ 2, 3.
31. Agnon, *Ir u-melo'ah*, 16.
32. Agnon, *Ir u-melo'ah*, 16. See also Kowalski, *Powiat Buczacki*, 26–27, 37–38; *Sefer Buczacz*, 47.
33. Dalairac, *Les Anecdotes*, 230; cited in Barącz, *Pamiątki Buczackie*, 12.
34. Barącz, *Pamiątki Buczackie*, 10.
35. Kowalski, *Powiat Buczacki*, 27–28, citing W. Urbański, *Buczacz i jego Powiat* (Buczacz, 1936); W. Urbański, *Przewodnik po powiecie buczackim* (Buczacz, 1931).
36. Barącz, *Pamiątki Buczackie*, 10.
37. Dalairac, *Les Anecdotes*, 228–30; cited in Barącz, *Pamiątki Buczackie*, 10–12.
38. Agnon, *Ir u-melo'ah*, 16. See also H. Bar-Itzhak, "Folklore as an Expression of Intellectual Communication between Jews and Poles," *Studia Mythologica Slavica* 7 (2004): 97n4.
39. Dalairac, *Les Anecdotes*, 232; Barącz, *Pamiątki Buczackie*, 13.
40. For context, see Magocsi, *A History of Ukraine*, 227–28, 290–95; Subtelny, *Ukraine*, 147–48, 153–54; Zamoyski, *The Polish Way*, 185–88; Stone, *The Polish-Lithuanian State*, 235–40; *Sefer Buczacz*, 47.

Chapter Four. Stones and Souls

1. Stotskyi, *Basilian Monastery*, 39, 143; Barącz, *Pamiątki Buczackie*, 27, 54; Kladochnyi, *Brief Sketch of Buczacz*, 4; Kowalski, *Powiat Buczacki*, 34, 49–50; "Bazylianie w Buczaczu," *Oriens* 5, no. 4 (Warsaw, 1 August 1937): 155.

2. *Sefer Buczacz*, 67–68, 72–73; Barącz, *Pamiątki Buczackie*, 14–16.

3. D. Neuman, "The Synagogues in the Town," *Davar Supplement*, 28 August 1938; response by M. Rabinowitz, *Davar Supplement*, 9 September 1938; both in *Sefer Buczacz*, 89–92. Kladochnyi, *Brief Sketch of Buczacz*, 12, claims that King Sobieski helped replace the destroyed synagogue with a new structure in 1685. "Buczacz," in *Pinkas Hakehillot, Poland*, vol. 2: *Eastern Galicia*, ed. D. Dąbrowska et al. (Jerusalem, 1980; Hebrew), 83, erroneously states that the Great Synagogue was designed by an Italian architect in the late seventeenth century. Agnon, *Ir u-melo'ah*, 17–18, suggests that construction began in 1715. *Polski Słownik Biograficzny*, vol. 26 (Kraków, 1984–85), 114, Italianizes the name of the city hall's architect to Merettini. For the Italian influence in Poland, see J. K. Ostrowski, ed., *Land of the Winged Horsemen* (New Haven, 1999), 60–62, 89–91; Zamoyski, *The Polish Way*, 189–205; G. Rąkowski, *Przewodnik po Ukrainie Zachodniej*, vol. 2, *Podole* (Pruszków, 2006), 263–65.

4. Kladochnyi, *Brief Sketch of Buczacz*, 7; Kowalski, *Powiat Buczacki*, 45–46.

5. B. Stern, "Austria," *Hamagid* 9, no. 34 (Łuck, 30 August 1865; Hebrew), 267; *Sefer Buczacz*, 91–92.

6. I. Duda, *Buczacz: The Guide* (Lviv: 1985; Ukrainian), praises the bas-relief by the sculptor V. Melnyk of Ternopil decorating the "Komsomolets" cinema as depicting "Komsomol members from the 1920s and contemporary life."

7. *Sefer Buczacz*, 89–90. In a 1921 photo of the Great Synagogue one can see in the background the Basilian Monastery and the Fedor Hill, where thousands of Jews were murdered in World War II. Reproduced in Bartov, *Anatomy of a Genocide*, 14.

8. Agnon, *Ir u-melo'ah*, 20.

9. Agnon, *Ir u-melo'ah*, 20–21, citing Psalm 130; *Sefer Buczacz*, 12; Kowalski, *Powiat Buczacki*, 54–67.

10. *Sefer Buczacz*, 12, 89–90.

11. Agnon, *Ir u-melo'ah*, 29.

12. Agnon, *Ir u-melo'ah*, 25–27.

13. Agnon, *Ir u-melo'ah*, 29–37.

14. Agnon, *Ir u-melo'ah*, 37–40, 43–56; *Sefer Buczacz*, 90–92.

15. Stern, "Austria."

16. Agnon, *Ore'ah nata lalun*, 11; *A Guest for the Night*, 9–10.

17. Agnon, *Ore'ah nata lalun*, 12–13; *A Guest for the Night*, 11–12.

18. More in Bartov, *Anatomy of a Genocide*, 295–96.

19. Barącz, *Pamiątki Buczackie*, 54. Some sources suggest that Mikołaj Potocki was born in 1706. Z. Zielińska, "Mikołaj Bazyli Potocki H. Pilawa, 1706?–1782–09–13," https://www.ipsb.nina.gov.pl/a/biografia/mikolaj-bazyli-potocki-h-pilawa.

20. See, e.g., A. Kowalczykowa, *Romantyzm* (Warsaw, 2008), 77–83.

21. *Sukcessya Xiążąt i Królów polskich* (Lwów, 1731); Barącz, *Pamiątki Buczackie*, 55–56; Kowalski, *Powiat Buczacki*, 70–71.

22. *Tygodnik Ilustrowany,* 1860, no. 24, Archiwum Państwowe w Krakowie (APK), zesp. Teki Schneidera, file 227, pp. 665–68.

23. Barącz, *Pamiątki Buczackie,* 33, 56.

24. Stotskyi, *Basilian Monastery,* 39–40.

25. Stotskyi, *Basilian Monastery,* 40; Barącz, *Pamiątki Buczackie,* 56–57. See also B. Voznytskyi, *Mykola Pototskyi, Bernard Meretyn, Ioan Heorhiy Pinzel* (Lviv, 2005; Ukrainian).

26. Stotskyi, *Basilian Monastery,* 40–41, 143–44.

27. Archives of the Lwów Episcopacy: *Directorium Divini Officii in Archidioecesi Leopoliensi* (Lwów, 1819), 73; *Schematismus Universi Venerabilis Cleri Archidioeceseos Metropolitanae Graeco Catholicae* (Lwów, 1832), 89; *Directorium Divini Officii in Archidioecesi Leopoliensi* (Lwów, 1835), 68–69, registering a population of 1,860 Jews and 1,558 Catholics.

28. Kladochnyi, *Brief Sketch of Buczacz,* 5–6; Kowalski, *Powiat Buczacki,* 49–52; "Bazylianie w Buczaczu," 155.

29. Barącz, *Pamiątki Buczackie,* 33–34; *Polski Słownik Biograficzny,* 113.

30. Lukowski and Zawadzki, *A Concise History of Poland,* 82–88.

31. *Polski Słownik Biograficzny,* 113.

32. Lukowski and Zawadzki, *A Concise History of Poland,* 88–96.

33. Barącz, *Pamiątki Buczackie,* 58; *Polski Słownik Biograficzny,* 113–14.

34. P. Krasny, "Osiemnastowieczne figury przydrożne w Buczaczu," *Prace z Historii Sztuki* 21 (1995): 65–75; Duda, *Buczacz,* citing Ukrainian art historian Hryhoryi Lohvyn (Gregory Logvin). See also Kladochnyi, *Brief Sketch of Buczacz,* 10–11; Voznytskyi, *Mykola Pototskyi,* 50–69; Kowalski, *Powiat Buczacki,* 28–32; A. Żarnowski, ed., *Kresy Wschodnie II Rzeczypospolitej: Buczacz* (Kraków, 1992), 16.

35. J. K. Ostrowski, "A Great Baroque Master on the Outskirts of Latin Europe," *Artibus et Historiae* 21, no. 2 (2000): 197–216, 211–12. See also Ostrowski, *Winged Horsemen,* 62, 86, 243; T. Kuznek, *Przewodnik po Województwie Tarnopolskiem* (Tarnopol, 1928), 222; Duda, *Buczacz;* Kladochnyi, *Brief Sketch of Buczacz,* 10–11. Pinsel's works were exhibited in the Louvre Museum in late 2012 and early 2013: https://life.pravda.com.ua/culture/2012/11/22 /116223/.

36. Agnon, *Ir u-melo'ah,* 231.

37. Agnon, *Ir u-melo'ah,* 231–32, referring to Psalms 119.

38. Agnon, *Ir u-melo'ah,* 233.

39. Agnon, *Ir u-melo'ah,* 235.

40. Agnon, *Ir u-melo'ah,* 235–36. See also M. Konyk, "'Jewish Faces of Catholic Saints,'" on Yevheniya Kononenko's novel *The Sacrifice of the Forgotten Master* (Kyiv, 2007; Ukrainian), https://ukrainianjewishencounter.org/en/jewish -faces-of-catholic-saints-yevheniya-kononenko-on-the-riddles-of-small -towns-and-great-artists/.

41. Agnon, *Ir u-melo'ah,* 236–38. Further in Bartov, *Anatomy of a Genocide,* 158–264.

42. S. Grodziski, *Wzdłuż Wisły, Dniestru i Zbrucza* (Kraków, 1998), 137; A. Johnston, "Libya 1911," *BBC News,* 10 May 2011, https://www.bbc.com/news/world-europe-13294524.

43. Duda, *Buczacz.*

44. Further in Bartov, *Anatomy of a Genocide,* 275–77. This version of the website no longer exists.

45. "Sensational find in Ternopil," *Den,* no. 9 (12 March 2008; Ukrainian).

46. Kowalski, *Powiat Buczacki,* 35–37; Kladochnyi, *Brief Sketch of Buczacz,* 8; Ostrowski, *Winged Horsemen,* 52. See also "Victims of the NKVD under the Church," Buchach city webpage, 16 May 2020, https://buchach.org.ua/home/novyny/876-zakatovani-liudy-pid-tserkvoiu.html.

47. *Słownik Biograficzny,* 114; Barącz, *Pamiątki Buczackie,* 34–35, 57–59.

48. *Słownik Biograficzny,* 114, citing F. Karpiński, *Pamiętniki* (Warsaw, 1898), 18, 66, 74–76. See also Grodziski, *Wzdłuż Wisły, Dniestru i Zbrucza,* 137.

49. *Słownik Biograficzny,* 114, citing J. U. Niemcewicz, *Pamiętniki czasów moich* (Paris, 1848), 81–83; N. A. Feduschak, "A Prince, Philanthropist and Playboy," *Kyiv Post,* 2 November 2011, http://www.kyivpost.com/guide/people/a-prince-philanthropist-and-playboy-an-exciting-li-116186.html, citing Voznytskyi, *Mykola Pototskyi,* implying that Potocki was Ruthenian.

50. Grodziski, *Wzdłuż Wisły, Dniestru i Zbrucza,* 136–37; Żarnowski, *Kresy Wschodnie,* 8; Miłosz, *Polish Literature,* 143–47. Wolff, *The Idea of Galicia,* 145, cites L. von Sacher-Masoch, *Graf Donski,* 2nd ed. (Schaffenhausen, 1864), 343, where the fictional Ruthenian giant Onufry recalls: "My father told me how the former master, the father of our count, made the peasants climb up into trees and cry 'cuckoo' and then shot them down like forest birds."

Chapter Five. Communities of Spirit

1. Agnon, *Ir u-melo'ah,* 308. The term "scattered and frayed" is my rendering of Agnon's citation from Isaiah 18:7 (King James Version: "A people scattered and peeled").

2. N. Sinkoff, *Out of the Shtetl* (Providence, RI, 2004), especially 14–23.

3. A. Teller, "Hasidism and the Challenge of Geography," *Association for Jewish Studies Review* 30, no. 1 (2006): 1–29; M. J. Rosman, *Founder of Hasidism* (Berkeley, 1996).

4. G. Dynner, *Men of Silk* (New York, 2006); M. Wodziński, *Haskalah and Hasidism in the Kingdom of Poland,* trans. S. Cozens (Oxford, 2005).

5. A. J. Brawer, *Galizien: Wie es an Österreich kam* (Leipzig, 1910), 104–7; G. Scholem, *Major Trends in Jewish Mysticism* (New York, 1995); G. Scholem, *The Messianic Idea in Judaism and Other Essays on Jewish Spirituality* (New York, 1995); G. Scholem, *Sabbatai Sevi,* trans. R. J. Z. Werblowsky (Princeton, NJ, 1975).

6. P. Maciejko, "Coitus interruptus in *And I Came this Day unto the Fountain*," in R. J. Eibeschütz, *And I Came this Day unto the Fountain*, ed. P. Maciejko, 2nd rev. ed. (Los Angeles, 2016), xix.

7. *Sefer Buczacz*, 52–53, and note 18, citing M. A. Perlmutter, *The Book "Va-avo ha-yom el ha-ayyin"* [and I Came this Day unto the Fountain] *and Its Authorship by Jonathan Eybeschütz* (Tel Aviv, 1947; Hebrew).

8. *Sefer Buczacz*, 52; P. Maciejko, "Frankism," *The YIVO Encyclopedia of Jews in Eastern Europe* (2010), https://yivoencyclopedia.org/article.aspx/Frankism; P. Maciejko, *The Mixed Multitude* (Philadelphia, 2011); M. D. Baer, *The Dönme* (Stanford, CA, 2010).

9. J. Emden, *Sefer Shimush* (The Guidebook) (Jerusalem, 1974 [1757–58]; Hebrew), fol. 6b–7a; cited in M. Bałaban, *On the History of the Frankist Movement* (Tel Aviv, 1934; Hebrew), 120–25, https://www.hebrewbooks.org/45492; Maciejko, "Frankism."

10. Maciejko, "Frankism."

11. *Sefer Buczacz*, 52n17, citing G. Scholem, "Baruchiah, the Sabbatian Heresiarch in Salonica," *Zion* 1, no. 3 (1941): 119–47 (part 1), and *Zion* 1, no. 4 (1941): 181–202 (part 2).

12. Agnon, *Ir u-melo'ah*, 214.

13. *Sefer Buczacz*, 53.

14. *Koło* means "circle" and *rów* means "ditch," so Agnon's interpretation is marginally plausible.

15. Agnon, *Ir u-melo'ah*, 214–15.

16. See, e.g., S. Sparrowhawk, "Plunge into the Magic of Kupala Night," *Reuters*, 4 July 2019, https://www.reuterscommunity.com/topics/content-discovery/plunge-into-the-magic-of-kupala-night/.

17. P. L. Taylor and C. Nicola, *The Secret of Priest's Grotto* (Minneapolis, 2007).

18. Further in G. D. Hundert, *The Jews in a Polish Private Town* (Baltimore, 1992); A. Teller, *Money, Power, and Influence in Eighteenth-Century Lithuania* (Stanford, CA, 2016).

19. Dynner, *Men of Silk*; Wodziński, *Haskalah and Hasidism*.

20. Agnon, *Ir u-melo'ah*, 305.

21. Agnon, *Ir u-melo'ah*, 306.

22. Agnon, *Ir u-melo'ah*, 307.

23. Agnon, *Ir u-melo'ah*, 315; *A City in Its Fullness*, 261–62.

24. Agnon, *Ir u-melo'ah*, 391–93; *A City in Its Fullness*, 365–67.

25. Dynner, *Men of Silk*, 137–95.

Chapter Six. When the Empire Came

1. M. Brawer, "Dr. Abraham Jacob Brawer (1884–1975)," *Eretz-Israel* (1983): 9–11 (Hebrew); M. Brawer, *Atlas*, 6th ed. (Tel Aviv, 1969; Hebrew); N. Achituv, "The Biography of Geography," *Haaretz*, 20 November 2019

(Hebrew), https://www.haaretz.co.il/magazine/.premium-MAGAZINE-1 .8156077.

2. Brawer, *Galizien*, 15–28; W. O. McCagg, *A History of Habsburg Jews, 1670–1918* (Bloomington, IN, 1992), 27. Higher estimates in Sinkoff, *Out of the Shtetl*, 201–25.

3. S. Grodziski, "The Jewish Question in Galicia," in Bartal and Polonsky, *Polin*, vol. 12, 61–72; Brawer, *Galizien*, 24–29, 40–49.

4. See, e.g., J. K. Fedorowicz, ed., *A Republic of Nobles* (New York, 1982).

5. A. Mickiewicz, *Pan Tadeusz*, trans. B. Johnston (New York, 2018), 211.

6. Brawer, *Galizien*, 35–39.

7. Brawer, *Galizien*, 98–102.

8. Brawer, *Galizien*, 39–43; S. Schnür-Pepłowski, *Cudzoziemcy w Galicyi, 1787–1841* (Kraków, 1898), 80–99, citing A. J. Schultes, *Lettres sur Galitzie* (Tübingen, n.d.), on his travels in Galicia in 1806–8.

9. Brawer, *Galizien*, 43–49, 103–4.

10. Wolff, *The Idea of Galicia*. See also Joseph Roth, *The Radetzky March*, trans. J. Neugroschel (Woodstock, NY, 1995 [1932)].

11. APK, zesp. Teki Schneidera, files 227–29, 19 March 1777; files 227–29, 2 April 1777, ref. to Halicz District Court ruling on 19 March 1777; file 228, pp. 395–440, Bürgermeister von Buczacz, filed in Lemberg, 4 August 1784; file 229, likely August–September 1777. See also M. Stoeger, *Darstellung der gesetzlichen Verfassung der galizischen Judenschaft* (Lemberg, 1833); W. Tokarz, *Galicya w początkach ery józefińskiej w świetle ankiety urzędowej z roku 1783* (Kraków, 1909).

12. *Sefer Buczacz*, 54–55; Barącz, *Pamiątki Buczackie*, 35–36.

13. Tsentralnyi derzhavnyi istorychnyi arkhiv, m. Lviv (TsDIAL), "K.k. Galizische Statthalterei, 1772–1854," fond 146, op. 78, spr. 1; fond 146, op. 88, spr. 183.

14. L. Schneider, *Das Kolonisationswerk Josefs II. in Galizien* (Berlin, 1989).

15. Barącz, *Pamiątki Buczackie*, 36.

16. Bartov, *Anatomy of a Genocide*, 158–69. More generally, see K. Struve, *Deutsche Herrschaft, Ukrainischer Nationalismus, Antijüdische Gewalt* (Berlin, 2015).

17. Agnon, *Ir u-melo'ah*, 441–47; *Sefer Buczacz*, 57; S. Y. Agnon, "Agunot" (1908), in Agnon, *Elu ve-elu*, 329–37.

18. Agnon, *Ir u-melo'ah*, 446–47.

19. Agnon, *Ir u-melo'ah*, 450–51; *A City in Its Fullness*, 373–74.

20. Agnon, *Ir u-melo'ah*, 456; *A City in Its Fullness*, 380–81.

21. Agnon, *Ir u-melo'ah*, 478–79; *A City in Its Fullness*, 409–10.

22. Agnon, *Ir u-melo'ah*, 479–80; *A City in Its Fullness*, 410–11.

23. Agnon, *Ir u-melo'ah*, 484; *A City in Its Fullness*, 416.

24. Agnon, *Ir u-melo'ah*, 485–86; *A City in Its Fullness*, 419.

25. Agnon, *Ir u-melo'ah*, 487–90; *A City in Its Fullness*, 421–24.

26. H. Bartov, *The Brigade*, trans. D. S. Segal (Philadelphia, 1967 [1965]). Generally, see D. J. Penslar, *Jews and the Military* (Princeton, NJ, 2013).

Chapter Seven. How to Love a Child

1. R. van Luit, "Homberg, Herz," in *The YIVO Encyclopedia of Jews in Eastern Europe* (2010), https://yivoencyclopedia.org/article.aspx/homberg_herz; *Sefer Buczacz*, 55.

2. K.u.k. Galizische Statthalterei, TsDIAL fond 146, op. 85, spr. 1903.

3. "Statystyczne podania szkół publicznych z r. 1854/5 w Galicyi wschodniej, czyli w lwowskim okręgu administracyjnym," in APK, zesp. Teki Schneidera, file 228, p. 243; "Bazylianie w Buczaczu," 155–56; Archives of the Lwów Episcopacy, *Schematismus des Königreiches Galizien und Lodomerien für das Jahr 1817* (Lemberg, n.d.), 595; Kladochnyi, *Brief Sketch of Buczacz*, 4–5.

4. Sinkoff, *Out of the Shtetl*, 201–25.

5. Sinkoff, *Out of the Shtetl*, 225–70.

6. Sinkoff, *Out of the Shtetl*, 269. See also J. Perl, *Sefer Megale Temirin* (Revealer of Secrets), ed. J. Meir (Jerusalem, 2013; Hebrew).

7. N. M. Gelber, "The History of the Jews of Tarnopol," in *Encyclopaedia of the Jewish Diaspora, Poland Series, Tarnopol Volume*, ed. Ph. Korngruen (Tel Aviv, 1955; Hebrew), 57–58 (hereafter cited as *Tarnopol Volume*), citing Österreichisches Staatsarchiv (ÖSA): Min. f. Kultus u. Unterricht, 23a 213 ex Sept. 1817.

8. *Tarnopol Volume*, 73–74. Further in N. M. Gelber, *Zur Vorgeschichte des Zionismus* (Vienna, 1927), 93–124.

9. Sinkoff, *Out of the* Shtetl, 228–31; *Tarnopol Volume*, 46–51, 55–83.

10. *Tarnopol Volume*, 95–96, 103.

11. M. Bernstein, *Einige Kulturhistorische Blicke über die Juden in Galizien nebst kleinen Andeutungen auf den Bildungszustand anderer Nationen* (Vienna, 1850).

12. "Nos erreurs deviennent encore plus dangereuses, et plus incurables, lorsqu'elles ont pour elles la sanction de la religion."

13. Bernstein, *Einige Kulturhistorische Blicke*, v, 11–12.

14. Bernstein, *Einige Kulturhistorische Blicke*, 13.

15. Bernstein, *Einige Kulturhistorische Blicke*, 14.

16. Bernstein, *Einige Kulturhistorische Blicke*, 15, 17–18.

17. Bernstein, *Einige Kulturhistorische Blicke*, 32–33.

18. Bernstein, *Einige Kulturhistorische Blicke*, 36–37.

19. Bernstein, *Einige Kulturhistorische Blicke*, 37–38.

20. M. Stanislawski, *A Murder in Lemberg* (Princeton, NJ, 2007), 3.

21. Bernstein, *Einige Kulturhistorische Blicke*, 39.

22. Bernstein, *Einige Kulturhistorische Blicke*, 41.

23. Bernstein, *Einige Kulturhistorische Blicke*, 41–43.

24. H. M. Green, "Adolf Stoecker," *Politics and Society* 31, no. 1 (2003): 110; "Heinrich von Treitschke Pronounces, 'The Jews are Our Misfortune' (15 November 1879)," *German History in Documents and Images* (GHDI), http://ghdi.ghi-dc.org/sub_document.cfm?document_id=1799. P. G. J. Pulzer, *The Rise of Political Anti-Semitism in Germany and Austria* (New York, 1964); J. Katz,

Out of the Ghetto (Cambridge, MA, 1973); M. Stoetzler, *The State, the Nation, and the Jews* (Lincoln, NE, 2008).

25. J. Korczak, *When I Am Little Again and The Child's Right to Respect*, trans. E. P. Kulawiec (Lanham, MD, 1992 [1925, 1929]); J. Korczak, *Jak kochać dziecko* (Warsaw, 2012 [1919]).

26. Cited by The Janusz Korczak Association of Canada, http://www.januszkorczak.ca/biography.html.

27. Kulawiec, Introduction, in Korczak, *When I Am Little Again*, xiv–xv, xvii.

28. J. Korczak, *Ghetto Diary*, trans. B. J. Lifton (New Haven, 2003), 39–40.

29. Korczak, *Ghetto Diary*, 92.

30. Korczak, *Ghetto Diary*, 94.

31. Korczak, *Ghetto Diary*, 100–101.

32. Korczak, *Ghetto Diary*, 103–5.

33. Korczak, *Ghetto Diary*, 111.

34. *Sefer Buczacz*, 55–56, also citing ÖSA, MdI, IV T. 11, 2579.

35. A. S. Ferziger, "Igra, Meshulam ben Shimshon," *The YIVO Encyclopedia of Jews in Eastern Europe* (2010), https://yivoencyclopedia.org/article.aspx/Igra_Meshulam_ben_Shimshon.

36. L. Ginzberg and A. Peiginsky, "Buczacz, Abraham David B. Asher Anshel," *Jewish Encyclopedia* (New York, 1901–6), citing E. Z. Shmerler, *Toledot ha-Rabi* (Lemberg, 1890), http://jewishencyclopedia.com/articles/3793-buczacz-abraham-david-b-asher-anshel.

37. Laor, *Agnon*, 21.

38. *Sefer Buczacz*, 56–58; R. Mahler, *Der kamf tsvishn Haskole un Khsides in Galitsie in Der Ershter Helft 19tn Jor-Hundert* (New York, 1942), 245–50; Y. A. Kamelhar, *Dor De'ah* (Jerusalem, 1969–70 [1932–33]; Hebrew), 74–81; Agnon, *Ir u-melo'ah*, 518–42.

Chapter Eight. The Fiction of History

1. J.-P. Himka, *Religion and Nationality in Western Ukraine* (Montreal, 1999); Magocsi, *The Roots of Ukrainian Nationalism*; K. Struve, *Bauern und Nation in Galizien* (Göttingen, 2005).

2. Shanes, *Diaspora Nationalism*, 31–37; J.-P. Himka, *Galician Villagers and the Ukrainian National Movement in the Nineteenth Century* (New York, 1988), 158–75; Struve, *Bauern und Nation*, 384–433.

3. I. L. Rudnytsky, "The Ukrainians in Galicia under Austrian Rule," in *Nation-building and the Politics of Nationalism*, ed. A. S. Markovits and F. E. Sysyn (Cambridge, MA, 1982), 46 and 24, citing O. Terletskyi, *Russophiles and Populists in the 1870s* (Lviv, 1902; Ukrainian). See also F. Hillis, "Children of Rus'," *Harvard Ukrainian Studies* 34, nos. 1–4 (2015–16): 313–42.

4. Y. Kirilyuk, "A Great Humanist Poet," introduction to *Taras Shevchenko: Selected Works, Poetry and Prose*, multiple translators (Moscow, 1979), 17.

5. Magocsi, *History of Ukraine*, 294–300.

6. K. Lada, "The Ukrainian Topos of Oppression and the Volhynian Slaughter of Poles, 1841–1943/44," PhD diss., Flinders University, 2012.

7. "Haidamaki," trans. J. Weir, in *Taras Shevchenko*, 92–97.

8. J.-P. Himka, *Socialism in Galicia* (Cambridge, MA, 1983), 57–85, 163–69; Rudnytsky, "The Ukrainians in Galicia," 55, 59.

9. Y. Hrytsak, "A Strange Case of Antisemitism," in Bartov and Weitz, *Shatterzone of Empires*, 232–35, discussing Franko's 1883 essay "The Jewish Question"; his popular 1884 poem, "The Travels of Schwindeles Parchenblütt"; and his 1887 essay "Semitism and Antisemitism in Galicia."

10. Hrytsak, "A Strange Case of Antisemitism," 231.

11. I. Franko, *Boa Constrictor and Other Stories*, trans. F. Solasko (Moscow, n.d.), 204–6. For context, see A. Fleig Frank, *Oil Empire* (Cambridge, MA, 2007); V. Schatzker, ed., *The Jewish Oil Magnates of Galicia*, including V. Schatzker, *The Jewish Oil Magnates: A History, 1853–1945*, and *The Jewish Oil Magnates: A Novel by Julien Hirszhaut* [1954], trans. M. Dashkin Beckerman (Montreal, 2015).

12. Franko, *Boa Constrictor*, 214.

13. Franko, *Boa Constrictor*, 241, 244, 255–56, 294.

14. I. Franko, *Fateful Crossroads*, trans. R. Franko (Winnipeg, 2006 [1900]), 178–79.

15. Franko, *Fateful Crossroads*, 36–37.

16. Franko, *Fateful Crossroads*, 38.

17. Franko, *Fateful Crossroads*, 32–33, 70.

18. Franko, *Fateful Crossroads*, 70, 72–73.

19. Franko, *Fateful Crossroads*, 74.

20. Franko, *Fateful Crossroads*, 72–75.

21. Franko, *Fateful Crossroads*, 109–11.

22. Franko, *Fateful Crossroads*, 156–57, 205.

23. Franko, *Fateful Crossroads*, 282–83.

24. Franko, *Fateful Crossroads*, 284–85, 288.

25. Franko, *Fateful Crossroads*, 287.

26. Hrytsak, "A Strange Case of Antisemitism," 233–37. See also I. Franko, *Zur Judenfrage* (Kyiv, 2002; Ukrainian), including the essays "Semitism and Antisemitism in Galicia," "The Jewish State," and "My Jewish Friends."

27. Franko, *Fateful Crossroads*, 288–89.

28. Franko, *Fateful Crossroads*, 354.

29. Franko, *Fateful Crossroads*, 363.

30. For later anti-Jewish depictions, see, e.g., I. Franko, "The Raging Tempest" (1907), in *Winds of Change*, trans. R. Franko (Winnipeg, 2006), 191, 207.

31. K. E. Franzos, *The Clown of Barnow*, trans. E. Lerdau (New Orleans, 2004), xi–xii; *Der Pojaz* (Frankfurt am Main, 1988), 5–6. Translation modified.

32. Franzos, *The Clown*, xii; Franzos, *Der Pojaz*, 6.

33. Franzos, *The Clown*, xiii; Franzos, *Der Pojaz*, 7. See also S. W. Baron, "The Impact of the Revolution of 1848 on Jewish Emancipation," *Jewish Social Studies* 11, no. 3 (1949): 195–248; A. Lichtblau and M. John, "Jewries in Galicia and Bukovina, in Lemberg and Czernowitz," in *Jewries at the Frontiers*, ed. S. L. Gilman and M. Shain (Urbana, IL, 1999), 29–66.

34. Franzos, *The Clown*, xiv–xv; Franzos, *Der Pojaz*, 8.

35. Franzos, *The Clown*, xv; Franzos, *Der Pojaz*, 8.

36. B. Phillips, "Preface to the American Edition," in *The Jews of Barnow*, trans. M. W. Macdowall (North Stratford, NH, 1999 [1883]), v–vi. A founder of the American Jewish Historical Society, Phillips joined the staff of the *New York Times* in 1872. His Jewish family emigrated from Bohemia to England in the mid-eighteenth century; his father became a prominent businessman in Philadelphia after moving to America in 1800. *The Universal Jewish Encyclopedia*, vol. 8, 490–91; *Publications of the American Jewish Historical Society* 6 (1907): 195–97; *The Jewish Encyclopedia*, https://jewishencyclopedia.com/articles/12109-phillips-barnet.

37. Phillips, Preface to *The Jews of Barnow*, vi, viii.

38. K. E. Franzos, *Leib Weihnachtskuchen and His Child*, trans. M. Mitchell (Riverside, CA, 2005 [1896]), 30, 52, 79, 102.

39. Franzos, *The Clown*, 355, 405; Franzos, *Der Pojaz*, 312, 354. On the real Dawison, born in 1818, see H. Rosenthal and E. Mels, "Dawison (Davidsohn), Bogumil," *The Jewish Encyclopedia* (1906), http://www.jewishencyclopedia.com/articles/5005-dawison-davidsohn-bogumil. See also K. E. Franzos, "The Shylock of Barnow" (1873), in *The Jews of Barnow*, 19–71.

40. Franzos, "Preface," *The Jews of Barnow*, xix–xx; S. Morris, "Introduction," in Franko, *Winds of Change*, 8–9. According to his widow, Franzos considered *The Clown of Barnow* "as needing no more revisions" after completing it more than a decade before his death. J. Hermand, "Nachwort," in Franzos, *Der Pojaz*, 360, 371–73. See also Pulzer, *The Rise of Political Anti-Semitism*.

Chapter Nine. Fathers and Sons

1. "David Heinrich Mueller," *Ost und West* 13, no. 2 (February 1913): 162; G. Kressel, "Professor David Zvi (Heinrich) Müller," in *Sefer Buczacz*, 109–10.

2. "Dr. Zvi Heinrich Müller," *Hatsevi*, 9 January 1913, 2 (Hebrew).

3. Kressel, "Professor Müller," 110, citing I. H. Teller, "Fragments of Memory," in *Miyamim Rishonim* 2 (1935): 166; "Dr. Zvi Heinrich Müller," *Hatsevi*, 2.

4. "David Heinrich Mueller," *Ost und West*, 163; Kressel, "Professor Müller," 111. See also D. H. Müller, *Die Propheten in ihrer ursprünglichen Form* (Vienna, 1896); D. H. Müller and J. von Schlosser, *Die Haggadah von Sarajevo* (Vienna, 1898); D. H. Müller, *Die Mehri-und Soqotri-Sprache* (Vienna, 1902); D. H. Müller, *Die Gesetze Hammurabis und ihr Verhältnis zur mosaischen Gesetzgebung sowie zu den XII Tafeln* (Vienna, 1903).

5. "David Heinrich Mueller," *Ost und West*, 164–66. *Hatsfirah* (1885): 34, cited in *Sefer Buczacz*, 111, commented that in being "raised to the rank of full professor," Müller became "one of very few of such outstanding accomplishment," but "despite his wisdom and his value in the world of scholarship," had not "abandoned his nation and [Jewish] learning and is one of the excellent writers [of Hebrew]."

6. "Dr. Zvi Heinrich Müller," *Hatsevi*, 2.

7. Letter sent by Müller from Vienna on 12 April 1893, in *Sefer Buczacz*, 118.

8. Franzos, *The Clown*, 37–38; Franzos, *Der Pojaz*, 44–45.

9. S. Y. Agnon, *Me-atsmi el atsmi* (From Myself to Myself) (Tel Aviv, 2000 [1947]; Hebrew), 18; D. Laor, "A Meeting in Vienna, May 1908," *Haaretz*, 8 August 2008 (Hebrew), http://www.haaretz.co.il/literature/1.1341697.

10. Brawer, "Dr. Abraham Jacob Brawer," 9; Laor, *Agnon*, 47–48, 160–68.

11. G. Sturm, *David Heinrich Müller und die südarabische Expedition der Kaiserlichen Akademie der Wissenschaften 1898/99* (Vienna, 2015); R. Calinger, review, *Isis* 110 (2019): 429–31.

12. J. Ficowski, *Regions of the Great Heresy*, trans. T. S. Robertson (New York, 2003).

13. Freud's and Franz Kafka's influence on Agnon is clearest in his stories collected under the title *Sefer ha-ma'asim* (The Book of Tales), in S. Y. Agnon, *Samukh ve-nir'eh* (Close and Seen) (Tel Aviv, 1998; Hebrew), 87–206. See also A. J. Band, *Studies in Modern Jewish Literature* (Philadelphia, 2003), 241–50.

14. *Sefer Buczacz*, 119; E. Jones, *The Life and Works of Sigmund Freud*, vol. 1: *The Formative Years and the Great Discoveries, 1856–1900* (New York, 1953), 1–3, 12–13.

15. M. Freud, *Sigmund Freud* (New York, 1958), 11.

16. H. Fry, *Freud's War* (Stroud, UK, 2009). See also J. Roth, *The Wandering Jews*, trans. M. Hofmann (New York, 2001 [1937]).

17. R. Patai, *Journeyman in Jerusalem* (Lanham, MD, 2000), 438; I. Singer, "Max Grunwald," *The Jewish Encyclopedia* (1906), http://www.jewishencyclopedia .com/articles/6911-grunwald-max. Grunwald founded the Society for Jewish Folklore in 1897, served as its president, and edited its journal, *Mittheilungen der Gesellschaft für Jüdische Volkskunde* (1897–1922), and its successor, the *Jahrbücher für jüdische Volkskunde* (1923–25).

18. M. Grunwald, "Encounters with Sigmund Freud," in *Sefer Buczacz*, 119–22. See also E. A. Grollman, *Judaism in Sigmund Freud's World* (New York, 1965); M. Schur, *Freud* (New York, 1972); M. Krüll, *Freud and His Father*, trans. A. J. Pomerans (New York, 1986); Y. H. Yerushalmi, *Freud's Moses* (New Haven, 1991); J. Derrida, *Archive Fever* (Chicago, 1996); E. J. Bellamy, *Affective Genealogies* (Lincoln, NE, 1997), 154–59; 24–25; A.-M. Rizzuto, *Why Did Freud Reject God?* (New Haven, 1998).

19. D. Cohen, *The Escape of Sigmund Freud* (London, 2009), 178, 205–7; S. Freud, *Moses and Monotheism*, trans. K. Jones (London, 1939).

20. W. Portmann, *Die wilden Schafe* (Münster, 2008), 12–15; K. Hödl, *Als Bettler in die Leopoldstadt* (Vienna, 1994), 123–24.

21. T. Andlauer, *Die jüdische Bevölkerung im Modernisierungsprozess Galiziens, 1867–1914* (Frankfurt am Main, 2001), 83; Hödl, *Als Bettler in die Leopold-stadt*, 273–76; M. Bałaban, "Buchach," *Yevreyskaya Encyclopaedia*, vol. 5 (St. Petersburg, 1912–14; Russian), 135–36; *Sefer Buczacz*, 222. On the "Kuchnia Ludowa" and its founder and director Regina Reiss, see TsDIAL, fond 146, op. 25, spr. 2068.

22. H. Roll, "The Hospital and the Old People's Shelter," in *Sefer Buczacz*, 180–82; Portmann, *Die wilden Schafe*, 15–17. On the massacre see deposition by Yitzhak Bauer, 10 January 1968, in Bundesarchiv Berlin (BAB), 162/5182, 6212–14.

23. M. Nomad, *Dreamers Dynamiters and Demagogues* (New York, 1964), 235; *Tydzień Robotnika*, no. 6 (Warsaw, Lemberg Edition, 6 February 1938), cited in Portmann, *Die wilden Schafe*, 18–19.

24. Agnon, *Ir u-melo'ah*, 646.

25. Undated letter by Siegfried Nacht, in Portmann, *Die wilden Schafe*, 11–12; Z. Heller, "From My Memories," in *Sefer Buczacz*, 158. A middle brother, Arthur, was born in 1880.

26. Portmann, *Die wilden Schafe*, 23–27, 30, citing "Curriculum vitae," in "Sieg-fried Nacht (Stephen Naft)," in the Max Nacht Papers, 1892–1973, Interna-tional Institute of Social History, Amsterdam, Netherlands; "Autobiograph-ical Sketch," in Max Nomad Papers, 1902–67, Tamiment Library, New York; N. Menatseach, "From My Youth in Buczacz," *Sefer Buczacz*, 173.

27. Nomad, *Dreamers*, 7.

28. Portmann, *Die wilden Schafe*, 28–30. Along with the "Brief aus Halb-Asien," Nacht also published "Die revolutionäre Bewegung in Russland," *Neues Leben* (1902). K. E. Franzos, *Aus Halb-Asien* (Leipzig, 1876). Arendt cited in A. Raz-Krakotzkin, "Jewish Peoplehood, 'Jewish Politics,' and Political Re-sponsibility," *College Literature* 38, no. 1 (2011): 72.

29. *Memoirs of a Revolutionist* was published in 1899; see also his *The Conquest of Bread* (New York, 1907). Kropotkin was arguably the most important ideo-logue of anarcho-communism.

30. Nomad, *Dreamers*, 8–9.

31. The Social Democratic Party of Galicia split in 1899 into Polish and Ukrai-nian parties; in 1905 Jewish members of the Polish party (PPSD) left to cre-ate the Jewish Social Democratic Party (ŻPS). J. Shanes, "Żydowska Partia Socjalno-Demokratyczna," *The YIVO Encyclopedia of Jews in Eastern Europe* (2010), http://www.yivoencyclopedia.org/article.aspx/Zydowska_Partia_Soc jalno-Demokratyczna; S. Yekelchyk, *Ukraine* (New York, 2007), 63.

32. J. Kornberg, *Theodor Herzl* (Bloomington, IN, 1993).

33. Nomad, *Dreamers*, 9.

34. Nomad, *Dreamers*, 9–10. Mosler might have been the son of "the experienced surgeon Maurycy Mosler" mentioned in Żarnowski, *Kresy Wschodnie*, 9.

35. *Służba dworska: Gazeta dla robotników rolnych powiatu buczackiego i innych powiatów podolskich*, nos. 1–5 (June–October 1905), Library of the Polish Parliament, Warsaw, P. 50730. Heller, "From My Memories," 150, recalls the Ukrainian gymnasium student Osyp Nazaruk, later minister of press and propaganda in the Ukrainian People's Republic (UNR), as co-organizer of the peasant strikes and co-editor of *Służba dworska*. See also "Służba Dworska," https://uk.wikipedia.org/wiki/S%C5%82u%C5%BCba_Dworska.

36. *Służba dworska*, no. 1, 1–3.

37. *Służba dworska*, no. 1, 3–4, 7–9, 11–14.

38. *Służba dworska*, no. 2, 1–7.

39. *Służba dworska*, no. 2, 10–12.

40. *Służba dworska*, no. 5, 6–10 (poem on 9).

41. Agnon, *Ore'ah nata lalun*, 228–31; *A Guest for the Night*, 312–17. Translation modified.

42. Agnon, *Ore'ah nata lalun*, 234–35; *A Guest for the Night*, 321–23.

43. Agnon, *Ore'ah nata lalun*, 235–37; *A Guest for the Night*, 323–25.

44. Agnon, *Ore'ah nata lalun*, 238–41; *A Guest for the Night*, 326–30. Y. Mosner, "Maine yugent yoren in Buchach," in *Pinkas Galitsye* (Buenos Aires, 1945), 476, recalls that Buczacz "had a labor movement even before it was officially recognized in other large towns in Galicia . . . The leader of the workers at the time was the lawyer Dr. Anshel Mosler, who was born in Buczacz."

Chapter Ten. Wild Sheep

1. Portmann, *Die wilden Schafe*, 30–34.

2. Nomad, *Dreamers*, 11.

3. G. Rossoliński-Liebe, *Stepan Bandera* (Stuttgart, 2014).

4. Nomad, *Dreamers*, 12–14. See also J. Kolasky, ed., *Prophets & Proletarians* (Edmonton, AB, 1990), 212–13.

5. Portmann, *Die wilden Schafe*, 55–58, citing M. Nacht, "Anarchistenjagd," *Neues Leben* 23 (6 June 1903); 24 (13 June 1903).

6. Agnon, *Ore'ah nata lalun*, 237; *A Guest for the Night*, 324–25.

7. Portmann, *Die wilden Schafe*, 117–18, 55–58, citing Nacht's "Anarchistenjagd." Buczacz had had a telegraph office since 1863, and a post office since 1781. Kladochnyi, *Brief Sketch of Buczacz*, 13; Stotskyi, *Basilian Monastery*, 42. For Siegfried Nacht's pamphlet, see https://robertgraham.wordpress.com/siegfried-nacht-the-social-general-strike-1905/.

8. "Stephen Naft Dies; Political Writer, 78," *New York Times* (13 December 1956): 37, https://www.nytimes.com/1956/12/13/archives/stephen-naft-dies-political-writer-78.html.

9. Nomad, *Dreamers*, 44.

10. E. Wilson, *To the Finland Station* (Garden City, NY, 1953).

11. E. Wilson, "Introduction," in M. Nomad, *Aspects of Revolt* (New York, 1961), vii, xvii–xviii.

12. Nomad, *Dreamers*, 235–38.

13. Letter from Dr. Alain Kanfer, Paris, 22 March 2010. I have made minor grammatical corrections to the English.

14. Kanfer's poetry collections include *A travers* (Paris, 1988); *D'autres . . . et de moi* (Paris, 1979); *Endurer la terre* (Paris, 1974); *Contes du milieu de la nuit* (Paris, 1972); *Ombre du soleil* (Paris, 1971); *Avant-être* (Paris, 1966). See also *Le Luth brisé: Première anthologie en français de poèmes du ghetto et des camps,* trans. from Yiddish and Polish by I. Kanfer (Paris, 1965). She was also involved in the "Treblinka affair" in 1966. See S. Moyn, *A Holocaust Controversy* (Waltham, MA, 2005), 94–95.

15. Heller, "From My Memories," 155–58; D. Pohorille, "Episodes of Life," *Sefer Buczacz,* 199–200; Laor, *Agnon,* 22; E. Prokop-Janiec, *Polish-Jewish Literature in the Interwar Years,* trans. A. Shenitzer (Syracuse, NY, 2003), 248; E. Prokop-Janiec, "Mojżesz Kanfer a teatr jidysz," in *Teatr żydowski w Krakowie,* ed. J. Michalik and E. Prokop-Janiec (Kraków, 1995), 125–50; E. Prokop-Janiec, "Kanfer, Mojżesz," *The YIVO Encyclopedia of Jews in Eastern Europe* (2010): http://www.yivoencyclopedia.org/article.aspx/Kanfer_Mojzesz.

16. As reported to me by Alain Kanfer at our meeting in Paris in December 2010.

17. Portmann, *Die wilden Schafe,* 85n522, 111n673.

18. Alain Kanfer mentions the admission card in an email dated 4 June 2010. Likely because she had not been a permanent resident, Sabina did not mention living in Paris before 1912 in her 1915 police registration.

19. *Sprawozdanie dyrekcyi C. K. Gimnazyum w Buczaczu za rok szkolny 1901* (Lwów, 1901), 36–39.

20. "Droga życiowa Ostapa Dłuskiego," no date, Akta Ostapa Dłuskiego, Archiwum Akt Nowych (AAN), 450/I-1, p. 1; "Dłuski Ostap—Langer Adolf (1892–1964)," *Słownik Biograficzny Działaczy Polskiego Ruchu Robotniczego,* ed. F. Tych, 2nd ed., vol. 2 (Warsaw, 1985 [1978]), 585–86. See also R. C. Nation, *War on War* (Durham, NC, 1989), 105–6, 112–14.

21. "Dłuski," *Słownik Biograficzny;* "Droga życiowa Ostapa Dłuskiego," 1–2. For a detailed account and analysis, see R. Solchanyk, "The Foundation of the Communist Movement in Eastern Galicia, 1919–1921," *Slavic Review* 30, no. 4 (December 1971): 774–94. See also *Proces komunistów we Lwowie* (Warsaw, 1958), 114–28; F. Świetlikowa, *Komunistyczna Partia Robotnicza Polski 1918–1923* (Warsaw, 1968), 279–306.

22. Solchanyk, "Foundation of the Communist Movement," 788–89.

23. Solchanyk, "Foundation of the Communist Movement," 789–91.

24. "Relacje tow. Dłuskiego," AAN, 450/I-3, pp. 1–5, written forty years after the events of 1919.

25. "Droga życiowa Ostapa Dłuskiego," 2.

26. "Relacje tow. Dłuskiego," 8–12.

27. "Dłuski," *Słownik Biograficzny.*" See, e.g., O. Dłuski, "Pan Beck oszukuje społeczeństwo polskie" (Warsaw, 1937), for the Parisian *Correspondance Internatio-*

nale, AAN, 450/IV-4. Dłuski also wrote for the Basel-based *Rundschau über Politik, Wirtschaft & Arbeiterbewegung.* Dłuski's interwar Polish police file includes a note from the Lublin Voivodship office, dated 4 January 1938: "At the beginning of 1937 Adolf Langer, pseudonym Ostap Dłuski . . . came to Prague from France or Belgium. He is an irreligious Jew who holds a very important position in communist organizations and has very good connections in Poland." AAN, 450/I-2. See also B. M. Lazitch, *Biographical Dictionary of the Comintern*, 2nd ed. (Stanford, CA, 1986), xxvi; K. McDermott and J. Agnew, *The Comintern* (Houndmills, UK, 1996).

28.   O. Ostenrode, "Die Rostowlüge und ihre Folgen," 7 January 1943, AAN, 450/VI-1, p. 4, emphases in the original. For a laudatory analysis, see T. Perl, "Z działalności Ostapa Dłuskiego w czasie II wojny światowej," in *Z pola walki* 1, no. 1 (1958): 125–32. See also K. Maj, *Polscy komuniści we Francji 1919–1946* (Warsaw, 1971), 107–35, 157–61, 276–78.

29.   After the war Stalin suppressed the compilation of evidence of Nazi crimes against Jews on Soviet soil that he had previously commissioned. See I. Erenburg and V. Grossman, eds., *The Complete Black Book of Russian Jewry*, trans. D. Patterson (New Brunswick, NJ, 2002); J. Rubenstein and I. Altman, eds., *The Unknown Black Book*, trans. C. Morris and J. Rubenstein (Bloomington, IN, 2008).

30.   Cited in J. Herf, *The Jewish Enemy* (Cambridge, MA, 2006), 56.

31.   Ostenrode, "Die Rostowlüge," 4–5.

32.   O. Dłuski, "Il n'y a qu'un seul chemin qui mène à la l'indépendance," AAN, 450/II-69, pp. 1–3 (undated); "Aux immigrations slaves en France," AAN, 450/II-69, pp. 2–3 (undated); "La Pologne nouvelle et la France en face de l'impérialisme germanique," 28 February 1945, AAN 450/II-71, pp. 9–10. In a questionnaire dated 17 July 1945, Dłuski identifies himself as "Andrzej Dłuski (Adolf Langer)," lists his pseudonyms as "Ostap, Adam Dłuski, Ostap Dłuski, Ostap Fedor," cites his nationality as "of Jewish origins, Polish," his mother tongue as "Jewish [żydowskiego], Polish," his spoken foreign languages as "Russian, German, French," his social origins as "son of a rural school manager," his wife's name as "Stanisława (Lasia)," née "Sara Herszkowicz," and notes that he "was leader of the Ukrainian resistance movement in France." AAN 450/I-1.

33.   J. T. Gross, *Fear* (New York, 2006), 35, 125; D. Engel, "Patterns of Anti-Jewish Violence in Poland, 1944–1946," *Yad Vashem Studies* 26 (1998): 43–85; J. B. Michlic, *Poland's Threatening Other* (Lincoln, NE, 2006), 211; D. Stola, "Fighting against the Shadows," in *Antisemitism and Its Opponents in Modern Poland*, ed. R. Blobaum (Ithaca, NY, 2005), 284–300.

34.   "Dłuski," *Słownik Biograficzny;* "Droga życiowa Ostapa Dłuskiego," 4. B. Szaynok, "The Role of Antisemitism in Postwar Polish-Jewish Relations," in Blobaum, *Antisemitism*, 274–75, points out that Gomułka attributed the pogroms to internal and external anticommunists.

35. The World Congress in 1948 hosted such celebrities as Pablo Picasso, Frédéric and Irène Joliot-Curie, Bertolt Brecht, Paul Éluard, Aldous Huxley, Julian Huxley, Ilya Ehrenburg, Julien Benda, Anna Seghers, and others. See also O. Dłuski, "Pour une vaste tribune de discussion," WPC journal, 1955, AAN, 450/IV-24.

36. O. Dłuski, "Aussprache während der 'Goethefeier in Warschau,'" AAN, 450/III-103, pp., 6–7.

37. M. Shore, *Caviar and Ashes* (New Haven, 2006), 305; Dłuski's lament in AAN, 450/IV-21, pp. 1, 9. J. Rubenstein and V. P. Naumov, eds., *Stalin's Secret Pogrom*, trans. L. E. Wolfson (New Haven, 2001); A. Vaksberg, *Stalin against the Jews*, trans. A. W. Bouis (New York, 1994).

38. "Dłuski," *Słownik Biograficzny;* "Droga życiowa Ostapa Dłuskiego," 5; Dłuski's death notice: AAN, 450/V-1. See also Polish newsreel of Dłuski's state funeral: http://www.repozytorium.fn.org.pl/?q=pl/node/11002.

Chapter Eleven. Bringing Light to the World

1. M. B. Stęczyński, *Okolice Galicyi* (Lwów, 1847), 147–48. Further in A. Czołowski and B. Janusz, *Przeszłość i Zabytki* (Tarnopol, 1926), 70; Żarnowski, *Kresy Wschodnie*, 13.

2. Z. Reich, *Worte des Dankes* (Lemberg, 1853), in Österreichische Nationalbibliothek (ÖNB): 486.076-B, pp. 7–8.

3. W. Kalinka, *Galicya i Kraków pod panowaniem austryackiem* (Kraków, 1898), 55–57, 71–72; new edition, ed. W. Bernacki (Kraków, 2001), 83–89.

4. P. Stebelski, *Ze statystyki przestępności Galicyi* (Lwów, 1892), 69–77. See also R. P. Hsia, *The Myth of Ritual Murder* (New Haven, 1988); H. W. Smith, *The Butcher's Tale* (New York, 2002).

5. E. Dubanowicz, *Stanowisko ludności żydowskiej w Galicyi wobec Wyborów do parlamentu wiedeńskiego w r. 1907* (Lwów, 1907), 6, 8–13.

6. J. J. Lerski, *Historical Dictionary of Poland, 966–1945* (Westport, CT, 1996), 119.

7. S. Gruiński, "Introduction," in *Materiały do kwestyi żydowskiej w Galiciyi* (Lwów, 1910), 35, 54–55.

8. S. Szczepanowski, *Nędza Galicyi w cyfrach* (Lwów, 1888), 130–35, 154–58.

9. Further in Wolff, *The Idea of Galicia*, 234–35, 275–79, 312–15.

10. R. Scholz, *Królewna Wiosna* (Buczacz, 1905), in ÖNB, 440690—B, 5–6, 9–11, 23–29, 33–36.

11. Agathon, "Les jeunes gens d'aujourd'hui," *L'Opinion* 13 (20 April; 7, 13, 27 May; 4 June 1912); H. Massis and A. de Tarde, *Les jeunes gens d'aujourd'hui* (Paris, 1913). Cited in P. M. Cohen, "Reason and Faith," *Historical Reflections / Réflexions Historiques* 13, nos. 2–3 (1986): 474–75.

12. R. Wohl, *The Generation of 1914* (Cambridge, MA, 1979).

13. Laor, *Agnon*, 103–14.

14. Duda, *Buczacz;* Himka, *Galician Villagers,* 284; "Solomia Krushelnytska and Italy," *Den* 37 (21 November 2006), http://www.day.kiev.ua/en/article/time -out/solomia-krushelnytska-and-italy.

15. L. Iuniverg, *The Publishing World of Iosif Knebel* (Jerusalem, 1997; Russian), 9–16; Duda, *Buczacz.* See also "Joseph Knebel's Publishing House," https:// content.lib.washington.edu/exhibits/russian-childrens-lit/5-knebel.html.

16. S. M. Carnicke, "The Knebel Technique," in *Actor Training,* ed. A. Hodge, 2nd ed. (New York, 2010), 99, 114; "The Cherry Orchard" (1968), Abbey Theater, https://www.youtube.com/watch?v=MtdObMWiOow.

Chapter Twelve. Galician Childhood

1. M. Orłowicz, ed., *Ilustrowany Przewodnik po Galicyi* (Lwów, 1919), 143–44; Kowalski, *Powiat Buczacki,* 219–23.

2. R. C. Lukas, *Forgotten Holocaust,* 2nd rev. ed. (New York, 1997), 131–34; T. Piotrowski, *Poland's Holocaust* (Jefferson, NC, 1998), 80–82, 97.

3. W. Szklarz, *Życiorysy Buczaczan* (Wrocław, 2007), 429; "Żołnierze Armii Polskiej zmarli w ZSRR w okresie IX 1941 r. do IX 1942 r.," https://genealodzy .pl/index.php?name=Web_Links&req=viewlink&cid=97&orderby=titleD; P. Żaroń, *Kierunek wschodni w strategii wojskowo-politycznej gen. Władysława Sikorskiego 1940–1943* (Warsaw, 1988). See also J. T. Gross, *Revolution from Abroad,* 2nd ed. (Princeton, NJ, 2002).

4. Hundert, *Jews in Poland-Lithuania,* 3. See also M. Barchana et al., "Trends in Colorectal Cancer Incidence and Mortality in the Israeli Jewish Ethnic Populations," and G. Y. Locker and H. T. Lynch, "Genetic Factors and Colorectal Cancer in Ashkenazi Jews," both in *Familial Cancer* 3 (2004): 207–14, 215–21, respectively.

5. S. Hnatkiwskyj, Buchach, Ternopil, Ukraine, contributed on 9 May 2005, BBC Learning Center Gloucester, WW2 People's War, https://www.bbc.co .uk/history/ww2peopleswar/stories/04/a4037104.shtml.

6. Orłowicz, *Przewodnik po Galicyi,* 143.

7. *Pinkas Hakehillot,* 512.

8. Orłowicz, *Przewodnik po Galicyi,* 200; slightly different figures in *Pinkas Hakehillot,* 481.

9. R. E. Gruber, *Virtually Jewish* (Berkeley, 2002).

10. E. Lohr, "The Russian Army and the Jews," *Russian Review* 60 (2001): 404–19; A. V. Prusin, *Nationalizing a Borderland* (Tuscaloosa, 2005).

11. S. Spector, *Prague Territories* (Berkeley, 2000); P. M. Judson, "Marking National Space on the Habsburg Austrian Borderlands, 1880–1918," in Bartov and Weitz, *Shatterzone of Empires,* 122–35.

12. Lichtblau and John, "Jewries in Galicia and Bukovina."

13. S. Ansky, *The Enemy at His Pleasure,* trans. J. Neugroschel (New York, 2003); S. An-sky, *The Destruction of the Jews in Poland, Galicia, and Bukovina,* trans.

S. L. Zitron, 4 vols. (Tel Aviv, 1929; Hebrew). See also A. Siewiński, "Memories of Buczacz and Jazłowiec during the Great War, 1914–20," in Bartov, *Voices on War and Genocide*, 21–137.

14. Orłowicz, *Przewodnik po Galicyi*, 141.

15. S. Bak, *Painted in Words* (Bloomington, IN, 2001).

16. T. R. Weeks, "From 'Russian' to 'Polish,'" National Council for Eurasian and East European Research (2004): 2, https://www.ucis.pitt.edu/nceeer/2004 _819-06g_Weeks.pdf.

17. *Drugi Powszechny Spis Ludności z dn. 9.XII 1931 r.* (Warsaw, 1938).

18. "Lithuanian 2011 Population Census in Brief," https://osp.stat.gov.lt/services -portlet/pub-edition-file?id=15930.

19. "All-Ukrainian Population Census 2001," https://web.archive.org/web/2011 1217151026/http://2001.ukrcensus.gov.ua/eng/results/general/nationality/. See also Z. Yavetz, *My Czernowitz* (Tel Aviv, 2007; Hebrew); H. Braun, ed., *Czernowitz* (Berlin, 2006); F. Heymann, *Le Crépuscule des lieux* (Paris, 2003); M. Hirsch and L. Spitzer, *Ghosts of Home* (Berkeley, 2010).

20. O. Bartov, *The "Jew" in Cinema* (Bloomington, IN, 2005), 23–24. See also A. O. Scott, "Unlikely Hero in an Underground Hideout, Away from the Nazis," *New York Times*, 8 December 2011, https://www.nytimes.com/2011 /12/09/movies/in-darkness-from-agnieszka-holland-review.html.

21. See, e.g., Michael Wilmington, "The Third Man," *Criterion Collection*, 8 November 1999, https://www.criterion.com/current/posts/25-the-third-man.

22. Michlic, *Threatening Other*, 58–68; Gross, *Fear*, 192–243.

23. Y. Shtern, "A Kheyder in Tyszowce (Tishevits)," in *East European Jews in Two Worlds*, ed. D. D. Moore (Evanston, IL, 1990), 51–70; E. Mendelsohn, *The Jews of East Central Europe* (Bloomington, IN, 1983), 65–68; S. D. Kassow, "Community and Identity in the Interwar *Shtetl*," and C. Shmeruk, "Hebrew-Yiddish-Polish," both in *The Jews of Poland between Two World Wars*, ed. Y. Gutman et al. (Hanover, NH, 1989), 2–6, 291–94, respectively; A. Bar-El, "Tarbut," trans. C. Friedman-Cohen, *The YIVO Encyclopedia of Jews in Eastern Europe* (2010), https://yivoencyclopedia.org/article.aspx/Tarbut.

Chapter Thirteen. Gate of Hope

1. Orłowicz, *Przewodnik po Galicyi*, 202; H. Tsins, ed., *Kitov, My Hometown* (Tel Aviv, 1993; Hebrew); E. Husen, ed., *Kittever Yiskor Book* (New York, 1958; Yiddish); Nosonovsky, *Hebrew Epitaphs*, 25.

2. *The Trial of Adolf Eichmann*, Session 21, 1 May 1961, http://www.nizkor.com /hweb/people/e/eichmann-adolf/transcripts/Sessions/Session-021-07.html; http://www.nizkor.com/hweb/people/e/eichmann-adolf/transcripts/Sessions /Session-021-08.html; http://www.nizkor.com/hweb/people/e/eichmann -adolf/transcripts/Sessions/Session-021-09.html; Bartov, *The "Jew" in Cinema*, 325–26n61.

3. N. Frank, *In the Shadow of the Reich*, trans. A. S. Wensinger (New York, 1991);
    A. Shapira, "Beisky's Court of the Righteous," *Haaretz* (English edition), 14
    April 2007, https://www.haaretz.com/israel-news/culture/1.4816146; G. Nis-
    sim, *Il tribunale del bene* (Milan, 2003).

4. I. Karmel, *Stephania* (Boston, 1953); I. Karmel, *An Estate of Memory* (Boston,
    1969).

5. D. Tidhar, "Yissachar Sidkov," *Encyclopedia of the Founders and Builders of Is-
    rael*, vol. 5 (1952; Hebrew), 2170–71, http://www.tidhar.tourolib.org/tidhar
    /view/5/2170.

6. On "mercurial" Jewish tradesmen, see Slezkine, *The Jewish Century*, 1–39.
    See also K. Stauter-Halsted, *The Nation in the Village* (Ithaca, NY, 2001);
    Himka, *Galician Villagers*; Struve, *Bauern und Nation*.

7. "Polonia," https://en.wikipedia.org/wiki/SS_Polonia_(1910); B. Gvirtsman,
    "Presentation" (Hebrew), http://www.slides.co.il/zoom.php?id=9610; D. Ro-
    govin Helberg, *The Shtetl and I*, trans. Z. Rogovin, http://www.vishnive.org
    /e_index.html.

8. See, e.g., M. Eliav, "The First Beginnings of Petah Tikva"; I. Bartal, "Petah
    Tikva"; and R. Yizrael, "Critique of the Historiography of the First Years
    of Petah Tikva," all in *Katedra* 9 (1978): 3–25, 54–69, 95–126, respectively
    (Hebrew).

9. The photo is in Bartov, *Anatomy of a Genocide*, 5.

10. D. Shumsky, "Czechs, Germans, Arabs, Jews," *Association of Jewish Studies Re-
    view* 33, no. 1 (2009): 71–100, citation on 97.

11. Y. Golstein and B.-S. Stern, "PICA," *Katedra* 59 (1991): 103–25 (Hebrew).

12. Y. Beilin, *Israel* (New York, 1993), 12–36; M. Gilbert, *Israel* (London, 1988),
    69; T. Segev, *One Palestine, Complete*, trans. H. Watzman (New York, 2000).

13. R. Burstein, "The Language War and the Hebrew Teachers' College," *Hed
    ha-ulpan he-chadash* 100 (2013): 22–34 (Hebrew).

14. D. Porat, *Beyond the Reaches of Our Souls* (Tel Aviv, 2000; Hebrew), 80–102,
    249–53, 361.

15. M. A. Kaplan, *The Making of the Jewish Middle Class* (New York, 1991);
    S. Friedländer, *Nazi Germany and the Jews*, vol. 1 (New York, 1997), 41–72;
    V. Klemperer, *I Will Bear Witness*, trans. M. Chalmers, 2 vols. (New York,
    1998–99); O. Bartov, *Germany's War and the Holocaust* (Ithaca, NY, 2003),
    192–215.

16. S. Y. Agnon, *Shira*, 3rd ed. (Tel Aviv, 1999; Hebrew), 296; *Shira*, trans. Z. Sha-
    piro (New York, 1989), 295. See also T. Segev, *The Seventh Million* (Jerusa-
    lem, 1991; Hebrew), 13–56.

Chapter Fourteen. We'll Never See the World We Came From

1. See, e.g., H. Bartov, *Whose Little Boy Are You?* trans. H. Halkin (Philadelphia,
    1978 [1970]); *Halfway Out* (Tel Aviv, 1994; Hebrew).

2. D. Sharfman, *Palestine in the Second World War* (Eastbourne, UK, 2014), 44–49; Beilin, *Israel*, 55.

3. "Seventeenth Report to Congress on Lend-Lease Operations: Reverse Lend-Lease Aid from the British Commonwealth of Nations," President F. D. Roosevelt, 24 November 1944, p. 18, in *Report to Congress on Lend-Lease Operations*, vols. 18–24 (1944), https://www.google.com/books/edition/Report _to_Congress_on_Lend_lease_Operati/yZVIAQAAIAAJ?hl=en&gbpv=1.

4. H. Blum, *The Brigade* (New York, 2001); I. Keynan, *Holocaust Survivors and the Emissaries from Eretz-Israel* (Tel Aviv, 1996; Hebrew); I. Zertal, *From Catastrophe to Power* (Berkeley, 1998); Y. Grodzinsky, *Good Human Material* (Tel Aviv, 1998; Hebrew); H. Yablonka, *Survivors of the Holocaust*, trans. O. Cummings (New York, 1999).

5. Yablonka, *Survivors of the Holocaust*, 199–230; Bartov, *The "Jew" in Cinema*, 258–62.

6. G. Almagor, *The Summer of Aviya*, trans. H. Halkin (London, 1991 [1985]); *Under the Domim Tree*, trans. H. Schenker (New York, 1995 [1992]); "Israel Prize recipient G. Almagor, 2004" (Hebrew), https://cms.education.gov.il /EducationCMS/Units/PrasIsrael/Tashsad/GilaAlmagor/NimokyHsoftim .htm.

7. D. Porat and Y. Weitz, eds., *Between the Star of David and the Yellow Star* (Jerusalem, 2002; Hebrew), 92–93; D. Porat, *The Blue and the Yellow Stars of David* (Cambridge, MA, 1990), 30.

8. Exodus 16:3.

9. Bartov, *The "Jew" in Cinema*, 257–58; O. Bartov, *Mirrors of Destruction* (New York, 2000), 199–201; Segev, *The Seventh Million*, 101–10; R. Stauber, *Lesson for This Generation* (Jerusalem, 2000; Hebrew), 14–33; O. Almog, *The Sabra* (Tel Aviv, 1997; Hebrew), 143–48.

10. See also, e.g., L. Holliday, *Children in the Holocaust* (New York, 1995); J. Marks, *The Hidden Children* (New York, 1993); I. Grudzińska-Gross and J. T. Gross, eds., *War through Children's Eyes*, trans. R. Strom and D. Rivers (Stanford, CA, 1985); Nicholas Stargardt, *Witnesses of War* (London, 2006); Bartov, *Anatomy of a Genocide*, 232–62.

11. McCagg, *History of Habsburg Jews*, 110; S. Stampfer, "Marital Patterns in Interwar Poland," in *The Jews of Poland between Two World Wars*, ed. Gutman et al., 173–97.

12. Numbers 16:32.

13. G. Kressel and L. Alicki, eds., *Sefer Kosov* (Tel Aviv, 1964; Hebrew and Yiddish), 397, 339–90.

Credits

The poem by Kochanowski, "On the Linden Tree," in *The History of Polish Literature*, updated edition, edited by Czesław Miłosz, copyright © 1983, University of California Press. Used by permission of University of California Press. All rights reserved.

Excerpts from *Ir U-Melo'ah* (*A City in Its Fullness*) by Shmuel Yosef Agnon copyright © 1973, Schocken Publishing House Ltd., Tel Aviv, Israel. Used by permission of Schocken Publishing House. All rights reserved.

Excerpts from *Guest for the Night* by Shmuel Yosef Agnon, translated by Misha Louvish, copyright © 1968, copyright renewed 1996 by Penguin Random House LLC. Used by permission of Schocken Books, an imprint of the Knopf Doubleday Publishing Group, a division of Penguin Random House LLC. All rights reserved. Translation directly from the Hebrew original, *Ore'ah Nata Lalun*, copyright © 1998, Schocken Publishing House Ltd., originally published in 1939.

Excerpts from *Taras Bulba* by Nikolai Gogol, translated by Peter Constantine, translation copyright © 2003 by Penguin Random House LLC. Used by permission of Modern Library, an imprint of Random House, a division of Penguin Random House LLC. All rights reserved.

Excerpts from *Fateful Crossroads* by Ivan Franko, translated by Roma Franko, edited by Sonia Morris, copyright © 2006, Language Lantern Publications. Used by permission of Language Lantern Books.

Index

References to photographs and maps are indicated by italicized page numbers.